The Sociology of English Language Teaching and Learning in the Age of AI

Mohammad Ali Al-Saggaf
https://orcid.org/0000-0001-7401-0509
Xiamen University Malaysia, Malaysia

Ali Sorayyaei Azar
https://orcid.org/0000-0003-3539-8250
University of Malaya, Malaysia

Tania Hossain
Waseda University, Japan

IGI Global
Scientific Publishing
Publishing Tomorrow's Research Today

Published in the United States of America by
IGI Global Scientific Publishing
701 East Chocolate Avenue
Hershey, PA, 17033, USA
Tel: 717-533-8845 | Fax: 717-533-7115
Website: https://www.igi-global.com E-mail: cust@igi-global.com

Library of Congress Cataloging-in-Publication Data

Names: Al-Saggaf, Mohammad Ali, 1979- editor | Sorayyaei Azar, Ali, 1967- editor | Hossain, Tania editor
Title: The sociology of English language teaching and learning in the age of AI / edited by Mohammad Ali Al-Saggaf, Ali Sorayyaei Azar, and Tania Hossain.
Description: Hershey, PA : IGI Global Scientific Publishing, 2026. | Includes bibliographical references and index. | Summary: "This book aims to explore the sociological aspects of English language learning and teaching in the context of AI, examining how AI technologies influence language acquisition, pedagogy, and the broader social implications"-- Provided by publisher.
Identifiers: LCCN 2025035587 (print) | LCCN 2025035588 (ebook) | ISBN 9798337337555 hardcover | ISBN 9798337337562 paperback | ISBN 9798337337579 ebook
Subjects: LCSH: English language--Computer-assisted instruction for foreign speakers | English language--Study and teaching--Social aspects | Artificial intelligence--Educational applications | LCGFT: Essays
Classification: LCC PE1128.3 .S626 2026 (print) | LCC PE1128.3 (ebook)
LC record available at https://lccn.loc.gov/2025035587
LC ebook record available at https://lccn.loc.gov/2025035588
British Cataloguing in Publication Data
A Cataloguing in Publication record for this book is available from the British Library.

Table of Contents

Detailed Table of Contents

innovation by de-mystifying, critically thinking, and pedagogically testing. This chapter documents the journey of the participants through four consecutive phases: awareness of AI in the beginning, conceptualization, operationalization within practice, and continuous mentorship. Drawing on excellent qualitative data from case studies, participant descriptions, and institution reports, the chapter documents measurable teacher confidence, inter-disciplinary teamwork, and student engagement gains. The chapter critically discusses the selection, adaptation, and piloting of the tools by teachers in different and resource-limited higher education environments. In addition, it also sets out the design principles that inform professional development experience, including co-construction of knowledge, iterative peer scaffolding, and responsiveness in context. The chapter concludes with a set of practical suggestions for institutional leaders, policymakers, and curriculum makers who want to expand such interdisciplinarity projects. Ultimately, the chapter provides a much-needed, practice-oriented guide to the integration of AI into language teaching in pedagogically grounded, ethical, and contextually aware manner.

This chapter examines the relationship between Artificial Intelligence (AI) and Contextual responsiveness in language learning for the sake of meeting increasing demand for flexible, inclusive and morally sound educational technology. It explores how AI can either help or hinder intercultural communication competence. As a researcher and educator who works with multilingual and multicultural students, I argue that AI systems must take into account a variety of linguistic norms, contextual values, and communication styles. This chapter provides solutions that could be used to improve contextual responsiveness through inclusive data practices, adaptive learning systems, teacher preparation, and community-driven design in addition to identifying cultural bias in training data and the danger of linguistic imperialism. The effects of AI contextual responsiveness on learner engagement, performance, and identity formation are illustrated empirically

Classrooms have always evolved along with prevailing social practices and technologies. Let us consider AI or artificial intelligence. This chapter insists that we do not consider it merely as a sophisticated form of automation. At the current moment, AI is rapidly becoming integrated into the English Language Teaching (ELT) discipline. Many assume that it will do little more than make lessons more personalized, more engaging, and more efficient. It may do even more. We discuss AI in, for instance, providing real time writing feedback, pronunciation, and vocabulary tutoring, and in generating tasks for learners to communicate for advanced learning. We examine the implications of these systems in SLA and the role of the ELT teacher as a learning facilitator and orchestrator of feedback versus a primary source of knowledge. We discuss perniciously important, practical, and ethical matters such as linguistic bias, teacher and student AI literacy, governing frameworks, data privacy, and inequitable systems to use advanced techniques.

This chapter explores the AI-human teacher mutual complementarity in Grade 3 English reading instruction. The chapter discusses this synergy in teaching and assessing the five foundational pillars of reading (phonemic awareness, phonics, fluency, vocabulary, and reading comprehension), through a balanced literacy framework of read-aloud, shared reading, group guided reading, and independent reading. It presents a ten-day lesson outline to demonstrate how teacher-led instruction can be practically and synergistically merged with AI affordances in reading instruction. The chapter synthesizes discrete, fragmented theoretical positions that inform AI-human teacher synergy in reading instruction. It positions AI as the scaffold that enhances access, efficiency, and personalization, and the teacher as providing sound pedagogy, critical engagement, emotional support, and contextually relevant instruction. The chapter highlights the transformative potential of the synergy in reading instruction and recommends the judicious and practical leveraging of AI in teacher-led reading instruction.

The pedagogical use of artificial intelligence (AI) tools in the classroom has been the buzzword for educators since the popularization of generative AI, ChatGPT, in the early 2020's. However, behaviorists and pragmatists argue that technology is only a tool especially in developing communication skills, as it requires regular human interaction in a real setting. Hence, this paper presents STEP Buddies+AI or Student Teacher Enhancement Program (STEP), a 5-week workshop series designed to improve cross-cultural communication skills of pre-service teachers by developing collaborative learning approaches with AI tools. As an action research, the conception of this program started with literature review and needs analysis. Before the implementation of the program, students underwent a diagnostics test (Pre-test) on cross-cultural communication. During the implementation, participants were interviewed, and documentary evidence was collected. After the implementation phase, students took the Post-Test and shared their reflective journal. The paired sample t-test analysis of the pre-test and post-test scores show a significant difference on their cross-cultural communication competencies. For the interviews and documentary evidence, the data analysed using ATLAS.ti rendered the following themes: cultural awareness development; cross-cultural communication techniques; benefits and challenges of using AI; and benefits and challenges of working in pairs. With the results of this study, developers of programs for student teachers and for the development of cross-cultural communication skills may propose the need to integrate a buddy system and AI tools in collaborative activities like Think-Pair-Share.

As digital natives evolve alongside innovation, educators must stay open-minded with tools like AI technology to enhance instruction and develop curriculum. In secondary English Language Arts (ELA) classrooms and other areas, AI use is becoming more common among teachers and students alike in daily writing, reading, research, and communication tasks. Globally, AI is finding its way into all of these pedagogical elements, yet access is not always reliable in more rural societies due to poverty, polarization, and isolation. Furthermore, ongoing AI interactions can lead to negative effects like suicidal ideation and depression (Hill, 2025). Project-based learning (PBL) counteracts this issue for digital native learners by encouraging interaction,

Preface

As editors of this volume, we are both excited and cautiously reflective about the moment in which *The Sociology of English Language Teaching and Learning in the Age of AI* appears. The convergence of artificial intelligence with English language education is no longer a distant prospect; it is an unfolding reality that is reshaping classrooms from rural Algeria to urban Malaysia, from primary reading lessons in South Africa to pre-service teacher training in Japan and the Philippines. What began as tentative experiments with chatbots and automated feedback tools has rapidly evolved into a complex sociotechnical ecosystem that touches every dimension of English Language Teaching (ELT): pedagogy, assessment, teacher identity, learner agency, cultural representation, and linguistic justice. This book emerges from a shared recognition among the contributing authors—scholars working across Asia, the Middle East, Africa, North America, and Europe—that the sociological implications of these changes demand urgent, nuanced, and context-sensitive analysis.

The chapters assembled here deliberately foreground voices from regions and institutions that are too often sidelined in global conversations about educational technology. Rather than offering another celebratory narrative of technological inevitability, the authors critically examine how power, access, identity, and ethics are being renegotiated when AI enters English classrooms. We see AI not merely as a cluster of tools but as a social actor that amplifies existing inequalities while simultaneously opening new possibilities for inclusion and creativity. Whether exploring algorithmic bias in multilingual datasets, the risk of linguistic imperialism embedded in large language models, or the quiet resilience of project-based learning in low-resource rural schools, the contributions insist on grounding technological discussion in lived educational realities.

This volume therefore serves three interrelated purposes: first, to map the current terrain of AI integration in ELT with intellectual rigor and geographical breadth; second, to propose frameworks, models, and practices that keep human agency and sociocultural context at the center; and third, to stimulate further research that is ethically aware, pedagogically imaginative, and attentive to the diverse worlds in which English is taught and learned.

CHAPTER OVERVIEW

The book opens with Sedigheh Shakib, Mohamadreza Jafary, and Azadeh Amoozegar's examination of AI as a sociotechnical force in ELT (Chapter 1), introducing the Curated Augmentation Framework as a principled alternative to unchecked automation. Chapter 2, by Hussein Assaggaf and colleagues, complements this by presenting the Freedom–Responsibility Spectrum and the Teacher-in-the-Loop model, offering practical guidance for balancing personalization with human oversight.

Chapters 3 and 12 shift focus to the enduring challenges of multilingualism, with Atyaf Ibrahim and Prodhan Mahbub Ibna Seraj analyzing World Englishes in diverse societies, and Malika Gheraissa exploring the rising yet contested position of English in Algeria's complex linguistic ecology. Both chapters illustrate how AI tools must be designed with deep awareness of local language hierarchies and cultural practices.

Professional development and teacher preparation form the core of Chapters 4 and 8. Houda Boumedienne and Ouafa Ouarniki describe an interdisciplinary training model co-facilitated by language educators and AI specialists, while Joseph Velarde and Vinothini Vasodavan present the innovative STEP Buddies+AI program that blends human paired collaboration with generative AI to strengthen pre-service teachers' cross-cultural communication competencies.

Ethical and inclusive design concerns are foregrounded in Mohammed Abdulkhaleq's exploration of contextual responsiveness (Chapter 5) and in the broader discussions of bias, equity, and identity that thread through the volume. Practical classroom applications appear in Jabulani Sibanda's detailed ten-day lesson sequence demonstrating human–AI synergy in Grade 3 reading instruction (Chapter 7) and in Froilan Mobo and Katarzyna Milek's analysis of AI's role in fostering innovative 21st-century pedagogies (Chapter 6).

Katrina Broughman provides a necessary counterpoint in Chapter 9, cautioning against over-reliance on AI among digital natives in rural and marginalized settings and making a compelling case for project-based learning as a socially grounded antidote. Broader synthetic perspectives are offered by Mohammed Alaqad and colleagues on future trajectories (Chapter 10) and by Sanjeev Kumar on the revolutionary potential—and persistent challenges—of AI integration across teaching and learning processes (Chapter 11).

We close with a quiet but firm conviction: the future of English language education will not be written by algorithms alone. It will be shaped by the teachers who decide when and how to invite AI into their classrooms, by the learners who accept or resist its presence, and by the communities that insist their languages, values, and histories remain audible amid the hum of machines. This volume is offered as both a mirror and a compass—reflecting the complexities of the present moment while pointing toward pathways that preserve the fundamentally human project of language teaching and learning. We invite readers to engage critically, to question enthusiastically, and to imagine generously as we collectively author the next chapter of this unfolding story.

Mohammad Ali Al-Saggaf
Xiamen University Malaysia, Malaysia

Ali Sorayyaei Azar
University of Malaya, Malaysia

Tania Hossain
Waseda University, Japan

Chapter 1
AI-Integrated Language Learning Transforming Pedagogical Paradigms in ELT

Sedigheh Shakib Kotamjani
https://orcid.org/0000-0001-6249-0293
Central Asian University, Uzbekistan

Mohamadreza Jafary
https://orcid.org/0009-0003-7816-1330
McGill University, Canada

Azadeh Amoozegar
https://orcid.org/0000-0003-4988-5113
INTI International University, Malaysia

ABSTRACT

This chapter critically scrutinizes the AI integration into English Language Teaching (ELT) from the perspective of critical CALL and explores AI as a sociotechnical matter that transforms pedagogical relationships, teacher agency, and ethical reflections in language education. Drawing on recent empirical studies and international case studies from three different cultural backgrounds, this chapter reports on the overall positive or negative perceptions and experiences of applying AI tools in ELT, as well as global practices for implementing AI tools. Our Curated Augmentation Framework for AI serves as a support role, rather than a replacement model, to enable AI as an aid for enhancing—not replacing—a human pedagogy, whether for foundational skills, formative assessment, or extended learning. Ethical issues,

DOI: 10.4018/979-8-3373-3755-5.ch001

such as algorithmic bias, linguistic justice, and cultural adaptation, are introduced, along with practical suggestions for teacher agency. The chapter concludes with future research agendas designed to ensure the adoption of AI for the humanistic core of language learning, particularly in under-researched contexts.

1. INTRODUCTION: THE CROSSROADS OF INNOVATION AND HUMAN CONNECTION IN LANGUAGE LEARNING

In English language teaching (ELT) classes, making use of artificial intelligence (AI) involves a lot more than merely switching out books for iPads. It signals a deep change in the connections that make up education. As Crompton et al. (2024) convincingly show, this change goes beyond just using new tools; it actively questions the long-standing power relations between teachers, students, and the mechanisms that control how knowledge is made and disseminated. This tension is nicely shown by the worldwide controversy that sprang up after ChatGPT was released in 2022. Teachers all over the world were torn between seeing its intriguing potential to make language practice more democratic by giving students more opportunities to interact and get feedback, and dealing with profound concerns about its ability to interfere with the basis of educational authenticity (Szczepanik, 2025). These different answers make Williamson's (2020) important point very clear: AI is not merely a new technology; it is also a complicated sociotechnical challenge that requires us to completely rethink what learning is and how it happens.

Learning a language is still something that only people can do. It requires the careful development of interconnected abilities including reading, listening, speaking, and writing, all of which require advanced cognitive and social interaction (Bimpong, 2020). Writing, in particular, requires a lot of critical thinking, which is the capacity to break down information, make logical arguments, and express ideas clearly and accurately (Wu, 2021). This is when AI tools show their most powerful dualism. Studies like Kristiawan et al.'s (2024) show that AI-powered writing aides and chatbots can be extremely beneficial by giving students guidance on structure, vocabulary, and grammar. This help, on the other hand, comes with a lot of cautionary remarks. Learners, like the ones Yılmaz Virlan and Tomak (2024) investigated in Turkey, have understandable concerns about losing their own voice and the constant threat of plagiarism when they rely too much on these tools. A lot of professionals are unsure concerning what they ought to do. A major study by the British Council in 2024 of 1,348 teachers from around the world shows that the field of teaching is at a very important point in its history. A large majority (76%) agree that AI could be beneficial, but more than half (54%) declare that they lack have the expertise they need to use it effectively in their teaching. This significant disparity is not just a hassle; it might make educational inequalities even worse, leaving both teachers and students left behind.

This chapter delves deep into this complex landscape, examining how two specific strands of AI technology – generative AI tools like ChatGPT and advanced voice-enabled chatbots – are actively transforming the teaching and learning of core language skills: argumentative writing and oral interaction within second language acquisition (SLA). We will go through the subject by looking at long-term global case studies and new research, carefully looking at both the clear transformational potential and the major issues that these technologies bring along. There is a single primary inquiry that guides our investigation: How can teachers effectively employ these powerful technologies while keeping the vital human elements—critical thinking, authentic voice, and meaningful interaction—that are at the heart of deep language acquisition experiences?

We use Selwyn's (2019) key point of view to pose this pressing issue. He wants us to see educational technology not as an unavoidable, impartial force for progress, but as a "pedagogically contested space." This means understanding that adding tools like AI to learning settings is never automatic or without benefit. It requires educators, institutions, and authorities to make careful, morally sound decisions about **how** these technologies are employed and **whose** interests they subsequently serve. As we examine AI's growing significance, this critical lens becomes increasingly necessary.

Consider the domain of writing. Writing persuasive argumentative essays remains an extremely challenging endeavor for college students, and they often require substantial, tailored feedback to get it right (Kerman et al., 2024). Since late 2022, generative AI tools like ChatGPT have gone from being brand-new to almost ubiquitous (Boudouaia et al., 2024). Their impact is undeniable. Khampusaen's (2024) work, along with others, demonstrates that using ChatGPT meticulously can enhance the quality and structure of EFL students' writing. Additionally, Alsofyani and Barzanji's (2025) empirical work with Saudi EFL learners demonstrated that feedback from ChatGPT was as effective as feedback from a teacher in developing writing abilities. This suggests that individualized support could be quite useful in large classes. This aligns with the views of some, who suggest that AI can significantly enhance ELT by making writing more fluent and facilitating faster feedback loops (Alhusaiyan, 2025). Tools like ChatGPT are helping students, especially those in high school, understand how to write persuasive arguments (El Wahabi & Belhaj, 2024; Bakri & Pongpalilu, 2025; Royani & Sihombing, 2024). Nevertheless, this assistance does have certain downsides. The simplicity of creating text makes teachers worry that students tend to grow excessively reliant on technology, which could lead to outsourcing their thinking and stunting the growth of their independent writing skills (Jiang & Hyland, 2025). Qualitative studies on how students feel, such as the one by Esmaeil et al. (2023), consistently demonstrate this contradiction, with students expressing both gratitude for the help and concerns about authenticity and skill development. One major challenge is finding the right proper balance between using AI to assist individuals with writing and developing genuine, independent writing skills (Khampusaen, 2024; Boudouaia et al., 2024).

Voice-enabled AI chatbots are also transforming the way people communicate with each other in oral interactions. These tools utilize advanced combinations of automatic speech recognition and text-to-speech technology to create systems that can engage in conversations with learners naturally and interactively (Koç & Savaş, 2025). Their primary application in language classes has been to transform the classroom experience, providing crucial aural input and, critically, creating safe, accessible spaces for practicing oral interaction – opportunities often scarce in traditional settings (Koç & Savaş, 2025). AI is particularly useful for enhancing speaking abilities because it can simulate conversations, provide immediate feedback on pronunciation and fluency, and construct interactive environments that evolve over time (Kristiawan et al., 2024). There is plenty of opportunity to deal with issues such not having enough time to practice speaking and getting personalized feedback in EFL and FLE (French as a Foreign Language) settings (Al-Sofi, 2024; Xiao et al., 2025).

However, as Case et al. (2025) point out, this change gets attention among individuals given that it is associated with the very human act of communicating with each other. Integrating AI into these main parts of language acquisition, including writing and speaking, is more than just a technical issue. It prompts us to consider more complex problems related to language, learning, and communication as a whole. Szczepanik (2025) states that AI-generated discourse may exhibit biases, such as "growthism." Xiao et al. (2025) emphasize that, in light of recent AI advancements in EFL, the most important thing to do is to carefully navigate this integration, maximizing benefits and minimizing risks to ensure that these powerful tools truly enhance the deeply human experience of learning a new language, rather than detracting from it. The objective of this chapter is to help teachers achieve a comprehensive understanding necessary to tackle this challenging job.

2. THE AI ECOSYSTEM: TOOLS, TRANSFORMATIONS, AND TENSIONS IN LANGUAGE LEARNING

There are now many different kinds of AI technologies that are strongly connected to the field of English Language Teaching (ELT). These are not merely digital additions; they are completely new ways to help individuals learn languages. Intelligent Tutoring Systems (ITSs), advanced chatbots, adaptive learning platforms, and automated writing assessment tools all give students various ways to study, changing how lessons are taught and learned (Kristiawan et al., 2024). This ecosystem is part of the larger topic of Computer-Assisted Language Learning (CALL). It utilizes features such as natural language processing, automatic feedback, and personalized instruction paths to meet specific language demands (Alhusaiyan, 2025). The potential for change is immense; it includes assistance in understanding the material you are reading, practicing skills repeatedly, and even correcting pronunciation in real time (Crompton et al., 2024). However, this very change creates much stress, which teachers and students must carefully navigate.

2.1 Conversational Agents: Simulated Humanity and Its Limits

Chatbots stand as one of the most visible and rapidly evolving AI applications in language education. Moving far beyond simplistic scripted interactions, modern platforms like Replika facilitate remarkably fluid, open-ended dialogues (Tolstykh & Oshchepkova, 2024; Kristiawan et al., 2024). This capability creates a unique "low-stress environment" for learners, often substantially reducing the speaking anxiety that many experience when practicing with human peers, particularly in the early stages of acquisition (Koç & Savaş, 2025). Picture a learner hesitantly forming sentences without the fear of immediate judgment from a classmate or teacher – this is the psychological space these tools can provide. Adding voice technology represents a significant step forward. Voice-enabled devices add important features that enhance this exercise by providing learners with real-time, precise feedback on the accuracy with which they pronounce words, the naturalness of their intonation patterns, and other markers of fluency (Dennis, 2024). The impact can be tangible. Research involving Korean EFL learners using such voice-based chatbots documented measurable gains in confidence, with a notable increase in their willingness to initiate and sustain communication in the target language (Koç & Savaş, 2025). This finding is reinforced by a broader analysis; Hwang et al. (2022) reviewed 24 empirical studies and found that a substantial 78% of participants reported a significant reduction in speaking anxiety when practicing with AI conversation partners. This effect was particularly pronounced when learners engaged in structured role-plays, which provided clearer frameworks than unstructured conversations.

However, the simulation of human interaction inevitably encounters boundaries. Learners quickly discern the limitations of even the most advanced systems. Japanese students, for instance, frequently encountered interactions that felt jarringly "unnatural" when chatbots failed to grasp subtle cultural nuances or the evolving context within a conversation (Koç & Savaş, 2025). This points to a core challenge: authentic communication relies heavily on shared cultural understanding and pragmatic competence – areas where algorithms still struggle profoundly. A more concerning limitation surfaces with speech recognition technology. As Liakina and Liakin (2023) meticulously documented, pronunciation assessment tools frequently stumble when encountering non-standard accents. Their study found that these algorithms misidentified important phonological features about 30% of the time when interacting with individuals who did not use English as their first language. This is not only a technical problem; it could push learners from different language backgrounds to the margins if their speech patterns differ from the "standard" models on which the AI was trained. These limits on technology are significant reminders. AI can simulate some parts of conversation, but authentic, meaningful communication needs a level of cultural and contextual understanding, as well as the capability to adjust to different speech patterns, which existing algorithms just fail to match. The HALEF chatbot's attempt to simulate a conversation at a coffee shop was creative, but it consistently struggled with the practical subtleties of indirect requests, such as respectfully asking for a refill without issuing a direct command. Sydorenko and colleagues (2019) attribute this limitation to AI's inherent difficulty in processing the rich tapestry of contextual cues that humans use effortlessly to infer meaning beyond the literal words spoken. The promise of simulated humanity remains compelling, but its current reality is distinctly bounded.

2.2 Writing Partners: The Co-Authorship Dilemma and the Search for Authentic Voice

AI's impact on writing instruction is arguably its most transformative and contentious aspect. Tools have advanced considerably. Grammarly implemented to be mostly a grammar and spell checker. Currently, it functions as a smart writing trainer, providing detailed feedback on issues such as sentence rhythm, clarity, and word choice. It suggests synonyms and points out phrases that are too similar (Giray, 2024; Kristiawan et al., 2024). Many individuals acknowledge that such an evolution is occurring; for example, Grammarly is often cited as a tool that helps students improve their writing mechanics and style choices (Yılmaz Virlan & Tomak, 2024; Crompton et al., 2024). However, this support has certain unintended negative consequences. As one composition instructor poignantly observed: "My students' mechanical errors decreased significantly, but I now spend considerably more time addressing a new issue – a homogenized voice. It is the unintended consequence of algorithmic editing smoothing out all the unique quirks" (Giray, 2024, p. 7). This dynamic becomes more intense with the emergence of generative AI, especially ChatGPT. ChatGPT is more than simply an editor; it can additionally assist you come up with ideas and organize your writing. It helps students generate ideas, organize complex arguments, and refine thesis statements. These are all extremely helpful for challenging tasks such as writing persuasive argumentative essays (Bakri

& Pongpalilu, 2025; Xiao et al., 2025; Royani & Sihombing, 2024). Its generative nature, powered by vast Large Language Models (LLMs), allows it to emulate human language and planning in ways that surpass earlier chatbot technologies, offering versatile pathways to support writing development (Kasneci et al., 2023; Case et al., 2025; Esmaeil et al., 2023).

Learners often experience this support as empowering. Saudi undergraduates, for example, found ChatGPT's ability to provide immediate feedback on persistent organizational challenges and tense usage "liberating," allowing them to iterate quickly (Alsofyani & Barzanji, 2025). Quantitative evidence supports these perceptions. Khampusaen's (2024) controlled study documented impressive improvements: a 63.2% boost in the overall quality of content and a 43.5% gain in organizational coherence when EFL writers employed ChatGPT strategically during their argumentative essay writing process. Similarly, Alsofyani and Barzanji (2025) provided compelling empirical evidence, finding that "ChatGPT-generated feedback was as effective as teacher-generated feedback" in improving the writing skills of Saudi EFL learners, highlighting its potential as a scalable solution for providing individualized support, especially in large classes where teacher workload is a major constraint. Students explicitly valued its role in "scaffolding and supporting learners within their ZPD [Zone of Proximal Development]," offering tailored guidance precisely when needed (Alsofyani & Barzanji, 2025, p. 453). They praised the "immediate and fast feedback anytime" and specific help with "punctuation, organization, and tense usage," describing the overall experience as "an amazing and enjoyable" one that fostered their sense of independence (Alsofyani & Barzanji, 2025, p. 451). ChatGPT-4 and other tools like it provide even more assistance by fixing particular sentence-level problems such as incorrect grammar and undesirable combinations and giving explicit advice on how to improve (Boudouaia et al., 2024). Many people suggest that it can enhance content and provide real-time feedback, making writing more efficient and effective (Xiao et al., 2025; Royani & Sihombing, 2024). In FLE settings, it has helped many students improve their argumentative writing; however, the study by El Wahabi and Belhaj (2024) makes it clear that pedagogical support remains crucial for ensuring authentic language use.

However, this powerful co-authorship introduces a profound dilemma. Despite appreciating the support, learners often display a clear preference for human feedback. As one participant in Alsofyani and Barzanji's (2025) study articulated, "ChatGPT corrects my grammar; my teacher understands *why* I broke that rule intentionally" (p. 451). This sentiment was reflected quantitatively in their findings, where "preferring ChatGPT over my instructor" received the lowest weighted score among students. This aligns directly with Ahmed's (2023) research, where participants preferred teacher feedback due to perceived ease of interaction and accuracy (Alsofyani & Barzanji, 2025, p. 457). The reasons extend beyond rapport. Researchers are identifying subtle but significant markers of artificiality in AI-assisted writing. Jiang and Hyland (2025) uncovered troubling evidence of "synthetic engagement markers" in texts generated or heavily influenced by tools like ChatGPT. These are overused transitional phrases and metadiscursive elements (words like "furthermore," "notably," "it is important to consider that") that create an illusion of coherence and reader engagement without the authentic voice and logical flow of human writing. Their detailed corpus analysis revealed a striking pattern: ChatGPT-produced arguments contained 37% more of these metadiscoursal markers compared to human-written essays. They term this artificial smoothness "facsimile cohesion" – a surface-level polish that masks potential weaknesses in genuine argumentative depth and originality. This risk of homogenization and fake fluency highlights the main problem: AI can be a great helper, but relying too heavily on it can hinder the learner's ability to develop their own voice and think critically independently, both of which are essential for genuine academic writing (Jiang & Hyland, 2025). Students have expressed concerns about the accuracy of their work, the risk of plagiarism, and the authenticity of their work when using these technologies (Esmaeil et al., 2023). The co-authorship is real, but the terms need to be discussed frequently to protect the learner's authentic language identity.

2.3 Adaptive Systems: The Personalization Paradox – Efficiency vs. Diversity

Adaptive learning platforms represent AI's powerful capacity for granular personalization. Systems like Duolingo, powered by sophisticated AI backends, or Carnegie Learning's courses, exemplify this approach. They continuously analyze individual learner behavior – response times, error patterns, correct answers – and dynamically adjust the difficulty and sequencing of content in real-time (Kristiawan et al., 2024). This hyper-personalization makes some tasks more efficient. For example, vocabulary retention can increase by approximately 30% when AI schedules reviews using optimal spaced repetition algorithms. This ensures that students review terms just when they are about to forget them (Gu, 2024). Controlled investigations have shown that this targeted approach is efficient. Wei (2023) concentrated on 60 Chinese university students and discovered that those who received training through an AI-adaptive system performed better at remembering grammar and vocabulary than the population getting conventional instruction. In terms of quality, students in these types of programs typically report that they appreciate being able to work at their own pace and that the system meets them where they are (Wei, 2023).

However, this very strength creates a significant paradox – the "Personalization Paradox". The algorithms execute an outstanding job of adapting to a learner's "demonstrated" skills and pace, but they may also unintentionally limit their language skills.

These systems can limit exposure to the wide range of language varieties, registers, accents, and cultural contexts that comprise real-world language use (Crompton et al., 2024), as they focus too much on individual advancement along predetermined paths. Consider South Korea's SpeakingMax platform. It excels at preparing learners for the specific demands of tests like TOEIC, drilling "standard" pronunciation, and formulaic responses. However, in doing so, it potentially devalues legitimate regional variations or less formal, but equally valid, communicative styles by implicitly presenting one variety as the sole target (Dennis, 2024). The equity implications become starkly visible in performance discrepancies. Dennis (2024) notes that such platforms might achieve impressive accuracy rates, say 95%, when evaluating speech that closely matches native-like "standard" models. When confronted with polished and clear, yet uniquely Korean-accented English, this accuracy can drop as low as 78%. This difference is not only a technical issue; it could put learners at a disadvantage due to their native language. Therefore, the most effective and fair implementations are those that purposefully combine the efficiency of algorithmic guidance with human-curated materials and activities designed to protect and promote linguistic diversity. Case et al. (2025) make a strong case for this: "Personalization should expand linguistic repertoires, not confine learners to algorithmic comfort zones" (p. 97). The objective is to leverage AI's capacity to open up the world of language, not to confine learners to a narrow path based solely on the algorithm's initial training data and predefined objectives. It remains a significant challenge to utilize adaptive AI systems responsibly, striking a balance between hyper-efficient customization and the need for diverse exposure to real-world language.

3. PEDAGOGICAL METAMORPHOSIS: REDEFINING ROLES AND RELATIONSHIPS IN THE AI ERA

Adding artificial intelligence to English and French language schools does not seem just like giving teachers new tools; it is changing the way education works at its core. This change takes us firmly away from traditional teacher-centered models and toward dynamic, learner-centered approaches based on real-time data and unprecedented personalization (Yılmaz Virlan & Tomak, 2024; Alhusaiyan, 2025). AI promises learning settings that are perfectly suited to each student, naturally adaptable, and possibly more engaging and welcoming (Alhusaiyan, 2025). AI's ability to micro-personalize, or tailor content and pacing to each learner's profile with incredible accuracy, is at the heart of this change. Advanced formative feedback loops also help learners become more metacognitively aware, which means they learn how they learn (Kristiawan et al., 2024). Platforms like Duolingo and Rosetta Stone use gamification elements like streaks, leaderboards, and interactive challenges to keep learners interested and motivated, by creating personalized routes (Kristiawan et al., 2024; Luckin et al., 2016). However, this new technology requires a deep rethinking of instructors' roles, how learning is evaluated, and what keeps individuals engaged.

3.1 Teacher Transformation: From Sage to Synthesizer and Ethical Navigator

In classrooms that utilize AI, the teacher's role undergoes a significant transformation. Teachers are becoming less like the main source of information and more like data scientists and ethical counselors for students. They must make sense of the complex learning analytics generated by AI systems, while also ensuring that ethics are adhered to, particularly when humans are involved (Case et al., 2025). Consider how Finnish teachers have utilized the AI-powered Eduten platform. Studies show that these instructors spend about 40% less time giving lectures on standardized subject. This extra time is deliberately reinvested—about 30% more—into planning and running real, collaborative projects where students use skills, they learned with AI help (Edmett et al., 2024). This change requires new skills that go beyond just knowing how to use technology:

- **Algorithmic Literacy:** The capacity to look at AI tools and datasets with a critical eye and see any potential biases they might have (for example, problems with recognizing accents or cultural blind spots).
- **Feedback Triangulation:** Putting together information from AI-generated feedback, peer review, and their own expert observations to get a whole picture of how well the learner is performing.
- **Strategic Intervention:** Knowing when technology is unable to assist and when you need human help, emotional support, or a more detailed explanation.

As one astute Finnish teacher characterized this shift: "I find myself curating rather than creating from scratch—my focus is on selecting which AI-generated suggestions or patterns merit deeper class discussion and which require critical interrogation" (Edmett et al., 2023, p. 27). The newly created role is like that of an orchestra conductor, skillfully bringing together the technology tools and the crucial human parts to make a learning experience that makes sense and has a beneficial effect.

The evolution shows how essential it is to have strong professional development. Zawacki-Richter and colleagues' (2019) systematic review presented a sobering picture: fewer than 17% of teachers received adequate training to navigate these complex new responsibilities. Initiatives like the British Council's (2024) advocacy for “pedagogical AI literacy” programs are essential. These programs must move well beyond simply teaching teachers *how* to operate the tools; they need to foster deep understanding of *when* and *why* automation serves genuine learning goals, and crucially, *what* the ethical implications might be. The European Commission's workshops in Barcelona are a good example of this approach. They combine hands-on exploration of AI tools with structured ethical debates on challenging topics, such as data privacy and the impact of “surveillance capitalism” within educational institutions (European School Education Platform, 2025). Teachers are becoming important synthesizers and moral guardians, ensuring that technology aligns with the fundamental ideals of education.

3.2 Assessment Reimagined: Shining the Spotlight on the Process

We need to radically rethink how we grade writing in light of the rise of generative AI, particularly tools like ChatGPT, which can swiftly generate excellent drafts. It is not enough to only look at the final product while teaching, and it could even be misleading. Progressive instructors are therefore shifting emphasis towards **process portfolios**. These portfolios require students to meticulously document their entire writing journey, including initial brainstorming notes, multiple iterative drafts that show evolution, revision trails highlighting specific changes, and, crucially, reflections that explain their choices and engagement with AI tools, if used (Bakri & Pongpalilu, 2025).

Building on this, Khampusaen (2024) advocates for the development and use of “AI-aware rubrics.” These rubrics explicitly reward the unique “human-added value” in student work. Criteria might focus on:

- **Cultural Adaptation:** How effectively the student adapts arguments or language to specific cultural contexts.
- **Personal Voice & Originality:** The presence of a distinct authorial voice and original synthesis of ideas that moves beyond predictable AI output.
- **Critical Intervention:** The quality of the student's revisions and additions that demonstrably improve upon or critically engage with initial AI-generated suggestions or structures.

Such frameworks might explicitly allocate significant weight—for instance, 30% of marks—to “algorithmic transparency,” where students clearly document how and where they used AI assistance. An even larger portion, perhaps 40%, could be dedicated to “human intervention analysis,” requiring students to articulate and justify the revisions, insights, and unique contributions they made beyond the AI's initial suggestions (Khampusaen, 2024).

This process-focused approach yields significant cognitive benefits. Students guided by frameworks such as the "ChatGPT Guideline for Critical Argumentative Writing" demonstrated remarkable gains, with up to an 82% improvement in argument development depth and complexity (Suh et al., 2025). Such advantages have not been achieved by having AI write the essays, which is a significant point. They arose because students had to critically evaluate their thinking by actively comparing their first drafts or outlines with AI-generated ones. All of this made them explain why their unique human perspective, experiences, or interpretations were valuable. Bakri and Pongpalilu (2025) expressed that "Students who actively defended their deviations from ChatGPT's suggestions, explaining their rhetorical choices, developed significantly stronger rhetorical awareness than peers who uncritically accepted all AI recommendations" (p. 2536). To further ensure authenticity and deepen understanding, some institutions are reintroducing or strengthening *viva voce* (oral) defenses. In these sessions, students must verbally justify their writing choices, explain their research process, and defend their arguments. This practice, as observed by El Wahabi and Belhaj (2024) in French composition courses, correlated with a dramatic 73% reduction in detected plagiarism. Assessment, reimagined, becomes pedagogy itself.

3.3 Cultivating Engagement: Moving Beyond the Gamification Mirage

Duolingo and other platforms employ gamification, such as streaks, points, and leaderboards, to boost initial motivation and keep individuals progressing. However, this sort of approach has some disadvantages. It can put more value on external rewards, such as gaining points or keeping a streak, than on the inward gratification that comes from truly being able to communicate and understand (Kristiawan et al., 2024). Research by Crompton and colleagues (2024) raises a critical concern: common engagement metrics used by such platforms often conflate simple "platform addiction" (logging in daily to maintain a streak) with authentic, deep learning. The danger arises when the drive for "streak maintenance" replaces the development of actual language proficiency for real-world use.

Research into voice-based chatbots suggests a more sustainable engagement model. Studies indicate learners persist with these tools not primarily for external badges, but because the low-stakes, private practice environment demonstrably builds authentic confidence in their speaking abilities (Koç & Savaş, 2025). This confidence then fuels a greater willingness to communicate (WTC) in real interactions. Furthermore, engagement tied to authentic need proves powerful. The HALEF coffee shop simulation study demonstrated a 22% higher retention rate for pragmatic language markers (such as polite request forms) when the AI practice tasks directly mirrored situations that learners genuinely anticipated encountering in their daily lives (Sydorenko et al., 2019).

The most important thing to remember from other contexts, like writing classes in Saudi Arabia, is that balance is essential for keeping individuals deeply engaged. Students accomplish more effectively when AI provides monotonous but necessary tasks, such as grammar drills, vocabulary review, and pronunciation repetition, because these tasks free up substantial instructional time. Classroom instructors can subsequently employ their skills to make complicated group projects which enable students to contemplate the societal implications of language use, negotiate meaning, have critical discussions, and come up with creative solutions to problems—things that no algorithm can do at the moment (Alhusaiyan, 2025; Koç & Savaş, 2025). This strategic division leverages the strengths of both. As Koç and Savaş (2025) aptly conclude based on their analysis of effective implementations: "Chatbots excel for *rehearsal*—providing safe, repetitive practice. Humans are indispensable for the *performance*—facilitating meaningful, socially embedded communication and complex cognitive tasks" (p. 17). True engagement stems from using technology to facilitate more profound human interaction and intellectual challenge, rather than merely gamifying routine practice.

4. GLOBAL IMPLEMENTATIONS: CULTURAL INFLECTIONS AND CONTEXTUAL NUANCES

The implementation of artificial intelligence in language training is not identical everywhere. It appears in a multitude of distinct ways around the world due to factors such as cultural values, educational priorities, economic realities, and political conditions. When you look at unique foreign case studies, you can see how these local variables change the way AI technologies are employed as well as what their ultimate implications are in English Language Teaching (ELT). These different uses demonstrate the flexibility of the technology and highlight the importance of local frameworks in its success and limitations.

4.1 South Korea: Precision Under Pressure – Efficiency and its Discontents

The "hagwon" (cram school) mentality in South Korea's highly competitive private education industry makes it a unique place to test out AI. In this case, technologies like Ringle and SpeakingMax are typically used with laser-like focus on getting ready for high-stakes tests (Crompton et al., 2024; Dennis, 2024). These platforms utilize advanced AI to achieve remarkable accuracy, particularly when examining small phonological details crucial for tests such as the TOEIC or TOEFL. Dennis (2024) suggests that they can carefully break down the differences, such as the sounds /r/ and /l/, providing specialized workouts that aim for perfection. This technical skill, on the other hand, reveals substantial cultural and educational gaps. The systems naturally place a higher value on grammatical precision and phonological conformity to a perceived "standard" than on communicative efficiency or expressive fluency. This reinforces a deeply ingrained test-centered approach to teaching that often prioritizes "correct" English over the ability to use the language in a natural and creative manner.

The search for this level of algorithmic accuracy causes real problems. There are clear differences in socioeconomic status. Families with money in areas like Gangnam can easily get high-end AI instructors that cost more than $100 a month. On the other hand, rural schools generally rely on tablet applications funded by donations, which offer more rudimentary features (British Council, 2024). This difference could exacerbate existing educational inequities. Also, the pressure to be flawless that these tools create might have negative effects on mental health. Han's (2020) study of 200 middle school students found that dedicated AI practice led to an impressive 18% increase in speaking exam scores. However, follow-up interviews showed that students were more anxious about "sounding robotic" or unnatural in real conversation. This encapsulates the main conflict in Korea: the need for quick, demonstrable progress through AI can sometimes come at the expense of real language growth and trust in communication. The technology is great at helping people improve in certain assessments, but its narrow focus in a high-pressure system might overlook the broader, more complex, and human-centered goals of learning a language.

4.2 Saudi Arabia: Enthusiastic Adoption with Emerging Critical Awareness

Saudi Arabia presents a contrasting picture characterized by widespread institutional enthusiasm for AI writing tools within higher education. Alhusaiyan (2025) reports that a striking 87% of Saudi universities have implemented AI tools, particularly like ChatGPT, in their composition courses, reflecting a national push towards technological integration in education. Tangible benefits back this enthusiasm. A revealing mixed-methods study by Alsofyani and Barzanji (2025) demonstrated that students receiving feedback that combined AI analysis and human instructor insights improved their writing scores by 37% more than peers relying solely on ChatGPT. Learners consistently praised the immediacy and constant availability of algorithmic feedback, appreciating its assistance with mechanics such as punctuation, tense consistency, and basic organization (Alsofyani & Barzanji, 2025). As one participant vividly described the experience as "liberating" for tackling persistent challenges (Alsofyani & Barzanji, 2025).

However, this enthusiasm coexists with a growing critical awareness. Despite valuing the AI's speed, students ultimately placed higher weight on the instructor's ability to contextualize suggestions and understand intent. One student articulated this distinction clearly: "ChatGPT gave me ten synonym options; my professor explained why **two** of them suited the specific tone and argument I was trying to build" (Alsofyani & Barzanji, 2025, p. 451). This highlights the irreplaceable value of human insight into rhetorical nuance and authorial purpose. Alsofyani and Barzanji's (2025) research uncovered an unexpected and crucial finding for implementation strategies: the benefits of AI feedback varied significantly by proficiency level. AI input that focused on grammar and mechanics was most helpful for learners with lower proficiency levels (approximately CEFR A2). On the other hand, advanced learners (CEFR B2 and above) gained significantly more from human input that addressed higher-order issues, such as how to construct an argument, how to employ style, and how to make an argument more persuasive. This makes it evident that we need to use AI in varied ways. For instance, we need to make use of AI to help beginners learn the basics, whereas we should additionally allow human teachers to provide more detailed feedback, particularly to advanced learners. AI is thought to be a useful tool to enhance Saudi EFL classrooms more effectively by promoting teamwork, autonomy in learning, and motivation. There are still problems, though. For example, some teachers are unfamiliar with how to implement some AI tools properly, and learners can lose motivation if they rely too much on the technology (Alhusaiyan, 2025).

4.3 Finland: Equity and Teacher Empowerment as Foundational Principles

Finland's way of integrating AI is very different from South Korea's, which is high-pressure and focused on tests. Finland's public education system is based on the idea that everyone should have the same opportunities. The country focuses on "teacher empowerment" and "systemic equity." AI is used strategically to handle mundane, repetitive tasks, such as correcting grammar and performing basic vocabulary drills, on platforms like Eduten (Edmett et al., 2023). This planned automation allows Finnish teachers to devote more time to higher-level teaching tasks, such as designing complex, collaborative projects, leading in-depth discussions, and providing detailed, personalized feedback on writing and complex communication skills (Edmett et al., 2023). A significant amount of government funding is being allocated toward this shift in focus. Finland spends approximately €35 million annually on extensive teacher training programs that teach teachers how to utilize pedagogical AI. This makes the Council of Europe (2024) ensure that teachers are not only consumers of the technology, but also informed and critical advisers (Council of Europe, 2024). The country also promises that every student would have accessibility an individual device, which removes some of the digital gap that other deployments have.

This idea firmly endorses "pedagogical sovereignty," which indicates that teachers have the authority and role to critically review and, when necessary, dismiss algorithmic recommendations based on what they actually have learned about their students' needs and overall academic goals. A classroom instructor from Helsinki provided an example of this notion by stating that "When the Eduten platform suggests another round of vocabulary drills based on an algorithm, I might look at my class and decide instead to redirect our time to a student-led debate about the ethical implications of AI, deliberately using that same vocabulary in a meaningful, critical context" (Edmett et al., 2023, p. 41). You can see the results of this fair and balanced approach. A significant 92% of Finnish teachers stated that AI technologies have made it much easier for them to do truly differentiated instruction that meets the needs of students with varying learning speeds and styles in the same classroom (Edmett et al., 2023). Perhaps most importantly, the achievement gap between native Finnish speakers and immigrant learners has been seen to close by about 15% after these AI-supported practices were carefully put into place. This shows that technology can help make education fairer when used in a system that is supportive, focused on teachers, and possesses a lot of resources.

4.4 Emerging Economies: Ingenuity and Resourceful Adaptation within Constraints

Vietnam, for example, has fewer financial resources and technological infrastructure than other countries, but they are quite creative in how they use AI to help individuals learn languages. Scholars call this "pedagogical bricolage." Teachers are innovative even when they have to deal with big problems, such not having enough bandwidth or access to premium resources. Pham and Dang (2025) write about how Vietnamese colleges use common tools like ChatGPT in new ways to get the most out of them. Instead of trying to copy adaptive systems that use a lot of resources, they focus on tailored, contextually relevant applications. Some ideas are using ChatGPT for advanced paraphrasing tasks, making reading passages and dialogue examples that are culturally relevant and resonate with local students, or making exercises based on current events in the area. At Ho Chi Minh City University, students compare AI-generated translations of culturally rich Vietnamese proverbs with translations made by literary sources or human experts, which is a very creative way to teach. This task has two goals: it helps students learn important language skills like translation, comparative analysis, and vocabulary, and it also helps them become more critical digital citizens by teaching them how to judge the strengths, weaknesses, and possible cultural biases in AI output (Pham & Dang, 2025).

It is impressive how well this clever adaption functions. Pham and Dang's (2025) study found that these low-cost, context-sensitive implementations, which were based on teachers' creativity instead of expensive technology, achieved about 89% of the core learning outcomes that are usually associated with much more advanced and expensive AI-powered language learning systems. This important study highlights an important rule for integrating AI around the world: Context-appropriate implementation, based on the needs of the students and the teacher's knowledge, is much more important than just having the latest technology or spending a lot of money. Success depends on using the tools you have in creative ways to solve specific local problems and meet learning goals, which shows that AI can be integrated in a meaningful way even without a lot of money. These different glimpses from around the world show that AI's path in language instruction is closely linked to local circumstances. This implies that answers need to be innovative with whatever resources they have, deal with unique challenges, and take into consideration cultural differences.

5. CRITICAL CHALLENGES: NAVIGATING THE ETHICAL LABYRINTH OF AI IN LANGUAGE LEARNING

Integrating AI into language learning creates a complex ethical dilemma that needs to be properly addressed. There are deep questions about fairness, authenticity, and human agency that go beyond technical problems and operational issues. These problems affect every level—technical, educational, and institutional—and require solutions that consider multiple factors and are grounded in critical thinking and ethical foresight.

5.1 Linguistic Justice: Confronting Algorithmic Hegemony and Bias

One of the most significant ethical concerns is AI's potential to reinforce linguistic hierarchies. Natural Language Processing (NLP) techniques, which are mostly trained on standardized Western corpora, sometimes treat real differences in language as problems. Blodgett et al. (2020) disclosed the fact clearly: their study observed that NLP systems marked elements of Nigerian English as "errors" in 65% of test cases, even though they were grammatically correct in Nigeria. There are similar biases in pronunciation evaluations. Liakina and Liakin's (2023) study indicated that speech recognition techniques deemed phonological characteristics of African American Vernacular English (AAVE) to be "incorrect" 3.2 times more often than similar structures in Standard American English.

These algorithmic biases lead to real-world unfairness. When AI scoring is used in institutional assessments, students who are already at a disadvantage are put at an even greater disadvantage. The British Council (2024) documented that Indian IELTS test-takers using AI writing evaluators received scores 23% lower on average than British peers—a discrepancy directly attributed to training data skewed toward Anglo-centric norms. As Amin (2023) argues, such tools risk "digitally colonizing" language by privileging dominant varieties while erasing linguistic diversity.

Addressing these demands requires concerted action:

- **Technical Diversification:** Developers must prioritize dialect-inclusive training datasets and provide transparent documentation of coverage limitations (Blodgett et al., 2020).
- **Pedagogical Vigilance:** Teachers should integrate critical AI literacy into lessons. Amin (2023) advocates a simple but powerful practice: "Dedicate five minutes in every AI feedback session to ask: "What might this algorithm misunderstand about my linguistic identity?" (p. 12).
- **Institutional Auditing**: Testing bodies must implement bias auditing frameworks "before" deploying automated assessment, ensuring tools are vetted for cross-dialect fairness (Blodgett et al., 2020).

5.2 Academic Integrity: Shifting from Punitive Measures to Pedagogical Process

The uproar over AI-assisted plagiarism typically hides serious issues with teaching. When Saudi students submitted essays written by ChatGPT as their own work, teachers noted that this was not only unethical but also a wasted opportunity to help students develop critical source evaluation and synthesis skills (Al-Sofi, 2024). Punitive approaches prove inadequate; progressive institutions now treat AI use as a teachable dimension of academic writing, akin to citation practices. The University of Dubai's composition program mandates "algorithmic transparency statements"—detailed appendices where students document **how** tools were used at each drafting stage, justifying their choices.

Process-oriented assignments transform AI from a threat into a metacognitive tool. Turkish EFL learners who documented their writing journey—comparing initial drafts, ChatGPT suggestions, and their final refinements—demonstrated 40% higher metacognitive awareness than peers writing without AI (Yılmaz Virlan & Tomak,

2024). One participant reflected: "Seeing how ChatGPT structured the argument mechanically made me realize why my own version, though less polished, resonated more deeply with our cultural context" (p. 16). In the same way, Université Paris Nanterre's use of "viva voce" defenses, in which students explain their writing choices out loud, cut down on plagiarism by 73% and, at the same time, improve students' oral argumentation skills (El Wahabi & Belhaj, 2024). This shift in perspective alters our understanding of integrity, transitioning from strict policing to encouraging "authentic authorship" through reflective practice.

5.3 Teacher Preparedness: Bridging the Empowerment Gap

The primary obstacle with integrating ethical AI is still the substantial disparity in the preparedness of teachers. Zawacki-Richter et al.'s (2019) global review revealed that 68% of teachers felt excluded from decisions regarding the use of AI in schools, and training is often limited to simple "click-through tutorials" that fail to provide context on how to effectively teach. This supports Crompton et al.'s (2024) "implementation paradox": expensive tools go unused even if institutions contributed money into them. The British Council's (2024) survey demonstrates the extent to which conditions are: only 24% of teachers stated they were ready, and rural teachers were especially adversely affected by the lack of professional development opportunities.

Effective solutions prioritize "collaborative empowerment":

- **Implementation Coalitions**: Canadian universities were the first to use "AI adoption coalitions," which let teachers test out tools in their own classrooms before they became prevalent in all schools. This bottom-up strategy makes sure that tools meet real teaching needs (Case et al., 2025).
- **Cross-Cultural Knowledge Sharing**: The "AI for Language Education" network run by the Council of Europe (2024) connects teachers from 30 nations to work together to make culturally responsive materials. A Bulgarian participant said, "Sharing how we adapted ChatGPT prompts for Roma English learners directly inspired Portuguese colleagues addressing similar equity challenges" (p. 15).
- **Pedagogical AI Literacy Programs**: Finland spends €35 million a year on more than just technical training; it also teaches individuals how to think critically about the ethical implications of tools (Council of Europe, 2024). In workshops, individuals can use tools and talk about data colonialism and algorithmic accountability at the same time.

5.4 The Path Forward: Ethics as Foundational Practice

These challenges all point to one important fact: integrating AI cannot only be a technological task. It calls for “ethically grounded pedagogy” that:

1. **Centers Linguistic Diversity:** Through inclusive design and critical student involvement, it actively struggles against algorithmic hegemony (Amin, 2023; Blodgett et al., 2020).
2. **Reframes Authenticity:** Of greater importance than keeping an eye on the product are being authentic about the process along with engaging in metacognitive reflection (Yılmaz Virlan & Tomak, 2024; El Wahabi & Belhaj, 2024).
3. **Empowers Teachers:** Considers the instructors as active partners in the change brought about by technology, not just passive recipients (Case et al., 2025; Council of Europe, 2024).

Szczepanik (2025) asserts that even the words generated by AI carry ideological weight. For example, ChatGPT's economic discourse is full of “growthism,” which makes neoliberal principles seem normal. Everyone involved needs to be constantly critical of these hidden curricula in order to stay vigilant against them. We can only utilize AI's full potential without compromising the humanistic foundation of language instruction if we navigate this moral maze with teaching wisdom and moral fortitude.

6. CONCLUSION: TOWARD SYMBIOTIC CLASSROOMS – HUMAN WISDOM IN THE AGE OF AI

Our study of how Artificial Intelligence can be used in English and French language instruction shows a world that is far different from simple utopian or dystopian ideas. It is complex terrain, demanding nuanced, context-sensitive navigation. The evidence points compellingly toward a model of “curated augmentation”: strategically deploying AI for discrete, mechanistic tasks—grammar drills managed by adaptive tutors, pronunciation practice via responsive speech recognition, instant feedback on structural elements—thereby liberating human educators for the relational, creative, and culturally nuanced work that algorithms cannot replicate. We see this balance embodied in Finnish teachers designing collaborative projects where AI-honed vocabulary is applied to debates on AI ethics; in Saudi professors expertly contextualizing automated feedback to preserve students' rhetorical voice; and in Vietnamese instructors ingeniously repurposing accessible tools like ChatGPT to generate culturally resonant materials within infrastructural constraints. These diverse educators exemplify a shift from technology "replacing" teachers to technology "empowering" deeper human interaction.

From this global tapestry, three core principles emerge for ethical and effective AI implementation:

1. **Contextual Intelligence Over Technological Imperialism:** Tools must adapt to local educational values, linguistic realities, and socio-economic contexts. This requires "educator-led redesign", not the imposition of standardized, one-size-fits-all solutions. Success hinges on teachers reshaping tools, like the Vietnamese "pedagogical bricolage," to serve specific community needs and cultural relevance, resisting the pull of technological determinism (Pham & Dang, 2025; Case et al., 2025).
2. **Radical Transparency Regarding Limitations:** Students and educators must possess a clear-eyed understanding of AI's inherent constraints. This means explicitly teaching about algorithmic biases against non-standard dialects (Blodgett et al., 2020; Amin, 2023), its struggles with cultural nuance and pragmatic language (Koç & Savaş, 2025), its potential for factual inaccuracy or "facsimile cohesion" (Jiang & Hyland, 2025), and its ideological leanings, such as the "growthism" identified by Szczepanik (2025) in AI-generated discourse. Understanding these boundaries is fundamental to critical digital literacy.
3. **Democratic Governance and Ethical Stewardship:** Meaningful voices for teachers and learners are non-negotiable in adoption decisions, pedagogical design, and crucially, regarding data rights and privacy (Kristiawan et al., 2024; Bertino et al., 2019). This includes transparent protocols for data usage, secure storage, and informed consent, alongside institutional support structures like the Finnish model of "pedagogical sovereignty" where teachers can ethically override algorithmic suggestions (Edmett et al., 2023; Council of Europe, 2024).

Significant "critical research priorities" demand attention. We urgently need longitudinal studies examining whether skills honed with AI assistance genuinely transfer to authentic, unassisted communication across different contexts. Investigations must explore how AI tools could be designed and used to "preserve" and "celebrate" linguistic diversity rather than inadvertently flattening it through standardized norms. The development and rigorous application of "bias-aware" assessment frameworks, building on the work of Blodgett et al. (2020) and Amin (2023), are crucial for equitable evaluation. As Szczepanik's (2025) incisive discourse analysis warns: "Unchecked, AI tools may standardize not just language but thought itself through algorithmic reinforcement of dominant ideologies" (p. 18). Vigilance against this hidden curriculum is paramount.

The path forward demands what Selwyn (2019) aptly terms "pedagogical courage"—the resolve to reject the narrative of inevitable technological dominance and instead insist on "human-centered design". It requires the courage demonstrated by Helsinki teachers who redirect AI vocabulary drills toward student-led debates on the ethics of the very technology they are using. It echoes in the critical work of students in Ho Chi Minh City who are analyzing ChatGPT's translations of Vietnamese poetry, looking at how well they stay trustworthy to the culture as well as the language (Pham & Dang, 2025). These classrooms are not only employing technology; they are also questioning it in a critical way to make sure it serves greater educational reasons.

The true measure of AI's value in language education lies not in its computational sophistication, but in its capacity to deepen the "human connection" that remains the irreducible core of meaningful language learning. As Al-Sofi (2024) succinctly advises, ChatGPT and similar tools should function as "responsible assistant[s]," working "in conjunction" with students' original ideas and teachers' expert guidance (p. 145). Likewise, Alsofyani and Barzanji (2025) affirm its value "when used appropriately" by critically aware users (p. 454). The ultimate objective is to establish "symbiotic classrooms" where AI handles the quantifiable items and humans concerned for the more qualitative things, like sparking critical thought, negotiating meaning, encouraging authentic voice, and building relationships across language and cultural barriers. To make this symbiosis happen, we need to constantly think about ethics, give teachers strong support, build things that are accessible to everyone, and most importantly, always put human learning and human connection at the core of everything that we perform with technology.

REFERENCES

Ahmed, M. (2023). ChatGPT and the EFL classroom: Supplement or substitute in Saudi Arabia's eastern region. *Information Sciences Letters*, *12*(7), 2727–2734. DOI: 10.18576/isl/120704

Al-Sofi, B. B. M. A. (2024). Artificial intelligence-powered tools and academic writing: To use or not to use ChatGPT. *Saudi Journal of Language Studies*, *4*(3), 145–161. DOI: 10.1108/SJLS-06-2024-0029

Alhusaiyan, E. (2025). A systematic review of current trends in artificial intelligence in foreign language learning. *Saudi Journal of Language Studies*, *5*(1), 1–16. DOI: 10.1108/SJLS-07-2024-0039

Alsofyani, A. H., & Barzanji, A. M. (2025). The effects of ChatGPT-generated feedback on Saudi EFL learners' writing skills and perception at the tertiary level: A mixed-methods study. *Journal of Educational Computing Research*, *63*(2), 431–463. DOI: 10.1177/07356331241307297

Amin, M. Y. M. (2023). AI and ChatGPT in language teaching: Enhancing EFL classroom support and transforming assessment techniques. *International Journal of Higher Education Pedagogies*, *4*(4), 1–15. DOI: 10.33422/ijhep.v4i4.554

Bakri, M., & Pongpalilu, F. (2025). Reclaiming the argument: Students' perceptions of ChatGPT's role in constructing argumentative texts in the age of AI. *International Journal of Multidisciplinary Research and Analysis*, *8*(5), 2531–2538. DOI: 10.47191/ijmra/v8-i05-29

Bertino, E., Kundu, A., & Sura, Z. (2019). Data transparency with blockchain and AI ethics. [JDIQ]. *Journal of Data and Information Quality*, *11*(4), 1–8. DOI: 10.1145/3312750

Bimpong, W. K. (2020). Teaching purposefully: Considering the perspectives of foreign language learners in language skill development. *Educational Resources Information Center*. https://eric.ed.gov/?id=ED598551

Blodgett, S. L., Barocas, S., Daumé, H.III, & Wallach, H. (2020). Language (technology) is power: A critical survey of "bias" in NLP. *Proceedings of the 58th Annual Meeting of the Association for Computational Linguistics*, 5454–5476. https://doi.org/DOI: 10.18653/v1/2020.acl-main.485

Boudouaia, A., Mouas, S., & Kouider, B. (2024). A study on ChatGPT-4 as an innovative approach to enhancing English as a foreign language writing learning. *Journal of Educational Computing Research, 62*(6), 1289–1317. DOI: 10.1177/07356331241247465

British Council. (2024). *Artificial intelligence and English language teaching: Preparing for the future.* https://www.teachingenglish.org.uk/sites/teacheng/files/2024-08/AI_and_ELT_Jul_2024.pdf

Case, R., Liu, L., & Mintz, J. (2025). Integrating AI technology into language teacher education: Challenges, potentials, and assumptions. *Computers in the Schools, 42*(2), 93–99. DOI: 10.1080/07380569.2025.2458950

Crompton, H., Edmett, A., Ichaporia, N., & Burke, D. (2024). AI and English language teaching: Affordances and challenges. *British Journal of Educational Technology, 55*(6), 2503–2529. DOI: 10.1111/bjet.13460

Council of Europe. (2024, Jan. 31). *AI and deeper learning in language education: Unlocking opportunities for sign languages users – The European Centre for Modern Languages launches new projects for 2024–2027.* https://www.coe.int/en/web/portal/-/ai-and-deeper-learning-in-language-education-unlocking-opportunities-for-sign-languages-users-the-european-centre-for-modern-languages-launches-new-projects-for-2024-2027

Dennis, N. K. (2024). Using AI-powered speech recognition technology to improve English pronunciation and speaking skills. *IAFOR Journal of Education, 12*(2), 107–126. DOI: 10.22492/ije.12.2.06

Edmett, A., Ichaporia, N., Crompton, H., & Crichton, R. (2023). *Artificial intelligence and English language teaching: Preparing for the future.* British Council. https://doi.org/10.57884/78EA-3C69

Edmett, A., Ichaporia, N., Crompton, H., & Crichton, R. (2024). *Artificial intelligence and English language teaching: Preparing for the future* (2nd ed.). British Council. DOI: 10.57884/78EA-3C69

El Wahabi, S., & Belhaj, L. (2024). Preparing learners for the higher education curriculum: Perfecting argumentative writing skills in French as a foreign language: An innovative teaching approach with ChatGPT and interactive in-class assessment. *International Journal of Sciences, Basic and Applied Research, 73*(1), 31–42. https://gssrr.org/index.php/JournalOfBasicAndApplied/article/view/16775

Esmaeil, A. A. A., Kiflee Dzulkifli, D. N. A., Maakip, I., Mantaluk, O. O., & Marshall, S. (2023). Understanding student perception regarding the use of ChatGPT in their argumentative writing: A qualitative inquiry. *Jurnal Komunikasi: Malaysian Journal of Communication*, *39*(4), 150–165. DOI: 10.17576/jkmjc-2023-3904-08

European School Education Platform. (2025, November 18). Integrating AI & ICT into the classroom (Barcelona, Spain). European Commission. Retrieved December 9, 2025, from https://school-education.ec.europa.eu/en/learn/courses/integrating-ai-ict-classroom-barcelona-spain-0

Giray, L. (2024). "Don't Let Grammarly Overwrite Your Style and Voice:" Writers' advice on using Grammarly in writing. *Internet Reference Services Quarterly*, *28*(3), 1–11. DOI: 10.1080/10875301.2024.2344762

Gu, J. (2024). Digital tools in language learning: Optimizing memory and attention for college students. *International Journal of Human-Computer Interaction*, *1*(11). Advance online publication. DOI: 10.1080/10447318.2024.2400384

Han, D.-E. (2020). The effects of voice-based AI chatbots on Korean EFL middle school students' speaking competence and affective domains. *Asia-Pacific Journal of Convergent Research Interchange*, *6*(7), 71–80. DOI: 10.47116/apjcri.2020.07.07

Hwang, W.-Y., Guo, B.-C., Hoang, A., Chang, C.-C., & Wu, N.-T. (2022). Facilitating authentic contextual EFL speaking and conversation with smart mechanisms and investigating its influence on learning achievements. . *Computer Assisted Language Learning*. Advance online publication. https://doi.org/10.1080/09588221.2022.2095406

Jiang, F., & Hyland, K. (2025). Does ChatGPT write like a student? Engagement markers in argumentative essays. *Written Communication*, *42*(3), 463–492. DOI: 10.1177/07410883251328311

Kasneci, E., Seßler, K., Küchemann, S., Bannert, M., Dementieva, D., Fischer, F., & Kasneci, G. (2023). ChatGPT for good? On opportunities and challenges of large language models for education. https://doi.org/DOI: 10.35542/osf.io/5er8f

Kerman, N. T., Noroozi, O., Banihashem, S. K., Karami, M., & Biemans, H. J. A. (2024). Online peer feedback patterns of success and failure in argumentative essay writing. *Interactive Learning Environments*, *32*(2), 614–626. DOI: 10.1080/10494820.2022.2093914

Khampusaen, D. (2024). The impact of ChatGPT on academic writing skills and knowledge: An investigation of its use in argumentative essays. *LEARN Journal: Language Education and Acquisition Research Network, 18*(1), 963–988. DOI: 10.70730/PGCQ9242

Koç, F. Ş., & Savaş, P. (2025). The use of artificially intelligent chatbots in English language learning: A systematic meta-synthesis study of articles published between 2010 and 2024. *ReCALL, 37*(1), 4–21. DOI: 10.1017/S0958344024000168

Kristiawan, D., Bashar, K., & Pradana, D. A. (2024). Artificial Intelligence in English Language Learning: A Systematic Review of AI Tools, Applications, and Pedagogical Outcomes. [TATEFL]. *The Art of Teaching English As a Foreign Language, 5*(2), 207–218. DOI: 10.36663/tatefl.v5i2.912

Liakina, N., & Liakin, D. (2023). Speech technologies and pronunciation training: What is the potential for efficient corrective feedback? In U. Kickhöfel Alves & J. Alcantara de Albuquerque (Eds.), *Second language pronunciation: Different approaches to teaching and training* (pp. 287–312). De Gruyter Mouton. https://doi.org/DOI: 10.1515/9783110736120-011

Luckin, R., Holmes, W., Griffiths, M., & Forcier, L. B. (2016). *Intelligence unleashed: An argument for AI in education.* Pearson Education. https://www.pearson.com/content/dam/one-dot-com/one-dot-com/global/Files/about-pearson/innovation/open-ideas/Intelligence-Unleashed-Publication.pdf

Pham, T. N., & Dang, T. X. (2025). An Investigation into the Application of Artificial Intelligence for Language Teaching and Learning in Vietnam. *Vietnam Journal of Education, 9*(2), 265–283. DOI: 10.52296/vje.2025.557

Royani, I., & Sihombing, M. R. (2024). ChatGPT in the academic writing classroom. *Esteem Journal of English Education Study Programme, 7*(2), 631–638. DOI: 10.31851/esteem.v7i2.14600

Selwyn, N. (2019). *Should robots replace teachers? AI and the future of education.* Polity Press.

Sydorenko, T., Hellermann, J., Thorne, S. L., & Howe, V. (2019). Mobile augmented reality and language-related episodes. *TESOL Quarterly, 53*(3), 712–740.

Szczepanik, R. J. (2025). The limits to growth(ism) in ChatGPT—Corpus assisted discourse studies in AI-generated texts. *Discourse & Society*, 1–20. DOI: 10.1177/09579265241308585

Suh, S., Bang, J., & Han, J. W. (2025). *Developing Critical Thinking in Second Language Learners: Exploring Generative AI like ChatGPT as a Tool for Argumentative Essay Writing*. arXiv preprint arXiv:2503.17013.

Tolstykh, O. M., & Oshchepkova, T. (2024). Beyond ChatGPT: Roles that artificial intelligence tools can play in an English language classroom. *Discover Artificial Intelligence*, *4*(1), 60. DOI: 10.1007/s44163-024-00158-9

Wei, Y. (2023). The impact of AI-mediated instruction on English learning achievement, L2 motivation, and self-regulated learning among Chinese university students. *Frontiers in Psychology*, *14*, 1–15. DOI: 10.3389/fpsyg.2023.1234567

Williamson, B. (2020). Education and the "datafication" of learning: Big data, AI and education governance. *Learning, Media and Technology*, *45*(3), 219–232. DOI: 10.1080/17439884.2020.1686014

Wu, Y. (2021). *Critical thinking in argumentative essays*. Babel Publishing., DOI: 10.52288/bp.27089851.2021.12.10

Xiao, F., Zhu, S., & Xin, W. (2025). Exploring the landscape of generative AI (ChatGPT) powered writing instruction in English as a foreign language education: A scoping review. *ECNU Review of Education*, *0*(0), 1–19. DOI: 10.1177/20965311241310881

Yang, C. T.-Y., Lai, S.-L., & Chen, H. H.-J. (2022). The impact of intelligent personal assistants on learners' autonomous learning of second language listening and speaking. . *Interactive Learning Environments*. Advance online publication. DOI: 10.1080/10494820.2022.2141266

Yılmaz Virlan, A., & Tomak, B. (2024). A Q method study on Turkish EFL learners' perspectives on the use of AI tools for writing: Benefits, concerns, and ethics. *Language Teaching Research*, •••, 1–24. DOI: 10.1177/13621688241308836

Zawacki-Richter, O., Marín, V. I., Bond, M., & Gouverneur, F. (2019). Systematic review of research on artificial intelligence applications in higher education—Where are the educators? *International Journal of Educational Technology in Higher Education*, *16*, 39. Advance online publication. DOI: 10.1186/s41239-019-0171-0

Chapter 2
Balancing Individual Agency and Systemic Oversight in AI–Powered English Language Learning Models

Hussein Taha Assaggaf
https://orcid.org/0000-0002-3991-5430
Al-Baha University, Saudi Arabia

Mesfer Ahmed Mesfer Alwadai
King Khalid University, Saudi Arabia

Mohammad Ali Al-Saggaf
Xiamen University Malaysia, Malaysia

Bader Abdulaziz Saad Altamimi
Prince Sattam Bin Abdulaziz University, Saudi Arabia

ABSTRACT

This chapter explores the ethical and pedagogical dimensions of AI-powered personalization in education, proposing a Freedom–Responsibility Spectrum to guide responsible implementation. This chapter adopts a pragmatic, evidence-informed approach to AI personalization in language learning. Drawing on empirical evidence and current frameworks, it emphasizes the importance of learner autonomy, teacher agency, and contextual safeguards. A practical framework is outlined, integrating transparency, equity, and curriculum alignment. The Teacher-in-the-Loop (TITL)

DOI: 10.4018/979-8-3373-3755-5.ch002

model is presented as a cornerstone for maintaining human oversight and pedagogical integrity. The chapter concludes by advocating for dynamic, human-centred AI partnerships that uphold educational values and foster meaningful learning outcomes.

1. INTRODUCTION

If freedom is to be genuinely preserved in AI-mediated learning, it must be structured rather than left to algorithmic drift.

Artificial intelligence (AI) has moved from peripheral experiment to everyday infrastructure in education. Adaptive platforms calibrate practice to learner performance; learning analytics flag students at risk; large language models (LLMs) now provide dialogic tutoring and feedback at scale (Al-Saggaf, 2025). Policymakers and professional bodies, meanwhile, have issued guardrails to reconcile innovation with learner rights and system integrity. These guardrails are synthesized into a practical Freedom–Responsibility Spectrum that situates common classroom uses by learner agency and governance duties (see Figure 1), in line with governmental and institutional bodies' guidelines and recommendation (UNESCO, 2021; ISO/IEC, 2023; NIST, 2023; OECD, 2023; U.S. Department of Education, 2023; European Union, 2024). In the European Union, the Artificial Intelligence Act lays down a risk-based regulatory regime for AI systems, i.e., risk management, data governance, transparency, and human oversight for high-risk use cases (European Union, 2024).

Human rights, fairness, transparency, and accountability are also very much emphasized by ethical global frameworks (e.g., the UNESCO Recommendation on the Ethics of AI) during the design and deployment of AI (UNESCO, 2021). Technical standards that go with them-a NIST AI Risk Management Framework and an ISO/IEC 23894 on AI risk management-are used to convert these standards into procedures that institutions and vendors may apply throughout the entire AI lifecycle (ISO/IEC 2023; NIST 2023).

We can observe a level of contradiction between the potential freedom provided by personalization i.e., more options, pace control and even voice learning, and the responsibilities and the responsibilities tied to algorithmic mediation (Chan and Hu, 2023; Al-Saggaf, 2024). However, personalized learning remains a potential promise derived by AI. This entails providing each learner with appropriate content at convenient time with enough support to improve learner's mastery.

Such ambition is neither new, nor an exception; classical private pedagogical studies confirm that such a model may contribute significantly in what is called gains-two sigma, when it comes to providing prompt feedback in the right time (Bloom, 1984). Medium and practically meaningful effects of intelligent tutoring systems (ITS) are shown in recent meta-analysis when these systems are implemented properly (Kulik and Fletcher, 2016). Besides, recent tests of low-stakes ITS, run by teachers (such as ASSISment) have shown progressive improvement after one year of usage, with promising effects for those students who are historically underserved, which highlight the promise of equity potential for the formative personalization (Arnold Ventures, 2024; WestEd, 2024).

This chapter examines how AI-enabled personalization can expand learner autonomy (freedom) while upholding ethical, legal, and pedagogical duties (responsibility). We synthesize the current evidence base, policy frameworks, and practical guidance to support balanced adoption in classrooms and institutions. This chapter is guided by the following questions: 1) Under what conditions does AI-enabled personalization genuinely enhance learner agency and outcomes, rather than simply optimizing short-term performance metrics? 2) How should responsibility be distributed among developers, institutions, educators, and learners to meet emerging regulatory and ethical expectations? 3) What practical design, governance, and classroom orchestration strategies allow educators to harness AI's benefits while preserving rights and equity?

In this chapter we argue for a right-forward, teacher-in-the-loop model that positions AI as assistive intelligence—a means to augment human pedagogy, not a replacement for it—especially in linguistically and culturally diverse settings relevant to applied linguistics and the sociology of language education.

2. CONCEPTUAL FOUNDATIONS

2.1 What do we mean by AI-driven personalization?

We define AI-driven personalization as the dynamic tailoring of learning experiences—content, pacing, feedback, and pathways—based on inferences from learner data through machine-learned models or generative systems. This spans: (a) rule-based adaptivity (e.g., item difficulty selection), (b) data-driven learner modelling (e.g., Bayesian knowledge tracing and recommendation policies), and (c) generative AI tutoring offering dialogic feedback and scaffolded explanations (OECD, 2023; U.S. Department of Education, 2023).

In this chapter, these patterns are treated not as interchangeable but as risk graded use cases, summarized on the Freedom–Responsibility Spectrum (Figure 1), where formative, explainable supports with teacher oversight differ categorically from automated, consequential decisions (OECD, 2023; European Union, 2024). In practice, mainstream platforms exemplify different parts of this spectrum: Duolingo's Birdbrain model uses ML to match exercise difficulty to learner proficiency and optimize practice sequencing, reporting improved learning signals through

A/B tests (Bicknell and Brust, 2020; Duolingo, 2020). Khan Academy's Khanmigo trials emphasize conversational scaffolding for reasoning and teacher-facing planning support, with early usage reports contingent on professional development and classroom norms (Khan Academy, 2024; Michigan Virtual, 2025).

When it comes to formative vs. summative uses, a key distinction for responsibility is the stakes of the decision. Evidence suggests AI can be most beneficial in formative contexts—hints, retrieval practice, and feedback loops—where teachers orchestrate interventions and learners maintain agency (U.S. Department of Education, 2023; WestEd, 2024). By contrast, high-stakes uses (e.g., placement, credentialing, grading) demand stringent safeguards, transparency, and contestability—if used at all (GDPR, 2016/Art. 22; European Union, 2024).

In language-learning contexts, AI personalization commonly manifests as (a) adaptive item selection calibrated to learner proficiency, (b) dialogic generative tutoring that scaffolds form, meaning, and use, and (c) recommendation policies that surface tasks and texts aligned to estimated needs (OECD, 2023; U.S. Department of Education, 2023). For example, Duolingo's Birdbrain uses machine learning to match exercise difficulty to learner ability, reporting improved learning indicators in A/B tests (Bicknell and Brust, 2020). Emerging classroom pilots with Khanmigo indicate potential for dialogic reasoning support when teachers receive professional development and retain orchestration authority (Khan Academy, 2024; Michigan Virtual, 2025).

2.2 Methodological Considerations

This chapter adopts a pragmatic, evidence-informed approach to AI personalization in education. It synthesizes findings from peer-reviewed studies, policy frameworks, and classroom pilots to derive actionable insights. The micro-scenarios are illustrative, grounded in applied linguistics contexts, and designed to reflect real-world instructional challenges. While not exhaustive, they aim to capture the diversity of learner needs and institutional constraints. The guiding questions are answered using internal logic and evidence from the chapter itself, ensuring coherence and relevance. To support responsible AI use in education, multiple policy instruments converge on key principles. The EU AI Act (2024) mandates risk management, transparency, and human oversight for high-risk educational AI systems. GDPR Article 22 (2016) grants learners rights against solely automated decisions with significant effects. The NIST AI Risk Management Framework (2023) outlines governance functions—MAP, MEASURE, MANAGE, GOVERN—to embed trustworthiness. ISO/IEC 23894 (2023) complements this with lifecycle-based risk treatment processes. Together, these frameworks provide a coherent structure for institutions to assess, deploy, and monitor AI tools in alignment with ethical and legal obligations.

2.2 Freedom: Autonomy, Agency, and Voice

In educational terms, freedom encompasses (a) Autonomy: authentic choices among tasks, texts, or strategies, (b) Agency: capacity to act on those choices with feedback and tools, and (c) Voice: the learner's ability to influence goals and representation in the learning process. Historical and contemporary evidence indicates that individualized, responsive support can produce substantial learning gains when it enables timely feedback and mastery pacing contributing to learners intrinsic and extrinsic motivational factors (Bloom, 1984; Kulik and Fletcher, 2016; Al-Saggaf 2020). Generative tutors potentially extend this responsiveness, giving learners on-demand explanation and practice opportunities aligned to their zone of proximal development (OECD, 2023; U.S. Department of Education, 2023).

Yet autonomy without intentional design can drift into algorithmic nudging—subtle steering by recommender policies that may privilege "easier" paths, reinforce prior interests, or narrow exposure. Filter-bubble concerns, widely discussed in information ecosystems, translate to curriculum exposure as an extrinsic motivational factor, if personalization lacks mechanisms for serendipity by design and exposure diversity. To keep personalization from collapsing into comfort zone routing, Figure 1 embeds exposure diversity constraints and a "challenge text" requirement in the mid to right configurations, preserving autonomy and breadth (Pariser, 2012; UNESCO, 2021; OECD, 2023). For language education, this matters as learners benefit from encountering diverse registers, dialects, and identities; personalization should expand horizons, not confine them.

In applied linguistics, preserving freedom entails exposure diversity—structured encounters with multiple registers, dialects, and identities—so that personalization broadens rather than narrows horizons. In sociolinguistics modules, teachers can set system-level constraints (e.g., a minimum proportion of texts from Global Englishes; alternation between academic and community genres) and track whether AI recommendations meet diversity quotas over time.

In a Micro-scenario (Sociolinguistic exposure, BM–ENG & CN–ENG), A Year-2 Sociolinguistics class explores English variation. The platform curates mini-corpora featuring Malaysian English (BM–ENG code-switching vignettes), Singapore English discourse markers, and English used by PRC-educated professionals in transnational firms (CN–ENG influenced lexico-grammatical patterns). Students select two corpora aligned to their interests and one "challenge corpus" beyond their comfort zone. The teacher reviews the AI's selection log to ensure breadth, then facilitates discussion on ideology and identity (UNESCO, 2021; OECD, 2023).

In another Micro-scenario (Identity-affirming production), learners compose short identity narratives (e.g., "My multilingual journey"), optionally asking an LLM for audience-aware feedback (tone, register, stance). The teacher requires students to (a) keep "voice markers" (discourse features signalling identity), (b) annotate changes suggested by the AI, and (c) justify accept/reject decisions—thus centring agency and metalinguistic reflection (Chan and Hu, 2023; Jisc, 2023; U.S. Department of Education, 2023).

2.3 Responsibility: Ethical, Legal, and Pedagogical Duties

In terms of responsibility, the first matter of concern is the ethical and human-rights framing. UNESCO's Recommendation articulates values—human dignity, fairness, transparency, and human oversight—that should guide AI in education (UNESCO, 2021). The OECD similarly calls for "opportunities, guidelines, and guardrails" co-developed with the teaching profession (OECD, 2023). These values anchor responsibilities across the AI lifecycle.

This raises the need for regulatory obligations. The EU AI Act (2024) codifies a risk-based model: educational AI systems that may determine access or progression can be classified as high-risk, triggering obligations on providers and deployers (risk management, data governance, transparency, post-market monitoring, and human oversight) (European Union, 2024).

Data protection regimes add learner rights. Under GDPR Article 22, data subjects have the right not to be subject to a decision based solely on automated processing that has legal or similarly significant effects, and they retain rights to human intervention and to contest decisions—critical for educational placement or grading (GDPR, 2016/Art. 22). In the U.S., FERPA constrains the disclosure and use of education records, requiring institutions to vet vendors and practice data minimization in AI workflows (Student Privacy Policy Office, n.d.; U.S. Department of Education, 2023).

Technical risk management is not left out; The NIST AI Risk Management Framework specifies governance and operational functions-MAP, MEASURE, MANAGE, GOVERN-to embed trustworthiness (validity, safety, security, interpretation, privacy enhancement, fairness, accountability) (NIST, 2023). ISO/IEC 23894 complements this with concrete processes (communication, scoping, assessment, treatment, monitoring) and mappings across the AI system lifecycle (ISO/IEC, 2023). For learning analytics, Jisc's Code of Practice (updated guidance) operationalizes institutional responsibilities: transparency and consent, validity of inferences, minimization of adverse impacts, and stewardship (Jisc, 2023).

AI comes with Pedagogical responsibility and human oversight. Therefore, the U.S. Office of Educational Technology advises teacher-in-the-loop orchestration: using AI to support formative feedback, reduce administrative load, and widen access—without ceding professional judgment to automated systems (U.S. Department of Education, 2023). The risks of removing human oversight are not hypothetical: the

2020 UK grading controversy demonstrates how opaque model decisions in high-stakes contexts can erode equity and public trust (CNBC, 2020). In practice, this means: (a) reserving consequential decisions for human deliberation; (b) providing explanations of AI outputs suitable for educators and learners; and (c) establishing appeal and override pathways aligned with regulatory expectations (GDPR, 2016/Art. 22; European Union, 2024).

Let us take a Micro-scenario (Pragmatics tutor with teacher-in-the-loop). In an EAP pragmatics module on email politeness, an LLM suggests revisions to mitigate negative politeness threats (e.g., hedging, indirectness). The system (a) shows why a change is recommended (highlighted pragmatic strategy), (b) records confidence/uncertainty, and (c) routes borderline cases for teacher review. Learners must submit an explanation note ("Why I accepted or rejected the AI's suggestion"), keeping the human as final arbiter. Operationally, it is recommended to aligning classroom decisions with the right half of Figure 1—teacher in the loop, formative deployments—while reserving left side configurations for exceptional cases with explicit risk management, transparency, and appeal (GDPR, 2016/Art. 22; Jisc, 2023; NIST, 2023; OECD, 2023).

2.4 Bringing the Concepts Together

For the purpose of this chapter, we will treat AI personalization as a space where freedom (autonomy, agency, voice) and responsibility (ethics, law, pedagogy, risk) co-determine legitimate practice. The analytic stance is pragmatic: use AI where the evidence of benefit is strongest (e.g., formative practice with teacher orchestration), and scale only with commensurate safeguards (Kulik and Fletcher, 2016; Chan and Hu, 2023; Al-Saggaf, 2024; WestEd, 2024).

Policy and standard-setting bodies have given us a common vocabulary and framework; the mission is to make these into workable routines for the classrooms and governance patterns for institutions that respect rights and create opportunities, especially in applied linguistics and language education where identity, variation, and inclusion are at the centre of concern (UNESCO, 2021; OECD, 2023).

2.5 Freedom–Responsibility Spectrum for AI Personalization in Education

The table below illustrates the spectrum of learner freedom and associated risk levels in AI-personalized education, ranging from AI-led autopilot to human-only instruction. Risk levels are color-coded to highlight the need for safeguards.

Table 1. Freedom–Responsibility Spectrum

Configuration	*AI-led Autopilot*	*Algorithm-first Pathwaying*	*AI-augmented Instruction*	*Human-led with AI as Tool*	*Human-only Instruction*
Decisions	Automated grading, placement, gatekeeping; minimal human review	Adaptive sequencing & nudging shape exposure/pacing	Teacher curates; AI supports hints, retrieval; dialogic LLM feedback	Teacher-only feedback/sequencing; selective AI for options	Teacher-only feedback, sequencing, assessment
Typical Uses	High-stakes exams, admissions, credentialing	Next-exercise routing; auto hinting without explanation	Formative feedback with teacher review; adaptive practice; AI writing/ reading support	Curated corpora; teacher-led dialogue; limited AI probes	Seminars; oral exams; portfolio assessment
Learner Freedom	Minimal	Mixed (steered)	High (with guardrails)	High (human curated)	High (human curated)
Risk Level	VERY HIGH	MED–HIGH	LOW–MED	LOW	LOW
Applied Linguistics Examples	CN–ENG placement decided by opaque model; appeal unclear	EAP recommender keeps surfacing comfort-zone genres; exposure narrows	Pragmatics tutor: learner drafts email; AI suggests repair strategies; teacher audits chat	Sociolinguistics: balanced Global Englishes corpora; students choose +1 challenge text	Identity narratives; dialogic human assessment
Safeguards Required	Prohibit sole automation for significant effects; human review & appeal (e.g., GDPR Art.22)	Explainability (XAI), teacher override; opt-out; monitor subgroup drift & exposure diversity	Teacher-in-the-loop; formative use only; data minimization; opt-in consent	Transparency on what AI does; optional use; Jisc-style LA code	Standard academic integrity; dialogic assessment

continued on following page

Table 1. Continued

Configuration	*AI-led Autopilot*	*Algorithm-first Pathwaying*	*AI-augmented Instruction*	*Human-led with AI as Tool*	*Human-only Instruction*
Policy/Standards Anchors	EU AI Act (high-risk); GDPR Art.22; FERPA (US)	EU AI Act risk mgmt. & transparency; Jisc validity	NIST AI RMF; ISO/IEC 23894; U.S. OET (teacher-in-the-loop)	Jisc LA Code (transparency, validity, minimising adverse impacts)	Professional standards & ethics
Evidence Cues	Ofqual 2020 crisis (trust & equity harms)	Personalization can overfit; risk of filter bubbles	ITS meta-analyses show medium effects; RCTs show sustained gains in low-stakes contexts	OECD guardrails + profession partnership	—

The following figure is a visualization of the balance between learner autonomy and governance duties. In Figure 1, which arrays five configurations from AI-led autopilot to human only instruction, with applied linguistics micro scenarios (sociolinguistic exposure diversity, identity affirming writing, pragmatics tutoring) mapped to each configuration.

Figure 1. Freedom – Responsibility Spectrum for AI Personalization in Education

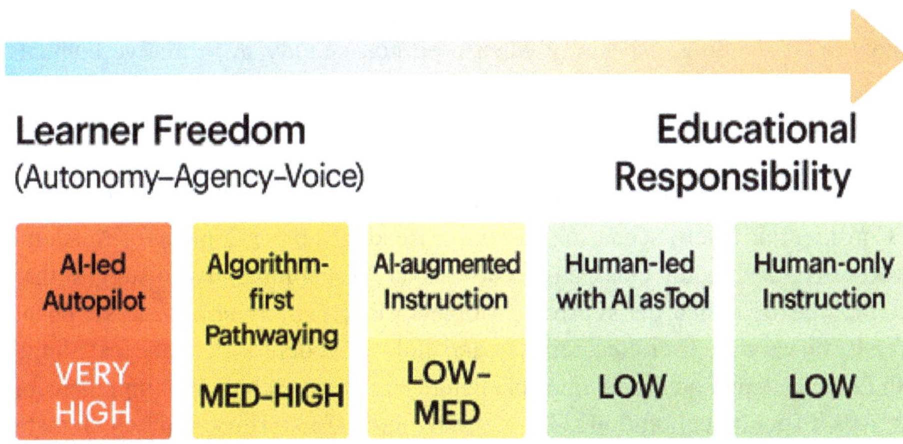

3. THE PROMISE OF AI-PERSONALIZED LEARNING

AI-enabled personalization possesses the credibility and evidence base to, given favourable conditions, strengthen learning outcomes, widen access, and aid in enhancing teacher work-through low-stake, teacher-orchestrated, and learner-agency-preserving implementations (see Figure 1) (Kulik and Fletcher, 2016; U.S. Department of Education, 2023). Across multiple strands of research and policy guidance, a converging message emerges: AI is most valuable as assistive intelligence for formative assessment, targeted practice, and timely feedback; it becomes problematic when used as an automated decider in high-stakes contexts (OECD, 2023; European Union, 2024).

3.1 Improved learning outcomes through responsive practice

A growing body of meta-analytic research on intelligent tutoring systems (ITS) demonstrates that when AI tools provide step-level feedback and adaptive practice aligned with instructional goals, they can lead to substantial improvements in student learning outcomes. For example, Kulik and Fletcher (2016) report that ITS implementations often yield moderate to strong gains in achievement, particularly when systems are designed to scaffold learning in real time.

More recent randomized controlled trials (RCTs) involving platforms like ASSISTments—which offer students immediate feedback and teachers' actionable insights—have shown that such systems can support long-term retention and conceptual understanding, especially when used consistently in formative contexts. These outcomes are particularly notable in settings where learners benefit from timely, individualized support that complements teacher instruction. This evidence supports the AI-augmented instruction zone in Figure 1, where AI is used formatively and remains teacher-in-the-loop, enhancing rather than replacing human judgment.

Consider this Micro-scenario (Formative Reading), in an English for Academic Purposes (EAP) reading class, a teacher uses an AI recommender to suggest three texts tailored to each learner's current proficiency level. The system ensures exposure diversity by varying discipline, register, and dialect. Students select one text aligned with their academic goals and one "challenge" text to stretch their comprehension. The AI's difficulty calibration is informed by models like Birdbrain, which match task complexity to learner ability (Bicknell and Brust, 2020). The teacher curates final choices to prevent over-reliance on familiar genres, thereby promoting broad literacy development and critical reading skills (Pariser, 2012; OECD, 2023).

3.2 Richer Engagement, Metacognition, and Feedback Loops

Personalization can increase time-on-task and perceived relevance by keeping tasks within a productive challenge window, while dialogic tutors foster metacognitive talk (e.g., 'explain your steps' or 'justify your revision') (OECD, 2023; U.S. Department of Education, 2023). Duolingo reports A/B-tested gains when Birdbrain feeds the session generator with learner-calibrated difficulty estimates, indicating more efficient practice sequencing (Bicknell and Brust, 2020; Duolingo, 2020). Early classroom pilots with Khanmigo suggest that prompted reasoning and reflective dialogue can help learners articulate strategies—provided teachers scaffold norms and review transcripts (Khan Academy, 2024; Michigan Virtual, 2025).

In a Micro-scenario (Pragmatics), a pragmatics tutor supports students drafting emails to professors, offering strategy-labeled suggestions (e.g., hedging, indirectness) and asking learners to explain accept/reject decisions. The teacher audits the chat and gives final approval—precisely the AI-augmented, formative pattern encouraged on the right of Figure 1 (OECD, 2023; U.S. Department of Education, 2023).

3.3 Accessibility and inclusion

AI can reduce access barriers by providing timely scaffolds (hints, exemplars, glosses), multimodal supports (audio, captions, translation), and pacing flexibility that benefits learners with diverse needs (OECD, 2023; UNESCO, 2021). The ASSISTments trial's stronger effects for students in higher-poverty schools underscore personalization's equity potential when combined with teacher oversight and formative use (Arnold Ventures, 2024; WestEd, 2024).

Looking at a Micro-scenario (Applied Linguistics, identity-affirming writing) where students compose short identity narratives (e.g., "My multilingual journey"), an LLM offers audience-aware feedback on tone and register, but learners are required to retain voice markers (stance features, discourse particles) and to justify all edits; the teacher grades the reflection, not the model's preference—maintaining agency and identity (UNESCO, 2021; U.S. Department of Education, 2023).

3.4 Teacher capacity: Insight without overload

Used well, AI can reduce routine workload (drafting practice sets, generating exemplars, first-pass feedback) and give teachers clearer insight into misconceptions via dashboards or explainable recommendations (NIST, 2023; U.S. Department of Education, 2023). Khanmigo pilot teachers reported utility in brainstorming questions, lesson hooks, and student activities, with the caveat that professional development is crucial for effective use (Khan Academy, 2024; Michigan Virtual,

2025). A useful practice tip in this regard would be to keep AI on diagnose-don't-decide tasks: formative hints, item generation aligned to learning objectives, misconception clustering—with teachers making the pedagogical calls (OECD, 2023; U.S. Department of Education, 2023).

3.5 Institutional benefits and responsible scale

At the institutional level, AI personalization can enable earlier, lower-cost interventions (learning analytics), data-informed curriculum improvement, and wider access to practice without requiring one-to-one human tutoring (Jisc, 2023; OECD, 2023). However, benefits scale safely only with governance routines—risk mapping, data minimization, transparency, appeals—as articulated in NIST AI RMF and the ISO/IEC 23894 lifecycle (ISO/IEC, 2023; NIST, 2023). In connection to Figure 1, institutional gains typically come from right-side configurations—teacher-orchestrated, formative deployments—where risks are low to low-medium and responsibilities are operationalizable through codes of practice (Jisc, 2023; OECD, 2023).

3.6 Boundary conditions: When the promise holds (and when it doesn't)

The evidence cluster suggests the promise is strongest when four (4) conditions are met:

- Formative focus (hints/feedback, not summative gatekeeping) AI should be used to support learning in progress—by giving hints, feedback, and scaffolding—not to make high-stakes decisions like grading or passing/failing. When AI is formative, it empowers learners and helps them grow. But when used for summative assessment, it can amplify bias, reduce transparency, and undermine trust. For instance, an AI tutor that gives real-time feedback on writing is formative. An AI that auto-grades essays for final marks is summative—and riskier. (OECD, 2023; U.S. Department of Education, 2023);
- Teacher-in-the-loop (TITT) orchestration with override and audit trails. Teachers must remain central decision-makers. AI should assist, not replace, their judgment. Systems should allow (a) Override: Teachers can change or reject AI suggestions. (b) Audit trails: There's a record of what the AI recommended and what was done. This ensures accountability, pedagogical integrity, and human oversight—especially when AI makes mistakes or recommendations that don't fit the learner's context. (Jisc, 2023; NIST, 2023);

- Transparency about recommendations and uncertainty, with learner choice and opt-out. This means AI systems must: (a) Explain how and why they make recommendations. (b) Show confidence levels or uncertainty. (c) Allow learners to opt out or choose alternatives. This supports learner autonomy and informed consent. Without transparency, learners may blindly follow AI, even when it's wrong or biased. (ISO/IEC, 2023; Jisc, 2023);
- Exposure-diversity design to avoid filter bubbles. AI should be designed to broaden learners' horizons, not narrow them. This means: Recommending diverse content, not just what aligns with past behaviour. Avoiding "echo chambers" where learners only see what they already agree with. Education should challenge learners, expose them to multiple perspectives, and foster critical thinking—not just comfort or confirmation. (Pariser, 2012; UNESCO, 2021).

Conversely, promises erode when systems are used for high-stakes automated decisions (placement, grading) without human review and appeal—precisely the left-hand "AI-led autopilot" zone in Figure 1, which recent policy treats as high-risk (GDPR, 2016/Art. 22; European Union, 2024).

3.8 Measuring the promise: Outcomes and agency, not just scores

AI-powered personalized learning systems are often judged by achievement metrics alone—like test scores or completion rates. But this narrow lens misses the broader educational goals of empowering learners, fostering autonomy, and exposing them to diverse ideas and voices. To evaluate AI personalization credibly, we need multi-dimensional metrics that reflect Cognitive outcomes (achievement), Learner agency (control, choice, reflection), and Exposure diversity (breadth of content and perspectives). To evaluate AI personalization credibly, programs should combine learning outcomes with agency metrics and exposure diversity indicators. Here are a few suggested measures:

- **Achievement**: classical learning system target mastery of the content and applying knowledge in new contexts as its tangible outcomes where evaluation and assessment are based on: (1) Unit tests that should be aligned to standards of the curriculum; and (2) Transfer tasks requiring implementation of skills learned for problems the students have never encountered before. The achievement of these two criteria is therefore a vital issue to ensure that learning is not only enhancing personalization, but also in the interest of engagement (Kulik and Fletcher, 2016; WestEd, 2024).

- **Agency**: refers to target learner autonomy, decision-making, and reflective thinking: hence, learning agency is core to personalized learning. That is, students are either active participants or passive recipients. A disagreement could arise as to what we need to consider as indicator(s) in this regard, for more research is still being done. However, the following indicators can be suggested for now. (a) Choice breadth: Number and variety of learning paths or content types the student selects. (b) Help-seeking behaviour: Frequency and timing of student-initiated requests for help or clarification. (c) AI suggestion acceptance rate with rationale: How often students accept or reject AI recommendations, and whether they provide reasons. (d) Metacognitive journal quality: Depth and insight in student reflections about their learning process. (OECD, 2023; U.S. Department of Education, 2023).
- **Exposure diversity**: distribution of registers/dialects/genres over time and proportion of challenge texts completed Breadth and richness of content exposure—linguistic, cultural, and cognitive. Exposure diversity combats filter bubbles and supports critical thinking, cultural literacy, and language development. Pariser (2012) suggests the following indicators: (a) Distribution of registers/dialects/genres over time: Tracks whether students are exposed to formal/informal language, regional dialects, academic vs. narrative texts, etc. (b) Proportion of challenge texts completed: Measures how often students engage with texts that are above their comfort zone or outside their usual interests. (Pariser, 2012; UNESCO, 2021).

3.9 Practical design heuristics

To ensure that AI-powered personalized learning systems fulfil their promise while upholding ethical and pedagogical responsibilities, educators and designers must adopt a set of principled practices that safeguard learner agency, equity, and diversity.

First and foremost, AI should be used *to diagnose, not decide*. This means keeping AI in the feedback lane—providing formative insights, identifying misconceptions, and suggesting next steps—while reserving final decisions about grades, placement, or advancement for human educators. Such a method goes in-line with the guidelines and directives of the US department of education and the European Union General Data Protection Regulations (GDPR), article 22, that prohibit any automation of any decision that significantly affect or influence individuals without human supervision. For instance, platforms such as the AI -Tutor in Khan Academy offer prompt feedback, but it holds and leaves instructional decisions and judgement in the hands of the teachers, considering making AI as mere support for the professional judgement, and not replacing it.

There is also another practice with a possibility of causing discrimination in personalization. Leaving algorithms to their own devices would continue feeding users with culturally filtered content with those disparate diasporic users being a minority group. Hence, the systems should take into account *exposure diversity* quotas, tagging learning materials with language, dialect, register and gender. For example, rotating contents in linguistically and culturally is among the UNISCO AI Literacy tool kit to expose learners to various voices and styles, and enhancing their horizons, therefore, with intercultural competence and critical thinking.

Hence, *transparency* may be taken as the second axis for responsible AI design. Systems ought to require some form of explanation from either the AI or the learner. AI systems may attempt some justifications with relation to its recommendations, for instance "Recommended because it builds on your previous work", while learners think of the reasons to accept or reject these recommendations.

This means that AI systems need to be designed to *audit equity*. In its turn, periodical evaluation and assessment of outcomes among sub-group learners is a prerequisite, as well as adjusting contents or prompts to ensure such discrepancies are not created. LearnPlatform's EdTech Equity Audit tools allow schools to track gaps in performance and intervene when those gaps begin closing, that is if personalization is ever found to accidentally exacerbate existing inequalities.

Thus, these four practices, diagnosing without deciding, constraining for diversity, requiring explanation, and auditing equity, become a strong framework within which the transformational potential of AI could be aligned with the ethical imperatives of education. They allow educators to realize the promise of AI: improved learning outcomes, deeper engagement, and broader inclusion, all while maintaining the integrity and responsibility mapped in Figure 1 of this chapter.

4. THE DEBATE: FREEDOM VS. RESPONSIBILITY

In light of the promise of AI-personalized learning, debate presents quite the attractively bold narrative debate: How do we counterbalance learner freedom--that is, autonomy, agency, and voice--with the duties of educators, institutions, and developers to ensure fairness, transparency, and accountability? (Al-Saggaf, 2024; Chan and Hu, 2023). That debate is not negligible; it conditions tangible design choices, policy paradigms, and classroom practices (see Figure 1).

Generally speaking, personalized learning is featured with learner's independency; it is alleged that students acquire mastery of the period needed to comprehend the content, its sequential learning position, and even the teaching method. This aligns with the focus on student-centred curricula, which prioritize agency and self-regulation (Luckin et al., 2016).

Thus, it is worth noting that placing algorithmic systems on the educational platforms creates undeniable tension that further enhances the contradicting dualism of autonomy and delicate control. These systems that are designed to allure and attract learners at any cost, try in an inadequate way to algorithmically push the learner towards a specific field or a direction based on the learner's earlier work or expected success. Although this would help in short-term empowerment, it may undermine in-depth learning and intellectual exploration (Rodríguez et al., 2022).

With time, such dynamics may pave the way for educational Filter-Bubbles (FB) to appear. Filter-bubbles is a well- documented phenomenon in digital media (Pariser, 2012) and is currently gaining more attention in the AI assisted teaching methods. These filter bubbles may appear when recommendation algorithms continue to distribute the same content varieties that learners have seen previously, which prevent their exposure to other varied groups of genres, registers, and dialects. Zhou et al. (2024) found that students using reading platforms that are AI-enhanced are rarely exposed to the opportunity of contents that with language or cultural varieties, unless these contents are deliberately considered and embedded in the system design.

He, Zou, and Du (2025) point out that while the use of EAP Talk enhances learners' speaking fluency and interaction, its drivers favour standardized academic registers, which narrows learners' language repertoire and hinders their ability to navigate diverse communicative contexts. This narrowing has serious consequences when it comes to designing educational materials. If we want to exercise the freedom to learn through AI, the teacher must intervene at a certain stage, and it must never be left to algorithmic deviation. Teachers and systems are required to set limits of exposure diversity to form something like security check, i.e., complex texts and dialect diversity must be maintained within a quota in the system. These security checks are vital to minimize algorithmic narrowing and also to prevent personalization from becoming a hindrance to critical inquiry, cultural literacy, and linguistic diversity (UNESCO, 2021; OECD, 2023).

When we look at the aspect of freedom in AI personalized learning, it is not an "either or" to use control as opposed to freedom. Rather, it is a negotiable space where autonomy should be protected from the background push of the hidden factions of the algorithmic propulsion. Hence, a responsible AI-driven learning is to put learners' empowerment at its core. Allowing them to choose, observe, reflect, and grow alongside with the constraints that their algorithms' predictions have set for preferences.

4.2 Responsibility Dimension: Ethics, Law, and Pedagogy

The first dimension of AI's responsibility in education is the interconnected set of ethical, legal, and educational layers. These three layers should be addressed with consideration for their interdependence, as well as the potential tensions between them. Such perspective allows for a better understanding an ultimately incorporation of Ai systems in education, rather than being treated separately or hierarchically, allowing for AI system to support learning, with human rights, professional integrity and pedagogical values first in its development.

Ethically, UNESCO's Recommendation on Ethics of Artificial Intelligence emphasizes fairness, transparency, and human oversight. In education, these principles are especially important when learners – usually minors – suffer from narrow and limited decision-making systems. Ethical AI must promote inclusion, avoid bias, and ensure that decisions affecting learners are explainable and contestable (UNESCO, 2021). Scholars such as Williamson (2025) argue that ethical frameworks must go beyond abstract principles and be embedded in the everyday design and deployment of educational technologies.

From a legal standpoint, the European Union's General Data Protection Regulation (GDPR) enshrines the right of individuals not to be subject to decisions based solely on automated processing that significantly affect them (Regulation (EU) 2016/679). This is especially relevant in educational contexts where AI systems may influence access to learning opportunities, progression, or certification. Colonna (2024) emphasizes that AI-based assessment systems must ensure that teachers remain "in the loop," capable of overseeing and overriding decisions when necessary. The newly enacted EU Artificial Intelligence Act classifies educational AI systems as "high-risk," requiring transparency, data quality, and human oversight in high-stakes decision-making (Saarela et al., 2025).

The pedagogical layer of responsibility is equally vital. According to the U.S. Department of Education (2023), educators must remain central to instructional decision-making. AI should enhance teaching, not replace professional judgment. The Department likens AI to an "electric bike"—a support mechanism that reduces effort while keeping the human in control—rather than a "robot vacuum" that operates autonomously. This aligns with wider educational principles that prioritize teacher agency, contextual judgment, and ethical reflection in the use of technology (Holmes et al., 2022). A striking example of what can go wrong when key safeguards are overlooked is the UK's 2020 grading algorithm debacle. Disrupted by the COVID-19 pandemic, the government decided to skip the traditional A-level and GCSE examinations and instead award grades generated by an algorithm run by Ofqual. For lack of transparency, the system offered no apparent method to appeal against the grades, a situation that turned out to be hugely problematic: almost 40% of the teacher-assessed grades were downgraded, with students from socially disadvantaged backgrounds much more likely to be affected. According to Leckie and Prior (2023), the algorithm performed very poorly in small schools, adding systemic bias to the assessment process. The public reacted quickly, violent protests erupted across the country, and the credibility of the education system was damaged. Even the prime minister recorded an official criticism of the model, calling it the infamous "mutant algorithm." The government had no choice but to admit defeat.

This event remains a plain reminder of the dangers inherent when leaving such high-risk educational decisions in the hands of an obscure AI system, deprived of sound human review and ethical safeguards. This failure is a result of robotic driving mode with almost no human intervention and with maximum risk. Preventing such failures from educational institutions must require the development of a multi-layered scope of responsibility that includes ethical design, legal accountability, and educational integrity. Only then would we be in a strong position to harness the power of AI for educational purposes; equality, equity, trust, and human dignity.

4.3 Risks of Overreach: Bias, Privacy, and Interpretation

As AI increasingly integrates into education, three core issues need to be urgently analysed: bias, privacy, and ease of explainability.

Bias: AI systems often show the inaccuracy of the data they have been trained on. When certain groups remain underrepresented, the results tend to deepen existing inequalities. Teaching the language may inadvertently favour British and American English at the expense of World Englishes, along with many other dialects and cultural expressions. Buolamwini and Gebru (2018) showed industries' commercial AI systems greatly misclassified darker-skinned individuals, laying bare the dangers of biased datasets. Baker and Hawn (2022) warn that such biases distort assessment, feedback, and even placement when systems fail to consider demographic diversity. For instance, biased AI systems could encourage assessments favouring standardized academic English of AI tutors, limiting the opportunity for linguistic variation, and thus hampering the acquisition of sociolinguistic skills.

Privacy: Student data are protected in the U.S. and Europe by laws such as FERPA and GDPR, which require transparency, consent, and strict data handling. The review of the AI Act and GDPR by the European Parliament highlights the difficult balancing act needed between allowing bias detection and protecting sensitive data. A solid governance framework and human oversight must come first.

Explainability: In the absence of explanation of how AI-driven learning platforms work, teachers and learners are left in complete misperception and they cannot understand, or even question automated decisions. Liu et al. (2024) argue that Explainable AI (XAI) allows teachers to interpret AI outputs and make informed decisions. On the other hand, Altukhi and Pradhan (2024) point to another reason for the slow adoption of AI in education: the lack of clear standards. When AI is a black box, trust and accountability don't thrive.

4.4 The Freedom–Responsibility Trade-off in Practice

The tension between freedom and responsibility in AI-mediated education is not a dichotomy at all—it is rather a continuum, as depicted in Figure 1, ranging from complete automation to greater human autonomy, with pedagogical and ethical considerations attached to these variants.

Now, the Far-Left Zone (AI on Autopilot) implies that such AI systems are being run almost ghost-like with very little human supervisory interference, if any. Mathematics is such that the automation is scalable and efficient, posing grave risks when such decisions are either opaque or irreversible.

According to Dumbuya (2025), over-reliance on AI systems completely disenfranchises the educator; teaching becomes just facilitation, and learning is standardized in a manner that completely overlooks the uniqueness of each individual learner. This discussion has important ramifications in formative assessment, as the best interest of the learners might be casually pushed by the AI toward certain algorithmic options without the informed consent of the learners themselves.

As for the Middle Zone (AI-Augmented Instruction), this balanced model blends AI support with human judgment. Teachers guide the process, AI offers feedback, and learners engage critically. Kim (2023) describes it as a collegial partnership, where the sharing of control allows the learner to adopt a reflective stance and engage in the ethical process of personalization. Learners hold agency; they can accept, reject, or reflect on AI suggestions, making this zone the most conducive to responsible innovation.

On the other hand, with the Far-Right Zone (Human-Led Instruction), teachers retain all the control with very little input from the AI. While this allows for maximum autonomy and creativity, it also limits the amount of scalability and personalization that can be offered by AI. According to Belloula (2025), teacher-led approaches offer a strong degree of context sensitivity but tend to be resource-heavy and less able to adapt to differing learner profiles.

Let us consider this hypothetical example from applied linguistics. An AI teacher recommends politeness strategies to his students to use these strategies in their academic writing. If this is done by a mere prompt to an AI-driven platform and changes are applied automatically, the learners are deprived of their freedom of action. If the modifications are identified and discussed, the responsibility is distributed. This is an example of the middle area to consider and put in practice. In this way, this approach facilitates cognitive development and language learning through transparency and choice.

Below is an attempt to conceptualize the balance to be retained as a solution to the debate of the nexus between Freedom and Responsibility when it comes to AI-Personalized learning. The figure is proposed as a design solution that respects both ends of the spectrum, assuring the implementation of choice, transparency, and diversity alongside human oversight, fairness checks, and vigorous data protection mechanisms.

Figure 2. AI Personalization Workflow

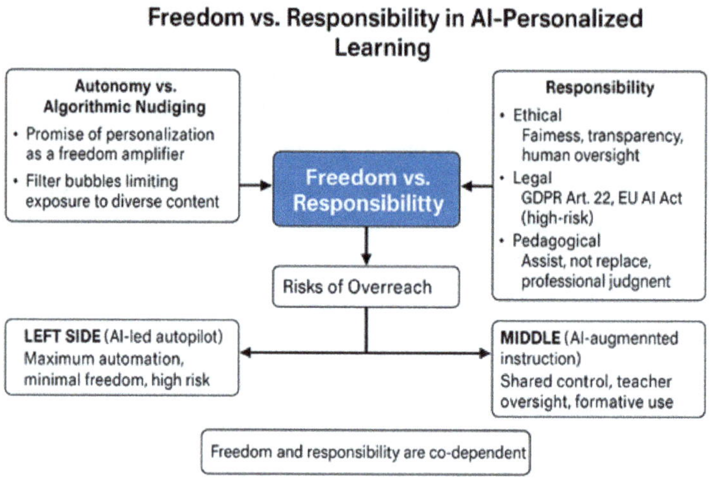

5. A PRACTICAL FRAMEWORK FOR RESPONSIBLE AI PERSONALIZATION

In order for AI to become more deeply embedded into personalized learning, we require a framework premised on ethical, pedagogical, and institutional responsibility. As AI increasingly becomes embedded in instruction, feedback, and engagement, educators must ensure that it supports human judgment and expertise rather than replacing it.

5.1 Human-AI Collaboration as a Foundational Principle

Responsible AI begins with the understanding that human-AI collaboration should be fundamental, where AI exists within the domain of supportive tools without assuming autonomous decision-making power. The AI should foster creativity, enhance efficiency, and provide personalization while retaining the responsibility of the educator for developing critical thinking among students and instances of academic honesty (Nguyen, 2025). This philosophy corresponds to the "teacher-in-the-loop" concept, where claims and decisions remain embedded within contextualized pedagogical expertise.

5.2 Ethical Guardrails: Transparency, Privacy, and Equity

A strong framework would embed ethical guardrails, especially transparency, privacy, and equity. AI systems need to be explainable and auditable so educators and learners can understand how decisions are reached. This is veritably essential in the adaptive learning context, in which opaque algorithms can inadvertently strengthen biases or restrict content exposure (Zhai et al., 2024; Ardito, 2025). Institutions must implement clear data governance policies and ensure learners retain agency over their data.

5.3 Pedagogical Alignment and Curriculum Integration

Instructional design for AI tools must be aligned with learning theories and goals. Rather than simply using AI standalone, an instructor might embed AI into a curriculum so that it supports formative assessment, differentiated instruction, and learner autonomy. Embedding AI ethics into curricula and faculty training creates an environment for educators to critically evaluate and adapt AI tools to their particular educational context (Nguyen, 2025).

5.4 Institutional Policy and Professional Development

Support for sustainable implementation depends on institutional policies that define the use of AI with responsibility, and which also encourage lifelong learning for professionals. Policies should delineate explicitly where AI can be deployed, outline processes to ethically review use cases, as well as guarantee equitable treatment with regard to access. Training for educators must be able to teach them how to comprehend AI outputs, evaluate risks, and create learning activities that responsibly use AI (Chan and Hu, 2023; Hutson and Rains 2024).

5.5 Student-Centred Design and Inclusive Access

Finally, responsible AI personalization must focus on the student, recognizing diversity in need and facilitating inclusive access. AI tools must cater to different learning styles, languages, and accessibility requirements. Equal access may avoid digital divides, which is a must for ensuring its benefits reach all students. (McDonald et al., 2024; Samala et al., 2024).

6. TEACHER-IN-THE-LOOP (TITL)

The Teacher-in-The-Loop (TITL) paradigm constitutes a pedagogy-grounded approach towards integrating AI into education. The emphasis under this paradigm lies on placing the educators at the centre of instructional decision-making. Unlike other systems that promote automation for replacing human effort, TITL is positioned as being bilaterally orchestrated, whereby human and artificial intelligences collaborate in obtaining increased personalization, feedback, and learner engagement.

6.1 From Automation to Augmentation

Initial efforts of integrating AI with education heavily emphasized automation—automated grading, adaptive sequencing, and predictive analytics—leading to concerns of displacing teachers and limiting their ability to affect pedagogical decisions. Present-day scholarship contends augmentation, wherein AI amplifies the expertise of a teacher rather than replacing it (Kim, 2023). The simplest of the AI methods may include tasks such as keeping track of a student's progress or elucidating possible misconceptions, while it is up to the teacher to interpret the presented evidence and decide how these insights are to be used in structuring or adapting teaching. This is paramount, as it preserves instructional flexibility; in fact, over-automation limits the capability of educators to decide on instructional goals or respond to situational dynamics in their classroom (Holstein et al., 2018).

6.2 Pedagogical Co-Design and Contextual Sensitivity

Effective TITL implementation depends on pedagogical co-design, where educators participate in generating the operational modalities that AI tools will have within their particular teaching environments. According to Daher (2025), teachers contribute essential knowledge of the learner's needs, the curriculum objectives, and the culture of the classroom—dimensions that AI cannot fully encompass. Joint design safeguards the responsiveness, ethical conduct, and contextual relevance of AI tools. Co-design, therefore, ensures that AI tools are co-engineered in terms of context sensitivity and address educational values. Moreover, TITL approaches emphasize adaptive scaffolding, where AI provides real-time feedback or suggestions, but teachers retain authority over pacing, content selection, and assessment. This balance supports learner agency while preserving the relational and dialogic aspects of teaching.

6.3 Professional Development and AI Literacy

For TITL to be effective, educators must be equipped with AI literacy—not just technical skills, but a deep understanding of how AI systems work, their limitations, and their ethical implications. The EQUIP framework (Ethical Governance, Qualified Professional Learning, Unified Collaborative Partnerships, Implementation Readiness, and Progressive Adaptation) offers a structured model for preparing teachers to engage critically and confidently with AI tools (Daher, 2025). Professional development should include hands-on experience with AI systems, opportunities for reflective practice, and collaborative inquiry into how AI can support diverse learners. Without such preparation, there is a risk of overreliance on opaque systems or uncritical adoption of tools that may reinforce bias or narrow learning pathways.

6.4 Dynamic Teacher-AI Partnerships

TITL is not a static model but a dynamic partnership that evolves over time. Kim (2023) outlines a three-stage progression: (1) teachers as passive recipients of AI outputs, (2) teachers as active users who interpret and adapt AI insights, and (3) teachers and AI as constructive partners in co-orchestrating learning. This final stage envisions a hybrid system where both human and machine intelligences contribute uniquely to instructional design, formative assessment, and learner support. Such partnerships require mutual understanding; AI systems must be transparent and interpretable, while teachers must be empowered to question, bypass, or modify AI recommendations. This ensures that AI remains a servant of education, not a master of it.

7. CONCLUSION

With the integration of AI into the education system, the conflict is no longer about whether AI should be introduced, but rather about how to introduce it responsibly, equitably, and pedagogically. This chapter has been coupled with the requirements of a basic AI allocation framework that values learner autonomy, teacher autonomy, and ethical checkpoints.

The scope of freedom and responsibility has been drafted in the text to clarify the level of risk and degree of control included in various AI systems, from full automation to full human education. In this way, AI can enhance learning outcomes, especially in formative contexts that keep teachers informed, such as intelligent teaching systems and adaptive platforms. In no way should allocation undermine transparency, fairness, or the voice of the learner. Thus, the framework should include the principles of human-AI collaboration, pedagogical compatibility, data ethics, and inclusive design.

The Teacher in the Loop (TITL) is a key pillar of this vision. This system keeps teachers up to date as AI is used to discriminate, provide feedback, and foster engagement. Thus, TITL is much more than a technocratic formative construct; it has come to represent an educational perspective that suggests that teachers cannot be substituted for anything in the process of building meaningful, equitable, and human-centred learning.

Ultimately, the future of AI in education depends not on algorithmic evolution alone, but on our collective ability to design, govern, and teach using AI in ways that elevate educational values. Responsible personalization is an ongoing process, requiring reflection, dialogue, and a shared commitment to the learner's prosperity. Freedom and responsibility are key pillars of ethical AI. Personalization must empower learners while safeguarding their rights. By aligning innovation with human values, educators can build learning environments that are inclusive, transparent, and effective.

REFERENCES

Al-Saggaf, M. A. (2020). Investigating the types of motivation of TESL students in a higher education institute in Malaysia. *TESOL and Technology Studies*, *1*(1), 55–69. DOI: 10.48185/tts.v1i1.105

Al-Saggaf, M. A. (2024). Freedom and Responsibility in Education 5.0. In *Preconceptions of Policies, Strategies, and Challenges in Education 5.0* (pp. 275-283). IGI Global. https://doi.org/DOI: 10.4018/979-8-3693-3041-8.ch016

Al-Saggaf, M. A. (2025). NLP in Action: Enhancing Translation and Interpretation. In *Role of AI in Translation and Interpretation* (pp. 175-204). IGI Global Scientific Publishing. https://doi.org/DOI: 10.4018/979-8-3373-0060-3.ch007

Altukhi, Z. M., & Pradhan, S. (2024). "Systematic Literature Review: Explainable AI Definitions and Challenges in Education" *ICIS 2024 Proceedings*. 11. https://aisel.aisnet.org/icis2024/lit_review/lit_review/11

Ardito, C. G. (2025). Generative AI detection in higher education assessments. *New Directions for Teaching and Learning*, *2025*, 11–28. DOI: 10.1002/tl.20624

Baker, R. S., & Hawn, A. (2022). Algorithmic bias in education. *International Journal of Artificial Intelligence in Education*, *32*(4), 1052–1092. DOI: 10.1007/s40593-021-00285-9

Belloula, S. (2025). Empowering Educators: Leveraging AI to Revolutionize Lesson Planning. *International Journal of Research in Education and Science*, *11*(2), 264–280. https://files.eric.ed.gov/fulltext/EJ1475735.pdf

Bicknell, K., & Brust, C. (2020, October 7). *Learning how to help you learn: Introducing Birdbrain!* Duolingo Blog. https://blog.duolingo.com/learning-how-to-help-you-learn-introducing-birdbrain/

Bloom, B. S. (1984). The 2 sigma problem: The search for methods of group instruction as effective as one-to-one tutoring. *Educational Researcher*, *13*(6), 4–16. DOI: 10.3102/0013189X013006004

Buolamwini, J., & Gebru, T. (2018). Gender shades: Intersectional accuracy disparities in commercial gender classification. *Proceedings of Machine Learning Research*, *81*, 1–15. https://proceedings.mlr.press/v81/buolamwini18a/buolamwini18a.pdf

Chan, C. K. Y., & Hu, W. (2023). Students' voices on generative AI: Perceptions, benefits, and challenges in higher education. *International Journal of Educational Technology in Higher Education, 20*(43). Advance online publication. DOI: 10.1186/s41239-023-00411-8

CNBC. (2020, August 21). *How a computer algorithm caused a grading crisis in British schools.* https://www.cnbc.com/2020/08/21/computer-algorithm-caused-a-grading-crisis-in-british-schools.html

Colonna, L. (2024). Human oversight in AI-based educational assessments: A GDPR perspective. *European Journal of Law and Technology, 15*(1), 1–18.

Daher, R. (2025). Integrating AI literacy into teacher education: A critical perspective paper. *Discover Artificial Intelligence, 5*, 217. DOI: 10.1007/s44163-025-00475-7

Dumbuya, E. (2025). Artificial Intelligence and Education: Preserving Human Agency in the World of Automation. *Online Submission.* https://files.eric.ed.gov/fulltext/ED664881.pdf

Duolingo. (2020). *Learning how to help you learn: Introducing Birdbrain!* https://blog.duolingo.com/learning-how-to-help-you-learn-introducing-birdbrain/

European Union. (2024). *Regulation (EU) 2024/1689 laying down harmonised rules on artificial intelligence (Artificial Intelligence Act).* Official Journal of the European Union. https://eur-lex.europa.eu/eli/reg/2024/1689/oj/eng

GDPR. (2016). *Article 22—Automated individual decision-making, including profiling.* https://gdpr-info.eu/art-22-gdpr/

General Data Protection Regulation (GDPR). (2016). *Article 22—Automated individual decision-making, including profiling.* https://gdpr-info.eu/art-22-gdpr/

He, Y., Zou, L., & Du, M. (2025). EAP Talk and the narrowing of linguistic diversity: A study of AI-driven academic English platforms. *Journal of Applied Linguistics and Technology, 42*(1), 55–72.

Holmes, W., Bialik, M., & Fadel, C. (2022). *Artificial intelligence in education: Promises and implications for teaching and learning.* Center for Curriculum Redesign.

Holstein, K., Hong, G., Tegene, M., McLaren, B. M., & Aleven, V. (2018). The classroom as a dashboard: Co-designing wearable cognitive augmentation for K–12 teachers. *LAK, 18.* Advance online publication. DOI: 10.1145/3170358.3170377

Hutson, J., & Rains, T. J. (2024). *Charting the AI transition in education and business environments: Navigating the generative inflection point for Industry 4.0 success.* Taylor & Francis., DOI: 10.4324/9781003512813

ISO/IEC. (2023). *ISO/IEC 23894:2023—Artificial intelligence—Guidance on risk management.* https://www.iso.org/standard/77304.html

Jisc. (2023, August 2). *Code of practice for learning analytics.* https://www.jisc.ac.uk/guides/code-of-practice-for-learning-analytics

Khan Academy. (2024). *Annual report 2023–2024: Khanmigo overview.* https://annualreport.khanacademy.org/khanmigo

Kim, J. (2023). Leading teachers' perspective on teacher–AI collaboration in education. *Education and Information Technologies*, *29*, 8693–8724. DOI: 10.1007/s10639-023-12109-5

Kulik, J. A., & Fletcher, J. D. (2016). Effectiveness of intelligent tutoring systems: A meta-analytic review. *Review of Educational Research*, *86*(1), 42–78. DOI: 10.3102/0034654315581420

Leckie, G., & Prior, L. (2023). The 2020 Ofqual algorithm and the politics of educational data: A secondary analysis. *British Journal of Educational Studies*, *71*(2), 145–163. DOI: 10.1080/00071005.2022.2104567

Liu, Q., Pinto, J. D., & Paquette, L. (2024). Applications of Explainable AI (XAI) in Education. In D. Kourkoulou, A. O. Tzirides, B. Cope, & M. Kalantzis (Eds.), *Trust and Inclusion in AI-Mediated Education: Where Human Learning Meets Learning Machines* (pp. 93-109). (Postdigital Science and Education; Vol. Part F3835). Springer. https://doi.org/DOI: 10.1007/978-3-031-64487-0_5

Luckin, R., Holmes, W., Griffiths, M., & Forcier, L. B. (2016). *Intelligence unleashed: An argument for AI in education.* Pearson Education. https://static.googleusercontent.com/media/edu.google.com/en//pdfs/Intelligence-Unleashed-Publication.pdf

McDonald, N., Johri, A., Ali, A., & Hingle, A. (2024). Generative artificial intelligence in higher education: Evidence from an analysis of institutional policies and guidelines. https://doi.org//arXiv.2402.01659DOI: 10.48550

Nguyen, K. V. (2025). The use of generative AI tools in higher education: Ethical and pedagogical principles. *Ethics and Education.* Advance online publication. DOI: 10.1007/s10805-025-09607-1

NIST. (2023). *AI Risk Management Framework (1.0) and Playbook.* National Institute of Standards and Technology. https://www.nist.gov/itl/ai-risk-management-framework

OECD. (2023). *Artificial intelligence in education: Promises and challenges.* OECD Publishing. https://www.oecd.org/education/artificial-intelligence-in-education.htm

OECD. (2023). *OECD Digital Education Outlook 2023: Opportunities, guidelines and guardrails for effective and equitable use of AI in education*. https://www.oecd.org/en/publications/oecd-digital-education-outlook-2023_c74f03de-en/full-report/opportunities-guidelines-and-guardrails-for-effective-and-equitable-use-of-ai-in-education_2f0862dc.html

Pariser, E. (2012). *The filter bubble: How the new personalized web is changing what we read and how we think*. Penguin. (Original work published 2011) https://archive.org/details/filterbubblewhat0000pari_z0d7

Regulation (EU) 2016/679 of the European Parliament and of the Council. (2016). *General Data Protection Regulation (GDPR)*. Official Journal of the European Union.

Rodríguez, F., Pérez, J., & García, M. (2022). Algorithmic nudging in adaptive learning systems: Balancing personalization and autonomy. *Educational Technology Research and Development, 70*(4), 1021–1040. DOI: 10.1007/s11423-021-10023-9

Saarela, M., Gunasekara, C., & Karimov, R. (2025). High-risk AI in education: Implications of the EU AI Act for learning analytics. *AI & Society, 40*(1), 89–104.

Samala, A. D., Rawas, S., Wang, T., Reed, J. M., Kim, J., Howard, N.-J., & Ertz, M. (2024). Unveiling the landscape of generative artificial intelligence in education: A comprehensive taxonomy of applications, challenges, and future prospects. *Education and Information Technologies*. Advance online publication. DOI: 10.1007/s10639-024-12936-0

Student Privacy Policy Office. (n.d.). *Protecting student privacy (FERPA & PPRA)*. U.S. Department of Education. https://studentprivacy.ed.gov/

UNESCO. (2021). *Artificial intelligence and the futures of learning*. United Nations Educational, Scientific and Cultural Organization. https://unesdoc.unesco.org/ark:/48223/pf0000377071

UNESCO. (2021). *Recommendation on the ethics of artificial intelligence*. United Nations Educational, Scientific and Cultural Organization. https://unesdoc.unesco.org/ark:/48223/pf0000381137

U.S. Department of Education. (2023). *Artificial intelligence and the future of teaching and learning: Insights and recommendations*. Office of Educational Technology. https://tech.ed.gov/ai/

Ventures, A. (2024, August 8). *A replication randomized controlled trial (RCT) of ASSISTments* (summary with link to WestEd report). https://www.arnoldventures.org/stories/a-replication-randomized-controlled-trial-rct-of-assistments-an-online-study-tool-to-improve-student-math-outcomes-in-seventh-grade

Virtual, M. (2025, August 13). *Have you considered AI in your classroom? A Khanmigo pilot story.* https://michiganvirtual.org/blog/have-you-considered-ai-in-your-classroom-a-khanmigo-pilot-story/

WestEd. (2024). *Implementing and evaluating ASSISTments…* (North Carolina RCT report). https://files.eric.ed.gov/fulltext/ED631720.pdf

Williamson, B. (2025). Governing AI in education: Ethics, policy, and the limits of automation. *Learning, Media and Technology*, *50*(1), 1–17.

Zhai, X., Guo, S., & Zheng, Y. (2024). Artificial intelligence in education research during 2013–2023: A review based on bibliometric analysis. *Education and Information Technologies*, *29*, 16387–16409. DOI: 10.1007/s10639-024-12491-8

Zhou, Y., Tan, R., & Lee, C. (2024). Breaking the bubble: Teaching AI literacy through filter bubble simulations in middle school. *Computers & Education*, *205*, 104589. DOI: 10.1016/j.compedu.2023.104589

Chapter 3
English Language Learning in Multilingual Societies

Atyaf Hasan Ibrahim
https://orcid.org/0000-0001-6261-0697
College of Arts, Al-Iraqia University, Iraq

Prodhan Mahbub Ibna Seraj
https://orcid.org/0000-0002-4483-6059
American International University-Bangladesh, Bangladesh

ABSTRACT

World English has maintained an undeniable presence for over 150 years. At the dawn of the 21st century, the advent of a new millennium and fears of a uniform world led to an unprecedented surge in interest in this phenomenon. This linguistic diversity encompasses bi/multilingualism, which results in population movement, language shift, and cross-cultural interactions, leading to difficulties in learning English. This chapter focuses on discussing the challenges posed by multilingualism in learning English as a global language. It outlines various teaching strategies, assessment, and evaluation processes for multilingual classrooms with a focus on learning English. Here, the discussion is held on how cultural considerations are integrated into language teaching. Finally, evidence is shown from case studies of successful programs to inform future directions in English language learning in multilingual contexts.

DOI: 10.4018/979-8-3373-3755-5.ch003

1. INTRODUCTION TO MULTILINGUALISM

As the world has become a 'global village,' the movement of peoples, cultures, and ideas has resulted in varying degrees of social, cultural, and linguistic diversity in many nations. This linguistic diversity consists of bi/multilingualism among minority groups, justified with an 'ethnic rights' argument, as well as the multi/language-ness of urban centers and contact zones as a result of population movement, language shift, and cross-cultural interactions between indigenous and settler communities. Such new multicultural societies raise evident challenges for the social cohesion of existing nations. This pressure has also been felt in the Asia-pacific region, where English-dominant and English-encroaching nations have responded with a unique blend of officially-stated 'celebrations' accompanied by a plethora of 'trials' through educational, largely monolingual/ monolithic policies, conflicting language priorities resulting in language endangerment, national curriculum mandates, calls for a standardization of educational resources, and 'correct' interpretation and distribution of curriculum documents, all in an apparent rush to drive a 'rational master' agenda of a re-colonization of minds through language. Such hybrid, ambiguous coherence creates an epistemological paradox of 'always already' knowing through 'never knowing' bilingualism, with numerous intersections of resulting marginalization and language obsolescence (Scarino, 2013).

2. CHALLENGES IN ENGLISH LANGUAGE LEARNING

Language learning has always faced numerous complicated factors related to broader sociocultural, historical, and political contexts. Based primarily on the widely accepted belief in the crucial role of language in shaping personal, social, and national identities, English language learning (ELL) is no exception. When considering language learning more locally, particularly in relation to English in a multilingual society, current challenges primarily involve three interrelated areas: policy, culture, and pedagogy (Ahmed & Qasem, 2019). On the one hand, the interface between a globally dominant language and a language of knowledge poses a continued challenge for achieving more prosperous and more equitable access to English. On the other hand, applying locally appropriate resources for English instruction in conjunction with complex existing languages and pedagogical frameworks becomes increasingly difficult (Albiladi, 2019).

In addressing three interrelated challenges regarding the interface between multilingualism and non-standardness, the researchers aim to contribute through theory-building within a reasonably broad scope of the multilingual society and English education. It is argued that ELL in multilingual societies is reflected in a complex interface among a globally powerful language and lesser or less widely spoken local language varieties or nonstandard dialects, which is necessarily theorized by adapting the concept of language interfaces and diversities. Furthermore, the political, normative, and instructional potential of the interface highlights three interrelated challenges regarding English access.

2.1. Interference of Native Languages

As learning English is a necessity for foreign language proficiency in some countries, such as Indonesia, this has led to the growth of English language courses in various communities. (Arifin, 2011) indicates that in the communication process of teaching and learning English at the course of Ikatan Alumni Yayasan Shinta, interference of the mother tongue (first language) with the target language (English) occurs. Before further discussing this issue, it is essential to consider the importance of English in this country. The socio-cultural-based proposal that English is viewed as a threat to local languages due to its everyday use in elite-class interactions remains debatable. However, frequent critiques, comments, and even a scientific forum on the tinges of English existence reveal that it is indeed viewed as a prestigious language. Those having English fluency, apart from the local language competency, are more respected and credited as worthy individuals who are likely to be perceived as having higher education. Furthermore, English is so sought after that any opportunities enabling its acquisition are exploited, including in the current global development of information and communication technology. Some preceding studies have primarily focused on examining aspects of English at the macro level, such as its influence on speakers and its relationship to local languages, which involve analyzing language variations.

2.2. Socioeconomic Factors

Numerous socioeconomic factors significantly influence the process of learning English in multidimensional and multilingual communities, impacting it either positively or negatively. The learning environment can either create a healthy, comfortable, safe, and secure space for students, which is conducive to effective language acquisition, or conversely, it can present barriers that hinder their performance. Social factors within the realm of EFL (English as a Foreign Language) learning encompass various variables characteristic of social communities that manifest apparent effects on the language acquisition process. These include the linguistic attributes of the community, the prevailing political climate regarding bilingualism and language rights, and the socioeconomic status of individual students participating in the learning process. Each of these dimensions plays a critical role in shaping the overall experience and efficacy of English language education.

The linguistic nature of the community is one of the factors believed to influence the learning of a foreign language. For instance, Morocco has always been known for its linguistic diversity. The successful usage of Arabic, Tamazight, Spanish, French, and English characterizes the Moroccan cultural and linguistic community. Concerning Arabic, the status of the language is one of the most complicated in the world due to its diglossic linguistic situation and the discrepancy between the standard form and the colloquial one. This difference hinders the language acquisition of local dialects, such as those spoken by Tamazight speakers. The struggle for universality and global respect by Modern Standard Arabic hampers its internal development as a lingua franca (Amiri & Karfa, 2021).

On the other hand, the contemporary promotion of the French language particularly accentuates the phenomenon of diglossia within the framework of multilingualism that exists in Morocco. In addition to this, it induces a colonial legacy that is vividly recognized as 'linguistic apartheid,' whereby the French-educated elite class has significantly profited from the thorough Francization of various civilian affairs. It is an overwhelming fact that the inherent difficulty in learning a foreign language (FL) is greatly enhanced by the complexities arising from L1 transfer. The former Minister of Higher Education in Morocco stated that the learning of English is currently on the rise, which is a positive trend, and that the language policy has been adjusted with the expectation that English will become the primary language of science. In this context, high school graduates are now required to study English rigorously to access opportunities in higher education. The Moroccan policymakers have strongly endorsed the promotion of foreign languages, with particular focus on the English language. The former Minister of Higher Education in Morocco proclaimed that English serves as the practical language for advancing scientific research, and it is widely believed to be the most effective solution to the country's educational challenges. Moreover, students who seek to continue their academic pursuits in critical fields such as Engineering and Medicine must acquire a high level of proficiency in the English language to ensure their success and competitiveness in these professional domains. (Hammou & Kesbi, 2024)

2.3. Access to Resources

Without the presence of affordable, user-friendly, and instructive professional preschool and childcare services that could assist them in developing or improving their English skills alongside their child, women faced difficulties finding promising careers (Wall, 2017). Although there are professional childcare services that assist immigrant parents, they are difficult to access due to the lack of resources. In

Mississauga and Toronto, for example, there is a lack of low-cost services for preschoolers and children up to sixteen years old, particularly for newcomers, including those from low-income backgrounds. Existing summer camps and daycare facilities are often expensive, and accessing them can be challenging due to distance and language barriers. This makes it more difficult for mothers to participate in school events. After-school programs in Ontario's school system, which are aimed at engaging immigrant children, are not offered in accommodations like refugee shelters where many immigrant families reside, despite the majority of women's complaints about their children's behaviors of being more physically assertive than unfocused, difficulties with task-switching, and being in trouble with teachers. Parents' lack of knowledge about advocating for their children at school or in the neighborhoods, particularly regarding extracurricular sports in school, was another concern raised by the women.

3. TEACHING STRATEGIES FOR MULTILINGUAL CLASSROOMS

A classroom with multilingual students offers excellent potential for unique and rich learning opportunities, but also presents complex challenges that require increased teacher knowledge and expertise. Recent research has revealed the processes through which gifted teachers plan, instruct, and assess learning in multilingual classrooms. Worldviews of action and culture, representational systems, and conditional systems mediate complex relationships among goals, context, and practice. Educators and researchers must take greater responsibility to broaden the professional discourse about bilingual and multilingual teaching and learning. The world is undergoing significant changes. Shrinking borders have rendered facets of language ubiquitous; immigration, colonization, and globalization have significantly increased the movement of people and languages. The coexistence of different languages, cultures, nation-states, and communities has become commonplace; hence, transcultural communication has become a key facet of the modern world (Lartec et al., 2014). Language, being central to the formation of meaning, communication, and understanding, is implicated in all of these processes. Some would argue from a utilitarian perspective that multilingualism is necessary for its economic benefits; others would consider it a greater social good, promoting communication and understanding among diverse groups of people and thereby avoiding contingencies based solely on a single language, which can foster various prejudices and conflicts. (Viesca et al.2022)

However, multilingualism is deeply problematic, and not only from social and political viewpoints. Language is seldom a neutral vehicle for conveying information. Language is also multidimensional; it can regulate and constitute perception of reality and experiences; it possesses indexicalities that map into entrenched social categories; it has social history and inhabits ideology. Given that our experience of the social world is fundamentally mediated by language, we are also privy to the social workings of language. The construction and sustenance of social meaning through language is a sophisticated and, at times, subtle process that any adequate social science must take seriously. Tragically, a priori analytical assumptions regarding the essential nature of the social universe lead to a neglect of detail in understanding it, thus misunderstanding it and oversimplifying the relationship between language and sociality. Multilingual education or education in multilingual settings has become increasingly prominent. By juxtaposing multiple languages and promoting the mindful integration of them through dialogue, multilingual education is considered a means of engaging with differences and cultivating conditions for the survival of diverse communities. (Kirss et al., 2021)

3.1. Differentiated Instruction

Differentiated instruction is widely discussed but not clearly defined. There are numerous approaches and teaching methods to ensure that all students learn in a way that suits them (Rogerson, 2018). Upon conducting a literature review of various differentiated instruction techniques, guided reading was identified as the primary strategy employed to differentiate reading instruction in the researched studies.

Two main approaches are often resorted to by L2 teachers: (1) select a homogeneous group of students or (2) accept the ad hoc levels of heterogeneity but incorporate differentiated instruction (DI). The former approach is likely to fail, as students are diverse, and their differences tend to grow over time. By definition, DI is a strategy that involves approaching every student as an individual. It is an alternative to a one-size-fits-all approach to education. DI is particularly prominent but remains elusive globally. Over the years, it has been misconstrued and misinterpreted by L2 teachers despite being promoted as a cornerstone of effective instruction and the gold standard that teachers should strive for. A hallmark of DI practice is when L2 teachers arrange two or more fluid instructional levels or tiers, differentiating students based on their proficiency levels. In this way, higher-ability learners are given more complex tasks, while middle- and lower-ability learners are assigned more manageable tasks tailored to their cognitive capacities. All alternate word usages depend on the context and need, being synonymous or interchangeable.

As traits perceived as disabilities become increasingly complex over time and across various social environments, L2 heterogeneity becomes increasingly daunting, particularly in multilingual contexts. Alluding to the capricious nature of external factors that regulate individual variations in L2 learning, these teachers emphasized the persistent, admirable qualities of L2 individuals themselves. They felt astonished by and envious of students' behaviors as autonomous meaning-makers, suggesting that well-crafted tests do not guarantee coverage of L2 knowledge, unlike the swift and robust adaptability of students. Obstructing DI intervention is a challenge that should be recognized and addressed in practice, specifically in determining what a learner knows beyond their current achievement level. These teachers felt burdened because of the demands stemming from their students' diversity. This entails more than cumulating ID knowledge and theory; the desire to adapt instruction to individual needs should be met with practical strategies on how to gauge students' prior knowledge before imparting knowledge to them and then determine the appropriate instructional level to use (Rafi & Pourdana, 2023).

According to Warner (2010), guided reading is a small-group reading instruction designed to provide differentiated teaching that supports students in developing reading proficiency. The teacher employs a tightly structured framework that enables the incorporation of several research-based approaches into a corresponding agenda. The teacher prepares for guided reading by planning, assessing, arranging the classroom, gathering appropriate materials, and partnering.

In a guided reading lesson, students are grouped into small groups based on their reading levels. This grouping takes place during the independent reading workshop. The teacher also plans book introductions and teaching points. When selecting an appropriate text for a guided reading lesson, the teacher constantly considers the lesson's purpose and the learning goals for the group of students. Good readers transpose their understandings of spoken language to print and have an understanding of the interrelationships among reading, writing, and language. Differentiated instruction is a broad process for classroom practitioners. Professional development that links theory with specific models and methods that teachers can directly incorporate into practice is essential.

3.1.1. Flexible Grouping

Flexible grouping allows you to mix and match students, fostering cooperation and collaboration, essential skills in a multilingual classroom. The grouping must be flexible, random, and change often. For instance, flexible grouping prevents children from having the same partner or group in each activity, as they are randomly assigned to different groups. Students must not handpick their partners or groups, as the same children will always end up together. Finally, grouping must change often so that students are not continually paired with friends or children they do not want to work with. ESL students can be paired with fluent English speakers or work with peers at the same level of learning.

The most effective grouping strategies are small groups of three to six and pairs or partners. Small groups allow quieter students to express their opinions and thoughts while also enabling the teacher to interact with every student during lessons. Usually, children are seated at tables with four or six chairs, making group formation easy. Many larger groups can be divided into smaller, homogeneous groups, allowing for more fluid movement within the classroom, as well as within the "home" and "expert" groups in jigsaw-style learning activities (Roberson, 2019). A good grouping strategy requires motivation, effort, and time, but can prove beneficial to the students and the teacher. Economic feasibility and class size will also contribute if larger drop-in centers exist.

3.1.2. Varied Assessment Methods

It has also been found that teachers often target low-level cognitive tasks in their assessments by requiring pupils to recall only what they have learned. In addition to tools that assess factual and procedural knowledge, teachers need to present learners with problems that involve transferring what has been discovered to new situations and applying related underlying concepts and principles (Chimpololo, 2010). Academic assessment must be an ongoing process that objectively informs both teachers and pupils about the pupils' academic language achievement. This paper proposes that, in a bilingual education classroom, teachers should utilize multiple assessment tools to measure various aspects of linguistic competence, thereby obtaining a comprehensive understanding of their pupils' performance. The study's findings and recommendations will enhance teachers' assessment practices in bilingual education, aligning them with the expectations outlined in the Bilingual Education Policy.

The qualitative data elicited through semi-structured interviews revealed that teachers perceived assessment as a formal process of measuring language proficiency through tests. In addition, teachers overwhelmingly preferred written exercises, oral tests, and end-of-semester examinations over continuous assessment methods. Results from the classroom observations are contrary to their expectations; teachers only use pre- and post-assessment methods, and participating pupils are only given informal tests at the beginning of the term. Classroom observations revealed that formal continuous assessment techniques were largely absent in the two primary schools. When opportunities for formative assessment were presented, teachers highlighted some factors that hindered their practical implementation in the classroom. These include the rigid syllabus structure, the large number of pupils enrolled in a class, the lack of training on how to implement formative assessment, and the inadequate time to compile results from different continuous assessment methods. Some students suggested that peer assessment could be employed in the classroom context. In the same vein, a suggestion was made for the use of continuous assessment techniques to help teachers evaluate the target behaviors of pupils. (Paloposki et al.2025).

3.2 Scaffolding Strategies

A scaffold is a temporary and supportive structure designed to help a student or group of students accomplish a task they could not achieve — or perform as well — without the scaffold. Scaffolding is not a strategy per se but rather an enabling structure or support that allows a student or group of students to transition from one level of performance to another. ELLs (English Language Learners) in mainstream classrooms require specific scaffolding, which can be thought of as a bridge between teaching and learning or as a systematic, gradual approach to managing tasks of increasing difficulty. Many mainstream classroom teachers with ELLs have used scaffolding instruction to help promote understanding of content subject areas. Teachers have implemented scaffolding strategies, utilizing cooperative learning groups to support student learning and achievement. Teachers can also find ways to use students' native language as a tool to enable access to the majority language. Scaffolding has been reported as one of the most effective strategies for enhancing reading achievement in ELLs (McKenzie, 2011).

Every teacher in the United States must work toward the special understandings, skills, and dispositions needed to facilitate the language and academic development of students for whom English is a new language. Researchers found that the majority of teachers' experiences were not consistent with their current beliefs regarding the educational characteristics of ELLs. Before their certification, teachers had little to no exposure to effective practices connected to ELLs. To achieve the progress of teachers, they need to become educated on practical strategies and methods to achieve the goal of increasing reading performance levels with ELLs.

Teachers who are accustomed to traditional teaching styles are more likely to accept teaching contemporary styles once they are exposed to them. Exposure includes strategies that are conducive to ELLs' learning styles, the theory of language learning, and their cultural background. Teacher learning can be characterized as problem-solving or inquiry that starts with teachers' special goals for their students. Teachers are required to extend their learning beyond the classroom. They must put forth extra effort to ensure that students are learning the material covered in the curriculum. In doing so, teachers need to constantly examine questions such as, 'Are they making any progress?' or 'How do they know?' Student achievement is further enhanced when teachers prioritize their professional development within the school during school hours and maintain regular contact with their students. (Liu & Ma, 2024)

3.3. Visual Supports

The brain utilizes distinct channels to process verbal and visual information: the left hemisphere handles verbal information, and the right hemisphere deals with visual information. Presenting new vocabulary through visual means can make the teaching and learning of English an active process, allowing students to grasp new information through images rather than just text. Since vocabulary learning is primarily a mental process mediated through images, visual aids can also help students retain the vocabulary longer and remember it more easily. Visual aids provide students with a visual representation of what they are learning, helping them understand the meaning of vocabulary (Skupeňová, 2017). Visual aids can be applied to assist in the teaching and learning of vocabulary, especially in ESOL contexts. Flashcards are teaching and learning resources made of cards on which valuable information for studying is written or drawn. Cards serve as visual aids, helping learners to organize information into memory folders. Flashcards are a specific type of card that is used as a teaching and learning aid. Flash cards can be used to teach words to beginner or elementary students who are studying vocabulary for the first time. Flash cards can be applied in various ways. Pictures can be used to teach target vocabulary items. A teacher holds flashcards in front of students, points to certain pictures, and says the corresponding words. Flash cards can be turned upside down and used as a vocabulary game. In vocabulary learning, introducing new words and utilizing realia in the classroom can be beneficial. Realia, which means a language or cultural object used as a teaching aid, refers to real objects that teachers utilize in the classroom. Realia can help students realize the meanings of new words. When a teacher teaches "bananas," "apples," "oranges," or "grapes," the teacher may take out fruits from a basket and hold one in front of the students. Sticking such images can create the atmosphere of a fruit shop. Realia can also be used to make students feel closer to their environments, thus motivating students to learn a second language.

3.4. Modeling and Demonstration

Beyond using audiovisual materials to facilitate second language learning, teachers can engage in small group work in front of the class and use modeling demonstrations to promote language learning. Educators can build their courses around hands-on activities that elicit an inquiry-based process, or they can prepare and select videos of experiments, simulations, or models that demonstrate phenomena or principles present in the model. Whiteboarding is one such interactive pedagogic technique, which involves using a whiteboard or large sheet of paper to carry out a demonstration, summary, or explanation with a marker (Schwaller, 2011). In recent studies, both modeling and whiteboard numeracy are given focus as student-centered approaches, consisting of small-group work or whole-class whiteboard modeling of demonstrations that leverage second language affordances and engage a diverse elementary school classroom in second language development. In addition, teachers use multisensory modalities, including visualizations, inquiries, modeling, gestures, and codes that feature temporality, emotions, and auditory motivation to mediate the students' sense-making and negotiating what they co-construct within the context of inquiry-through-modeling. It is argued that promoting learning-by-doing involves actively seeking participation to co-create knowledge and socially construct insights. Such a reform-based practice supports an epistemic community of questioning (together "what"), modeling (together "how"), and explanation (+ "why") grounded in spontaneously constructed artifacts, ameliorating deep engagement through scaffolding and the opportunity to revisit issues for instruction and assessment. In summary, teachers utilize Whiteboarding as a formative assessment tool, in conjunction with modeling, which leverages agency through individual ownership, collaborative work, and a sequence of multilateral input, thereby providing support for co-construction and becoming a pedagogical tool that expands the teaching repertoire.

3.5. Collaborative Learning

Collaborative learning is any instructional method that involves positive social interaction between learners in groups. There are two kinds of collaborative learning situations. In formal collaborative learning, small groups are established with a specific task for two or more lessons. Students have particular roles and responsibilities and are expected to complete assigned tasks. Peer evaluation ensures accountability. In informal collaborative learning, the instructor asks students to form pairs or small groups for a short period to practice a new concept or skill, followed by whole-class feedback. Since collaborative learning was introduced and adopted by educators, its principles have captured the attention of scholars, researchers, and practitioners in EFL. Collaborative learning is based on the social constructivist theory of learning and attempts to promote learning through interaction among students engaged in shared tasks (Babiker, 2018). While collaborative learning has been practiced in various contexts and across different branches of education, it has led to the success of many EFL learners and groups. This technique helps develop fluency and allows effective mediation of learned structures. Collaborative learning is beneficial to those who struggle with uttering even simple sentences. This will help them start using the language and gain confidence for future conversations. It allows group work to be organized in various ways within a single class, such as by grouping stronger learners with weaker ones or mixing different levels. This will help keep the progress of all levels. Effective collaborative learning directly leads to a knowledge-building community. The critical role of the teacher as a designer of the learning environment ensures that the learning opportunities provided are appropriately engaging, which requires a thorough understanding of the varied products of collaborative learning and the characteristics of practical group work. Collaborative learning is a technique in which small groups of learners work together to promote their learning and that of others. Collaborative learning relies on social interaction between learners to encourage them to take active roles in the learning process. Successful collaborative learning experiences promote mutual support, equal participation, cohesion, cooperation, and interdependence. In contrast, cooperative learning is more structured owing to its emphasis on formal group organization and positive interdependence supported by a reward system based on group accomplishments. Several learning approaches can be classified as collaborative or cooperative. One of the well-studied groups of collaborative learning approaches is based on interaction design principles adopted from the fields of social psychology and sociolinguistics by designers.

4. ASSESSMENT AND EVALUATION IN MULTILINGUAL CONTEXTS

Assessment and evaluation of learners' language performance have always been an interrelated process to gather information on students' progress, needs, and the efficacy of teaching. To some extent, it is done to aid learning; however, assessment has traditionally been conceived as a testing or evaluation process rather than a learning one. In the context of first and foreign language assessment, evaluation, or testing, it has been found desirable to design appropriate tests (Afitska, 2014). Measures have also been proposed for assessing the success or otherwise of language teaching, which typically involves measuring language proficiency attainment at some stage.

The issue of assessment has recently gained significance in the context of migration. This global phenomenon has sparked the interest of researchers in assessing the language of instruction in increasingly multicultural environments. Interest in this area intensifies because a great deal of economic and sociopolitical activity relies on native fluency in a language. However, unlike the extensive literature on general testing issues, language testing in the context of migration still requires research to develop principled EAL assessments that take into account the sociolinguistic circumstances of the individual. These involve the impact exerted by cognate language proximity, the relative status of languages in society, and the language of instruction on EAL education achievement.

Communication is increasingly conducted in L2. Enumeration of the new ELT challenges in various settings, including the EFL one, has revealed a shift in focus from the message transmitter to the interlocutor, the gradual introduction of new genres, such as aural, multimodal, and computer-mediated texts, and the need for L2 listening assessment. However, situations where language specialists are non-native speakers and the media, whether predominantly oral or digital, remain unexplored.

4.1. Formative Assessment

Assessment refers to a wide range of methods used in gauging students' progress in learning. A distinction is often drawn between formative and summative evaluation, although it would be more correct to do so in a broader sense: formative assessment includes a variety of assessment practices that support learning; summative assessment consists of those that follow and assess learning. Formative assessment is explicitly acknowledged in the standards of the Professional Teaching and Competency Framework in England, in the key indicators of successful primary schools in Singapore, as well as in the underlying principles of the revised curriculum in Hong Kong SAR (Afitska, 2014). This form of assessment counters the teaching-to-the-test debate and mitigates risks of IQ inflation.

Formative assessment is a broader term than formative use of assessment. It includes many assessment practices, only some of which can inform subsequent teaching and learning. Formative uses of assessment may consist of assessment tasks, individual feedback (e.g., from peers and parents), or various forms of feedback. Assessment for learning precisely describes the formative use of assessment. Criterion-based growth analysis was employed to investigate pedagogy and professional development in four British school clusters, focusing on their impact on pupil learning and identifying areas for improvement, as well as the problems and challenges encountered.

There had been significant growth in the formative use of assessment in information detail, and the schools exhibited widely different approaches, interpretations, and beliefs. It was concluded that more professional development time is required to improve the quality of assessment practice. Formative assessment can only be used if the use is principled. Formative assessment necessitates adjustments to both pedagogical and evaluation processes. Implementation advice regarding formative assessment should concentrate on a small number of elements to maximize beneficial instructional effects.

4.2. Summative Assessment

Wong (Afitska, 2014) formulates criteria to assess students' speaking skills in a second language. The assessment consists of two main criteria: fluency and accuracy, which can be further subdivided into 14 subcategories: quantity, pace, length, self-repair, grammar, word form, spelling, word choice, locution, pronunciation, stress, intonation, and volume. Because the criteria are too comprehensive, Wong has to select several criteria when evaluating assessments among students to avoid assigning too many subcategories. Ultimately, the 2-by-2 matching characteristics (fluency vs. accuracy and group work vs. individual work) result in a complex set of 1-by-7 assessable criteria in the final trade-assessing activity. Using the speaking assessment as an example, Wong illustrates how assessments can become impromptu events.

Furthermore, it would be difficult for students to learn the criteria and assess their own oral proficiency and progress through such an assessment. Wong proposes that tasks be purposely designed with a focus on determining only one criterion when collecting plans, making evaluation more straightforward for students. Wong adds that clear teaching and learning objectives should be set first, and then criteria questions should be developed to assess the extent to which these objectives have been achieved.

Based on the findings from shared cases, which aim to design and conduct formative assessments of students' foreign language skills in a primary language classroom, it is recommended that formative assessments should be designed based on students' life-world experiences and their experiences with various tasks. The foreign language skills that teachers want to assess should be selected and integrated into the overall picture to plan for assessments; the potential knowledge and skills that students can mobilize to conduct the assessment should be considered; and the format and procedure of the assessment should take into consideration of students' previous experiences with the same or similar assessments. In addition, teachers should provide purposeful guidance and scaffolding to each group during the first round of assessments, allowing them to explore and experiment with the formative assessment tasks without an explicit focus on the assessment itself. Furthermore, planning for the trade of formative assessments should be structured and clarified to students by introducing the progressive refinement of decision-making when working on a similar assessment task collectively in the whole class.

4.3. Standardized Testing Issues

Standardized testing has been and is the most dominantly used measurement in all high-stakes ELT contexts globally. It is behind almost all language policies relating to educational and immigration systems in postcolonial southern societies, where lower classes can be marginalized through gatekeeping power, and middle classes can gain access to better academic and job opportunities through "well-studied" or "well-remembered" test-taking strategies. IELTS has gradually developed this authority for assessment and begun to impose its standards for testing and evaluating ideologies in terms of what constitutes English, taking into account societal values that are not static but continually changing (Badwan, 2017).

With the rise of globalization since the mid-20th century, the fabric of societies has been and continues to change. The advent of the internet and the World Wide Web had been heralded as opening borders and democratizing power, allowing all to gain access to knowledge and a global voice. However, as new modes of communication were brought by technologies originally developed in the Global North, they were unevenly incorporated in southern countries. What once were clear borders of groups A (monolingual speakers, mainly residing in the Global North), B (speakers using an L2 ultimately in a larger L2 community, normally but not necessarily under the aegis of group A countries), and C (speakers of the L2, but using it mainly for international, intragroup communication, primarily domiciled in the Global South) are now fuzzy. Time lags and unequal development in economic, political, and power resources have hindered the dream of a borderless world.

5. CULTURAL CONSIDERATIONS IN LANGUAGE TEACHING

While many researchers acknowledge the relationship between language and culture, the nature of the relationship is unclear. Nambiar (2017) posits that culture is socially acquired as the "know-how" needed for daily living. Thus, the acquisition of one presupposes the acquisition of another. In language teaching and learning, the importance of integrating culture is explicitly acknowledged. There are several reasons for this. First, learning a language without knowing the culture of a language will produce a 'fluent fool' (Chenoweth, 2014). Second, it will not be sufficient for insight into the political, social, religious, and economic systems in which the language functions if students master only linguistic structure. Finally, it is well known that the language being taught carries a knowledge system different from that of the learners and their perspective toward nature. Therefore, language learning and teaching should never be held in isolation from culture. A critical issue in integrating culture into the teaching and learning of a foreign language is which culture to use: local, target, or international. In situations where learners intend to migrate to a country where the target language is spoken or seek employment in that country, it is common for the teaching of the language to be accompanied by the teaching of the target culture, to acculturate them as quickly and efficiently as possible into that culture. This view assumes that one cannot teach a foreign language without teaching its target culture. Some views focus on teaching a foreign language using the local culture because it provides learners with a better understanding of their own culture, especially in a language such as English, which is widely used globally. As a lingua franca learned by many non-native speakers around the world, it seems essential to mention that local culture should be incorporated more into the language learning process, as it forms the base for effective communication within their community. Learners should be able to understand that the new language can be used to describe their local culture, which will help in promoting the values of the language in their societies. The value of the target culture should also be conveyed, as learners need to have an understanding of their own culture to comprehend the national culture of the target language. In language learning, therefore, the material used to learn English with a communicative approach should not focus solely on the linguistic aspect but instead on how this language can be used appropriately in various communicative events.

5.1. Cultural Sensitivity

In global societies where linguistic and cultural differences coexist, teachers, particularly those of English as a Second Language (ESL), face the challenge of educating students whose linguistic skills vary significantly, ranging from limited to fluent English. Language teaching involves not only oral and written skills of a foreign language but also its use in different social contexts. Linguistically diverse students of English may feel embarrassed or ashamed to engage in conversations. Some become nervous, preserving silence in public encounters with native speakers, while others overcome this language barrier to express themselves freely and feel liberated. In this study, relevant literature examined how national and cultural backgrounds affect students' experiences learning English. Additionally, students were interviewed in multiple dialogues to gather their perceptions about their linguistic explorations of the English language.

In such multilingual nations, adolescent English language learners (ELLs) form an extremely heterogeneous and diverse group characterized by the languages spoken, cultures, religions, literacy levels, social classes, and prior schooling (Chenoweth, 2014). Attending secondary school is a new experience for many families, with no model on how to proceed. Compared to the motivation for education among U.S.-born individuals, the motivation for education may differ in some ways in Asian and Middle Eastern countries. Cultural contexts create very different lenses through which perceptions and understanding are viewed among ELLs and U.S. teachers. Exploring an outsider's perspective on the culture of schooling may provide new insights for reflection and enhance culturally responsive teaching.

Language policies aim to stabilize national identity and promote an equal post-colonial space that upholds non-English official languages. In cultural refractions of colonization, hybrid identities are wrought of English in terms of struggle, disadvantage, passivity, and conformity. Under colonialism, English shifted from a mere linguistic tool toward a hybrid gate of opportunity in which a native-like accent induces self-doubt and second-guessing for ELLs. This postcolonial ambivalence concerning English highlights the moral complexity of parenting, as it simultaneously desires ELLs to be proficient in English. Hidden from ELLs, however, is an Anglo-centric belief system that espouses English as the key to success in the global economy.

5.2. Integrating Culture into Language Learning

Many researchers acknowledge the relationship between language and culture. The importance of integrating culture into the English language, specifically in teaching and learning, is further reinforced by Nambiar (2017). They propose that learning a language without knowing the culture is a troublesome yet common phenomenon in learning a foreign language. The authors posit that understanding the target culture explicitly provides insight into the systems within which the language functions. Language jokes, proverbs, idioms, and insults, for example, evoke elements of the culture that are difficult to explain in terms of linguistic structures. As such, non-native speakers of English who look only to learn the linguistic structure of the language may do so at their peril. This underexposure may result in them becoming a 'fluent fool' or a naïve speaker of the language, who may use correct language forms within an inappropriate cultural context. They argue that in this multicultural world, where English serves as the lingua franca, it is almost impossible to teach and learn a language without its associated culture and to encounter two cultures that are the same or even somewhat similar. Consequently, language learning and teaching should not be conducted in isolation from culture.

In language teaching, it is suggested that the target culture must necessarily be taught in a process referred to as cultural assimilation. On the other hand, there is a view that focuses attention on teaching the language by incorporating the local culture to enhance familiarity for learners. The proponents of this view argue that incorporating local culture in the English language teaching process is essential, as it will help the learners communicate and function smoothly and effectively in the society where the language is used. Awareness of how the new language can describe one's own culture will offer validity to one's learning and provide a different and broader perspective on the new language and its culture. Understanding their culture is as important as understanding the target culture.

6. CASE STUDIES OF SUCCESSFUL PROGRAMS

Different contexts where coherent English language instruction has been implemented successfully, and that should be adapted to the various isolated or fragmented situations of need, on which the contributors agree, are described in this chapter. The first case study describes how a teacher successfully supported the literacy of English language learners in a predominantly Spanish-speaking school. For nearly two decades, the teacher has pursued a dual language certificate and worked to build relationships with students and their families, ensuring that all students participate in high-level instruction. Constructions taken up include "supporting English language learners' literacy development," "delivering multimodal instruction," and "building community," with the last shifting from being articulated in terms of agency to being couched in a more fundamental sense of the conditions for community. Situated in an interview where the teacher is asked how they accomplish this feat, an understanding of the reflexive dimensions of their work is irreversibly established; the teacher's well-founded, agency-centered constructions of conscious decisions, commitment to professional development and perseverance cohere with evocations of relationships, warmth, care, love, faith, and belief. The second case study describes a school whose leadership made changes to its use of English. It draws on systemic functional multilingual theory, multimodality, and genre to show how the English curriculum was transformed from one imported, in which students passively received input through broadcasts and materials, to one locally designed by teachers, in which they engaged in communicative practices of their choosing through popular culture. In this interracial case study, partnerships constructed between the school's human resources and afforded by the labor market are considered and situated within a changing sociopolitical landscape.

6.1. Bilingual Education Models

A variety of experiences and languages create multilingual societies that require equitable and robust English language learning opportunities for all. Bilingual education models vary in their levels of academic content area instruction in the native language and desired outcome goals for English language learners. A program can be more bilingual than another in that it allows students to retain and develop their first language in addition to English. Adding a second language to one's first language enhances cognitive processes, social interaction with a wider variety of peers, and access to a larger amount of information (Garcia-Bautista, 2010). Language and cognition are interrelated; therefore, this model is based on the premise that the better the child acquires the first language, the better the cognitive performance in the second language. These are the various bilingual education models, along with their outcomes and the research supporting their conclusions (Ozimek, 2014).

6.2. Community Language Programs

In many parts of the world, there is a growing understanding of the importance of maintaining multilingualism in childhood and of the adverse effects of prioritizing the acquisition of an international language over minority languages. More people are also becoming aware of the fact that there are many 'Englishes' and that there are varieties of English language in multilingual nations that have features different from those of the varieties used in native-speaking nations. The recognition of the respective skills of local English teachers in Asia, along with the understanding that such teachers may not require native fluency, may help stem the tide of the exportation of TESL teachers to Asia. This will eventually lead to a more balanced and less dependent relationship between native-speaking and non-native-speaking communities. As there is a greater awareness of the importance of a 'bottom-up' approach to educational reform, community language programs are evolving and, in many cases, being developed (Baldauf et al., 2013).

In many parts of the world, especially in Europe, Australia, New Zealand, North America, and South Africa, monolingualism is giving way to bi- and multilingualism. In many regions of Africa, Asia, and South America, multilingualism is the norm. There is, in fact, a growing recognition that remaining multilingual is essential in childhood and a corresponding understanding that the acquisition of a world language during childhood can lead to a decline in attention to home and community languages. As a consequence, there is growing awareness of the adverse effects of early learning of a world language at the expense of minority languages. There is also increasing awareness, across many societies, of the fact that there are many 'Englishes .'There is growing recognition that non-native varieties of English exist in many multilingual nations, which often feature distinct characteristics that can evoke negative attitudes among members of these nations when they encounter native-speaking varieties of English.

7. FUTURE DIRECTIONS IN ENGLISH LANGUAGE LEARNING

For several decades, a large number of English teachers in Thailand and many other non-Anglophone countries have adopted native-speaker pronunciation as the standard in teaching English language and pronunciation classes. Promoting native-speaker pronunciation is thought to be a way of enhancing the quality of one's English, particularly in the context of global English and global English studies, which have brought about new notions of English as a lingua franca and native/non-native English speakers as a sociocultural construct (Assalihee et al., 2019). The enormous growth in the teaching and learning of English for communication purposes as a global language within and outside today's globalized marketplace, along with increasing awareness that English learners in Thailand, as well as in ASEAN and non-English speaking countries, are learners and users of English as a lingua franca in multilingual, or World Englishes contexts has intensified criticism of the native-speakerism debate.

While a good command of the English language has been known to be key to a bright future, including better job opportunities and career prospects, growing concerns over the native-speakerism debate have replaced the one-size-fits-all principle of using the so-called standard accents and native-speakerism as the gold standard in the English language learning and teaching community, including that of native-spoken varieties of English. A similar need for a non-deconstructive paradigm is being called for in the context of teaching pronunciation in all three EFL contexts. As the controversy over native-speakerism continues, new frontiers in the teaching of pronunciation in established ESL and EIL contexts require empirical studies of the dynamics of deconstructing two interrelated constructs: native-speakerism and accentedness, about accent discrimination, language ideologies, and a sense of language ownership. In addition, along with the growing acceptance of multilingualism, a paradigm of plurilingual/translingual perspective in the study of the teaching of English pronunciation in Thailand and other similar EFL contexts is emphasized, where various pedagogical implications of English as a lingua franca and the multimedia principle as a (self-) product of such awareness will be investigated.

7.1. Innovative Pedagogies

Innovative pedagogies are crucial for ensuring students' acquisition of high levels of English proficiency and their ability to utilize English in various real-life contexts and situations. The proposed innovative pedagogies are: (1) Active, profound, relevant, and realistic learning, (2) Technologically-assisted learning, (3) Practical and locally relevant learning, (4) All-inclusive learning and environment, and (5) Various measures of performance assessment. The first innovative pedagogy is that learning should be active, profound, relevant, and realistic. Learners should not only see English as an additional or optional subject, but they should also realize that English is a necessity. Teaching topics and materials should also be readily available in English. Such contexts help learners appreciate the learning, heighten their participation in English learning, and enhance their productivity (Assalihee et al., 2019). Furthermore, classroom learning should foster meaningful connections between in-class activities and out-of-class experiences, enabling learners to appreciate its value.

The second innovative pedagogy is that learning and teaching should be technologically assisted, with technological solutions seamlessly integrated into the learning and teaching processes. It is indisputable that technology has taken hold of language education, especially in the ways languages are taught and learned. Entry to numerous online platforms specializing in general and English learning is free and learner-centric. The ubiquitous access to portable information and communication technologies, on the other hand, creates numerous opportunities for learners to learn English at any time and from anywhere. Enabling and empowering learners to fully harness these opportunities ensures their fluency in English usage in the 21st century. Nurturing the current generation of technologically intelligent learners to become individual knowledge creators and information communicators is essential, given the moderate amount of screen time in class in today's highly competitive world. The third innovative pedagogy is that learning and materials should be practical and locally relevant. Instead of teaching learners what they are less likely to have the opportunity to utilize, it is suggested that they be taught what would be practically needed in their locales (Ntelioglou et al., 2014). Such pedagogies and materials, on the one hand, enhance the effectiveness of English learning while, on the other hand, increasing the likelihood that learners will apply what they learn to navigate through the complexities of their societies as responsible citizens.

7.2. Policy Recommendations

The policy recommendations provided herein should serve as an encouragement for further dialogue on how language policies can be effectively implemented within South Africa's multilingual society and, of course, elsewhere. All decisions regarding these recommendations need to be debated widely. Concrete actions or pathways forward in terms of policies, frameworks, guidelines, and protocols will be developed using the scenarios as a loose framework. However, further dialogue is needed regarding fundamental issues, such as the decision to pursue strong bilingual education or a more gradual transition to a commercial multilingual model, the nature and scope of proficiency monitoring, socio-environmental influences on learning, the types of learning routes required, and many other points. The recommendations are offered with the hope that they will stimulate ideas and debate about how universities can effectively implement their language policies (Nkabinde, 2002). Implementing a language policy in practice entails several communicative actions to create conditions that facilitate language usage guided by and co-constructing the language policy, which is interpreted and translated into local procedures and practices, as well as how it aligns with users' actual language practices. These communicative practices highlight the dynamic interaction through which the language policy is constructed and reconstructed by the language policy-implementing agencies and the contexts or communities in which they operate. A local framework of policy actions will then be provided to offer implementers a best-practice overview of communicative acts to make a language policy effective. The viability and long-term sustainability of languages are closely tied to the formulation and implementation of public language policy. It is, therefore, crucial that language in education policies be inclusive and fair, lest the cycle of indifference, neglect, and marginalization of languages be perpetuated in the arena of higher education. (Hughes, 1994).

8. CONCLUSIONS

It is concluded that navigating the complications of English language learning within multilingual societies is very challenging. As the underlying forces of globalization and migration continue to shape the linguistic landscapes, it becomes increasingly vital to recognize and address the unique needs of learners situated in these diverse environments. The interplay of policy, culture, and pedagogy highlights the importance of developing inclusive educational frameworks that value linguistic diversity while fostering effective English language acquisition. By embracing a holistic understanding of multilingualism and integrating cultural considerations into teaching methodologies, educators can foster richer learning experiences that respect learners' backgrounds and identities. Additionally, ongoing research and fruitful case studies highlight the potential for advanced approaches that not only improve language learning results but also contribute to social cohesion in multicultural societies. Ultimately, confirming that English language education is open to the actualities of multilingual settings will lead to more unbiased and effective language learning, enabling individuals to engage in an interconnected world.

REFERENCES

Afitska, O. (2014). Formative Use of Language Assessment: Supporting Learning through the Medium of a Second Language. *US-China Education Review A, 4*(8), 517–535.

Ahmed, S. T. S., & Qasem, B. T. A. (2019). Problems of Teaching and Learning English as a Foreign Language in South Yemen: A Case Study of Lahj Governorate. *ELS Journal on Interdisciplinary Studies in Humanities, 2*(4), 485–492. DOI: 10.34050/els-jish.v2i4.7458

Albiladi, W. S. (2019). Teaching English Pronunciation Revisited: The Challenges of Teaching EFL in Non-English-Speaking Countries. European Journal of Foreign Language Teaching.

Amiri, E., & El Karfa, A. (2021). The Impact of Learning Environment on EFL Students' Academic Achievement: A Study of Sociocultural Factors Affecting Academic Achievement. *Arab World English Journal, 12*(4), 387–400.

Assalihee, M., Boonsuk, Y., Bakoh, N., & Sano, I. L. (2019). Reconceptualizing the 21st Century English Pedagogies for Islamic School Teachers in Asean. *Journal of Nusantara Studies, 4*(1), 401–421.

Babiker, A. (2018). Improving Speaking Skills in EFL Classes through Collaborative Learning. [ASRJETS]. *American Scientific Research Journal for Engineering, Technology, and Sciences, 44*(1), 137–154.

Badwan, K. M. (2017). "Did We Learn English or What?"A Study Abroad Student in the UK Carrying and Crossing Boundaries in Out-of-Class Communication. *Studies in Second Language Learning and Teaching, 7*(2), 193–210.

Baldauf, R. B., Kaplan, R. B., Kamwangamalu, N., & Bryant, P. (2013). Success or Failure of Primary Second/Foreign Language Programmes in Asia: What Do the Data Tell Us? Language Planning in Primary Schools in Asia, 205-219.

Ben Hammou, S., & Kesbi, A. (2024). Exploring Multilingual Education in Morocco: Official Documents and Teachers' Perceptions. *International Journal of Multilingualism, 21*(4), 1906–1927.

Chenoweth, N. H. (2014). *Cultural and Linguistic Obstacles for ELLs.* Beyond Words, 2(2), 91–120.

Chimpololo, A. (2010). Assessing Pupils ' Language Proficiency in a Bilingual Education Programme: Insights from Two Primary Schools in Malawi. *The Buckingham Journal of Language and Linguistics, 3*, 1–10.

Garcia-Bautista, M. G. (2010). A Washington State Elementary Teachers' Guide to Bilingual Education. All Graduate Projects.84. https://digitalcommons.cwu.edu/graduate_projects/84

Hughes, S. (1994). *The Change of Language and the Language of Change: A Consideration of Some of the Assumptions Behind Non-Governmental Language Planning Projects: Implications for Language in Education Policy*. Unpublished dissertation.

Kirss, L., Säälik, Ü., Leijen, Ä., & Pedaste, M. (2021). School Effectiveness in Multilingual Education: A Review of Success Factors. *Education Sciences, 11*(5), 193.

Lartec, J. K., Belisario, A. M., Bendanillo, J. P., Binas-o, H. K., Bucang, N. O., & Cammagay, J. L. W. (2014). Strategies and Problems Encountered by Teachers in Implementing Mother Tongue-Based Instruction in a Multilingual Classroom. *IAFOR Journal of Language Learning*, 1(1).

Liu, G., & Ma, C. (2024). Measuring EFL Learners' Use of ChatGPT in Informal Digital Learning of English Based on the Technology Acceptance Model. *Innovation in Language Learning and Teaching*, *18*(2), 125–138.

McKenzie, L. D. (2011). Scaffolding English Language Learners' Reading Performance. *Walden University ProQuest Dissertations & Theses, 2011*, 3482138.

Nambiar, R. M. (2017). Integrating Local Knowledge into Language Learning: A Study on the Your Language My Culture (YLMC) Project. *Arab World English Journal (AWEJ)*, 8(4).

Nkabinde, C. T. (2002). *An Assessment of the Impact of Current Language Policy About Adult Basic Education and Training at Phindangene Adult Education Centre (Lamontville)* (Doctoral dissertation, University of Natal, Durban).

Ntelioglou, B. Y., Fannin, J., Montanera, M., & Cummins, J. (2014). A Multilingual and Multimodal Approach to Literacy Teaching and Learning in Urban Education: A Collaborative Inquiry Project in an Inner City Elementary School. *Frontiers in Psychology*, *5*, 533. PMID: 24994986

Ozimek, S. (2014). *Advocating for a Transitional Bilingual Education Program for English Language Learners*. Policy Advocacy.3. https://digitalcommons.nl.edu/pa/3

Paloposki, T., Virtanen, V., & Clavert, M. (2025). From a Final Exam to Continuous Assessment on a Large Bachelor Level Engineering Course. *European Journal of Engineering Education, 50*(1), 164–177.

Rafi, F., & Pourdana, N. (2023). E-Diagnostic Assessment of Collaborative and Individual Oral Tiered Task Performance in Differentiated Second Language Instruction Framework. *Language Testing in Asia, 13*(1), 6.

Roberson, A. C. (2019). *A Self-Study of Purposeful Grouping for Collaborative Learning*. University of Mississippi.

Rogerson, J. (2018). *Differentiated Reading Instruction: Strategies to Reach All Students.* In *BSU Honors Program Theses and Projects.* Item 267. Available at: https://vc.bridgew.edu/honors_proj/267

Scarino, A. (2013). *Changing Perspectives on Language Learning: Towards Multilinguality. Leksika: Jurnal Bahasa, Sastra dan Pengajarannya*, 7(1).

Schwaller, T. (2011). *Occasional White Boarding: Examining the Effects of Physics Students' Understanding of Motion Graphs.* Michigan Technological University., DOI: 10.37099/mtu.dc.etds/535

Skupeňová, M. Š. (2017). Visualizing Literary Texts in University Language Courses. *CASALC Review*, *6*(3), 82–82.

Viesca, K. M., Teemant, A., Alisaari, J., Ennser-Kananen, J., Flynn, N., Hammer, S., & Routarinne, S. (2022). Quality Content Teaching for Multilingual Students: An International Examination of Excellence in Instructional Practices in Four Countries. *Teaching and Teacher Education, 113*, 103649.

Wall, T. (2017). L1 Literacy and Its Implications for LESLLA Immigrant Women in Canada.Hamline University. https://digitalcommons.hamline.edu/hse_all/4400

Warner, R. M. (2010). Differentiation in the Content-Area Classroom for English Language Learners. (Master's Thesis). University of Nebraska–Lincoln. https://digitalcommons.unl.edu/cehsdiss/78

Chapter 4
From AI Concepts to Classroom Practice:
How Professional Training by AI Experts Transforms Language Teaching

Houda Boumediene
https://orcid.org/0000-0002-3264-7867
University of Laghouat, Algeria

Ouafa Ouarniki
University of Djelfa, Algeria

ABSTRACT

The rapid integration of Artificial Intelligence (AI) into education systems has brought unprecedented opportunities and challenging dilemmas, mainly in language teaching. As more AI-powered tools become increasingly accessible, language instructors are increasingly confronted with the challenge of understanding, critically evaluating, and effectively integrating these technologies into instructional practice. Yet, many teachers, especially those who lack technical reports to base their decisions on, are not confident they have the necessary knowledge to make informed decisions regarding AI deployment in their schools. This chapter solves this critical need with the presentation of a new, interdisciplinary professional development model designed to prepare language teachers with conceptual knowledge and procedural skill in AI. Central to this model are a series of co-facilitated collaborative workshops and seminars between language learning specialists and AI experts. Training initiatives aim to bridge the long-standing gap between pedagogic realization and technology innovation by de-mystifying, critically thinking, and pedagogically testing. This

DOI: 10.4018/979-8-3373-3755-5.ch004

chapter documents the journey of the participants through four consecutive phases: awareness of AI in the beginning, conceptualization, operationalization within practice, and continuous mentorship. Drawing on excellent qualitative data from case studies, participant descriptions, and institution reports, the chapter documents measurable teacher confidence, inter-disciplinary teamwork, and student engagement gains. The chapter critically discusses the selection, adaptation, and piloting of the tools by teachers in different and resource-limited higher education environments. In addition, it also sets out the design principles that inform professional development experience, including co-construction of knowledge, iterative peer scaffolding, and responsiveness in context. The chapter concludes with a set of practical suggestions for institutional leaders, policymakers, and curriculum makers who want to expand such interdisciplinarity projects. Ultimately, the chapter provides a much-needed, practice-oriented guide to the integration of AI into language teaching in pedagogically grounded, ethical, and contextually aware manner.

1. INTRODUCTION

1.1 Framing the Urgency of AI Integration in Language Education

AI has graduated from being a specialist innovation in industry and computer science to a force of change in world education. AI no longer only refers to predictive analytics or automation but has evolved to become an accomplice in the production of epistemologies of learning, interaction forms, and pedagogy design. Yet integrated within adaptive learning platforms, intelligent feedback platforms, or conversation language models, AI is transforming into what it means to teach, learn, assess, and communicate (Holmes et al., 2019; Cukurova et al., 2020). Higher education has witnessed the mushrooming of AI uses build upon unprecedented possibility for tailoring, productivity, and scalability—along with issues of equity, teaching, and teacher identity.

AI is highly common in language learning and language teaching. It relies on advances in natural language processing (NLP), speech recognition, machine translation, and semantic analysis that AI presently facilitates input and output of language in many interactive, fun, and personalized forms.

Students can practice pronunciation with real-time acoustic feedback (e.g., ELSA Speak), receive precise syntactic and lexical assistance with tools like Write & Improve or Grammarly, and compose or edit advanced text with models like ChatGPT, Claude, or Gemini. These resources extend learning beyond the confines of the traditional classroom through provision of just-in-time support, multilingual scaffolding, and corpus-based analysis that would otherwise remain confined in the limits of expert commentary or specialist pedagogy (L o et al., 2024).

As Boumediene and Hamadi (2024) note, AI technologies have progressed rapidly from optional additions to infrastructural bases in most tertiary learning environments. However, while these technologies provide more participation and autonomous learning, they replace habitual epistemic structures of language teaching. AI writing, for instance, disturbs customary ideas of authorship, assessment, and voice. When computers can simulate discourse registers or hone argument patterns, the role of the teacher as a linguistic model or sole arbiter is rewritten. That requires a wholesale rethinking of learning goals, course assumptions, and even the ontological status of language acquisition.

But even while AI is so full of promise as educational technology, there is still a critical need to balance technological enthusiasm with ethical sensitivity and pedagogical humility. The uses of AI are not merely technological advances but cognitive and cultural transformations that require teachers to interrogate critically what is offered, what is lost, and for whom. Derakhshan and Zhang (2024) warn that whether or not AI can become successful at learning languages will not depend on the degree of tool sophistication but on educators' willingness to become responsible for its pedagogical, epistemological, and cultural implications. The issue is technological in a narrow sense, human and institutional in scope: How do we educate teachers to teach with not through AI technologies? How do we weigh them as not just passive learners but as critically active co-designers of digital learning futures?

1.2 The Gap Between Technological Development and Pedagogical Practice

There has been exponential growth in AI in education, but there is a widening gap between classroom practice and technological innovations. The gap is not merely a question of digital access or infrastructure—it is a sign of deeper epistemological divides between language pedagogy and computational rationality in AI. AI applications are traditionally created in abstraction from classrooms, motivated by concerns such as grammatic correctness, user scaleability, or optimization processes—but not from the dialogic, situated, and relational pedagogy of language education (Zhang & Zhang, 2021).

Language instruction in practice is usually accomplished by the majority of language instructors who perceive AI to be a "black box" system—that is, inscrutable to comprehension, culturally disorienting, and consonant-harmonious to their teaching responsibilities (Serholt & Barendregt, 2020).

The teachers point to inadequate transparency of algorithmic choice-making, arbitrariness of AI responses, and substitution of teacher-student interaction. It is not resistance to technology but the lack of pedagogical framing in how AI is delivered to educators, Bouakkaz and Boumediene (2025) say. The tools arrive unaccompanied by background, training, or calibration to the pedagogical objectives of the curriculum—and allow teachers to ignore them or misuse them.

These are subsequently aggregated in marginalized and under-resourced settings. As UNESCO (2021) suggests, educators in the Global South are subjected again and again to infrastructural challenges to successfully incorporating AI: outdated infrastructure, digitally illiterate training provision, weakly supportive policy, and insensitive curricula that fail to respond to technology. There, AI risks entrenching digital colonialism—externally devised systems foisting linguistic formats, pedagogical models, or content hierarchies onto indigenous knowledge practices.

The gap also represents opposing sets of values: objectivity and scalability-based engineering culture and context and empathy and dialogism-based pedagogical culture. Wang (2023) points out that these logics have to be made compatible only through co-designing and interdisciplinarity-as-continuation. This will not be enough to expose the teachers to the AI tools, rather, they must be brought in to help them design, challenge their presuppositions, and find their application in the contexts of their own classrooms. Without such engagement, even the most recent systems are pedagogically inert.

1.3 Rationale for Interdisciplinary Professional Development

In order to address these misalignments and enable productive integration, this chapter advocates for a co-constructed model of professional development (PD) that brings together AI experts, language teaching researchers, and classroom teachers in dialogic collaboration. It is not a question of retraining teachers as data scientists or programmers, but of building AI literacy as a complex competence that encompasses technical skill, critical insight, and pedagogical agency.

AI literacy, Long and Magerko (2020) argue, theory is not applied know-how with tools; it is learning about algorithms, about how biases come to be encoded, and about how answers are constructed from data structures. As language teachers, it is questioning how AI computes "correctness," what language norms it prefers, and how these judgments can exclude some dialects, identities, or rhetorical practices. This article will answer these questions. Moreover, they hold that without such consciousness, educators will in effect reconsolidate hegemonic discourse and stifle linguistic diversity with careless but kind-hearted uses of AI.

Interdisciplinary PD models represent a good solution. Cross-disciplinary collaboration-focused training programs that combine design elements into working, iterative back-checking processes and reflective mentoring—are likely to yield durable pedagogical change, as suggested by Chiu's (2022) meta-analysis. Boumediene et al. (2025) also cite that language teachers become more confident, more creative, and more critically engaged when they are not just users but reviewers and co-designers of AI content.

Furthermore, interdisciplinary training encourages ethical reflexivity. Educators learn to notice asking hard but essential questions: Who owns the data in AI systems? How does machine response build learner identity? What are the unintended consequences of AI application for assessment or remediation? Such questions are particularly pertinent in multilingual and multicultural classrooms, where algorithmic generalizations have the potential to annihilate nuance, flatten complexity, or silence local knowledge (Chapelle & Sauro, 2017).

In reality, AI integration teacher professional development must move beyond task-level preparation. It must foster an intellectual position, one that situates teachers as designers, critics, and moral agents in a rapidly changing digital environment. By grounding AI integration in interdisciplinary dialogue, contextual facts, and pedagogical values, we build the conditions for technology to augment, rather than destabilize, the professional agency of teachers.

1.4 Chapter Objectives and Scope

This chapter develops a systematic, evidence-based approach to interdisciplinary, AI-centered professional development program design and implementation for language teaching professionals at the post-secondary level. With concrete examples from multi-institution collaborative training projects, the chapter illustrates how language pedagogy experts and AI experts worked together in conceptualization, implementation, and assessment of training models that prepared educators for a transition from basic AI literacy to pedagogically meaningful experimentation in the classroom.

The specific objectives of the chapter are four-fold:

- To examine the theoretical underpinnings of artificial intelligence in the context of language teaching, explaining the need for inter-disciplinary collaboration between technologists and educators to develop adaptive and sustainable professional learning pathways.
- To share outstanding case studies and practitioner reports, showing how co-construction of workshops resulted in increased teacher agency, critical reflection upon new technologies, and more student engagement and motivation.
- To introduce and critically assess some selected AI tools—like ChatGPT, Grammarly, Write & Improve, and corpus-based platforms—against particular learning objectives, teacher agency, and classroom interactions.

- To offer practical strategic recommendations to institutional leaders and policymakers, with specific attention to the principles of scalability, adaptability, and ethical incorporation in resource-constrained settings.

The outline of the chapter is as follows:

- Section two presents the theory for interdisciplinary professional development of AI integration in a broader pedagogy, technology, and theory of adult learning context. It gives models such as TPACK, teacher learning sociocultural theories, and AI literacy frameworks to encourage interdisciplinary collaboration.
- Section three describes organizational and functional dynamics of the collaborative training model, including typology of workshop formats, why particular choices of AI tools are made, and curriculum development design heuristics.
- Section four outlines the path of teacher learning in four interlocking stages: initial introduction and growing awareness, conceptual consolidation, enactment in practice, and mentoring or peer-assisted follow-through. This path is sensitive to personal development as well as to institutional learning cycles.
- Section five illustrates reflective accounts and qualitative data of participant educators and facilitators. Their accounts reveal developments and challenges encountered, for example, epistemological tensions, ethical issues, and strategies in operation against context constraints.
- Section six summarizes significant findings of the field implementation and transmutes these results into actionable strategies for institutional reform, faculty development activities, and policymaking and framework reforms at a national level, particularly in the Global South and marginalized education systems.
- Chapter seven ends by throwing AI integration into language teaching forward-looking visions. It calls for the establishment of long-term, cross-disciplinary alliances that place teachers not only as end-users of AI tools, but as co-designers of pedagogical futures.

By situating language teachers' professional knowledge and identities center stage, and bridging disciplinary chasms between education and artificial intelligence, this chapter envisions an inclusive, ethically attuned, co-designed education future. In this envisioned system, AI is less about substituting teacher knowledge than a catalytic agent, supplementing human judgment, inspiring creativity, and enabling distributed agency on the part of teachers, learners, and technology developers collaboratively working together.

2. THEORETICAL AND CONCEPTUAL FRAMEWORK

Meaningfully incorporating Artificial Intelligence (AI) into language instruction entails more than technological additive; it must be theoretically and conceptually undergirded by an understanding that addresses how instructors absorb, reinterpret, and reimagine knowledge back into dynamic class settings. While AI is generally framed in computational or engineering terms, its successful integration into instructional settings is inherently socio-cultural and pedagogical. Teaching is not merely a knowledge transfer—it is a human, interpretative process, and the coming of AI in this context has to be critically mediated. The following section addresses four pillars of professional development that form the basis of the professional development model proposed in this chapter: AI literacy, the TPACK framework, theories of adult learning, and interdisciplinarity in teacher training. Each pillar is unpacked to illustrate its conceptual importance and practical implications in the contemporary language-teaching situation.

2.1 Defining AI Literacy in Language Education

AI literacy in the context of language teaching must be envisioned as an integrative and evolving cluster of competencies beyond familiarity with digital tools. It is the capacity of the teacher to engage critically with the logics of AI systems, discern their affordances and limitations, and introduce them into pedagogical practice with discernment and creativity. Recent literature emphasizes that AI literacy includes cognitive and ethical aspects. It encompasses not only knowledge of AI operation—how large language models process inputs and produce outputs—but also of how those outputs compare to or diverge from learning objectives. Ng, Li, and Wang (2023) argue that AI literacy entails the capacity to place, judge, and co-design with intelligent systems, a skill obviously required in education where such systems are increasingly intervening in human learning.

In language teaching as a discipline in particular, AI literacy is most immediate about understanding how language is generated, organized, and processed by computers. Teachers need to learn about the algorithms behind tools such as ChatGPT, Grammarly, and ELSA Speak, both in order to use them fruitfully and to counteract the uses to which they might be put as manipulative pedagogical tools. For instance, while such programs can be used to give grammatical proofreading or conversation simulation, they are also less capable in their awareness of cultural pragmatics, idiomatic usage, or affective sensitivity, those which lie right at the heart of language fluency. As Pangrazio and Selwyn (2019) clarify, the distinction between functional AI implementation and critical AI literacy is essential: whereas the former is about the implementation of the tool, the latter challenges its assumptions, bias, and social implications.

With the increasing use of generative AI in the language-learning setting, learners will tend to use such systems independently without appropriate teacher intervention. Lo, Hsu, and Chien (2024), in their review of the literature, observe students utilizing AI for writing, practicing pronunciation, and acquiring vocabulary. If left without a teacher intervention, this utilization has the potential to further reinforce surface learning and detachment from real communicative contexts. As it stands, then, teacher AI literacy must entail the cultivation of critical digital citizenship, where teachers are not only able to use AI but also model reflective, ethical, and contextual AI use for students.

2.2 Technological Pedagogical Content Knowledge (TPACK) and AI

TPACK continues to be a central theoretical model of conceiving the type of knowledge that teachers must bring to their practice as they integrate technology. Mishra and Koehler (2006) developed TPACK, which conceptualizes the zone of intersection of content knowledge (CK), pedagogical knowledge (PK), and technological knowledge (TK) as the sweet spot of effective technology-integrated instruction. With the emergence of AI in the new century, this model was even more advanced. Language instructors not only need to understand the language content they are teaching and pedagogical practices they are employing, but also the working mechanism and limitations of AI systems which are increasingly being employed in pedagogic activities.

The challenge lies in moving from a general familiarity with technology to a nuanced ability to integrate AI in such a way that it enriches, rather than replaces, human interaction. This is where the idea of TPACK-AI comes into crystal clear focus. As Lin (2023) demonstrates, integrating AI involves shifting the technological domain in order to include an understanding of machine learning, algorithmic feedback, and data-driven personalization. For language teachers, this involves learning how to interpret AI-generated feedback, how this relates to second language acquisition theory, and how it can be integrated into communicative pedagogies. The onus is not just to accept AI tools but to incorporate them into a pedagogy that is situated and pedagogically valid.

The case of AI writing aids such as Ecree, Write & Improve, or automatic pronunciation correction systems is a good example. Unless educators are extremely well-acquainted with how such types of devices operate and how the computational decisions they make differ from pedagogically informed human response, they will either not use them or misuse them. Chiu (2022) and Chen et al. (2023) indicate that unless pedagogical training is offered in employing AI in general, piecemeal or reluctant adoption is the most probable outcome.

. Teachers may apply AI superficially or spasmodically, hence not fully achieving its potential for transformative impact. Establishing TPACK-AI capacity requires more than individual training activities; it requires profound, recursive processes where teachers discuss how AI both slots into—or overturns—their pedagogical convictions with each other. Through such exposure, teachers can be assured of dealing with the technological, ethical, and pedagogical dimensions of AI-augmented language teaching.

2.3 Theories of Adult Learning and Professional Development

Any effective model of teacher preparation will have to be underpinned by a clear conceptual grasp of the adult learning principles. Knowles' andragogy model (1984) remains leading in this debate with the argument that adults are driven by relevance, experience-centered, and problem-centered learning settings. Current andragogy definitions such as Merriam and Bierema (2022) still center on learning settings that are participatory, flexible, and learner-real-world-issue-based. To the challenge of integrating AI, this means that the teacher is not only a passive learner of technical data but a co-designer of knowledge who, with his or her own pedagogical concerns and classroom practice, intersects with the learning process.

Besides that, constructivist professional development has an emphasis on the social and dialogic nature of learning. Vygotsky's (1978) and Bruner's (1996) theories remain applicable here. Learning, constructivist theory holds, is not an internalization process that occurs in isolation but an intersubjective one guided by discourse, interaction, and contextual meaning. In AI-enhanced teacher development, this may take the form of collaborative workshops where teachers experiment with AI tools, compare outputs, and reflect on their pedagogical fit. It also includes inquiry-based learning opportunities where educators investigate the biases, assumptions, and linguistic tendencies of generative models.

Professional development toward actual engagement with AI must be sustained and recursive as well. Desimone and Garet (2015) have shown that isolated, short workshops rarely lead to lasting change. Instead, improvement should take time, with reinforcement for reflection, mentoring, and sustained application. The training model described in this chapter puts these principles into practice, cycling through phases of exposure, conceptualization, experimentation in practice, and reflection-in-action in the community. Similarly, instructors learn not only about AI, but with it, through it, and in spite of it, and in the process build a nuanced and ethically sensitive teaching practice that respects innovation while neither sacrificing professional mastery.

2.4 Interdisciplinarity in Teacher Training

Interdisciplinarity is not an administrative necessity but a pedagogical practice that fruitfully places different epistemologies in tension, and in pursuing AI integration, this interdisciplinarity is nothing short of required. Successful AI integration into learning environments requires the co-labor of computer scientists, linguists, teachers, cognitive psychologists, and data ethicists. Each discipline has its specific features and methods, and it is in their intersection that new pedagogical concepts become possible. Repko and Szostak (2021) explain interdisciplinarity as a synthesis of certain ideas and approaches across many different fields for the purpose of finding solutions to large and complicated issues, like the integration of AI in education.

The intersection of AI technologists and language teachers can be particularly productive. As technologists discover classroom realities from teachers, they begin to reformulate their own assumptions about user needs and tool design. As teachers learn from developers, they gain insight into AI systems' internal workings and how to critically challenge their outputs. These interactions, or "boundary-crossing encounters" as they have been named by Akkerman and Bakker (2011), facilitate co-construction of hybrid knowledge beyond disciplinary boundaries. Criticism is given to the inaccuracy of ChatGPT's genre-based writing recommendations, as illustrated, prompted developers to enhance prompt-engineering practices, making the tool more educationally valuable.

Zhang and Zhang (2021) show how this kind of interdisciplinary teacher professional development not only enacts technical competency but also teacher agency. Through the process of involving teachers in the design and testing of the AI tool, they gain a critical understanding and sense of ownership that informs more pedagogically creative and contextually appropriate classroom pedagogy. Interdisciplinarity is not a matter of combining expertise, it is a matter of creating new ways of thinking, new ways of discourse, and new avenues for transformatory education. In the age of AI, these collaborative approaches are not preferred, they are a strict necessity.

3. THE COLLABORATIVE TRAINING MODEL

The collaboration model proposed in this chapter hopes to walk teachers step by step from the earliest introduction to AI concepts to the strong infusion of AI tools into their language classrooms. The model draws on the theories explained above and is grounded in real-world training activities co-facilitated by AI technologists and language education specialists.

3.1 Structure of the Model: AI Experts + Language Educators

At the heart of the model is the collaborative pairing of two expertise domains: on one side, AI specialists who provide accessible explanations of how AI systems work—focusing on machine learning, natural language processing, and speech recognition—and on the other, experienced language educators who translate these technical affordances into pedagogical scenarios. At the heart of the model is the collaborative pairing of two expertise domains: on one side, AI specialists who provide accessible explanations of how AI systems work, focusing on machine learning, natural language processing, and speech recognition, and on the other, experienced language educators who translate these technical affordances into pedagogical scenarios.This dual facilitation avoids the remoteness and technocentrism of workshops.

The framework is versatile and adaptive to various settings of postsecondary education. It has been piloted in national faculty development programs and university teaching centers, with cohorts ranging from beginning instructors to experienced lecturers. Sessions are instructed in hybrid formats to accommodate various levels of access, particularly in low-resource settings.

3.2 Workshops and Seminars

The learning cycle is supported progressively, week after week through a sequence of workshops at various levels of professional progression. Foundation seminars deal with foundational concepts in AI, stripping away the hype associated with "transformer models," "prompt engineering," and "learning analytics."

As experience grows, they proceed to tool-specific workshops where they get introduced to AI tools such as ChatGPT, Grammarly, and essay grading tools through live demonstrations and hands-on experimentation. Hands-on design labs follow, in which teachers work together to redesign lesson designs, create AI-empowered activities, and test classroom rollouts as prototypes. Microteaching sessions within the lab, during which students pilot-test their AI-enhanced lessons and receive constructive critiques from their peers and facilitators. Implementation clinics follow up for troubleshooting, experience-sharing, and revisiting designs.

3.3 Pedagogical Goals and Challenges of AI Conquered

The main educational objective is to prepare language teachers not just to use AI tools, but to use them intentionally. Rather than training teachers to adopt technology for technology's sake, the training asks teachers to go in search of particular learning challenges that AI can address. For example, ChatGPT can be used for brainstorming in the process of writing arguments, whereas ELSA Speak for practicing pronunciation in speaking classes.

Each meeting aligns with a sequence of learning outcomes: learning to grasp how AI works, learning to grasp how it maps onto learning objectives, gauging how it impacts learner engagement, and adapting assessment criteria for its use. Ethics, equity, and the responsible use of AI are integrated throughout.

3.4 Phases of Training

The training model progresses through four different but integrated phases. At the awareness stage, teachers are exposed to the educational value and ethical nuance of AI. Guided readings, discussions, and short video clips assist teachers in placing AI within their own classrooms. At the conceptual understanding phase, the learners develop an enhanced knowledge of how AI operates, often by reverse-engineering tool behavior or system output analysis. In a specific example, tutors would consider how a tool like Write & Improve gives feedback and then compare this with marking strategies.

Practice application phase is characterized by co-design. Educators tried out AI tools, prototyped lesson materials, and received formative peer critique. Representative work includes setting peer review processes utilizing AI or utilizing AI chatbots within role-plays for language practice. Finally, follow-up and mentoring keep the initiative going. Members receive continuous mentoring, share best practices on online forums, and collaborate to sort out problems emerging while embracing in the classroom.

This incremental, guided path allows educators to move from initial exploratory reserve to confident agency in the use of AI—a transition that is crucial to facilitate long-term integration of AI in language acquisition.

4. FROM KNOWLEDGE TO IMPLEMENTATION

Although raising awareness and conceptual knowledge about AI among language teachers is of paramount significance, the true secret to successful professional development design rests in the ability to convert that knowledge into usable, context-dependent classroom practice.The journey from knowing AI tools at a theoretical level to their pedagogical application in teaching is not a linear or one-way process. Teachers' emergent identities, institutional constraints and affordances, and learners' responses and needs construct it. This section elucidates teachers' journey of evolving from AI awareness to pedagogically using it and how their utilization of certain tools progresses through a process of iterative reflection.

Professional growth is generally conceived as a process—a continuum of growth as teachers progress through successive stages of participation. In this chapter, the collaborative training model draws on Desimone and Garet's (2015) model of effective professional development and incorporates findings from empirical studies on AI adoption in education (Zhang & Zhang, 2021; Chiu, 2022), and it is structured around four iterative steps: AI awareness, conceptual command, application, and mentoring and follow-up. Each of these phases represents a critical element of teacher learning and a bridge to movement from learning to classroom innovation.

At the awareness phase, teachers learn about the broader discourse surrounding AI in education. This includes fundamental concepts—algorithmic decision-making, machine learning, and natural language processing—policy positions and ethics concerns. Brief readings from UNESCO (2021) on responsible use of AI, complemented with video tutorials and interactive discussion, help teachers situate AI within their pedagogical reality. Of particular interest, this phase is not merely about getting to know technical AI jargon. It creates an opportunity for reflection during which teachers challenge their own presuppositions, ask questions on data privacy, and consider how automation might remodel learner agency. During one of the workshops, for example, teachers talked about how generative AI could help low-proficiency learners generate ideas but also about its ability to homogenize authentic voice in students' writing.

The conceptual understanding stage proceeds this question further with consideration of how AI software actually works. Teachers talk about input-output design of large language models, examine examples of machine-written feedback, and observe how software such as ChatGPT or Write & Improve are trained on a representative sample of writing. Instructors provide live demonstrations where participants try a number of various prompts and see how small variations in wording yield dramatically diverse results. This step also addresses the limitations of AI, such as not being aware of cultural nuance or that it "hallucinates" facts. Teachers begin questioning tool transparency, the source of training data, and bias—shifts from consumer to critical reviewer.

The third phase, practical application, is where teachers begin to develop and test AI-enhanced learning activities. In lab classes involving hands-on activities, teachers are encouraged to develop language tasks that incorporate AI tools in pedagogically significant manners. For instance, in a writing module, a teacher designed a peer review process where students edited their draft based on AI-created comments and thereafter weighed whether the feedback was good or bad before submitting to a human peer. A second teacher developed a pronunciation clinic using ELSA Speak, in which students practiced difficult sounds, monitored their progress, and contrasted AI-supplied feedback patterns across time. Such practices illustrate how teachers begin to appropriate AI technologies—not only as replacements for instruction, but as tools that enhance specific aspects of language acquisition when properly integrated into lesson design.

Most importantly, the application stage also involves small-scale classroom piloting. Teachers integrate their AI-based activities into teaching contexts and record student reactions, levels of engagement, and learning outcomes. They collect informal data—such as learner feedback, patterns of error, and participation rates—to evaluate the effectiveness of the tool. This information guides future revisions of their lesson plans and informs their developing pedagogical position on AI.

The final phase, follow-up and mentoring, continues where training impact is sustained beyond launch. After workshops conclude, participants remain connected with each other through online communities of practice, where they share classroom updates, tool tips, and troubleshooting concerns. Ongoing mentoring sessions with facilitators structure reflection and emergent problem-solving. For instance, one instructor discussed how students became too dependent on AI feedback and started to design around her feedback. Through coaching, she reworked the lesson to incorporate more metacognitive scaffolding, in which students had to explain the revisions they accepted from AI-generated feedback.

This mentoring stage depicts the recursiveness of enactment: teachers do not proceed linearly from knowledge to action yet return to previous stages as they encounter new pedagogical issues. The follow-up process also acknowledges that the embedding of AI is not a one-time occurrence but a continuous process of alignment among technology, content, learner needs, and teaching values.

Cumulatively, the transition from knowledge to implementation in the best way possible occurs when teachers undergo conceptual clarity, guided experimentation, contextual relevance, and continuous feedback. By organizing professional development around these principles, the collaborative model allows teachers to be not only consumers of AI but also informed pedagogical designers who incorporate AI with intention, reflectivity, and professional agency.

5. VOICES FROM THE FIELD

However well conceptualized or empirically supported a model of professional development is, however, its true test resides in the lived, complex experiences of the educators who work with it. Teacher learning, especially regarding new technologies such as Artificial Intelligence (AI), is not a linear process of information transfer. Instead, it is a complex, identity-forming process that is cognitive, affective, social, and profoundly contextual. The inclusion of AI within language classroom environments long characterized by human engagement, interpretive subtlety, and relational teaching—necessarily unsettles traditional norms and provokes diverse reactions ranging from interest to resistance, trial to skepticism.

This chapter is based on a large body of qualitative data gathered both during and following the enactment of the interdisciplinary training model. These sources consist of post-workshop interviews, reflective diaries, online forum discussions, and mentoring session transcripts. From these accounts, we discern prominent themes of initial anxiety, growing empowerment, collaborative innovation, ethical strain, and contextual modification. Not only do they offer an insight into the internalization and integration of AI tools, but they also reveal how teachers negotiate their own evolving professional identities in the process.

In the awareness stage, educators are introduced into the general discussion of AI in education. These incorporate underlying principles—like algorithmic decision-making, natural language processing, and machine learning—and policy directions along with ethical implications. Brief readings from UNESCO (2021) on AI ethical use, augmented by video explainers as well as discussion forums that are interactive, aid teachers in placing AI within pedagogical lives. Notably, this phase is not confined to presenting the technical jargon of AI. It also provides a reflective arena where educators question their own assumptions, express concerns over data privacy, and ponder how automation may redefine learner agency. In one workshop, for instance, educators discussed how generative AI could assist low-proficiency learners with idea generation but also argued over its potential to flatten authentic voice in student writing.

The conceptual stage enhances this engagement by going deeper into the way AI systems truly operate. Teachers discover the input-output paradigm of large language models, examine examples of machine-generated feedback, and explore how tools such as ChatGPT or Write & Improve are trained on language corpora. Facilitators guide live walkthroughs in which participants try out various prompts and watch as subtle changes in wording yield radically different outcomes. This phase also broaches the limitations of AI, including its inability to discern cultural nuance or its tendency to "hallucinate" facts. Educators start to ask questions about tool transparency, the origin of training data, and the possibility of bias—shifting from consumer to critical evaluator.

The third step, the stage of practical application, is where the instructors start actively developing and experimenting with a range of learning tasks that are embedded with artificial intelligence. At this stage, through hands-on laboratory work, instructors have the critical task of designing language tasks that successfully integrate AI tools in pedagogically useful and productive ways.For example, in a writing module, one instructor created a peer review task in which students first revised drafts based on AI-generated feedback and then reflected on its quality before submitting work to a human peer. Another participant created a pronunciation clinic with ELSA Speak, where students practiced problem sounds, recorded their progress, and compared AI-generated feedback over time. These tasks show how instructors start to appropriate AI technologies—not as substitutes for teaching, but as tools supporting certain facets of language development when purposively woven into lesson design.

Most significant, the application phase also includes small-scale limited classroom piloting. The educators incorporate their AI-based activities into instructional settings and document student responses, engagement levels, and learning outcomes. They gather informal data—such as learner reflections, error patterns, and participation metrics—to ascertain the impact of the tool. Such evidence drives future versions of their lesson plans and guides their developing pedagogical position on AI.

The last stage, follow-up and mentoring, is where the effects of training are consolidated beyond the first year of implementation. Once the workshops are complete, participants are not left alone but are kept connected through online communities of practice, where they discuss classroom updates, swap tool adaptations, and troubleshooting problems. Systematic reflection and solving emergent issues are addressed through regular mentoring sessions with facilitators. For instance, one instructor noted that her students relied too heavily on AI feedback and started to work around her instructions. She redesigned her lesson plan through mentoring to incorporate additional metacognitive scaffolding in which students were required to justify the revisions they accepted from AI suggestions.

This phase of mentoring reflects the recursive nature of use: teachers do not move linearly from knowledge to practice but revisit earlier phases as they struggle with new pedagogical issues. The follow-up mechanism also recognizes that AI integration is not a one-shot and forever deal but an ongoing process of coordination between technology, content, learner needs, and teacher beliefs. Cumulatively, the transition from knowledge to practice is best supported when teachers are provided with conceptual clarity, guided experimentation, contextual relevance, and ongoing feedback. By organizing professional development around these principles, the collaborative model allows teachers to be not only consumers of AI, but also knowledgeable pedagogical designers who incorporate AI with purpose, reflectiveness, and professional competencies.

No matter how well conceptualized or empirically validated a model of professional development may be, its ultimate test lies in the lived, situated experience of the educators who use it. Teacher learning, especially in terms of new and evolving technologies such as Artificial Intelligence (AI), is not a linear process of information transfer. It is, instead, a complex, identity-forming process that is cognitive, affective, social, and profoundly contextual. The insertion of AI into language classroom environments long configured by human contact, interpretive subtlety, and relational teaching—necessarily unsettles traditional norms and provokes diverse reactions that range from interest to resistance, trial to suspicion.

This chapter draws on a large body of qualitative data collected both during and after the presentation of the interdisciplinary training model. These include post-workshop interviews, reflective diaries, online forum discussions, and mentoring session transcripts. From these testaments, we extrapolate general themes of early resistance, developing empowerment, communal creativity, ethical unease, and contextual alignment. These themes not only offer an insight into internalization and integration of AI tools but also into how teachers negotiate their own evolving professional identities in the process.

5.1. Apprehension Meets Curiosity: Entering AI Space

Among the most frequent reactions expressed in early workshops was a mix of fascination and apprehension. Educators conveyed a feeling of cognitive dissonance as they were faced with terminologies like "neural networks," "natural language generation," or "transformer models", terms that, up to that point, had appeared remote, intangible, and irrelevant to their daily pedagogical life. A widespread misconception was that AI was either science fiction or menacing. As one secondary school teacher from Oran explained during a roundtable:

> *"I truly believed AI was about robots taking our place. I did not know it could also mean having assistance from an app that grades writing more quickly or provides my students with real-time pronunciation assistance."*

This quotation encapsulates the psychological remove that a number of instructors felt from AI, a remove recapitulated in the tech-focused terminology routinely surrounding AI discussion. What was most effective at closing this remove, then, was the model's dialogic and hands-on nature. Educators were encouraged to engage directly with AI tools in a sandboxed, low-stakes space: inputting prompts into ChatGPT, evaluating ELSA Speak's accuracy of feedback, or scrutinizing the wording of AI-generated rubrics in Grammarly. These micro-experiments rendered the invisible visible. As one instructor noted in her journal:

It's one thing to read about machine learning; it is another thing to see it misunderstand a student's sentence and recognize that it still needs me. This moment of realization, that AI, while powerful, is not infallible, opened the door for what could be described as critical appropriation rather than blind adoption.

5.2.Pedagogical Control and Co-Mediation

One of the most paradigm-shifting consequences of the training program, perhaps, was its reframing of Artificial Intelligence not as a pedagogical nemesis or substitute, but as a co-mediator of the learning process, a term that came to define the ways in which teachers learned to negotiate control, collaboration, and creativity with AI tools. Instead of seeing AI as an independent tutor or an omniscient fount of knowledge, educators came to see it more as a "cognitive scaffold", a notion loosely derived from Vygotskian learning theory, in which external supports are utilized to augment learners' ability until internalization is achieved.

In an activity in the training, teachers were prompted to utilize ChatGPT to create comprehension questions for canonical literary works they usually taught in their classrooms. A literature teacher at a university level shared her experience in a follow-up session:

"I typed in 'Create comprehension questions for Toni Morrison's Beloved.' It gave some great literal questions but did not have emotional and symbolic depth. That is when the lightbulb moment occurred: I am still the teacher. The machine can help, but I must guide it."

This awakening was representative of a broader change in attitude seen in most participants.

Far from ceding pedagogical control to automation, teachers started to reassert interpretive control, curating, editing, and sometimes challenging the output of AI systems. As one participant commented in a reflection circle, "*The AI provides raw material, but pedagogy is still mine. It is like co-authoring with a very literal co-author.*"

These insights are in line with Tondeur et al.'s (2017) argument that technology becomes pedagogically meaningful not when it operates independently, but when it is integrated in ways that enhance and extend the agency of educators. Educators began referring to AI tools as "pedagogical amplifiers" or "assistants," in the sense that they could help with sub-tasks such as lexical variation, grammar enrichment, and content scaffolding, but still had to be managed by humans in order to be responsive to learning outcomes and student needs.

This is also in agreement with Boumediene and Bouakkaz (2025), as they point out that "*AI becomes effective in language instruction not when it replaces instructional insight, but when it serves as a companion in a teacher's creative process.*" In this co-mediated model, AI does not substitute pedagogical judgment, it mirrors it, at times even making teachers aware of their own tacit expectations or blind spots more clearly.

A teacher explained that trying out AI-generated summaries made her aware of the unconscious reading strategies she wanted her students to learn—strategies that she had never knowingly taught. "*ChatGPT summarized the article in a way that made me realize my own criteria for relevance and nuance. I was expecting my students to know these things intuitively. That's when I decided to teach them explicitly.*"

This reciprocal dynamic, where teachers not only direct the tool but also learn from its limitations, is what distinguishes pedagogical co-mediation from mere tool usage. It transforms AI into a site of reflection and pedagogical self-awareness, rather than a shortcut or substitution.

5.3. Ethical Dilemmas and the Ghostwriter Problem

Even as the training created opportunities for educators to try out AI integration, it also brought to the surface a number of ethical issues that demanded immediate and ongoing professional debate. First among these was what the participants started referring to as the "ghostwriter problem"—the unsettling awareness that students were now capable of generating highly wrought texts with minimal or no personal involvement, comprehension, or authorship.This issue came to light repeatedly, particularly in English for Specific Purposes (ESP) and academic writing contexts. One technical writing instructor described grading a student report that seemed, on the surface, exemplary:

"Everything looked perfect: grammar, organization, references. But when I asked the students to explain their analysis in class, they had no idea what the report meant. It was like I was making a ghostwriter, rather than the student."

This gap between textual polish and intellectual ownership provoked deep anxieties regarding academic integrity and the loss of genuine student voice. Instructors explained that they felt "betrayed," "confused," or "disoriented" by the dissonance between the written products' fluency and the students' own knowledge or ability. As Boumediene et al. (2025) caution, unethical use of AI can lead to "performance without process," whereby students employ systems to produce deliverables while bypassing the necessary intellectual work of synthesis, analysis, and interpretation.

One group of educators redesigned their writing courses to incorporate oral defenses, revision diaries, and reflective logs in which the students were required to describe how they utilized AI tools and what choices they made during the process. Another educator added a "prompt audit," in which students were required to submit the very prompts they input into AI systems, along with a critique of the produced output. These strategies were not punitive; they aimed to re-center metacognitive engagement and reinforce learner agency.

As one instructor explained during the post-training debrief:

"I told my students, 'You can use AI, but you must be smarter than it. Show me that you know when to trust it, when to challenge it, and what you learned by working with it.' That's the real learning now."

This reframing encouraged teachers to shift from a binary stance of "AI is cheating" toward a more nuanced position: AI use can be ethical, pedagogical, and developmental—if framed transparently and embedded within reflective structures.

This level of thinking is also apparent in Wang's (2023) suggestion that teachers embrace "process-based evaluation models" to document how students engage with AI, not just what they create.

Additionally, these conversations compelled educators to reexamine fundamental questions regarding authorship, originality, and learning itself. When does AI usage constitute support instead of substitution? What is the meaning of "owning" an idea or sentence that has been generated by an algorithm trained on millions of unidentified texts? How do we design tests that honor creativity, authenticity, and critical thinking in a context where help is always a prompt away?

Lastly, the current crisis of ghostwriting has revealed not just a profound threat to academic integrity, but it has also revealed a valuable opportunity for transformation of pedagogical culture in general. Educators began to think of assessment differently, not merely as a gatekeeping function, but as a serious conversation, a two-way dialogue that occurs between the student, the machine, and the learning process as a whole.

5.4. Mutual Transformation Through Interdisciplinary Exchange

Interestingly, change was not only for teachers. AI facilitators also commented on how their assumptions changed. One computer scientist conceded:

"I once equated explainability with code transparency—making algorithms understandable to developers. But collaborating with teachers taught me that pedagogical explainability is something else. It's about making AI readable in human, classroom-focused terms."

This realization captures the two-way learning that characterizes genuinely interdisciplinary efforts. The training did not merely impart knowledge to educators; it was a zone in which disciplinary borders dissolved, and novel hybrid identities formed. Educators became technologists as much as they were able to break down AI procedures, whereas developers started thinking more like teachers—attuned to pedagogical flow, student diversity, and assessment subtlety.

5.5. Peer Support as Confidence Catalyst

A second striking observation arising from our conversations was the powerful manner in which peer dialogue enabled and supported teacher experimentation in their practice. In several sessions, we observed that teachers who were quite subdued and quiet started to contribute energetically with their ideas and comments after they had a chance to hear how their peers had successfully integrated AI into familiar activities that they were already undertaking. One participant reflected insightfully on this shift:

"What brought about a feeling of courage in me was not just the tool itself, but the experience of seeing my colleague successfully use ChatGPT to design a vocabulary quiz. She continued by discussing how this new technology saved her a considerable amount of time in preparing her lesson."That made it real."

This reflects Wenger's (1998) community of practice theories, where meaning and identity are constructed through ongoing, collective motivation. The model took advantage of this by creating post-training forums, WhatsApp groups, and online resource banks in which ideas could be preserved. This novel social scaffolding converted early adopters into what can be viewed as de facto mentors, thus effortlessly enabling the diffusion of innovation throughout different institutional contexts.

5.6. Contextual Constraints and Local Adaptation

Last but not least, the contributors throughout Algeria and elsewhere argued that the implementation of AI cannot be separated from infrastructural and cultural contexts. Access and connectivity remain a big problem in low-resource or rural settings. A teacher from one of the southern provinces related:

"We don't have stable internet all the time. So, I used ChatGPT on my phone at home, printed out a set of prompts, and had students role-play the conversations. Then we analyzed them together in class."

This type of innovative adaptation highlights the value of context-responsive design in professional learning. Rather than offering AI use as a one-size-fits-all solution, the course encouraged adaptive professionalism, whereby teachers customize tools, pedagogy, and assessment practices to learner needs, local infrastructure, and cultural appropriateness. In multiple sessions, educators who were initially quiet started to contribute after listening to how peers incorporated AI into familiar tasks. One participant reflected:

"What gave me courage wasn't the tool itself; it was watching my colleague use ChatGPT to generate a vocabulary quiz and tell me how it saved her prep time. That made it real."

This echoes Wenger's (1998) theory of communities of practice, in which meaning and identity are negotiated through sustained, collective participation. The model exploited this by establishing post-training forums, WhatsApp groups, and online resources banks where ideas could continue to circulate. This social scaffolding transformed early adopters into unofficial mentors, disseminating innovation throughout institutional contexts.

5.6. Contextual Constraints and Local Adaptation

Finally, but not least, delegates from across Algeria and beyond emphasized that AI adoption can't be separated from infrastructural and cultural realities. In rural or low-resource environments, connectivity and access are still a major issue. A teacher from a southern province explained:

"We don't have stable internet all the time. So, I used ChatGPT on my phone at home, printed out a set of prompts, and had students role-play the conversations. We then had a reflective discussion on those subjects together in the class."

This adaptive innovation highlights the imperatives of context-sensitive design in teacher education. Far from representing AI adoption as a one-size-fits-all activity, training was premised on adaptive professionalism, where teachers tailor tool utilization, pedagogy, and assessment practices to the needs of learners, available local infrastructure, and cultural suitability.

6. LESSONS LEARNED AND STRATEGIC RECOMMENDATIONS

The main insights of both the process of designing and implementing the interdisciplinary professional development model, and from participants' reflective practices, some several key lessons whose applicability extends beyond the local context where this model was tested. These lessons point not only to the potential of AI infusion in language education, but also to the structural, epistemological, and relational changes required to make such infusion pedagogically fruitful, ethically sound, and contextually feasible. This section synthesizes these lessons into five overarching themes and deduces important implications for policymakers, institutional leaders, teacher educators, and professional development organizers.

6.1 Lesson One: Demystification is a Prerequisite for Adoption

Perhaps one of the most obvious lessons of the training program is that the incorporation of AI in education starts with demystification. Most language educators began approaching AI tools with a combination of fear, confusion, and skepticism, perceiving them as black-box systems meant for technologists instead of educators. This impression constitutes a serious obstacle to adoption and needs to be directly addressed in any AI-themed professional development program. The most effective way to demystify AI is through hands-on experience, critical conversation, and interdisciplinary mediation. When teachers are shown, for instance, how a transformer model produces text, how a grammar-checking algorithm balances surface accuracy, or how a chatbot like ChatGPT reads prompts, they begin to understand not only the possibilities of AI but also its limitations. Demystification turns instructors into critical users and informed pedagogical designers from reluctant adopters.

Strategic recommendation:

Institutions need to integrate AI literacy modules in pre-service and in-service teacher education programs. These modules need to be not just about "how to use AI" but also about "how AI works" and "how AI fits (or clashes) with pedagogical objectives." Co-teaching between AI experts and educators needs to be institutionalized, especially in digital teaching and curriculum design courses.

6.2 Lesson Two: Interdisciplinary Conversation Produces Pedagogical Innovation

The partnership model foregrounded in this chapter illustrates that dialogue across disciplines—among AI developers, linguists, educators, and digital learning designers—can spur innovation that neither party could create alone. Educators offer deep knowledge of student behaviors, classroom contexts, and curricular needs, while technologists bring algorithmic and design know-how. In areas where these knowledge bases converge, they open up possibilities for emergent pedagogical imaginaries: AI is less a tool to be used, but rather a medium to rethink and reimagine.

This was the case in tasks where educators asked for AI tools to model conversations, simulate rhetorical moves, or scaffold feedback in peer review situations. The emergent practices were not determined by the tools themselves, but by pedagogical innovation enabled through interdisciplinary collaboration. The discussions also promoted epistemological humility, engineers became more attuned to classroom subtleties, and teachers felt more comfortable asking technical questions.

Strategic recommendation:

Policy initiatives need to support the establishment of cross-disciplinary nodes in universities where computer programmers, applied linguists, and education researchers work together to develop AI-based learning solutions. Grants and project funds must be allocated to collaborative projects that combine research, classroom piloting, and iterative development.

6.3 Lesson Three: Teachers Require Continuous Mentorship, Not One-Time Training

Another key takeaway is that AI-centered professional learning needs to be ongoing and recursive, rather than periodic. Short-term workshops are useful for awareness and tool introduction, but actual changes take place over time through trial and error, failure, reflection, and iteration. Educators who were involved in the follow-up mentoring stage of the training model showed considerably greater levels of classroom implementation compared to those who had been present only for the introductory workshops.

Mentoring also provided a sanctuary to grapple with the unforeseen side effects of AI integration, such as student over-dependence, moral uncertainty, and tool mismatch. Through peer discourse and expert facilitation, instructors were capable of reframing these issues as learning opportunities rather than barriers. This concurs with the general literature on professional development, which calls for extended, supported scaffolding mechanisms (Desimone & Garet, 2015).

Strategic recommendation:

Organizations need to invest in long-term professional learning ecologies that blend face-to-face and virtual mentoring, peer learning networks, and classroom-based action research. Teacher-leaders who effectively incorporate AI need to be trained as coaches or mentors, developing a recursive professional development model that expands from within the teaching profession.

6.4 Lesson Four: Ethical Reflection Needs to Be Central, Not Peripheral

AI technologies are not ideologically neutral. They embody the prejudices of the data they are trained on, the presuppositions of the developers who create them, and the sociocultural contexts of their usage. Teachers' pedagogical concerns regarding training involved such things as plagiarism, student dependency, cultural erasure, and algorithmic opacity. These are not technical problems, they are pedagogical and ethical imperatives.

The training's emphasis on ethics—learning with texts such as the UNESCO Guidance on AI in Education (2021), allowed instructors to pose their own questions and develop responses. Some, for instance, developed student-facing policies for the ethical use of AI, while others wrote reflective writing prompts asking students to critically evaluate AI feedback. In fact, these responses echo a deeper desire to develop greater educational agency within an AI-permeated world.

Strategic recommendation:

Education leaders need to insist that AI ethics and critical digital literacy are mandatory competencies in language teacher education that involve learning to recognize algorithmic bias, protect students' data, and educating students to critically evaluate AI-generated content. Organizations have an important duty to create and enact internal policies regarding the ethical adoption of artificial intelligence that also include overarching procedures for gaining student consent, in addition to being transparent during the whole process.

6.5 Lesson Five: It Is Crucial That AI Tools Are Adapted and Contextualized to Address the Specific Needs and Demands of Local Communities.

Last but not least, among the most significant lessons to come out of this project is that AI tools need to be contextualized to local realities. Not every language teaching environment is digitally privileged. In most Global South contexts, as in Algeria, real constraints are presented by such factors as slow internet connectivity, unavailability of institutional licenses, or low digital literacy among learners. Teachers underlined that effective integration hinged not on having access to the most sophisticated tools, but on innovative repurposing and context-sensitive modification. For example, some instructors decided that they would use offline AI writing tools as a way of offering effective support to their students' writing activities. Conversely, there were other educators who decided to use role-playing activities, which involved interactive interaction with chatbots enabled through peer discussion among students in groups. In another example, one instructor went ahead and used ChatGPT to generate sample dialogues, which they then printed out so they could be discussed and analyzed in class. Such adaptations only serve to highlight the need to treat technology not as a fixed and prescriptive solution, but instead as a mobile and pliable resource that can be modified and negotiated within both pedagogical structures and infrastructural contexts.

Strategic recommendation:

The national education policy must encourage open-access, low-bandwidth AI solutions that are adapted for use in low-resourced areas. Local teacher educators need to be empowered to localize content for training, and international partners need to be encouraged to create scalable AI tools that address linguistic diversity, offline use, and curriculum relevance.

In conclusion, we believe that the activation of this collaborative AI-focused training model has provided crucial insights that must guide future directions in education reform, technological advancement, and teacher empowerment. AI will certainly continue to influence the future of education, but its success will hinge not on technological advancement by itself, but on the ability of educators to combine it with criticality, creativity, and contextual sensitivity. The lessons we have derived here lead to a clear imperative: if we are to make AI a tool for pedagogical transformation, we must place the professional development of teachers as its moral and intellectual cornerstone.

7. CONCLUSION

As Artificial Intelligence goes on reshaping the boundaries of human cognition, social life, and communicative practices, language education stands at a critical juncture. What was a speculative horizon earlier, the possibility of AI transforming classrooms, is today an urgent pedagogical necessity. The integration of AI tools into learning and teaching is not a question of technological fashion but a structural change that reaches all levels of the educational process. This chapter contended that such a change cannot be undertaken as a simple act of technology adoption, but as an eminently pedagogical, ethical, and human-centered endeavor.

The thesis of the chapter is that effective AI integration in language education cannot be separated from transformative teacher professional development, one that is interdisciplinary in design, dialogic in process, critically reflective in practice, and sensitive to institutional and teacher contextual specificities. Standing right at the center and core of this revolutionary and transformative process is none other than the teacher, who represents an active and involved.

participant and not a passive receiver of ready-to-use digital solutions that happen to be conveniently available for one and all. Rather, the teacher acts as an active catalyst for pedagogical innovation, stimulating new ideas and practices in education. This fundamental role identifies and celebrates the immense worth of having critical interactions with the subject matter being taught, while at the same time developing and giving sustenance to genuine human relationships in the classroom setting.

The co-design training model developed here, forged through strategic collaborations among AI specialists and language teachers, presents a strong prototype for this emerging paradigm. It demonstrates that interdisciplinary training has the potential not only to demystify AI but also to catalyze a teacher's ability to engage critically with its possibilities, localize it, and reinvent the classroom in the process. Educators who had once experienced AI as opaque or alienating were now co-designers of learner-centered, AI-supported pedagogies. Their journey underscores the importance of recursive learning cycles, in which exposure, reflection, application, and re-evaluation are interwoven, not linear steps but evolving phases of professional and pedagogical growth.

This chapter's theoretical grounding in AI literacy frameworks, the TPACK model, adult learning theory, and interdisciplinary co-construction—has stressed that AI competence is not technical alone. It is epistemological, ethical, and pedagogical. In order for educators to incorporate AI in a meaningful way, they need to be prepared not just to comprehend how AI works but to question its logics: Whose knowledge is inscribed in these systems? What biases will be replicated? Who are the beneficiaries—and who are disadvantaged by their use? These questions require a type of AI literacy that is emancipatory and critical, not just operational.

Most importantly, this chapter has reasserted a basic truth: pedagogy needs to lead, and technology should follow. No algorithm, no matter how advanced, can match the subtle judgment, emotional intelligence, and socio-cultural sensitivity of a committed teacher. AI tools, whether generative text models, grammar feedback engines, or corpus-based platforms, are useful only insofar as they are embedded in considered teaching practices and guided by ethical judgment. When placed within pedagogical objectives and used with care, AI can augment feedback, prolong scaffolding, diversify inputs, and even individualize learning paths. But it cannot—and should not—substitute for the human labor of teaching.

At the same time, field observations and teacher reports have yielded ongoing and nontrivial concerns. Among these are infrastructural shortages, digital literacy disparities, ethical ambiguities around data utilization and student privacy, and enormous disparities in institutional support. Especially in under-resourced environments, frequently throughout the Global South, AI adoption threatens to widen current gaps if not led by equity-oriented design and inclusive policy structures. These concerns highlight the imperative for a global conversation that prioritizes not merely innovation, but justice; not merely tools, but the social systems in which they are situated.

Moving forward, the sustainable future of AI in language teaching depends on constructing ecosystems—not isolated training or toolkits, but long-term, adaptive infrastructures of support. These ecosystems need to be expansive enough to encompass mentoring networks, teacher-driven inquiry, peer-to-peer learning, interdisciplinary research, and spaces for ethical reflection and curricular experimentation. They need to invest in local capacity-building and treat educators as not merely implementers of innovation, but as knowledge producers, design partners, and ethical stewards of their classrooms and communities.

Finally, getting ready for an AI-driven future in language teaching is not just a matter of tech preparedness. It's a matter of developing an educational culture in which instructors feel visible, valued, and empowered to design the tools that define their classrooms. It's a matter of creating dialogic spaces in which innovation and inclusion are not opposed, but complementary. It's a matter of ensuring that, in welcoming smart machines into our classrooms, we don't lose focus on the human narratives, relationships, and hopes that make education worth doing in the first place. The future will be AI-augmented, but whether it is teacher-guided, ethically grounded, and student-centered is a decision. This chapter argues that the decision rests in our collective hands.

REFERENCES

Akkerman, S. F., & Bakker, A. (2011). Boundary crossing and boundary objects. *Review of Educational Research, 81*(2), 132–169. DOI: 10.3102/0034654311404435

Boumediene, H. (2025). The AI Evolution in Higher Education: Enhancing Teaching with ChatGPT. *Journal of Studies in Language* [JSLCS]. *Cultura e Scuola, 8*(1), 15–29.

Boumediene, H., & Bouakkaz, M. (2025). Artificial Intelligence in Education: Emerging Trends, Ethical Considerations, and Future Directions. In Cela, E., Vajjhala, N., & Fonkam, M. (Eds.), *Next-Generation AI Methodologies in Education* (pp. 407–438). IGI Global Scientific Publishing., DOI: 10.4018/979-8-3693-7220-3.ch014

Boumediene, H., & Hamadi, N. A. (2024). Integrating artificial intelligence into language learning to enhance proficiency through adaptive and ethical AI solutions. *Akofena, 4*(14), Article 32. https://doi.org/DOI: 10.48734/akofena.n014.vol.4.32.2024

Boumediene, H., Ouarniki, O., & Supran, A. (2025). Exploring the Effectiveness of Problem-Based Learning in Improving English for Specific Purposes (ESP) Proficiency: The Case of EAP Students. *Revue Algérienne des Sciences du Langage, 10*(1), 116–134.

Bruner, J. S. (1996). *The culture of education*. Harvard University Press.

Chapelle, C. A., & Sauro, S. (Eds.). (2017). *The handbook of technology and second language teaching and learning*. Wiley-Blackwell.

Chiu, T. K. F. (2022). Teachers' professional development and AI integration in education: A systematic review. *Computers & Education: Artificial Intelligence, 3*, 100066. DOI: 10.1016/j.caeai.2022.100066

Cukurova, M., Luckin, R., & Kent, C. (2020). *Artificial intelligence and the future of learning: Expert panel report*. UCL Institute of Education., DOI: 10.14324/000.rp.10100222

Derakhshan, A., & Zhang, L. J. (2024). Applications of psycho-emotional traits in technology-based language education: An introduction to the special issue. *The Asia-Pacific Education Researcher, 33*(4), 741–745. DOI: 10.1007/s40299-024-00881-y

Desimone, L. M., & Garet, M. S. (2015). Best practices in teachers' professional development in the United States. *Psychology, Society, &. Education, 7*(3), 252–263. DOI: 10.25115/psye.v7i3.515

Knowles, M. S. (1984). *The adult learner: A neglected species* (3rd ed.). Gulf Publishing.

Lo, C. K., Yu, P. L. H., Xu, S., He, W., & Zheng, J. (2024). Exploring the application of ChatGPT in ESL/EFL education and related research issues: A systematic review. *Smart Learning Environments*, *11*, 50. DOI: 10.1186/s40561-024-00342-5

Long, D., & Magerko, B. (2020). What is AI literacy? Competencies and design considerations. *Proceedings of the 2020 CHI Conference on Human Factors in Computing Systems*, 1–16. https://doi.org/DOI: 10.1145/3313831.3376727

Mishra, P., & Koehler, M. J. (2006). Technological pedagogical content knowledge: A framework for teacher knowledge. *Teachers College Record*, *108*(6), 1017–1054. DOI: 10.1111/j.1467-9620.2006.00684.x

Selwyn, N. (2019). *Should robots replace teachers? AI and the future of education*. Polity Press.

Serholt, S., & Barendregt, W. (2020). Teachers' views on AI in education: Challenges and possibilities. *British Journal of Educational Technology*, *51*(6), 1965–1980. DOI: 10.1111/bjet.12936

UNESCO. (2021). *AI and education: Guidance for policymakers*. https://unesdoc.unesco.org/ark:/48223/pf0000376709

Vygotsky, L. S. (1978). *Mind in society: The development of higher psychological processes*. Harvard University Press.

Wang, X. (2023). Bridging the gap between AI and EFL teacher education: Challenges and pathways. *Language Learning & Technology*, *27*(2), 123–140. DOI: 10.10125/ltl.13160

Wenger, E. (1998). *Communities of practice: Learning, meaning, and identity*. Cambridge University Press.

Zhang, Q., & Zhang, X. (2021). Bridging the gap: Interdisciplinary AI training for educators. *Educational Technology Research and Development*, *69*(4), 2117–2136. DOI: 10.1007/s11423-021-10026-9

Chapter 5
From Ethical Awareness to Inclusive Practice:
How AI Enhances Contextual Responsiveness in Language Learning

Mohammed Mohammed Ali Abdulkhaleq
https://orcid.org/0000-0002-4579-8963
Xiamen University Malaysia, Malaysia

ABSTRACT

This chapter examines the relationship between Artificial Intelligence (AI) and Contextual responsiveness in language learning for the sake of meeting increasing demand for flexible, inclusive and morally sound educational technology. It explores how AI can either help or hinder intercultural communication competence. As a researcher and educator who works with multilingual and multicultural students, I argue that AI systems must take into account a variety of linguistic norms, contextual values, and communication styles. This chapter provides solutions that could be used to improve contextual responsiveness through inclusive data practices, adaptive learning systems, teacher preparation, and community-driven design in addition to identifying cultural bias in training data and the danger of linguistic imperialism. The effects of AI contextual responsiveness on learner engagement, performance, and identity formation are illustrated empirically

DOI: 10.4018/979-8-3373-3755-5.ch005

1. INTRODUCTION

Artificial intelligence has revolutionized language learning through providing students with the capability to unprecedented access to educational interactive, adaptive and personal environments. Some of the examples that work with AI and have become more popular in the formal and informal educational settings are chatbots and smart teaching systems, and generative language patterns. These tools assist with learning vocabularies, help with grammar practice, and give feedback on pronunciation (Pérez-Paredes et al., 2025). The sensitivity of cultural related matters of AI systems in learning languages is an important issue that is still poorly understood despite the advancements in modern technologies.

Language is strongly connected with cultural discourses used in it. It is not just a group of grammar rules and symbols. As a teacher and research in the field of languages I have observed that learners often suffer from specific pragmatic, cultural and social differences that play a role in daily language interactions rather than linguistic structure per se. My experience in developing curricula for multicultural classrooms shows that the students who receive culture- rich language education show higher level of contextual awareness and communication competency in comparison to those students who receive dictionary and grammar education only. This study ascertains the importance of immersing contextual responsiveness in language learning programmes supported with artificial intelligence.

Recent studies highlight the deficiencies of AI traditional models in understanding cultural differences. Most Large Language Models such as GPT-3 and BERT generate biased cultural outcomes or inappropriate in non-western contexts as they were trained on a group of datasets that represent primarily western viewpoints using English language (Wei, 2025). For instance, idiomatic expressions, context greetings, and complements styles differ greatly among cultures. However, AI systems usually cannot understand or replicate such nuances. In addition to hindering students' capacity to authentic communication, this shortcoming of contextual responsiveness may lead to sustaining wrong information or wrong notions (Lewis, 2025).

Capacity of computer systems to identify language differences, understand them, and respect them through cultural discourses under the name of contextual responsiveness in AI in the context of language acquisition means constructing AI models that can immerse a group of language criteria and present appropriate remarks for the targeted culture and enhance capability among cultures. One of the possible methods that work in improving language competency and cultural awareness is the Cross-Cultural Intelligent Language Learning System (CILS) that uses adaptive algorithms to specify content as per learners' cultural backgrounds (Xia et al., 2024).

Considerable hindrances still exist despite such developments. The deficiency of training dataset groups of multicultural backgrounds is one of the major challenges.

Text collections are usually used in AI models and hence the models produced are consistently biased when non-dominant cultures are not represented in these corpora (Perez-Paredes et al., 2025). Furthermore, systemic biases in the algorithms themselves can lead to altered outcomes for students who belong to underrepresented cultures. Lewis (2025) found that when cultural biases were visible, minority students were 30% less likely to use AI language tools, highlighting the critical need for inclusive design practices.

For the sake of solving these problems, researchers have proposed frameworks such METAL (Multicultural Education through Technology-Assisted Learning). These frameworks encourage the use of multicultural data and adaptive algorithms that are sensitive to cultural differences (Lewis, 2025) in order to create AI systems that are not only technically sound but also ethically and socially responsible. These frameworks highlight the importance of collaboration between engineers, educators and cultural specialists.

Contextual and cultural sensitive AI systems have serious ethical implications. Ignoring cultural diversity in language learning resources may unintentionally marginalize non-Western perspectives, entrench hegemonic norms, and jeopardize educational equality for students from around the world (Alsaggaf, 2024). Therefore, underlying assumptions and beliefs must be carefully examined as AI is increasingly integrated into educational infrastructure. This necessitates examining the pedagogical concepts, algorithm design, and data sources used in AI-enhanced language learning (Pérez-Paredes et al., 2025). Moreover, culturally sensitive AI systems can be employed in educational settings for goals other than language acquisition. These resources improve intercultural competence, foster understanding between individuals from different backgrounds and enhance cross-cultural communication. The ability to communicate across linguistic and cultural barriers has become more important than ever in the era of globalization and digital interconnectedness.

Using existing empirical research, theoretical frameworks, and practical applications, this chapter examines the relationship between AI and contextual responsiveness in language learning. It aims to highlight the challenges and possibilities involved in creating culturally sensitive AI systems and to offer suggestions for improving the efficiency and usability of language learning resources. The chapter will contribute to the current debate on equitable and culturally aware language learning in the digital age by adopting an interdisciplinary approach encompassing applied linguistics, educational technology, and AI ethics. AI has been used in language learning as a result of decades of pedagogical experimentation and technology progress.

The foundation for today's intelligent systems, which now include machine learning, natural language processing, and generative artificial intelligence was laid by early computer-assisted language learning (CALL) applications in the 1990s. according to Son, Rozic, and Philpott (2023), these developments have led to a shift in focus from static, rule-based training to dynamic, learner-centred environments that adapt to each individual's needs and preferences. The demand for multilingual communication skills has increased in the context of globalization. Intercultural competence is now an essential part of language proficiency due to transnational education, digital collaboration, and international mobility. Students can greatly benefit from culturally sensitive AI tools to prepare for these cross-border interactions. They can expose students to a range of linguistic registers and dialects, mimic culturally diverse situations, and provide feedback on practical relevance. Moreover, there are particular opportunities and difficulties at the intersection of AI and multilingualism. AI must address problems of code-switching, language transfer, and sociolinguistic variation, although it can help learners acquire multiple languages simultaneously. In addition to enhancing linguistics proficiency, culturally adaptive AI system, in my experience as a researcher working with multilingual students, help students who often feel excluded in monolingual classrooms feel more included and like themselves.

The following sections cover the foundations of the contextual responsiveness pedagogical approach in learning a language. Furthermore, the effect of cultural biasness on the learning outcome will be investigated. The current AI applications with their shortcomings will be summarized in addition to presenting advantageous suggestions to establish culturally adaptive AI systms. This chapter seeks to enhance a more comprehensive and culture-sensitive approach for educational innovation and development of language acquisition supported by AI through visions of vocational practice and up-to-date research.

2. THEORETICAL FRAMEWORK

Providing a strong theoretical framework that takes into consideration the social and technological factors as an important matter when integrating AI with language learning. There is a necessity for combining learning theories and computational models, and intercultural frameworks in order to address the numerous intersections between AI and as a pedagogical necessity. In this section, the main theoretical pillars that support discussing AI and contextual responsiveness in language training is described.

2.1 Intercultural competency and contextual responsiveness

The ability to identify and estimate cultural differences and adapt with them is known as communicating with contextual responsiveness in learning languages. It is closely connected with the notion of competency between cultures that encompass attitudes, skills, and the knowledge required to effective socially acceptable cross-culture communication. To guarantee leaners' exposure to respectful and culture appropriate content in environments enhanced with AI, these competencies must be integrated into interfaces and algorithms.

The Technology-Organization-Environment (TOE) framework, the Technological Pedagogical Content Knowledge (TPACK) model, and the Diffusion of Innovation theory could be used to understand how to integrate culture sensitivity in AI systems (Tarisayi, 2024). These frameworks shed light on the necessity for culturally responsive design in pedagogical technology by emphasising the interaction of technological capabilities, institutional settings, and teaching strategies. The following section highlights the AI models and the learning theories.

2.2. AI models and the learning theories

AI uses a number of styles in teaching such as machine learning algorithms, rule-based systems, and generative AI tools. These models used natural language processing, adaptive content, and personal feedback to interact with students. Gibson et al. (2023) present three level approach that integrate developmental psychology, computational biology, learning design, and the sociocultural theory to understand how to enhance AI for learning. This model presents a comprehensive framework to study the effect of AI on the learning processes through specifying its responsibilities at the micro (individual), meso (society), and macro (culture) levels. The Generative AI platforms (GenAI) such as ChatGPT and Gemini have revolutionized language learning through simplifying instant communication and creating dynamic content. While arguments say that GenAI technologies can enhance learners' motivation and engagement, Noroozi et al. (2024) assert that GenAI has moral risks such as biasness, misconception of context. Their work present fundamental framework for GenAI moral integration highlighting the importance of culturally aware algorithms and human supervision.

From the theoretical aspect, AI-enhanced learning can coexist with constructivist theories which perceive that students generate knowledge actively through participation and contemplation. However, using AI requires re-evaluation of traditional learning theories. Finkenstadt (2025) presents the idea of AI-augmented theory building, showing how generative AI can facilitate the creation of conceptual models and interdisciplinary synthesis. This method shows how AI might improve human reasoning in educational settings rather than replace it.

Theoretical frameworks show the importance of designing AI when incorporated with taking into account contextual responsiveness in language learning. AI systems must be able to comprehend language differences, cultural pragmatism, and context specific communication standards. This requires multidisciplinary collaboration between linguists, educators, and AI developers in addition to technical sophistication. Technologies that culturally adapt AI boost learner involvement and retention, according to my experience as a language researcher who work with multicultural learners. Learners would be motivated to actively participate and hence acquire language competence when they are exposed to information related to their cultural identity. The theoretical emphasis on learner cantered and culturally oriented instruction is consistent with this observation. At this point, it is relevant to discuss the sociocultural theory and AI.

2.3. AI and the sociocultural theory

The sociocultural theory which confirms that social interaction and cultural resources mediate learning, was established on Vygotsky's work. AI is transformed into a cultural tool that influences a learner's perception and understanding AI-supported language learning. To make sure that this tool represents a variety of criteria and cultural values is the difficult part. It is important to match AI responsibilities with the historical and cultural activities, according to Gibson et al. (2023), who asset that AI systems are supposed to be created to enhance individuals and group cultural engagement in addition to individual learning.

Moreover, integrating AI into classroom looks like the previous technological advancements such as IT, telecommunication, and using the calculator. These cycles of resistance and eventual acceptance are compared by Tarisayi (2024), who claims that the theoretical frameworks used to study ICT, such as the socio-technical systems theory are still applied in AI. The necessity to have comprehensive and flexible theoretical frameworks that can take into consideration the growing technologies is further supported by some historical perspectives. The critical pedagogical approach provides a beneficial perspective to test power dynamics that are available in the AI systems in addition to the socio-cultural theory. Critical pedagogy which relies on Paulo Freire's work, emphasize learner agency, cultural identity, and defiance of hegemonic norms. Based on that, some concerns have been raised about whose language norms are being prioritized, whose voices are being amplified and whose voices are being repressed when AI is involved in language acquisition. As a researcher, I think that it is important to look at how to support AI tools for language imperialism or oppose to them. Additionally, through shifting the focus of teaching control led by teachers to the participation led by learners. AI challenges the traditional models of language acquisition. Despite the fact that such a shift goes in line with the constructivist ideas but it requires developing new systems to support, evaluate and provide feedback. Theoretical frameworks must adapt to these developments by integrating knowledge from multicultural communication, cognitive science, and human-computer interaction. By that we can completely understand AI's pedagogical consequences and ensure that its incorporation into language teaching is both fair and successful.

2.4 Technical Outline of Adaptive Algorithms

Language learning systems that are supported with AI centre around adaptive algorithms. These algorithms use techniques such as reinforced learning and natural language processing to examine input generated by learners and then dynamically adjust instructional content (Son, Park, & Kim, 2023). Nonetheless, there are still technical limitations despite the rapid advancement. There is a difficulty interpreting contextual pragmatics, idiomatic expressions, and many systems struggle to interpret non-standard dialects (Pan, 2025). Therefore, researchers advocate for explainable AI and contextually annotated training data (Tenzer, Feuerriegel, & Piekkari, 2024). The following section highlights the current AI apps in language learning.

3. THE CURRENT ARTIFICIAL INTELLIGENCE APPS IN LEARNING LANGUAGES

Artificial Intelligence has developed in learning Languages rapidly; now numerous of platforms and tools are available to help students to improve their skills in language and consider the cultural factors increasingly. These applications include the Generative Artificial Intelligence, systems of smart teaching, environments of adaptive learning, and tools of Natural Language Processing (NLP). The present state of AI-driven language learning tools is examined in this section, with an emphasis on how well they can promote international competency and contextual responsiveness.

3.1 Language Learning Resources Consolidated by Artificial Intelligence

Enormous language learning websites, such as Rosetta Stone, Duolingo, Busuu, and Hello Talk have incorporated Artificial Intelligence Technology. These systems use AI to specialize the paths of education, provide real-time feedback, and edit the content to meet the needs of each student individually. To enhance the participation and memorization, Duolingo, for instance, utilizes machine learning algorithms to predict learner performance and adjust the levels of difficulty accordingly (Son et al., 2023). A key component of many AI language tools is Natural Language processing (NPL).

Applications like speech recognition, conversational agents, and Automatic Writing Evaluation (AWE) have become possible thanks to its ability of allowing robots to understand and produce human language. These resources imitate the real world situations during teaching grammar and vocabulary. Son et al. (2023) insist on how enabling Natural Language Processing (NPL) from context-sensitive reactions from chat applications and digital tutors which is pivotal for promoting the pragmatic efficiency.

3.2 Generative AI and Contextual Responsiveness

By facilitating the dynamic and interactive conversations, Generative AI (GenAI) systems like ChatGPT, Claude, and Gemini have opened new vistas for language learning. These tools may generate idiomatic expressions related to certain cultures, change the tone and the recording in response to the user's input, and simulate conversations with individuals from different cultural backgrounds. Pan (2025) claims that the application of GenAI tools to enhance cultural immersion, writing learning, and producing personalized content is increasing. For example, Franziska Lys's work clarifies how possible for GenAI to work as a writing teacher, as it helps them to produce appropriate writings for both language and culture. However, contextual responsivess for GenAI stands as a problem. These technologies often depends on the training data which may not be representing a range of cultural contexts, even though they may simulate the cultural expressions. According to Pan (2025), heavy reliance on a range of data which is west-centred may results culturally insensitive or biased outputs. Some platforms work with teachers to make AI outputs suitable to specific cultural contexts and incorporate culturally various corpora in an attempt to decrease that.

3.3 Cross-Cultural Intelligent Language Learning Systems (CILS)

The Cross-Cultural Intelligent Language Learning Systems (CILS) is one of the most exciting developments in culturally sensitive AI applications CILS, which was created by Xia et al. (2024), use adaptive algorithms to specialize language learning to the linguistic and cultural backgrounds of his students. Technology improves the linguistic ability and cross-culture competence by adjusting interaction patterns, feedback, and content dynamically according to cultural criteria. The learner's interacting, and communicating skills are improved considerably as a result of CILS usage on websites such as Hello Talk, and Busuu. The students who used CILS showed significant improvements in vocabulary, grammar, pronunciation, and increased cultural awareness, according to experimental studies conducted with more than 1000 participants from 20 colleges (Xia et al., 2024). The effectiveness of the system is credited to the Technology Acceptance Model (TAM), which ensures that the understanding of the learner is driven by tangible benefit and ease of use.

3.4 Artificial Intelligence in Assessing and Correcting

AI is also making a revolution in language assessing by making it possible to assess the students' performance automatically and immediately. Programs of speech recognition and mechanic essay correction systems are examples of tools that provide immediate feedback about coherence, fluency, and pronunciation. Moreover, cultural considerations are increasingly taken into account in the assessment criteria of these systems. For instance, Pan (2025) discusses the assessment criteria creation supported by AI to evaluate language usage, so that it is linguistically correct, and culturally appropriate.

In addition, AI supports the formative assessment techniques which encourage learner autonomy. Student's progress can be observed, shortcomings identified, and targeted curative solutions are provided through Intelligent Teaching Systems (ITS) . because of the ability of these systems to adjust the teaching strategies to suit the learners' cognitive and cultural preferences, they are highly effective in assessing the students from various cultural backgrounds (Son et al., 2023). Ai is used increasingly in social and informal language learning environments, away from well-known electronic websites as Duolingo, and Hello Talk. For example, language teachers and students now are sharing mini cultural rich lessons on social media platforms such as Instagram and TikTok. These platforms are utilizing AI supported recommendations algorithms repeatedly to customize the content according to the user's behavior, in which effects indirectly on how the students are affected by the linguistic variety, and cultural criteria. Although these tools were not designed to be used in education, they represent a rapidly growing field of informal education by AI. AI is also used to help who wants to reconnect with their heritage languages., which were lost because of assimilation or migration. I have witnessed the adaptation of AI tools to teach languages as Arabic, Tagalog, and Yoruba through oral traditions and culturally themed stories in my work with diaspora groups. These resources support the students to use the language to regain their cultural identities, as well as vocabulary and grammar. Initiatives like " AI for original languages", which are leading the efforts to utilize natural language processing and speech synthesis to save the endangered languages, model to develop a culturally considering AI. Additionally, AI has been integrated into collaborative learning systems which help students from different cultural backgrounds to connect with each other. Students are linked through these systems which work by AI according to their linguistic aims and cultural interests, and communication preferences. These systems support mutual learning and communicating between cultures, which is in align with the aims of global citizenship education. Therefore, these applications present AI as a bridge between cultures rather than just being a teacher, I find them encouraging specially as a researcher.

3.5 Obstacles and Limitations

Several obstacles are still there regardless of these developments. The lack of transparency in AI decision making processes is a major concern because of the cultural factors which can be hard to be understood appropriately and apply them. Furthermore, lots of Ai systems are still facing difficulty to get the expressions of politeness, humor, and other certain cultural expressions. As a result of this, it may give correct notes on grammar, but inappropriate culturally to the students.

The digital gap is another barrier limiting access to learning resources which is supported by AI, the students in low resources environment may not have the digital knowledge and technological basis which is needed to benefit from these developments. This arise questions about inclusivity and equity in AI-assisted language training systems. Linguistic Imperialism, or the preferring some languages and cultural criteria stands over other in Ai systems, is a more serious issue when discussing AI and contextual responsiveness. AI systems are mainly trained on English language tend to marginalize the languages and dialects of minority, while empowering English language. This effect maintains the cultural homogeneity while effecting linguistic varsity. AI tools may unintentionally encourage Western communication norms which may lead the student to decrease the value of using their mother tongue language, according to my research with my students from postcolonial contexts, AI tools might inadvertently encourage Western-centric communication norms, which can cause students to undervalue their native language usage.

Another difficulty is the ambiguity of algorithms, or the ambiguity of decision-making in artificial intelligence. Many AI-powered language tools function as "black boxes," producing results without revealing their logic. Teachers and students find it difficult to determine whether cultural factors are considered or ignored because of this ambiguity. According to Liu (2024), in the absence of explainable AI, people are unable to critically interact with the system or question its assumptions. During my teaching career, I have seen situations where students receive grammatically correct but contextually inappropriate feedback, without any means of verifying or correcting the underlying logic. Beyond theory, there are practical implications of culturally insensitive AI. Students in multilingual classrooms may internalize biased feedback, leading to identity conflict, lack of participation, and diminished self-confidence. Testing can have a lasting impact on students' academic performance and self-perception because it is based on cultural bias rather than linguistic errors. For example, a student from Latin America may be criticized for "overusing" emotional language, while a student from East Asia may be told that their indirect communication style is "unclear." The shift from technological improvement to ethical and cultural responsibility is essential to overcome these obstacles. Developers must prioritize transparency, inclusivity, and cultural representation at every stage of AI development. Educators must be vigilant and apply their knowledge to mediate AI outputs and speak on behalf of students whose voices are often ignored.

3.6 Ethical Governance and Data Privacy

Since AI has become increasingly included in language learning and teaching, there is an urgent demand for systematic ethical governance and data privacy framework. While AI provides a potential for a better educational environment, there are some critical concerns related to the biasness of algorithms, data misuse and concerns about imbalanced access.

Embedding AI into language education requires ethical governance and a policy that governs advancement with ethical responsibility. An Ethical AI Governance Framework for Adaptive Learning (EAGFAL) was proposed by Umok, Nwandgbo, and Onwe (2005). This framework highlights strategies for mitigating biasness and ensuring transparent, fair AI adoption in education (Umok, et al 2025). Likewise, Kashyap et al. (2024) advocate for Human-Centered AI in the field of education in order to enhance human capabilities not to replace them. Such frameworks propose policymaking that reflects contextual responsiveness and cultural principles.

3.7 Case studies: Asia and Africa

It is necessary to highlight some studies that are non-western and examine how AI is adapted in Asia and Africa. Tenzer, Feuerriegel, and Piekkari (2024) argue that AI should be improved to contextually reflect specific cultural meanings such as indirectness in Japanese or hierarchical politeness in Korean. In Africa, there are some efforts to train AI to align its development with African moral traditions such as fairness, Ubuntu and community solidarity (Abiero, D. (2024). Similarly, Barnes, Zhang, and Valenzuela (2024) argue that cultural identity forms reactions to AI systems noting that individualist cultures could perceive it as a threat to autonomy while collective cultures may perceive it as part of the self or an extension to its culture. Such findings reveal that it is crucial to align AI as a language tool to be adapted as context-specific.

4. BIASES AND DIFFICULTIES IN LEARNING AI LANGUAGES

While AI has revolutionized language learning, there are a number of drawbacks, particularly regarding contextual responsiveness, ethical design, and equitable access. Ironically, I have seen firsthand how tools designed to democratize learning can reinforce systemic biases and cultural hierarchies if not critically examined. This is because I am a researcher focusing on the intersection of educational technology and language pedagogy. The many issues surrounding AI in language learning are examined in this section, with a focus on ethical dilemmas, cultural bias, and effects on students from diverse backgrounds. Building on this, the next section delves into cultural bias of AI systems.

4.1. Cultural Bias of AI Systems:

The presence of cultural bias in Large Language Models (LLMs) is one of the most pressing issues in the field of AI-enhanced language learning. Like GPT-4 and related structures, these models are trained on a vast amount of electronic content, most of which represents dominant cultural narratives, particularly those of Western English-speaking societies. According to Liu (2024), the dynamics of user interaction, algorithm design, and data quality are the three main reasons for cultural bias in LLMs. Examples of how these biases appear subtly but noticeably are the focus on specific idiomatic terms, conversational styles, or literary standards that may not be appropriate for learners' cultural contexts. Feedback generated from AI has misinterpreted ambiguity or cultural error in my classroom research. As a result, students become less confident, and their cultural communication standards may become less legitimate. These exchanges highlight the need for AI systems that are culturally sensitive, in addition to being linguistically accurate. While this section discussed the cultural biasness of AI systems, it is essential to highlight the ethical and cultural challenges encountered in designing AI tools in addition to the limitations and of Pragmatic and Contextual Understanding.

4.2. Ethical and Cross-Cultural Design Challenges

The use of AI tools in classrooms that are not culturally relevant to individuals has serious ethical implications. According to Liu (2023), the widespread use of AI calls for a cross-cultural ethical framework that considers different communication styles and values. In the absence of this framework, AI systems risk reinforcing digital colonialism, where globally dominant cultural values are exported under the guise of neutrality and are encoded in algorithms. In their comparison of five well-known Master of Laws programs, Tao, Liu, and Wang (2024) found that the outputs of these programs consistently aligned with the cultural values of English-speaking, Protestant European countries. By giving non-Western students a limited definition of "appropriate" or "correct" language use, this alignment could inadvertently harm them. To guide AI outputs, the authors propose "cultural prompting," a mitigating technique in which users incorporate cultural contexts into their prompts. This method disregards structural design flaws while burdening users, despite its potential. I believe that inclusive data practices are the first step in ethical AI design. This entails selecting training datasets that represent a variety of cultural perspectives and integrating linguists, cultural experts, and educators into the development process. In order to foster trust and accountability, algorithmic decision-making in educational environments must also be transparent.

4.3. Limitations of Pragmatic and Contextual Understanding

The AI's inability to understand context and pragmatics, which are essential elements for culturally sensitive communication, represents another major obstacle. Generative AI algorithms often struggle to complete tasks that require a comprehensive understanding of social hierarchies, politeness techniques, or specific cultural humor. In a study of Sino-foreign collaborative education programs, Zhang (2025) found that when generative AI systems were prompted to create content for multicultural scenarios, these systems typically produced outputs that were semantically valid but culturally incorrect. These limitations are particularly problematic in language learning because context plays a role in participating in meaning-making. In real-life interactions, learners may internalize AI-generated solutions that are theoretically sound but practically incorrect, potentially leading to misunderstandings. As an instructor, I have had to intervene multiple times to debunk these misconceptions, emphasizing the importance of human oversight for AI-mediated learning.

In addition to ethical and cultural considerations, there are issues of access and equity. Not all students have equal access to AI-powered resources, especially in environments with weak digital infrastructure. While AI can improve Intercultural Communication Competence (ICC), its benefits are not evenly distributed due to differences in digital literacy and access to technology, as Klimova and Chen (2024) argue. By favoring students who are already proficient in digital technology and marginalizing those who are not, the digital divide exacerbates existing educational disparities. Having discussed such limitations and the contextual understanding, human-AI collaboration along with the teachers' roles will be discussed in the next section.

4.5. Human-AI Collaboration and the Roles of Teachers

Finally, the application of AI in language education raises important questions about the changing nature of the teaching career. AI can not replace teachers in critical thinking and cultural mediation, although it can automate repetitive tasks and provide personalized feedback. Teachers must function as coordinators of cross-cultural learning, guiding students through cultural nuances and the use of technology, according to Zhang (2025). I completely agree with this view. From my experience, when AI is used to complement human instruction rather than replace it, the best learning outcomes are achieved. In order to contextualize AI outputs, correct cultural errors, and foster critical dialogue about language and identity, teachers are essential.

5. MAKING AI-BASED LANGUAGE LEARNING MORE CULTURALLY SENSITIVE

It highlights the necessity of culturally sensitive design and implementation through the increasing integration of artificial intelligence (AI) in language education. The language outcomes will be enhanced via culturally adapted AI tools which can also promote greater cross-cultural understanding, as evidenced by my experience as a researcher and teacher working with multilingual learners in a variety of cultural contexts. In conformity with current empirical research and theoretical insights, this section aims to present significant strategies to boost language learning through the use of AI.

5.1 Culturally Contextualized Adaptive Learning Systems

Changing content based on learners' cultural backgrounds, Adaptive learning systems are among the best methods to augment cultural awareness. The Cross-Cultural Intelligent Language Learning System (CILS) is a good example (Xia, Shin, and Kim, 2024). CILS enhances linguistic proficiency and intercultural competency by employing artificial intelligence to customize learning resources, feedback, and interaction methods in accordance with learners' cultural norms. Having worked with international students, I have learned that they become more motivated and confident when engaging with materials sensitive to their cultural identity. Adaptive systems like CILS work to decrease the alienation often experienced in standardized language programs by validating the cultural experiences of learners.

5.2 Training teachers on the AI integration and cultural competence

Teachers are instrumental in mediating AI tools and ensuring their cultural relevance. Li (2025) underscores the importance of English language instructors who are trained on cultural competence, especially in technologically advanced environments. According to her research, teachers who have received specialized training are more capable of adapting their methods for different student groups and integrating cultural elements into their lessons.

I fully support professional development programs that integrate intercultural education and AI literacy. Additionally, teachers need to understand how AI works, and should be able to critically evaluate the cultural appropriateness of the outcomes. When AI-generated content is culturally inappropriate, teachers equipped with skills can effectively guide students and intervene.

5.3 Intercultural Communication Competence (ICC) with the Help of Artificial Intelligence

Huang (2025) offers a framework for improving intercultural communication AI-assisted competence in the process of teaching English in colleges. The use of scenario-based simulations and personalized learning are two elements to achieve this competence. Artificial intelligence is believed to enhance intercultural communication competence by simulating real-world scenarios and providing feedback on the appropriate, cultural usage of language. The evidence shows that it has assisted learners in navigating culturally intricate real-world scenarios through AI-driven role-playing tools. The said scenarios include the negotiation of meaning in multilingual teamsters or cultural responses to sensitive feedback. In order to amplify the competence of AI-assisted communication between cultures, students are enabled through this simulation to experience a variety of communication methods and receive quick, context-aware feedback.

5.4 Comprehensive Data Practices and Cultural Representation

Contextual responsiveness in artificial intelligence commences with the data used to train models. Numerous, employed AI systems produce biased outcomes due to their training on datasets that disproportionately reflect certain viewpoints, that is, Western viewpoints. Liu (2024) asserts that the way to alleviate bias and promote equality, the AI training tools should include varied ranges of linguistic and cultural databases.

5.5 User-Controlled Context and Cultural Priming:

When users set cultural standards when interacting with AI systems is called "Cultural priming." It is another interesting approach. Using this method, students can guide AI responses to produce culture-appropriate results. They can also express their ethnic identity online, although this is not the ideal solution.

Through the inclusion of contextual signals in the AI inquiries, such as "How would a Japanese speaker respond in this situation?", I encourage, through the instructions, students to experiment cultural priming. This approach makes the AI more relevant and improve the cultural awareness of cultural communication variations.

5.6 Community-Oriented Design and Learner Agency:

Community-oriented design is regarded as one of the promising strategies to foster contextual responsiveness in acquiring language through the use of AI. Such strategies necessitate the inclusion of regional teachers, cultural specialists, and students in creating AI tools. Instead of enforcing top-down solutions, community-led design guarantees that AI systems reflect the values and real-world experiences of the served communities. I would like to assert that the collaborative creation of AI interfaces with local beneficiaries produces more culturally relevant and pedagogically effective outcomes. To improve the learner's ability to make decisions in AI interactions is a critically important tactic. What the majority of AI systems convey is only content; very few AI systems let students design the learning process to suit their cultural preferences. It is possible that students participate and express themselves authentically when they are in control of the tone, registry, and responses generated by AI. For example, should the users be able to choose the regional dialects and cultural filters, their interaction will improve, giving a chance for more personalized experiences. The principles of critical pedagogy, which emphasize the value of empowerment, choice, and voice in education, are emphasised.

5.7 Development of Multilingual Artificial Intelligence and Multidisciplinary Collaboration:

It is also essential to build multilingual AI systems. Many modern technologies, which favor high source languages such as English and other languages, frequently ignore speakers of low source languages. The cultural diversity and representation can be augmented through the improvement of AI to support linguistic plurality including language switching, interlingual translation, regional linguistic diversity. As a model for building equitable AI, projects such as "Common Voice" and "Masakhane" set a standard for open-source datasets for African and indigenous languages. Finally, interdisciplinary teamwork is essential and collaboration among linguists, educators, technologists, and ethics experts is vital for the development of technically robust and culturally sensitive AI systems. As a researcher, I advocate for interdisciplinary collaboration in AI-augmented language training education, which can prioritize learners' empowerment, cultural diversity, and ethical innovation.

6.0 EVALUATION AND EMPIRICAL EVIDENCE

Emphasizing the ability of AI to foster contextual responsiveness in language acquisition needs to be empirically verified. As a researcher dedicated to evidence-based practice, I think thorough evaluation is crucial to supporting theoretical assertions, enhancing educational choices, and advancing technology. This section summarizes the modern empirical studies that have dealt with how AI technologies affected learners' language skills, their abilities to deal with multicultural people, and how they interact with different learning settings.

6.1 Intercultural Communication Competence (ICC) and Artificial Intelligence

The development of intercultural communication competence (ICC) is one of the AI-augmented language acquisition aspects that has been studied extensively. A thorough examination of 11 experimental studies was conducted to determine the potential of AI tools, including chatbots and virtual reality simulations (Klimova and Chen, 2024). It also aims at improving ICC among university students. The research illustrates that students can benefit from AI in navigating cultural differences more effectively, particularly if teachers mingle the use of AI with conventional teaching methods. Having said that, they warned that AI can augment unintentionally cultural biases or overlook complicated cultural processes if not supervised by humans. These sources helped students understand cultural conventions, change the way they communicate, and think about their own cultural preconceptions. The findings indicate that AI can be a valuable tool for intercultural learning, consistent with what Klimova and Chen concluded.

6.2 Impact on Student Performance and Engagement

Alhusaiyan (2025) conducted a systematic review for 15 empirical studies regarding the AI-augmented language acquisition with the focus on the interaction of learners, preciseness of evaluation, and quality of writing. The review used activity theory to analyze the interactions between students, resources, and learning environments. The findings indicate that AI tools can improve writing coherence and fluency, especially when students receive personalized feedback. Having said that, there are still some obstacles in enhancing interactive competence and collective learning. I believe that AI technologies work better when they are incorporated with the teachers' feedback and peers' interaction. For instance, automated writing assessments can provide immediate feedback on the grammatical rules and structure, but it overlooks subtle details such as tone, targeted audience, and cultural appropriateness. So, I agree with hybrid techniques that mix AI's speed with human comprehension.

6.3 Integration of Teaching Methods and Mediation by Teachers

A 2025 study, which employed a quantitative approach, on the impact of cultural competency training on high school English language teachers involved more than 385 participants. The study demonstrated that teachers who went through the training were better able to change how they communicate and add cultural richness to their lessons. This proves that trainers need to be involved, since it is not possible to fully automate contextual responsiveness concerns in AI-enhanced environments.

In the professional development seminars I conduct, I emphasize the importance of teachers engaging critically with the outputs of artificial intelligence and helping students understand them. By acting as cultural mediators, teachers help students deal with problems arising from the use of language in various contexts. Empirical studies validate the mutually beneficial relationship between technical innovation and human competence, lending credibility to this strategy.

6.4 Fairness and Bias in AI Language Tools

Lewis (2025) conducted a mixed-methods study using four platforms to investigate the impact of cultural bias in AI language learning tools. The research determined that minority pupils' participation rates declined by 30% when cultural biases were apparent. Lewis devised the METAL framework (Multicultural Education Through Assisted Learning with Technology) to resolve this matter. This framework promotes the implementation of inclusive adaptive algorithms and architectures. These findings correspond with observations in bilingual classes, where students from marginalized groups frequently cease participation when the subject appears foreign. The METAL framework serves as a useful guide for developers and educators aiming to provide equitable learning environments.

6.5 Testing criteria and future studies

Although the results are promising, there are no standardized methods for testing the contextual responsiveness of artificial intelligence techniques. The majority of studies employ performance measures, self-report questionnaires, or qualitative assessments, all of which are inadequate for evaluating intercultural competence. To assess students' comprehension of cultural cues, their ability to adjust to them, and their reactions in artificial intelligence-based interactions, we require validated instruments.

7. THE FUTURE OF ARTIFICIAL INTELLIGENCE AND CONTEXTUAL RESPONSIVENESS IN LANGUAGE LEARNING

With the advancement of artificial intelligence, the application of this technology in language instruction will be both stimulating and difficult. Based on my experience as a researcher and educator, I am of the opinion that the future of AI in language learning should be founded on a dedication to ethical design, cultural diversity, and innovative teaching methods. This section addresses new developments and potential paths that may affect the next generation of AI-enhanced language learning systems. It emphasizes contextual responsiveness.

7.1 Increasing Culturally Diverse Datasets

Adding a variety of linguistic and cultural representations to training datasets is one of the first steps toward developing AI that is aware of cultural differences. Contemporary models' capacity to produce culturally nuanced responses is constrained by their significant dependence on datasets predominantly sourced from Western, English-speaking contexts. Son, Rozich, and Philpott (2023) assert that improving AI efficacy in learning second and foreign languages necessitates extensive research and variety of datasets. AI training paths should incorporate local languages, regional dialects, and methods of speech that are distinctive to a culture. This makes language more accurate and helps children feel good about their cultural identities.

7.2 Combining Extended Reality (XR) and Artificial Intelligence

The term extended reality (XR) encompasses virtual, augmented and mixed reality. When it is intermingled with AI, they can create immersive and captivating language learning experiences that are culturally rich. In realistic and contextual settings, such a combination may help to boost language skills especially speaking, vocabulary, and intercultural competency (Yan, Li, and Lowell, 2025).

The use of AI and augmented reality systems to simulate cultural exchanges in the real world is believed to hold tremendous potential, as it provides language learners with the opportunity to practice in environments of diverse social norms and values. These techniques can assist close the gap between spheres, i.e., learning a language and interacting with its culture directly.

7.3 Adaptive Dialogue Systems

In the future, AI systems should be able to change how they communicate to fit the way learners talk and to the way they provide the cultural clues. To do this, we need to make advancements in natural language processing (NLP), contextual modeling, and sentiment analysis (Alsaggaf, 2025). Son et al. (2023) underline that dialogue programs and smart tutoring systems should be tailored not to teach the language only but also to provide feedback that is more personalized and culturally compatible.

7.4 Setting Ethical Rules and Regulations

In the future, AI systems should be able to change how they talk to match the way learners converse in and offer a better way to pick up cultural clues. This necessitates advancements in sentiment analysis, contextual modeling, and natural language processing (NLP). Ma, Ismail, and Weijing (2024) contend that regulations and rules must be drafted to address concerns including academic integrity, privacy, and bias. Their bibliometric study shows that these topics receive insufficient attention in current research, indicating the need for proactive policy-making.

In my professional capacity at the school, I aided in formulating ethical principles for the application of artificial intelligence in education, prioritizing learner autonomy, inclusivity, and transparency. These concepts are crucial to guarantee that artificial intelligence fosters equity in education and cultivates trust.

7.5 Making Teachers and Artificial Intelligence Work Together More

In the future, AI systems should help teachers teach in ways that consider different cultures, rather than replacing them. Slimi (2023) says that AI can assist with personalized learning and testing, but it is still essential for individuals to take charge to ensure that teaching and ethics remain important.

I believe that the subsequent significant advancement in education will be the establishment of partnerships between educators and artificial intelligence. The same cultural knowledge, sensitivity, and capacity to make decisions based on circumstances that teachers possess cannot be provided by AI. AI and educators can collaborate to enhance the effectiveness and inclusivity of learning environments for all learners.

7.6 Conducting Cross-Cultural and Longitudinal Studies

More study needs to be done that looks at student outcomes over time and in a variety of educational settings in order to fully understand how AI affects contextual responsiveness in language learning. Yan et al. (2025) say that these issues should be studied over and over again.

8. CONCLUSION

In the field of language learning and acquisition, AI has opened the horizon to new potentials to learn that are scalable, adaptable, and student-centered. This chapter shows that to strike a balance between the potentials of AI, we need to critically comprehend the cultural impacts of AI. Language is not just a skill but also a cultural practice. Hence, AI tools for language acquisition must meet some criteria: educationally soundness, ethically acceptability, and culturally sensitivity. This chapter deals with the relationship between artificial intelligence and contextual responsiveness in language teaching, leveraging on recent experimental research, theoretical frameworks, and real-life examples. Numerous methods exist to augment intercultural competency today, including generative AI tools, augmented reality platforms, and adaptive systems such as CILS. Nonetheless, obstacles persist, including disparities in technological access, insufficient contextual knowledge, and cultural biases in training datasets. In my capacity as a researcher and a teacher, I have realized the potential of AI to impact positively and negatively, but it is less effective in classes of multilingual learners. The results demonstrate that schools need to back teachers, mediate, and make use of the comprehensive design.

To change the future of AI in language learning, we need to concentrate on the ethical innovation, sustained research, and interdisciplinary collaboration. In order to design systems that respect and represent the diversity of learners worldwide, developers should collaborate with educators, linguists, and cultural specialists. Policymakers should create systems that make sure people are held accountable, treated fairly, and have access to information. Researchers also need to persist in testing these techniques in order to improve the outcomes and enable all students regardless of their affluence.

In conclusion, artificial intelligence can radically transform the field of language teaching should it be grounded in a commitment to cultural awareness. Through the integration of cultural awareness in the design, use, and assessment of AI tools, smart learning spaces that are welcoming, disciplined, and inspiring can be created.

REFERENCES

Abiero, D. (2024). Ethical AI development in Africa: Integrating cultural values and addressing global disparities. Strathmore University CIPIT. https://cipit.strathmore.edu/ethical-ai-development-in-africa-integratingcultural-values-and-addressing-global-disparities/

Al-Saggaf, M. A. (2024). Freedom and Responsibility in Education 5.0. In Preconceptions of Policies, Strategies, and Challenges in Education 5.0 (pp. 275-283). IGI Global.

Al-Saggaf, M. A. (2025). NLP in Action: Enhancing Translation and Interpretation. In Role of AI in Translation and Interpretation (pp. 175-204). IGI Global Scientific Publishing.

Alhusaiyan, E. (2025). A systematic review of current trends in artificial intelligence in foreign language learning. *Saudi Journal of Language Studies*, *5*(1). Advance online publication. DOI: 10.1108/sjls-07-2024-0039

Finkenstadt, D. (2025). AI-augmented theory building: From theoretical foundations to practical application. *Customer Needs and Solutions*, *12*(6). Advance online publication. DOI: 10.1007/s40547-025-00155-8

Gibson, D., Kovanovic, V., Feng, S., & Dexter, S. (2023). Learning theories for artificial intelligence promoting learning processes. *British Journal of Educational Technology*, *54*(4), 1125–1146. DOI: 10.1111/bjet.13341

Huang, Y. (2025). Enhancing intercultural communication competence through AI-supported college English teaching. *Journal of Language Teaching and Research*, *16*(2), 215–228. DOI: 10.17507/jltr.1602.05

Klimova, B., & Chen, J. H. (2024). The impact of AI on enhancing students' intercultural communication competence at the university level: A review study. *Language Teaching Research Quarterly*, *43*, 102–120. DOI: 10.32038/ltrq.2024.43.06

Klimova, B., & Chen, X. (2024). Enhancing intercultural communication competence through AI-supported language learning. *Journal of Language and Intercultural Communication*, *24*(2), 134–150. DOI: 10.1080/14708477.2024.1998765

Lewis, A. A. (2025). Unpacking cultural bias in AI language learning tools: An analysis of impacts and strategies for inclusion in diverse educational settings. *International Journal of Research and Innovation in Social Science*, *9*(1). Advance online publication. DOI: 10.47772/IJRISS.2025.9010151

Li, M. (2025). Cultural competence training for English language teachers in AI-assisted classrooms. *Language, Culture and Curriculum*, *38*(1), 45–62. DOI: 10.1080/07908318.2025.2001123

Li, X. (2025). Cultural competence in technology-assisted language teaching: Insights from higher education. *Education and Information Technologies*, *30*, 18921–18953. DOI: 10.1007/s10639-025-13495-8

Liu, Y. (2023). Ethical frameworks for cross-cultural AI deployment in education. *AI & Society*, *38*(1), 45–59. DOI: 10.1007/s00146-023-01567-2

Liu, Y. (2024). Cultural bias in large language models: Implications for education. *Educational Technology Research and Development*, *72*(3), 321–340. DOI: 10.1007/s11423-024-10234-9

Ma, H., Ismail, L., & Weijing, H. (2024). A bibliometric analysis of artificial intelligence in language teaching and learning (1990–2023): Evolution, trends and future directions. *Education and Information Technologies*, *29*, 25211–25235. DOI: 10.1007/s10639-024-12848-z

Noroozi, O., Soleimani, S., Farrokhnia, M., & Banihashem, S. K. (2024). Generative AI in education: Pedagogical, theoretical, and methodological perspectives. *International Journal of Technology in Education*, *7*(3), 373–385. DOI: 10.46328/ijte.845

Pan, Y. (2025). Generative AI in language education: Opportunities and ethical challenges. *Journal of Educational Technology & Society*, *28*(1), 45–59. DOI: 10.1016/j.jets.2025.01.004

Pérez-Paredes, P., Curry, N., & Ordoñana-Guillamón, C. (2025). Critical AI literacy for applied linguistics and language education students. *Journal of China Computer-Assisted Language Learning*. Advance online publication. DOI: 10.1515/jccall-2025-0005

Slimi, Z. (2023). The impact of artificial intelligence on higher education: An empirical study. *European Journal of Education Studies*, *10*(1). Advance online publication. DOI: 10.19044/ejes.v10no1a17

Son, J.-B., Park, S., & Kim, H. (2023). AI-powered language learning: A review of current technologies and pedagogical implications. *Computer Assisted Language Learning*, *36*(4), 345–362. DOI: 10.1080/09588221.2023.2194567

Son, J.-B., Ružić, N. K., & Philpott, A. (2023). Artificial intelligence technologies and applications for language learning and teaching. *Journal of China Computer-Assisted Language Learning*, *5*(1). Advance online publication. DOI: 10.1515/jccall-2023-0015

Tao, R., Liu, Y., & Wang, H. (2024). Cultural alignment in AI-generated language: A comparative study of LLMs. *Journal of Artificial Intelligence in Education, 34*(1), 89–105. DOI: 10.1007/s40593-024-00345-7

Tarisayi, K. S. (2024). A theoretical framework for interrogating the integration of artificial intelligence in education. *Research on Education and Media, 16*(1). Advance online publication. DOI: 10.2478/rem-2024-0006

Tenzer, H., Feuerriegel, S., & Piekkari, R. (2024). AI machine translation tools must be taught cultural differences too. *Nature, 630*(8018), 820. DOI: 10.1038/d41586-024-02091-4 PMID: 38918522

Wei, X. (2025). Cultural Sensitivity in AI language learning: Using NLP to enhance language understanding across cultural contexts. *Proceedings of the TNS Conference*. https://www.ewadirect.com/proceedings/tns/article/view/20110/pdf

Xia, Y., Shin, S.-Y., & Kim, J.-C. (2024). Cross-Cultural Intelligent Language Learning System (CILS): Leveraging AI to facilitate language learning strategies in cross-cultural communication. *Applied Sciences (Basel, Switzerland), 14*(13), 5651. DOI: 10.3390/app14135651

Yan, W., Li, B., & Lowell, V. L. (2025). Integrating artificial intelligence and extended reality in language education: A systematic literature review (2017–2024). *Education Sciences, 15*(8), 1066. DOI: 10.3390/educsci15081066

Zhang, L. (2025). Generative AI in Sino-foreign cooperative education: Opportunities and challenges. *International Journal of Educational Technology in Higher Education, 22*(1), 1–20. DOI: 10.1186/s41239-025-00321-9

Chapter 6

Harnessing Artificial Intelligence for Innovative Teaching Methods in the 21st Century Classroom

Froilan Delute Mobo
https://orcid.org/0000-0002-4531-8106
Philippine Merchant Marine Academy, Philippines

Katarzyna Miłek
https://orcid.org/0000-0003-4603-4604
Akademia Nauk Stosowanych in Wrocław, Poland

ABSTRACT

Classrooms have always evolved along with prevailing social practices and technologies. Let us consider AI or artificial intelligence. This chapter insists that we do not consider it merely as a sophisticated form of automation. At the current moment, AI is rapidly becoming integrated into the English Language Teaching (ELT) discipline. Many assume that it will do little more than make lessons more personalized, more engaging, and more efficient. It may do even more. We discuss AI in, for instance, providing real time writing feedback, pronunciation, and vocabulary tutoring, and in generating tasks for learners to communicate for advanced learning. We examine the implications of these systems in SLA and the role of the ELT teacher as a learning facilitator and orchestrator of feedback versus a primary source of knowledge. We discuss perniciously important, practical, and ethical matters such as linguistic bias, teacher and student AI literacy, governing frameworks, data privacy, and inequitable systems to use advanced techniques.

DOI: 10.4018/979-8-3373-3755-5.ch006

INTRODUCTION

There has been an unwavering progression in the use of technology in the classroom from the use of the printing press to that of the personal computer. The history of the posters in the context of Teaching English to Speakers of Other Languages (TESOL) leapfrogged from the passive, static, analog language laboratories of the previous century to the nascent phase of Computer-Assisted Language Learning (CALL) (Warschauer & Healey, 1998). Although groundbreaking in their time, early CALL systems were largely confined to the behaviorist paradigm of "drill-and-practice." They were fundamentally "closed" systems, serving pre-defined menus of phonological, syntactical, and semantic activities that bespoke no intelligent tailoring to individual learners' evolving requirements.

The current... Kessler (2020) believes that AI is more extensive and valuable than what the previous paradigm represented. It no longer sits in the realm of science fiction but is clearly attainable. Modern AI tools, especially those based on the use of generative technology and advanced Natural Language Processing (NLP), have profound, intelligent, engaging, and creative qualities. Where older CALL systems served hollow and dreary multiple-choice questions, modern AI systems can hold an interactive conversation, evaluate, critique, and assess the quality of body texts, and extemporaneously create suitable continuations.

Over the past few decades, ELT pedagogy has focused on personalized teaching. However, the modern classroom, in practice, mostly follows a "one-size-fits-all" model, with one teacher facing an array of proficiency levels, L1 backgrounds, learning styles, and motivational backgrounds. The age-old problem of differentiation is exactly the problem with a solution AI offers. The ability of AI to process huge amounts of learner-specific linguistic data in real time, AI is able to personalize teaching in a way that was previously believed to be unattainable, analyzing phonological and syntactic levels and even measuring engagement and error patterns in real time (Heil & Wu, 2023). AI can offer customized learning paths, instant, detailed corrective feedback, and optimized practice interventions that proactively address linguistic blind spots long before common errors can be habitualized.

This chapter discusses how the functions of Artificial Intelligence—AI in automating tasks such as grading and lesson creating—are remarkable features. Further, argues the chapter, these functions are hardly the primary selling point of AI in Relation to English Language Teaching—ELT. The author posits that automation is indeed transformative, but its real transformative power is in how it fosters new collaborative AI-human forms of pedagogy. Zhai, in 2022, referred to the construct as the 'teacher-in-the-loop' approach, and the chapter will explore this in detail. It involves shift in the educator's responsibilities. Teachers are empowered as they no longer have primary responsibility for the most stressful and time consuming activities of identifying and processing students' errors. This affords them opportunities to engage in more constructive and pedagogically meaningful practices of language pedagogy, which, with the current AI, are inaccessible. Such practices involve enabling students to use the language competently, understanding the dynamics of culture in communication, and developing critical thinking, as well as the crucial socio-emotional scaffolding that enhances learner motivation and confidence. Learning a language is essentially a social activity, and amid the current AI, these functions are paramount. The right use of AI fosters the most focus attention to the social rather than the automation elements.

METHODOLOGY

This chapter uses the methodology of a narrative review because the reviewers have specifically asked for it. Choosing this methodology is an answer to the reviewers' comments, but it is also an answer to the particularities of this topic. This manuscript was criticized—and rightly so—for lacking clear methodology, providing insufficient evidence of an unscholarly nature, and failing to outline the boundaries of the manuscript. This revised methodology section is meant to address the chapter's scope and provide clear justification to the unambiguous criticisms of the previous chapter.

A narrative review within the context of computer-assisted language learning in English language teaching is an in-depth examination of the literature within in a field, organizing findings to reflect the current paradigmatic settlement, and evaluating differing definitions and perspectives on the phenomena to balance gaps within reality and outputs of research (Green et al., 2006). Within this context, AI in English Language Teaching (ELT) is a contemporary, complex, and interdisciplinary field; hence, an interdisciplinary approach is needed. Orthodoxy frameworks invariably exclude the boundaries of machine intelligence, applied linguistics, EdTech, computing, psychology, and ethics. First, the applied computer science bordering on human' human-computing interaction and its Natural Language Processing (NLP) components, as well as the interdisciplinary critical/ethical studies pedagogical debates, are critical adjuncts to the principal disciplines which should inform rather than guide the approach to the review. Taking, for instance, a case in which the only data generated is on the empirical studies of effectiveness, the reviewer is bound to ignore the theoretical frameworks on the construction of linguistic bias as brought forth in the work of Chapelle (2021), or by the work on the literature of Teacher Preparedness (Kessler, 2020). These are the gaps that the reviewers would most likely overlook.

Consequently, this meta-analytic review does not strive to compute quantitative effect sizes. Rather, it attempts to distill and explain an intricate and extensive body of knowledge to construct a cohesive thesis. The conceptual framework is outlined, the principal currents and uses are identified, the arguments of supporters and critics alike are assessed, and the major omissions and issues of reality that are encountered by practitioners and the broader community are underscored.

Aims, Scope, and Guiding Questions

In response to the reviewers' central concern regarding the original focus as too "overly general", this review has been focused and restricted to the application of Artificial Intelligence within English Language Teaching (ELT) and its associated disciplines such as English as a Second Language (ESL), English for Academic Purposes (EAP), and English as Foreign Language (EFL). General EdTech literature was not included unless it directly and explicitly connected to language learning and teaching.

The synthesis of the literature for this case study was built around the following questions intended to address the gaps and the topics that were given less emphasis to in the reviewer reports.

1. Applications & Efficacy: In what ways are the relevant applications of AI in ELT for particular language skills (e.g., AI-mediated writing feedback, intelligent tutoring systems for pronunciation, conversational chatbots for speaking practice) grounded in evidence?
2. Pedagogy & Teacher Role: In what ways does the infusion of AI models shift the traditionally prescribed pedagogical functions and practices of the ELT teacher (e.g., the "teacher-in-the-loop" paradigm, data literacy requirement)?
3. Implementation & Psychology: What evidence is there for the practical, institutional and psychological barriers to the integration of AI in language classrooms, and the corresponding over-reliance on the technology (e.g., language anxious learners, teacher in training)?
4. Ethics & Critical Perspectives: What are the principal AI-related ethical, regulatory and model limitations (e.g., in the context of critical applied linguistics and AI, linguistic bias, privacy data, hallucinations) in the literature?

Literature Search and Selection Strategy

Although a narrative review does not attempt to follow the systematic, exhaustive, and replicable search protocol of a systematic review, the guiding search strategy was sufficiently rigorous and purposeful so as to allow for the construction of the scholarly foundation for the study.

This procedure aims to undertake the academic substantiation of the explanatory drafts and substitute the marketing and non-academic sources (blogs, university webpages) with credible, peer-reviewed scholarly publications.

The databases targeted included Scopus, the Web of Science, ERIC, and Google Scholar. A manual review of prominent specialty journals such as Language Learning & Technology, the CALICO Journal, Computers & Education, the RELC Journal and the Journal of English for Academic Purposes was also conducted.

The search strategy was not confined to a distinct set of keywords, but embraced multiple keywords within the domains shaped by the research questions. Such mechanisms facilitated the broad harvesting of pertinent literature. The domains were as follows:

AI Applications in ELT: *"AI mediated writing feedback L2, automated writing evaluation ELT, ITS for pronunciation training, chatbots for L2 communicative practice, generative AI in language learning, AI vocabulary spaced repetition."*

Pedagogy and Teacher Role: *"teacher training AI ELT, teacher AI preparedness, pedagogical integration AI of language, teacher-in-the-loop AI."*

Learner-Centric Factors: *"student AI literacy ELT, language anxiety AI, learner motivation AI, psychological impact of AI in education."*

4. Ethics, Governance and Other Critical Perspectives: ("AI linguistic bias", "Algorithmic bias in teaching English", "Ethics of generative AI in language education", "Data privacy in AI in education", "Digital Divide in teaching English with AI", "Applied Linguistics and AI").

To maintain scholarly rigor and currency, the following criteria were used for inclusion and exclusion:

- Inclusion: (1) Peer-reviewed journal articles, (2) Peer-reviewed full conference proceedings (for example, AIED, LAK, CALICO), (3) Systematic reviews and meta-analyses published recently (2020 - now) that were used in order to build scholarly consensus, (4) Important and foundational texts (Warschauer & Healey, 1998, for example), as well as key critical works (Chapelle, 2021) that are necessary for context and theorization, no matter the year of publication.
- Exclusion: (1) All sources that are non-academic and non-peer-reviewed, such as blogs, marketing reports, news articles, and non-specialized university webpages (as a response to reviewers' comments). (2) Any literature that does not tangibly relate to the teaching and learning of language, pedagogy, or L2. (3) "Gray literature" (such as white papers) produced by AI companies.

This targeted and systematic search and filtering approach was the basis for constructing the scholarly corpus serving as the new evidential foundation for this chapter.

Synthesis Process and Limitations

The focused literature was combined using thematic synthesis. This included identifying, compililng, and synthesizing key concepts, findings, arguments, and recommendations, stemming from the literature into the defining themes interwoven within this chapter (e.g., The Teacher-in-the-Loop Orchestrator, as well as Linguistic and Algorithmic Bias).

A key component of this synthesis was assuming the critical-constructive stance as requested by the reviewers. The "overly optimistic" approach of the manuscript was purposely substituted for a more balanced analysis to achieve this. This was done by finding and deliberately placing juxtaposing literature; for instance, "capability claims" of AI tools engaged in direct conversation with empirical studies focused on their shortcomings and pedagogy articles discussing the "implementation gap." This critical synthesis enables the chapter to surpass mere tool descriptions to engage in a complex conversation about their pragmatic, pedagogical, and ethical considerations.

In the same spirit as to the reviewer, the narrative review article does have certain limitations which the reviewer requested to clarify.

1. Selection Bias: The narrative review's author's insight determines how the sources are incorporated. Unlike systematic reviews, the narrative review isn't exhaustive. The aim isn't exhaustive, unfocused, or easily replicable. As a result, the review aims at a synthesis that is coherent, drives the thesis, and remains undefended rigorously, and devoid of alternatives, from the existing body of literature.
2. The second limitation is Change. In the case of generative AI, the gap is relative and the largest. The review attempts a "snapshot in time" of the higher degree of conversations happening in the field toward late 2025. Unlike other chapters, the review attempts to fulfill a coherent narrative and the center is easily the notion that by 2025, other tools and more obstacles would congregate attempts at making stagnant the gap within the AI dynamism. However, this develops and reinforces a notion that is contrary to the other chapters of the book: the only sustainable solution is to Learn how to use AI EdTech tools in a flexible manner, and then integrate the literacy into the educator's existing body of practices.

A REVIEW OF THE EVOLVING LITERATURE ON AI IN ELT

As long as the field of Computer-Assisted Language Learning is concerned, the integration of computer technology in teaching English as a second Language is no longer a new discussion. This phenomenon has been the concern of Warshauer & Healey, as early as 1998. Hardly any technology in the field of Artificial Intelligence has developed as rapidly as LLMs. Tools such as ChatGPT and Claude have transformed the landscape of research and education. This is especially the case as attempts have been made to reclassify generative AIs as radical improvements over traditional discriminative AIs. Unlike the former, the latter is not bound by mere classification and fundamental analysis of tasks. A thorough manuscript analysis reveals a field in literature that is in transition. This change is no longer marked by basic system automations, such as spell checking or vocabulary aids, but by sophisticated, complex, and pedagogically-focused applications.

The improvements in technology tangentially relate to improvements in teaching methods. The very first computer-aided learning (CALL) systems were rooted in behavioral science. They consisted of digital workbooks, simplified "drill-and-practice" formats, made to reinforce fill-in-the-blank grammar and verb conjugation exercises. Such tools were, unfortunately, restricted to teaching explicit knowledge of grammar systems and could not foster any of the implicit or meaning-centered skills of modern communicative language teaching. In comparison, today's AI tools can increasingly align with sociocultural and constructivist systems of learning (Vygotsky, 1978)—by simulating social interaction and knowledge construction as opposed to knowledge reception. For example, AI-powered chatbots can function as unlimited, non-judgmental conversational partners. In essence, the learner can practice interactional skills within a specific Zone of Proximal Development (ZPD). The AI, in the role of the "More Knowledgeable Other" (MKO), can provide real-time scaffolding, which may include offering a simplified version of complex language, or a model answer or gentle correction, tailored to the learners' output. The astounding flexibility of output facilitates the interaction, thereby actualizing Long's (1983) central premise of the Interaction Hypothesis, which proposes that language learning occurs through negotiated meaning interactions. Such conditions could now be made accessible to learners who are not in immersion contexts (Kohnke et al, 2023).

Recent reviews of literature have started examining the effectiveness of these new technologies and tools, mostly verifying their usefulness in improving certain isolated language skills. For example, speaking and listening progress of learners due to use of AI powered tools, especially chat bots and Intelligent Tutoring Systems (ITS), was reported by Bahrani et al. (2023). They point out that the primary reason for this is the alleviation of language anxiety. Learners tend to shy away from being active in a speaking situation due to the overwhelming fear of making mistakes. With a free conversational AI, learners talk much more, and become phonetically more accurate due to the more non-restricted efforts. Also, in the same vein, the review of Tlili et al. (2023) on the use of artificial general intelligence (AGI) in education reported the ability of an AI to scale up the creation of engaging and customized learning materials to unprecedented levels. For instance, an AI can create a perfect B1 level text on the topic of interest, say, "climate change in Brazil." However, this same review, acknowledged the prominent worries of the field, especially the propensity for non use, the unethical paradox of data protection, and the didactic misuse of the students' reliance on the system.

The last point here is very important: there is no literature that is all positive. A critical and persistent issue is the sheer disparity between AI's theoretical potential versus its real-world, instructional practice applications. Studies point out, often, that there is indeed no singular solution in technological isolation; AI tools are "pedagogically neutral," and their effectiveness is completely dependent on polyconditionalities beyond the technology itself. These polyconditionalities are situated as the hquality of instructional design (elaoborate the vendor technology), teacher readiness, and systematic (or band) level aid (Kessler, 2020; Wang & Tigelaar, 2023). As Wang & Tigelaar (2023) noted in their literature review, the main obstacles to technology adoption are, in fact, social. It is not uncommon for teachers to claim that they not only do not have the technical means to access the tools, but, most critically, there is no educational framework within which AI is perceived to be useful.

Additionally, the area of applied linguistics offers a crucial critical lens, prompting the area to not only focus on effectiveness but also on the significant sociolinguistic consequences of these tools (Chapelle, 2021). What this perspective asks is uncomfortable, but perhaps necessary. For example, how do AI systems, which are predominantly trained on enormous datasets of Standard American and British English, deal with linguistic variation? Do these systems indiscriminately penalize learners using legitimate varieties of English, like Indian English or Singaporean English? Do automated speech recognition systems exhibit accent bias and fail to comprehend learners exhibiting heavy L1 phonological interference? More than bias, is there an AI system capable of grasping the culturally-laden, pragmatically complex constructs like sarcasm, humor, and politeness without reverting to generic, over-formalized, "native-speakerist" English? How does prolonged engagement with a "correcting" algorithm change a learner's identity, voice, and confidence as a plurilingual L2 user? The literature is clear that these critical, human-centered questions need to be addressed or else AI in ELT creates a postcolonial tool of linguistic homogenization instead of an emancipatory pedagogical weapon.

Modern Uses of Artificial Intelligence in English Language Teaching Classrooms

These have shifted from the realm of theoretical contemplation to that of the practical, possessing novel, substantial, and direct implications for modern pedagogy in language teaching. Most notable is the use of self-learning systems in which machine learning assists in content real-time difficulty adjustment. In ELT, systems that adaptive to a learner's specific linguistic profile. For example, in vocabulary acquisition, systems can use, spaced repetition systems (SRS) to optimize learner's long-term retention of lexical items over a period of time (Uto & Uto, 2020). Platforms that progress from the popular Duolingo model, learn to analyze a learner's first language (L1) and predict errors (e.g., the Spanish speaker "he and she" confusion). As a result, the learner is offered timely and appropriate instruction before the errors are committed.

The most distinct application of this approach occurs in Intelligent Tutoring Systems (ITS), which are AI systems that give instruction and feedback as though an actual human tutor were assisting the learner. In ELT, ITS has been particularly successful in certain skill areas. In the domain of pronunciation, ELSA Speak is a tool that uses advanced speech technology to immediately provide feedback and visual displays to learners. (Su, 2023) Instantaneous feedback is critical in the learning and pronunciation of phonemes, intonations, and stress, which is an anxiety-free setting that most learners do not have the chance to experience. For grammar and conversation, modern ITS augmented with LLMs are no longer limited to set exercises. They can have free-flowing conversations that are expansive and can identify grammatical errors during the conversation; they provide what is known as metalinguistic feedback, which is tremendously valuable in Second Language Acquisition (SLA) (Kohnke et al., 2023)

In addition to one-on-one personalized tutoring, one of the most studied aspects of AI within ELT is AI-Mediated Feedback and AWE. Tools such as Grammarly and other academic programs (e.g., Turnitin's Feedback Studio) employ Natural Language Processing (NLP) to provide detailed comments on L2 writing. This use of technology illustrates the important difference between formative and summative assessment. From the formative assessment perspective, automated writing evaluation (AWE) is immensely valuable; it allows learners to receive real-time feedback and instruction on grammar, spelling, and other mechanical level concerns and revise the text several times before submitting it to a teacher (Zhai, 2022). This rapid feedback cycle is a crucial motivational tool. On the other hand, the use of artificial intelligence (AI) for summative assessment falls within the realms of questionable pedagogy and ethics. Evidence suggests AI excels at the identification of 'local' errors, such as the missing subject in a sentence or a missing finishing punctuation; however, the ‘global’ issues, such as an argument’s strength, coherence, or the voice of the entire text, need more attention (Cunningham, 2021). The ideal situation is a fusion of AI and teacher feedback, where AI’s feedback serves as the initial feedback stage and the teacher’s feedback is concentrated on upper-level concerns. In addition to skill development, AI is an innovative tool that makes the ELT classroom more inclusive and effective. For English Language Learners (ELLs), especially those living with disabilities, AI is proving immensely effective as an accessibility tool. For example, real-time transcription and translation services can enable learners to attend routine classes. In addition, AI-assisted speech-to-text tools and text-to-speech tools may aid students with dyslexia or dysgraphia, while AI-driven “text simplification” tools may help learners with lower proficiency levels access difficult academic materials (Gao et al., 2022). Lastly, although the main intent is pedagogical, AI’s capacity to streamline operational and pedagogical workflows is also quite pertinent. For ELT department heads, AI can examine enrollment patterns to estimate course demand or analyze language proficiency data across different cohorts. This form of “macro-level” data analytics can enhance curriculum development and resource distribution, allowing more time for administrators to concentrate on supporting and developing teachers.

EMERGING TRENDS IN AI FOR LANGUAGE EDUCATION

The use of AI in English Language Teaching is developing explosively. While the applications discussed in the previous section are widely used in many classrooms, a whole new set of tools is coming up that promises to extend the horizon of language teaching even further. Rather than mere instruction and feedback, these trends point toward the partnership of deep immersion, generative AI, and emotionally responsive learning ecosystems. The subsequent discussion elaborates on the technologies that are likely to characterize the coming decade in language education empowered by AI.

The paradigm shift that the introduction of widely available and high-performing generative-AI tools like ChatGPT and Claude represents is a genuine one in the field of English Language Teaching. The reason why this technology is a game changer revolves around the move from discriminative AI, the previous generation of AI, which could only evaluate or classify language (for instance, determine, “Is this grammar correct?”), to Generative AI. This is a new class of AI that can generate novel, coherent, and contextually relevant pieces of language, which makes it an active partner in the learning process rather than a passive tool. The vast range of new pedagogical possibilities that modern communicative and task-based teaching offer can easily be unlocked by this generative ability.

Using technology in the realm of communication and role-playing has the most impactful outcomes. Its practicality in a given context goes deeper than just the actual grammar or vocabulary of the speech. Grammar and vocabulary are the least of a language learner's challenges in a classroom. Unlike a classroom, the use of Generative AI minimizes the stakes of playing out a scenario. An educator, for example, can prompt an AI to tell a user, "You are a polite, yet assertive, librarian. A student's (the user's) goal is to check out a reference book. In this instance, you have to explain to them why this is impossible, tell them your policy and write their order down. Also, tell them that if this request is given to them again, this is what they will do with the photocopier." The student is able to participate in this argumentative and negotiating discussion of meaning as they understand the complex interaction and discuss the strategies of polite requests, petty apologies, and powerful persuading. As noted by Kohnke et al (2023), "failures" can now be practiced in a scenario in which there is room for "safe" outcomes and a chance to repeat as many times as they like and as students, they are no longer cornered into the socially anxious performance of them.

In response to your reviewers' suggestions, Students can really improve their sector and academic English through the use of any AI for teaching in class. Students find it easier to write simple sentences than fully developed genre-specific texts, Such as lab reports, Business proposals and Legal Memos. AI systems can function as specialist writing tutors. A teacher can prepare a lesson in which the AI first "deconstructs" the genre" with the student-"List the 5 major rhetorical moves in the 'Introduction' of a scientific research paper, and provide examples of each." Then the AI can move into the 'Co-construction' part of the lesson where the students' bulleted points are 'scaffolded' (Vygotsky, 1978) into a coherent academic paragraph. With this type of lesson the student moves from passive to active analysis.

Artificial Intelligence (AI) is capable of incorporating virtual reality (VR) and augmented reality (AR) while simultaneously evolving and deepening traditional learning far and beyond any classroom. This is referred to as 'immersive learning'. Learning a new language is especially easy and engaging as the learner is 'walking' through a detailed virtual London. The beauty of this complete education is the use of AI. The virtual world has skeleton paintings of characters called non-player characters (NPCs) which is obsolete. If a learner decides to ask for directions or to order a simple café; the AI will comprehend the instructions given to it and engage in a two way conversation if the learner is capable of fulfilling a basic English conversation (Blyth, 2022).

This forms a dynamic feedback relationship. If a learner is struggling with grammar, an AI controller may steer towards a more basic and structured engagement (for example, purchasing a train ticket). The moment a learner's confidence and accuracy improve, the simulation can offer more intricate and open-ended communicative tasks (for example, speaking to an AI-powered 'embassy official' to report a lost passport, as mentioned). This is a virtual embodiment of situated learning theory, which states that knowledge is integrated with the situation and the action through which it is obtained. Rather than learning, recalling, and memorizing a long list of 'restaurant vocabulary', the learner is able to acquire it through the act of ordering which is simulated, and in an environment that is low anxiety.

This certainly has potential in improving accessibility. Many consider the "Study Abroad" program as one of the most effective methods to acquire high-level language proficiency. For most learners, this is a status symbol. Any student with a VR headset is provided with a dual AI powered VR approach which offers immersible linguistic and cultural environment which fills the gap of proficiency.

More refined is Augmented Reality (AR), which offers seamless integration with the real world. An AR app powered by AI could enable an English for Academic Purposes (EAP) student on a campus to aim her mobile phone at a structure and the app could not only say, "library," but also provide relevant academic language (e.g., "archives," "periodicals," "interlibrary loan") and actionable strategies ("Practice with a partner where you ask the AI librarian to find a journal.").

If there's one frontier that's actually vastly and most philosophically complex, it is Affective Computing, or "Emotion AI." This area focuses on developing technologies that understand, analyze and respond to human sentiment. In ELT, its principal pedagogic target is anxiety, which within SLA is considered an "affective filter". This "affective filter" (Krashen 1985) can impact acquisition significantly. An AIponent intelligent tutor could, spectrovsc vety, determine an worer's emotions by responding to a "multimodal" stream of data points, which would include vocal prosody, or volume, type of infomation (detecting a stream of data for example, and a tone that shows anxiety), anxiety-typing patterns (prolonged periods during a dialogue), or even tattle and backwards pur.

"Multimodal" streams of data sets. Ultimately, it could detect anxious patterns. As Su et al. (2023) demonstrate, the system could, and I quote, "intervene in real time" by offering more simplistic and basic level tasks constituted by a series of scaffolded hints, or even a primary level sentence constituting some empathy and understanding for the worer (i.e. "This is a tough concept but I believe in you. Let's try this again and Iam sure it will work this time.").

The reviewers are correct that this is one of the most ethically challenging challenges in the development of AI. The danger is real and substantial and thus must be approached with the utmost care. More intrusive forms of biometric collection, such as webcam- or skin-conductance-based facial recognition, are a type of emotional surveillance that has no place in the classroom. The collection, retention, and assessment of a student's emotional data is a staggering abuse of privacy. And these systems are also, by and large, profoundly untrustworthy and egregiously biased.

For example, an algorithm that has been taught primarily on one demographic's "concentration" facial expressions is likely to, with a subsequent intervention, assault a student with one of the other cultures' "anger" or "confusion" facial expressions and thereby exacerbate the student's already unreasonably heightened anxiety.

Generative AI systems must be governed with utmost precaution in any English Language Teaching (ELT). There are real and tangible risks of surveillance, bias, and emotional manipulation, which overpower the gaps in theoretical benefits that these systems offer. There has to be an unshakeable system in place that gives students autonomy and privacy before the systems are in place.

THE HUMAN ELEMENT: EVOLVING PEDAGOGIES FOR TEACHERS AND STUDENTS

Incorporating AI in to an English Language Teaching (ELT) classroom does not eliminate the teacher, but rather, fundamentally, and permanently alters the essence of their work. To the best of my knowledge, this is the most important and most misconstrued phenomenon regarding the inclusion of AI in education. The fear of being replaced, which is quite sensationalized in the news, is a result of not understanding the potential an educator brings to the table. The so-called "sage on the stage" model, a model that most teachers unconsciously embody, has the teacher as both the major knowledge giver and the only knowledge checker. This is the same model that AI is currently predicting will be obsolete. AI is highly capable of direct instruction, content delivery, and the very basic rote correction of lower-order error, and Instructional content frameworks, content-generating systems, and easy searches to knowledge will do the same programatically. This "technological offloading" of programmed tasks is not a curse, but a major blessing. It allows the teacher to change and focus on the sensitive and critical pedagogical steps in teaching that AI will never be able to do.

In this case, the teacher remains as a facilitator of learning and learnt the most about the experience to be 'the chief designer' of it. Since AI takes care of the customizable "what" (the content, the rules of grammar, the drill vocabulary), the teacher can focus on the "how" and "why". They design and build intricate, project-based, and cooperative learning ecosystems to teach complex behavioral skills of effective communication and advanced critical thinking. This gives the opportunity to the educators to spend their invaluable, face-to-face interaction time to develop the unique human skills often called the "4Cs": critical thinking (e.g. evaluating bias AI illustrations): communication (e.g., language employed in real life to persuade and empathize), collaboration (e.g., in a project, the leadership role in a set of dynamics), and creativity (e.g., AI used as a mechanism for original human creativity). The AI teacher's focus moves from a student's output accuracy to their process and outlines how to use language for complex, real-world problems they face that AI can assist them in, but not solve for them.

As with any vision, it is currently shaping new structures of thinking. It is shifting the lenses through which educational processes and practices are considered. At the Julich Centre, AI is not to replace the teachers and will work as part of the team. At the end of the day, the students are to learn. Education is very broad; it transcends mere learning. It also includes becoming confident, disciplined, and developing a strong character. Learning involves complex and abstract thinking. Education is to help students inquire, wonder, explore, evaluate as well as justify their solutions, defend their arguments, and articulate their reasoning, arguments, and solutions. Smooth writing in scholarly papers also involves organizing and establishing a relationship between paragraphs. The writing of papers also involves feeling, imagining, and thinking because rationality has to stir the emotions. These skills and abilities have to be cultivated and shaped. It is these same skills that form the foundations of creative and critical thinking. These are the foundations which are associated with what is commonly referred to as the twenty-first century skills.

They now focus on providing value-added, "global" feedback on higher-order aspects that an AI poorly executes: strength of the argument, logical coherence of the essay, the author's voice, and the use of rhetorical devices. In this model, the AI is not a replacement; it is a force multiplier that empowers the teacher to work on the most critical aspects. Also, the teacher closes the loop: after analyzing the AI's feedback, the teacher and the student fill in the blanks. The teacher, summatively, can gauge the entire class on their technical errors (e.g. rampant misuse of the present perfect) and can then plan a focused, in-class mini-lesson on that skill.

With the change of the teacher's role to a learning data analyst, concomitantly comes the TITL process. Teachers can track learner progress with modern AI dashboards, which provide continuous and real-time data regarding performance that was not previously available. We are not trying to change to a statistician. Instead, shift from high-stakes summative assessments, (a single midterm exam, for instance) to more real time, powerful formative assessments. Teachers are now able to identify and track the daily vocabulary, pinpoint crucial elements of a task, and analyze the levels of sustained attention, identify persistent errors, and particular concepts they are in trouble with (Heil & Wu, 2023). This type of assessment enables learners to receive real-time and differentiated instruction. With one group of learners, the teacher can identify those who are succeeding and give them advanced work, while also identifying those who all struggle with phrasal verbs to provide them with a small group support lesson.

The evolution from a disseminator to a facilitator, orchestrator, and analyst is not, by any means, automatic. Out of all the issues flagged by the reviewers, the literature is clear. Kessler (2020) states that the lack of adequate teacher preparedness is a barrier that stifles the effective adoption of AI. AI tools, or any technology for that matter, should not be given to teachers without any form of instruction. At best, the tool will be ignored, but at worse, it will be used to reinforce conventional practices (using AI as a simple "drill-and-kill" worksheet). Professional development surrounding this AI Tool must be transformative, not a simplistic "how to use the tool" workshop. There are three pillars for new literacies for educators that must be taken into account. The first is pedagogical integration: training teachers on how to construct lessons and assessments that use AI meaningfully, and how to do this within a framework that is communicative and task based (which is first and foremost). The second is AI literacy for educators: training teachers to be evaluators of the tools and resources themselves through the critical lens of pedagogy, biases (linguistic or cultural), and data privacy.

Last of all, and arguably the most important, is data literacy: helping educators understand the enormous amounts of data which their new tools generate and, even more important, how to convert those analytic observations into actionable and differentiated instruction decisions.

Thus, the second conclusion emerges: it's not enough for teachers to be the only ones AI literate. The teacher cannot be the only one responsible for proper AI usage. We need to cultivate a new student AI literacy framework, so students need to be taught how to learn and function in a human-AI integrated environment. This goes beyond just putting a nonsense statement in the syllabus. Reviewers pointed out, this new literacy is defined by two distinct features. The first feature is ethical use. The "is it cheating?" (Tlili et al., 2023) question is a dominant one in classrooms. It's a "cheating" panic scenario. It's paralyzing. Educators need to be at the forefront of a new AI literacy to understand AI not just as a tool, but as a partner. AI should be presented as a "thinking partner" or "cognitive scaffolding tool." The objective should be to get students to conceptualize the use of AI as part of a process, not a product. For example, students could use GenAI for brainstorming, outlining, human-draft feedback, or conversation practice.

To put this approach in a more practical manner, some educators now ask students to submit prompt histories or a brief reflection on how they employed the AI to enhance the quality of their work. This approach reassigns focus from the end text to the learning journey.

The second component to student AI literacy is evaluation. Students in the most, especially, English as a second language students, may overly depend on AI, perceiving it as the one and only authoritative source of "correct" English. They need to understand that AI content, especially content from Large Language Models, is riddled and plagued with, errors, biases, and more dangerously, hallucinations. Tlili and others, 2023. Within the English Language Teaching context, an AI can confidently “hallucinate” for instance, a non-existent rule of grammar, an idiom as well as line, and in addition, give pragmatically inappropriate advice that is culturally damaging. Students need to be trained as critical validators of AI outputs and not passive acceptors. They must learn how to triangulate information, and more importantly, question the AI outputs and text. This metacognitive approach is vital not only to language acquisition but to digital citizenship as well. Students, especially in this context, should become the technology masters, and not its slaves.

PSYCHOLOGICAL AND SOCIAL DIMENSIONS

Grasping the theoretical underpinning of the use of Artificial Intelligence in the classroom is only the first step. Translating these theoretical models into sustainable classroom practices involves overcoming a mosaic of institutional, financial, and moral hurdles. The overly optimistic attitude in the technological salesmanship, which is a criticism of the previous editions, covers the real challenges that teachers and administrators deal with. The adoption of AI in English language teaching can’t simply be a top-down “bottom-up” approach where the individual teacher is left alone to “play” with the new technology. Such a patching-up approach is inequitable and contributes to the already widening gaps. Adequate and effective use is an institutional responsibility that must be strategically “top-down” to first develop a clear organizational policy, governance, and strategy.

With the goal of maintaining adopting new technologies safely and effectively, this parts of http's governance proved vital. Educational supervisors can't just buy new software; they have to devise policies on how the new software is going to be used. The policies focus on today's most important problem on consent and data privacy. Students' data is sensitive, including records of their academic achievements, their behavioral engagement (which some people consider controversial), and even biometric or emotional data. Our policies have to be unambiguous and comply with both internationally and locally (e.g., Europe – GDPR, US - FERPA), specifying what data is captured, who controls the data, how the data is used in teaching and learning, and the third-party vendors in the teaching and learning ecosystem with whom the data is shared. These policies must be governed. There must a numerous policies on what AI tools to buy and how to set the purchasing or assessing criteria. There is no emphasis on, but also extensive data security practices, pedagogical practices, and, importantly, reduced algorithm bias.

Lastly, It is essential that any and all Artificial Intelligence governance should include an appeals procedure. Having an appeal procedure is essential so that students can use it effectively and efficiently. It is not sufficient for students to be automated essay scorers and simply submit appeals for their work to be reviewed by a trained professional. They must be guided on the procedure necessary to prepare the appeal.

Safeguards still have to be implemented and, as such, while adopting a system of governance, institutions are still confronted with a myriad of practical issues that arise. These issues were thoroughly identified by the reviewers to be the digital divide, which the war breaks out over the gap of the digital divide, the gap which AI threatens, an "AI dystopia. Numerous forms of the divide exist. Suffices to say that the divide is "social," especially regarding an economy. The AI system is severely priced. This sets a divided system, setting a high priced personalized resources for the wealthy institutions, and the non affluent institutions are offered "AI gap." Also, the divide is drastically "economically" divided. The divide is divided under the category of "Improvements In Technology." AI works efficiently over VR, immersive VR, and complicated data sets, robust and high speed data, and internet data, more so the internet, and often a one, is still captured devices which is still a phenomenal concept. It is the devices which pose a challenge, which is termed inertia, and human, whom as discussed in the earlier portion, is the "Skeen" is the disconnection of AI systems which is a well-known pattern. AI systems, which still have to be predicted and, as such, is still under discussion.

Your reviewers are correct. § As they suggested, practical, classroom-focused vignettes and case studies need to be funded, produced, and disseminated. § These specific "teacher-in-the-loop" orchestration instances are crucial to showing AI as a useful copilot in teaching and, therefore, demystifying the technology to remove faculty resistance.

These obstacles are intertwined with the serious ethical issues and boundary-defining limits associated with any model of AI that must be addressed with any AI in ELT discussion—bias in language education: linguistic and algorithmic. As reviewers of this work pointed out, this is not a footnote; it is a headline. AI systems are not "objective" and "neutral," and their training datasets—often scraped from the internet or developed from some academic or corporate sited corpus—are biased and dominated by Standard American or British English. This "native-speakerist" bias has grave pedagogical and ethical consequences for the worldwide English language teaching context. This means that these AI systems can and do incorrectly "flag" non-standard English varieties (like Singaporean English, Indian English or even African American Vernacular English) that are grammatically correct and valid. This penalizes learners for being plurilingual, defending a colonial, simplified model of "correct" English, and is contrary to decades of instructional progress in ELT pedagogy, particularly English as an International Language (EIL) (Chapelle, 2021). This bias is present in speech recognition systems, where learners with strong L1 accents experience feeling frustrated and a lack of confidence due to the recognition systems not assisting them as they should.

As is so, educators and students must be trained, along with the models, to be able to demonstrate the limitations to the models themselves. Unlike some other AI tools, AI LLM models are prone to 'hallucinations'. These models operate as a probabilistic system that generates text that seems plausible. They do not hold the capability to retrieve and report the actual 'truth'. As a result, they 'hallucinate' facts, citations, and even grammar rules (Tlili et al, 2023). An LLM might issue to a language learner, asking for an explanation of a complex grammar rule, an answer that is logically coherent and articulate but is totally wrong. Further compounding this unreliability is the so-called 'black box' problem. For many deep learning models and even their creators for some models, it is simply the case that they do not understand the rationale behind a specific choice (e.g. why a student's essay gets 4.5 when the maximum score is deemed to be 5.0, and the average score is 4.5). It's quite clear that the lack of transparency is the reason why accountability becomes impossible in educational settings. AI's lack of contextual and pragmatic understanding is not as profound. AI can parse the sentence, but fails to understand the pragmatic layer of human communication, such as humor, sarcasm, cultural subtlety, understatement, and, on the other hand, suppression (Cunningham, 2021). It is a tool for essence, not grammar.

These constraints are not shortcomings of the technology itself, more so an advancement of critical literacy skills. It further shows that AI is an immensely useful, yet negligent assistant. It can manage the more algorithmic aspects of language, but it is an tool that can only be effectively used by both a critical human teacher and a critical human student who, together, perform the indispensable, human-centered work of sense making.

IMPLEMENTATION: FROM THEORY TO CLASSROOM PRACTICE

In response to the "agreeable" generalization around the new technology, this section takes a quite practical, institutional, and economic analysis of the Artificial Intelligence (AI) adoption in English Language Teaching (ELT). The reliability and the promise of the theoretical model is far from the reality of a classroom that is equitable, effective, and sustainable and is conditioned on far more than the purchase of software. It is a wholly institutional problem and one that needs to be treated deliberately and strategically from the top. As the reviewers pointed out, the adoption of AI is not something that may be undertaken in a disorderly and chaotic way from the bottom. The "experimentation" of teachers, some of whom may be deemed "innovative", leads inescapably to a patchwork of inequitable access, inconsistent pedagogical practice, and high risks around data privacy. Thus, the adoption must commence from the top and in an ethical manner in order to mitigate the rigid and lapse policies on data.

Every decision that is made moving forward related to pedagogy and its connectivity with technology is grounded within this governance framework. The first and most important pillar of that framework is data privacy and consent. Data-driven educational tools, particularly intelligent tutors and adaptive learning tools, are data-driven by nature. They operate on the basis of collecting, processing, and analyzing gargantuan volumes of sensitive student information in real time. This information is not limited to the mere passing of tests. It may also include behavioral and engagement indicators such as the time spent on a task, the error rate, the data the student submits in the form of text and audio, and in some extreme and unethical cases, biometric and affective data. This means that educational leaders have an undeniable ethical and legal responsibility to implement policies that are completely transparent in regard to data compliance and collection policies, especially the GDPR and FERPA policies. Students, teachers, and parents, must be clearly notified on what data is collected, for what specific pedagogical purpose, owned by who, and with what third parties is data shared with. This must be active opt-in consent with the policy, rather than a passive, buried clause in a user agreement.

This branch leads to the next underlying tenet - 'data minimization'. In the world of perpetual data collection, educational institutions should practice the opposite of data hoarding - a policy that permits the maximum data that can be collected to serve a defined educational purpose to be collected, a policy of data correspondence. If a pronunciation app does not function unless it knows a student's name or their geo-coordinate position, it should not be permitted to collect those data. This is the strongest form of data protection against misuse or unauthorized use. In addition, the governance model must stipulate an appeals process. If any form of summative assessment employs an AI system - for instance, an AI-enabled proctor or an auto-essay grading system - it is the responsibility of the educational institution to ensure that the students have been provided with a reasonable, accessible, and well-structured process to appeal the AI score to a real educator. The use of an impenetrable "black box" system is against the principles of fair assessment. The final aspect requires a change to the purchasing policy. School and program administrators, along with program leads, are expected to have developed and implemented an appropriate and rigorous assessment framework prior to any procurement of a new AI system.

This rubric should make vendors step away from abstract marketing opinions and demand to know their tool's nurturing pedagogy, data security, and, especially, processes for self-audit and bias mitigation of language and demographics. The vendor, not the school, must demonstrate safety and effectiveness.

Ineven with achieving any form of equity within a perfect governance policy, institutions face immediate equity, cost, and infrastructure concerns. A particularly persistent issue is the "digital divide," which has the potential of becoming a "digital chasm." The economic barriers are among the foremost. The best, most sophisticated, and effective AI platforms, ethically-vetted, are costs prohibitive. This creates a deeply inequitable system: a tiered system in which well-resourced institutions have access to AI pedagogy along with premium automated, safe, and effective AI tutors. On the other hand, under-resourced schools have access to "free" resources, which monetize student data, or no access at all. This dynamic is the very achievement gap that AI is said to be solving. This economic divide is further compounded by infrastructure issues. AI is not magic; it works with dependable hardware. It requires high speed, high-bandwidth internet and access for all students, not just in a computer lab, along with one-to-one devices for any personalized accessible, or immersive learning. These requirements are not uniformly meet, which results in a inequitable divide between the students and the "haves" and the "have-nots." Lastly, in achieving full funding along with perfect infrastructure, all other institutions are deeply stalled with funding, perfection, and pother barriers. These institutions have full control of the funding without any barriers, yet the implementation has full infrastructure barriers.

In the case of Kessler (2020), the phenomenon of this type of resistance from teachers, administrators, and parents is much more nuanced than simply luddism. It is, instead, the result of rational misunderstanding, distrust, and, above all, an absence of sustained, high-quality professional development. Too often, teachers are expected to reconstruct their entire approach to teaching to integrate these tools, and are expected to do so without any added time or even more professional development. It is completely rational to expect resistance to what feels like yet another top-down, "silver-bullet" approach that no one is going to care about in two years. This attitude resembles the attitude that many people adopt to overcome the human barriers that often pose the biggest challenges.

Understanding abstract policies and framing them within the context of actual classroom practices tend to create severe cognitive dissonance. It is, therefore, of paramount importance to keep the curriculum collaborative. Out of this veil of the elusive technology, what emerges is the role of the technology and the initial stresses the teacher is likely to experience, concerning the teacher's role as the teacher of the class. Thus, let's take, for instance, the L2 writing "Teacher in the Loop" scenario. This particular scenario concerns itself with the teacher stress for an undergraduate EAP (English for Academic Purposes) for the teacher assigning a five paragraph argumentative essay. This whole process has been redesigned into three stages. In Draft 1, students only submit the first draft of their essays to an Automated Writing Evaluation (AWE) tool. The Artificial Intelligence (AI) gives them immediate and personalized formative feedback and revision on "local" errors of grammar and mechanics, sentence structure, and the like. In the absence of any teacher intervention, the students spend a class period or a homework session to make these revisions, thus engaging in an immediate feedback loop. In Draft 2, students who have AI-revised drafts engage in structured peer review.

In this case under review, we are more interested in the ideas developed in the 'AI vs. Human' essay. The initial instructions were issued in the hope that the AI would somehow figure out the instructions. Peer reviewers will be instructed that the AI has already formed the first draft of the essay and 'corrected' the most visible surface errors. Given that, reviewers will be instructed to focus on 'global' issues that the AI is lacking: the clarity of the thesis statement, the supporting evidence, and the whole argument. At lastly, in Draft 3, students hand in their final, clean draft to the human teacher. The teacher in this case, relieved from the tedious task of copy editing, will focus on the more complex parameters of the work and how the critical analysis is developed, the reasoning, and the author's voice and how distinct it is.

The second vignette demonstrates how Generative AI can be used for practical competence, one of the most difficult skills to teach. Students in an intermediate ESL class are learning the skill of making polite and formal requests. The teacher in this instance, as the educational designer, gives the chatbot a particular prompt: "Act as a university professor. I am a student who needs to request an extension on a paper. Respond to my requests. You must refuse the request and, for the request you refuse, give an explanation as to why the request was inappropriate as well as a more appropriate request you can suggest. This is only allowed if I am too rude or informal." Students have the opportunity to practice this type of session independently on their devices where they can modify the terms and formality levels in an atmosphere that is non-threatening. They can productively "fail" without the fear of embarrassment in a public situation. After this individual practice, the teacher asks the class to participate in a metapragmatic reflection, sharing what actually transpired. They conduct a collective analysis on why for the phrase "I need an extension" bluntly and freely, was a rejected phrase, while "I was wondering if it might be possible to..." was somewhat more complex and accepted.

Within this model, the AI supports practice through an interactive simulation at scale, but the human instructor provides the higher-order teaching on the cultural and social "why" that grounds the language.

ETHICAL CONCERNS AND MODEL LIMITATIONS

When discussing artificial intelligence in English Language Teaching (ELT), there is no room for naive optimism. A discussion of this sort must defend against and foreground the severe limitations and the risks of these technologies. As for the scope of language education, the most pressing and severe challenge is the phenomenon of bias, both linguistic and algorithmic. As reviewers have pointed out, this is not an oversight, a minor flaw that can be easily fixed, but a challenge at the deepest level. Artificial intelligence models do not function as objective and neutral judges of language 'correctness'. Rather, they are statistical models of the corpus they have been trained on. The challenge, however, is that the predominant linguistic data, which overwhelmingly constitutes the corpus, is data that has been subsumed under the ideological nonsense of Standard American and Standard British English. The systemic bias, predicated on an idea of 'native speakerism', is a powerful, almost hegemonic linguistic settlement. The pedagogical and ethical consequences are damning. The prescriptivist standards that dominate the ideological superstructure of artificial intelligence are a single, unified standard, which is globally hegemonic.

Time and again, it will incorrectly "flag" legitimate, grammatically correct, and non-standard varieties of English, like those spoken in Singapore, India, Nigeria, or the Caribbean, as "wrong" or "unnatural." This kind of technologically enforced prescriptivism punishes learners for their plurilingualism and denies the existence of English as an International Language. In addition, some of this bias is phonological; the speech recognition component of pronunciation tutors has been shown to poor at recognizing or appropriately modeling speech from language learners with strong L1 accents, and is often worse at recognizing and modeling their speech. This increases the learners' frustration and reinforces the colonialist notion that the accent is a "deficit" that needs to be "corrected" instead of embraced as part of one's identity. As a result, the tools that are applied uncritically serve to reinforce a prescriptive approach to pedagogy which counters decades of development in English language teaching in the communicatively oriented approach which includes plurilingualism and English as a Lingua franca (Chapelle, 2021). It poses a real risk to learner motivation and confidence because it reinforces the notion that their linguistic identity is "wrong." This goes beyond the bias crisis. As reviewers requested, educators are obliged to set the critical agenda around the models' basic flaws.

Instructing AI systems does not come without challenges and this is what we must articulate. In the context of LLMs or large language models, "hallucinations" or making things up is what is discussed the most. These models probabilistically generate text, and thus they aim to be plausible, not true like an automated "search engine" or "database." In doing so, they "hallucinate" or fabricate evidence, citations, scholarly documents, and various rules of grammar, and do so without any semblance of doubt (Tlili et al., 2023). Explaining the nuances of two phrasal verbs to an English language learner will reveal they have no phrasal verbs, and the structures they provide are articulate, coherent, and well-structured, yet entirely incorrect. Because the output of generative AI is not fact-checked by a human or a reliable external source, it assumes the role of an unreliable "tutor." This unreliability is compounded by the "black box" problem. In the case of many complex deep learning models, even the people that create them do not have insights that are sufficient enough to justify the reasoning behind a specific conclusion. In the everyday example we began with, an automated essay grader might provide a score, but offers no solid or pedagogically sound rationale as to "why." The less there is of this in education systems the more accountable they will have to be.

When a teacher is unable to justify the mark attained or to clarify Board comments on a particular piece of work, the assessment feedback cycle becomes functionally useless from a pedagogical standpoint. This lack of opacity is one of the many reasons why the application of artificial intelligence to any high-stakes, summative assessment is particularly troubling. Anyway, and with the greatest emphasis on language learning, AI does not possess pragmatic and cultural understanding on a human level. AI knows how to put words in a sentence but does not comprehend their meanings in the context of human reality. It does and will continue to struggle with the multi-layered and often unspoken human interactions: the humor, the sarcasm, the irony, the emotional tone one is trying to convey, or the unique voice of a writer. This, in turn, produces feedback that is often described as "tin-eared" or "tone-deaf" (Cunningham, 2021). For example, the AI may "correct" a stylistically creative sentence as being "non-standard," or it may "appreciate" a boring, formulaic, and uninspired piece of writing for being syntactically perfect. These biases, fallibility, opacity, and decontextualization are not simply bugs or glitches. They are the defining characteristics of " tech " today, which requires human criticality to always use a teacher within the context of it.

CONCLUSION: THE PATH FORWARD FOR A HUMAN-CENTERED AI PEDAGOGY

It's important to recognize that Artificial Intelligence will not address the complex, human-centered, and multifaceted challenges that accompany language learning. The idea of one technology solving all needs is a misunderstanding of the "wicked problems" of education and its intersections with psychology, sociology, and culture. AI in and of itself is not a solution, but a potential catalytic tool that, if thoughtfully and critically integrated with truly transformative pedagogy, can deeply improve and reimagine English Language Teaching (ELT) classrooms. The most immediate benefits lie in the AI automating some of the tedious cognitive work that is repetitive and time-consuming, and in offering personalized practice that scaled instruction could not achieve. AI's features that address "first-pass" writing error corrections, drill vocabulary through spaced repetition, and provide personalized grammar instruction help offload work. This technology's promise is to allow educators to direct their time and cognitive effort toward the more impactful work of teaching students authentic communication, critical thinking, socio-emotional learning, and mentorship.

It handles the mechanics of the language. The teacher can be relieved of that task to focus on the guidance of the art of its application—fostering pragmatic competence, navigating intercultural understanding, managing language anxiety, rapport building, and mentoring the development of a student's voice and identity.

This potential can be realized, but only under certain conditions. It requires a critical, human-centered approach, one that deeply understands the need to avoid the passive, "plug-and-play" approach to new technologies. AI, as outlined in this chapter, is nothing but a powerful, but deeply flawed, resource that lacks a pragmatic contextual grasp of problems, is culturally and linguistically biased, "hallucinates," and is incapable of rational understanding. It is not a tool to be used uncritically. It is a dangerous tool, as it can promote inequity, misinformation, and the degradation of the skills of teachers and learners. Consequently, the only ethically and pedagogically defensible model for the future is human-AI collaboration. This reframes the educator as the expert orchestrator, the "teacher-in-the-loop," who supervises, curates, authenticates, and mediates the AI. As a pedagogical designer, the teacher chooses the appropriate tool, designs the task, and critically responds to the tool's output. This ensures that pedagogy dominates the technology, not the other way around. The aim is thoughtful, directed use of a tool to avoid "technological solutionism" and achieve well-defined and human-centered learning goals.

Moving forward will require a consolidated, committed effort by all parties involved. From this review, the following practical recommendations target three main groups. For ELT educators, the call to action is to engage in small-scale, immediate, pedagogical experimentation. The aim isn't to transform your entire curriculum in one go, but to develop your own critical AI literacy. Begin with one non-threatening AI tool. For instance, play with a chatbot to collaboratively generate a lesson and a set of differentiated reading questions. It is not the AI's output you want to use, but the AI's output you want to critique, adapt, and refine. Use an Automated Writing Evaluation (AWE) tool for single, low-stakes formative assignments and analyze the feedback it generates. Assess the remarks against your own, identifying the strengths (e.g., the thoroughness in locating comma splices) and weaknesses (e.g., inability to address the author's voice or the logic of the argument) of the tool. This small-scale engagement is the first towards the chapter's main emphasis: the shifting focus from the tool to mastering integration pedagogically within a communicative framework.

Responsible leadership from school administrators and institutional leaders are more foundational and strategic. You need to build the appropriate policies and avoid quick technological fixes from vendors. Your first policies should be governance policies that address the comprehensiveness and the transparency of institutional policies on AI. You can only purchase platforms after there is a policy on ethical

AI frameworks. This scaffolding should include all legal standards and address student data, parental consent, data minimization, and appeals on AI assessment. You should be able to purchase platforms that are secure, transparent, and on a rubric that mitigates bias after which you can start purchasing. Professional development should also not be a single workshop. You should also focus your development on the integration of data literacy, AI literacy, and instructional design. This is also a net waste to invest in technological capital. There should also be a sustained investment in the human capital of your institution that is aligned to technological investments.

State, national, and international policymakers must shape the entire ecosystem. You can't remain neutral. You must fund independent, academic research that examines the claims, effectiveness, and risks of the proprietary, "black-box" tools. We cannot expect vendors to self-audit. This funding must address the crisis of linguistic and demographic bias in AI models. The next generation of tools must serve all learners, including those who do not speak a standard, hegemonic English. You must also use policy tools—grants, funding for infrastructure and training, and other initiatives—to close the digital divide. AI, without deliberate intervention, will be inequity's accelerator. It will create a two-tier system of AI-enriched, well-resourced schools and under-resourced schools that are devoid of tools. Policies must ensure equitable access not just to the devices, but also to the high-quality training for teachers that makes the devices pedagogically valuable.

There must be some mention of the limitations of this review. As this chapter utilizes the approach of a narrative review, it is not intended to be a systematic or exhaustive review of the existing literature. It is, by intention, a synthesis and an argument, aiming to outline the conceptual landscape and highlight the essential debates within the domain. Nevertheless, the most critical limitation is the order of magnitude of the rapid change in the domain itself. The pace of change in Generative AI, in particular, is faster than the normal cycle of the academic publishing industry. It is safe to say the chapter is in print, new tools and models will be available and new challenges will arise. This limitation, in itself, serves to reinforce the chapter's most fundamental argument: a sustainable pedagogy cannot be built around a particular, transient tool, but rather around core, foundational. critical thinking, adaptive pedagogy, and human-centered ethics.

The future of our profession relies on how we react to this moment. AI will not take the place of the English Language Teaching educator. AI will not take the mentor, guide, facilitator, or the human connection essential to meaningful education. However, ELT professionals who use AI effectively, ethically, and critically will—and they will be the ones who define the future of the profession. They will be the ones who successfully embrace this new human-AI collaboration in pedagogy to provide a personalized, responsive, effective, and equitable learning experience to all language learners.

REFERENCES

Bahrani, T., Qadery, S., & Bahrani, D. (2023). The impact of artificial intelligence-based chatbots on (EFL) learners' speaking and listening skills: A review of recent studies. *International Journal of English Language and Literature Studies, 12*(2), 89–102. DOI: 10.18488/ijels.v12i2.3385

Blyth, C. (2022). Immersive technologies and language learning. In *The Routledge handbook of second language acquisition and technology* (pp. 377–390). Routledge.

Chapelle, C. A. (2021). The role of applied linguistics in the age of AI. *Applied Linguistics, 42*(5), 957–963. DOI: 10.1093/applin/amab040

Cunningham, K. (2021). Automated Writing Evaluation in the EAP classroom: Exploring the interplay between teacher and machine feedback. *Journal of English for Academic Purposes, 50*, 100966. DOI: 10.1016/j.jeap.2021.100966

Gao, J., Wang, Y., & Li, J. (2022). Artificial intelligence in supporting students with special needs: A systematic review. *Computers & Education: Artificial Intelligence, 3*, 100062. DOI: 10.1016/j.caeai.2022.100062

Heil, J., & Wu, J. (2023). A systematic review of AI-based personalized learning and the teacher's role. *Computers and Education: Artificial Intelligence, 5*, 100155. DOI: 10.1016/j.caeai.2023.100155

Kessler, G. (2020). Preparing language teachers to effectively use technology. In *The Routledge handbook of language and technology* (pp. 512–525). Routledge.

Kohnke, L., Moorhouse, B. L., & Zou, D. (2023). ChatGPT for language teaching and learning. *RELC Journal, 54*(2), 537–550. DOI: 10.1177/00336882231162868

Su, J., Wang, Y., & Yang, Y. (2023). Artificial intelligence in second language pronunciation training: A systematic review. *Education and Information Technologies, 28*(1), 197–221. DOI: 10.1007/s10639-022-11197-0

Tlili, A., Shehail, M., & Asoodar, M.. (2023). What if the devil is in the details? A systematic review of the challenges of generative AI in education. *Computers and Education: Artificial Intelligence, 6*, 100197. DOI: 10.1016/j.caeai.2023.100197

Uto, M., & Uto, H. (2020). A system for visualizing the effects of spaced repetition learning on students' vocabulary retention. *Research and Practice in Technology Enhanced Learning, 15*(1), 2. DOI: 10.1186/s41039-020-0125-z

Vygotsky, L. S. (1978). *Mind in society: The development of higher psychological processes*. Harvard University Press.

Wang, Y., & Tigelaar, D. E. H. (2023). Understanding the complexity of language teachers' adoption of AI: A systematic review of the literature. *Education and Information Technologies, 28*(10), 13349–13380. DOI: 10.1007/s10639-023-11756-3

Warshauer, M., & Healey, D. (1998). Computers and language learning: An overview. *Language Teaching, 31*(2), 57–71.

Zhai, X. (2022). A 'teacher-in-the-loop' approach to using artificial intelligence for automated writing evaluation. *Assessment in Education: Principles, Policy & Practice, 29*(4), 481–501. DOI: 10.1080/0969594X.2022.2091484

ADDITIONAL READING

Afolabi, O. S., & Labase, M. (2024). A systematic review of AI in English Language Teaching: Tools, challenges, and future directions. *Journal of Educational Technology & Society, 27*(1), 120–138.

Aljuaid, M. (2024). AI in academic writing instruction: A systematic review of pedagogical applications and learner outcomes. *International Journal of Computer-Assisted Language Learning and Teaching, 14*(1), 1–18.

Bailey, D. R. (2024). Ethical challenges of AI in education: Bias, privacy, and equity. *Journal of Learning Analytics, 11*(1), 1–5.

Fitria, T. N. (2023). The impact of AI-powered tools on EFL learners' writing performance: A systematic review. *Journal of English Language Teaching and Linguistics, 8*(2), 335 350.

Hsu, T. C., & Chen, C. M. (2023). The effects of AI-assisted language learning on EFL learners' vocabulary knowledge and reading comprehension. *Computers & Education, 207*, 104928.

Kalantzis, M., & Cope, B. (2024). *AI for humans: A new curriculum for cyber-social literacy learning*. Cambridge University Press.

Khlaif, Z. N., & Salha, S. (2025). Exploring educators' AI literacy: A necessity for integrating generative AI in higher education. *Journal of Applied Research in Higher Education*. Advance online publication. DOI: 10.1108/JARHE-07-2024-0320

Mishra, P.. (2023). The new digital era: Reassessing skills for effective language teaching with AI. *Educational Technology Research and Development, 71*(4), 1321–1345.

Pegrum, M. (2022). *AI in language education: A critical literacy approach.* Springer.

Sharadgah, T. A., & Sa'di, R. A. (2022). A systematic review of research on artificial intelligence in English Language Teaching (2015-2021). *Computers and Education Open*, *3*, 100101.

Chapter 7
Human-AI Synergy in English Reading Instruction:
Leveraging AI to Enhance Teaching

Jabulani Sibanda
https://orcid.org/0000-0001-5328-5888
Rhodes University, South Africa

ABSTRACT

This chapter explores the AI-human teacher mutual complementarity in Grade 3 English reading instruction. The chapter discusses this synergy in teaching and assessing the five foundational pillars of reading (phonemic awareness, phonics, fluency, vocabulary, and reading comprehension), through a balanced literacy framework of read-aloud, shared reading, group guided reading, and independent reading. It presents a ten-day lesson outline to demonstrate how teacher-led instruction can be practically and synergistically merged with AI affordances in reading instruction. The chapter synthesizes discrete, fragmented theoretical positions that inform AI-human teacher synergy in reading instruction. It positions AI as the scaffold that enhances access, efficiency, and personalization, and the teacher as providing sound pedagogy, critical engagement, emotional support, and contextually relevant instruction. The chapter highlights the transformative potential of the synergy in reading instruction and recommends the judicious and practical leveraging of AI in teacher-led reading instruction.

DOI: 10.4018/979-8-3373-3755-5.ch007

INTRODUCTION

Artificial Intelligence's invasion of the education landscape and its proliferation has revolutionized teaching and learning, and reimagined and reconfigured delivery of, and engagement with, content. The area of reading instruction has received a significant boost from a range of AI-powered tools responsive to the needs of diverse learners. The tools have addressed some of the persistent challenges of traditional instruction like personalization, differentiation, real-time feedback, and scale.

Reading competence is foundational to all learning across disciplines, and it is imperative that human, digital, algorithmic, and computational resources are deployed in its instruction. Reading has evolved courtesy of technological advancements that have occasioned changes in reading texts. Texts have undergone a shift from the exclusively printed or paper-based static texts to digital, adaptive, and interactive texts amenable to instruction through more inclusive, engaging, and learner-centred AI tools. With such texts, "Learners can engage in dialogues with AI-driven annotations embedded within printed texts, receiving context-aware clarifications, scaffolded questioning, and adaptive feedback tailored to their learning progress" (Kılıçkaya & Kic-Drgas, 2025, para. 2).

The deployment of AI holds promise for enhancing reading instruction and learning. However, AI use comes with attendant challenges teachers and learners must navigate. At a general level, AI has been hailed for personalizing learning based on identifying individual needs and customizing instruction to such needs; for virtual environments and conversational agents that simulate reality and allow for real-time language practice and feedback; for automation of important language tasks, and streamlining of administrative tasks; for its global accessibility and scalability facilitative of cross-cultural communication; and for ushering in dynamic, interactive, engaging, and adaptable material; among others. On the contrary, AI's failure to replicate human attributes that are emotional, social and cultural; bias in AI systems algorithms; the digital divide that creates disparities in learning opportunities owing to differential technological access; teachers' conservatism and inadequate training; and over-reliance on, and excessive use of AI have been the major downsides of AI use. An appreciation of the strengths and challenges implicit in AI use necessitate a consideration of both the prospects AI brings to the teaching of English reading.

This chapter presents artificial intelligence (AI) as a disruptive and transformative force in reading instruction within English Language Teaching (ELT). The main argument the chapter advances is that, despite the transformative reading instruction capacity of AI tools, they cannot replace human effort. Optimal benefit from reading instruction can only be realized if there is a judicious and balanced deployment of both AI-powered tools and human effort. Passive and mechanical adherence to AI instruction can diminish relationships and render the tools counterproductive.

The two augment each other and should not be seen as mutually exclusive. Duggan (2020, p.5) makes the apt observation that "Far from becoming sidelined by the emergence of these exciting new technologies the primacy of the teacher's role has been reasserted, and the role of the educator will be enhanced rather than displaced by technology." This chapter explores the possibilities for leveraging AI to enhance and complement traditional reading instruction and assessment within the framework of a balanced literacy approach.

RATIONALE FOR FOCUSING ON ENGLISH

The rationale for a focus on reading in English in this chapter is threefold. First, English is a global lingua franca considered a gateway to learning in most education contexts. Reading competence in such a language gives one a headstart that reading in any other language does. English also keeps positioning itself as a gateway language for cross-linguistic transfer to the other languages. Second, the complexity of its opaque orthography and syntax with its vast vocabulary, irregular spelling patterns, and intricate grammar distinct from the African indigenous languages that are phonemically regular, add a reading instruction and assessment complexity that make the need for leveraging AI resources urgent. African indigenous languages have a transparent, phonemic and regular orthography facilitative of word decoding. "English… is an extremely deep orthography (one of the deepest alphabetic orthographies), meaning that the grapheme–phoneme correspondences are much less reliable and less consistent" (Miller, 2019, p. 3) rendering word decoding difficult. However, its consistent orthography and predictable patterns are adaptable to pattern identification by AI tools than may be the case with languages characterised by much morpho-phonemic variance. Third, the language has a strong AI presence than, for instance, African indigenous languages, and so the choice of AI-powered tools that can be used to augment the human teacher is wide. English has a global presence in standardized AI and digital resources. The digital resources AI tools draw from are enormous, which makes AI tools more adaptable in English than in any other language. It is also clear that most AI technologies for language education have been designed in English. Its pivotal role in global standardized assessments that keep growing in scale and demand has given impetus to AI innovations.

READING AND READING INSTRUCTION

A plethora of adjectives aptly describe the process of reading. It is complex, multifaceted, nonlinear, interactive, strategic, recursive, deliberate, personalized, incremental, and engaging act. Instruction and assessment of such an embodied and multidimensional art requires a commensurate multi-thronged approach. Reading instruction is as multilayered as reading is. It comprises multiple but interconnected sub-skills of phonemic awareness, phonics, fluency, vocabulary, and comprehension, holistically integrated to constitute the act of reading. At the foundation phase, its instruction is conducted within the balanced reading approach of read aloud, shared reading, group guided reading, and independent reading.

The choice of reading instruction to discuss the leveraging of AI tools is deliberate, seeing that every teacher is a teacher of reading, and that access to all learning is mediated by reading for meaning. From a review of many studies related to AI and language teaching, Mohebb (2025) observes that the language arts of reading and listening have been the least explored, an observation that justifies this study's focus on reading.

NEED FOR LEVERAGING AI IN READING INSTRUCTION: WHAT RELATED STUDIES HAVE SHOWN

Jin (2024, p.30) summarizes the AI affordances for education generally by saying "AI-driven learning environments are designed to optimize learning experiences, support individualized instruction, foster collaboration and social interaction, and promote motivation and engagement among learners." AI tools are strong on personalizing instruction and assessment, providing real-time feedback, assessing many learners efficiently (scalability), providing targeted interventions informed by diagnostic assessment, offering holistic assessment (comprehensively evaluating multiple reading skills simultaneously), and using engaging and less stressful assessment formats (compared to traditional tests). They continuously collect data on learner performance to base feedback on, make targeted instructional decisions, scaffold the reading process, proffer recommendations, give rewards, and so forth. The data-driven insights from AI tools also enhance human teachers' instruction. AI tools are also good at providing multimodal support (combining audio, visual, and textual features), which ensures inclusivity. They also scaffold texts through simplification, where necessary, or using cues to support the struggling readers. The built-in mechanisms within the AI tools encourage perseverance, a vital ingredient to the development of a growth mindset.

Sun, Tam, and Lim (2025, p.4) fault the traditional language classroom for adopting a "...one-size-fits-all, teacher-centered approach." AI-powered tools personalize both reading instruction and assessment allowing "...children to receive tailored instruction and feedback" (p.4). In their scoping review, Sun, Tam and Lim (2025, p.13) found evidence from eight studies that "AI was deemed effective and better in approximately 75% of the studies (n = 6), where the AI group performed significantly better than the non-AI group." They also report on Yueh et al.'s (2020) study "... where children performed better in a reading comprehension test when they engaged in the task with the robot reading companion rather than with the human reader (p.15). They further report that "All articles on non-L1 interventions found that the AI group was more effective" (p16), and "Of studies that conducted inferential statistics in comparing AI and non-AI groups, the AI group was always either better or on par with the non-AI group" (p.17), and,

> *For outcome measures, children similarly largely benefitted from AI more than they did from non-AI, with all studies finding greater or similar improvements when AI was used as opposed to non-AI methods. This was found regardless of whether the outcome measure was phonological awareness (Goffredo et al., 2016; Hooshyar et al., 2018) ... or alphabet knowledge/vocabulary (Hooshyar et al., 2018; Park et al., 2019) (p.17).*

In their systematic review of 47 instances of computer-assisted instruction for reading skills programs, Kurzeja et al. (2024) report that 34 evinced positive outcomes in the form of active responding, sequenced systematic instruction, immediate feedback, customization, and automated progress monitoring. The AI affordances in reading instruction cannot be overemphasized.

This chapter seeks to demonstrate how AI can be judiciously employed to complement teacher efforts at engendering adaptive, personalized reading instruction and assessment.

GAPS

Much research on AI and reading focuses on individualized reading instruction and assessment, at the expense of specific strategies for implementing the balanced reading approach components. Not many studies have explored how teachers can integrate AI tools into their reading pedagogy despite teachers being central to reading literacy development. The AI affordances have largely been seen as an end in themselves, a kind of substitute for the teacher, rather than a pivotal support complementing the teacher's instructional strategies. This has created a needless binary between either teacher-led reading instruction or AI mediated reading instructions. Studies have focused on AI tutoring systems and adaptive reading apps that scaffold reading and personalize real-time feedback to automate routine reading assessments (Karatzas and Zogopoulos, 2024), and use of interactive and game-based reading tools, among other aspects actuated, in part, by a desire to replace the teacher. Sun, Tam, and Lim (2025, p.3) observe that "... there is a major gap in the understanding for AI in early childhood education for the purpose of language learning." Studies have also focused on isolated reading components like reading speed, vocabulary, and comprehension (Kondrateva et al., 2024). From their scoping review, Sun, Tam, and Lim (2025, p.18) note studies that focused on "...outcomes for writing (Bonneton-Botté et al., 2020), phonological awareness (Hooshyar et al., 2018) and vocabulary (Park et al., 2019)." No study or theoretical paper known to the researcher has focused on all the foundational building blocks of reading within a balanced literacy framework as this chapter seeks to do. This chapter also seeks to discuss how the teacher and AI tools can complement in reading instruction.

CONFLUENCE OF AI AND TEACHER-LED READING INSTRUCTION PRACTICES ON PILLARS OF READING

Jin (2024, p. 31) observes that "AI complements traditional instruction and accelerates students' language acquisition journey." It is important to see teacher-led and AI-supported practices as intersecting and complementing in the teaching and assessment of phonemic awareness, phonics, fluency, vocabulary, and comprehension.

Phonemic Awareness

In the traditional and solely teacher-led approach to phonemic awareness instruction, there is much oral activity of a game-like or kinaesthetic nature through rhymes, clapping or tapping to syllables, and sound segmentation. Musical chants and play with word sounds assists learners to distinguish and manipulate individual word sounds. With the advent of AI-powered speech recognition technologies, the identification, blending, and isolation of phonemes in words can be done using Apps through interactive games and exercises that offer corrective feedback. Reading Rockets provides interactive lessons that allow learners to manipulate phonemes by segmenting and blending sounds. GraphoGame (GG) is an example of a game that adapts its difficulty level to a learner's progress, ensuring that tasks are both challenging and achievable. Bora et al. (2025) compared the effect of combining classroom phonics lessons with GraphoGame on Grade 2 English phonological awareness and reading skills to phonics instruction alone. The GraphoGame group performed significantly better than the control group in letter-sound knowledge, rime-unit recognition, and word recognition.

From their synthesis of research on GraphoGame, a highly recommended tool for word-reading acquisition, McTigue et al. (2019) warn that "Despite great potential, the effect of educational technology on classroom learning has overpromised..." They note that GG should be used as a "supplemental intervention" (p.54). The authors' review of several studies attests to high adult interventions having statistically significant effect compared to low adult interaction at a 0.47 to 0.07 ratio respectively. This is despite GG prescribing that it should be played in solitude. Ecochard's (2015) ethnographic study showed that the internal GG reward system was inadequate to sustain learner motivation, and her involvement through verbal and nonverbal encouragement is what sustained their motivation, testimony to the requisite synergy between the artificial and the human. On the one hand, the AI powered tools provide the requisite real-time, consistent, personalized feedback, and customized learning pathways (Binu, 2024), and on the other hand, the conventional teacher-led instruction provides rich interaction that transforms reading literacy into the social practice that it is. The conventional approach's incapacity to personalize attention in large classes is the gap AI tools can fill. Because AI tools have the capacity for misinterpreting heavily accented speech, the physical teacher's presence and intervention would ensure that learners' linguistic diversity does not work to their disadvantage. The monotony typical of AI games needs to be broken through teacher interaction and input.

Phonics

Traditionally, the teaching of phonics has been through a direct mapping of sound units (phonemes) to their corresponding written symbols (graphemes) using media like flashcards and worksheets of decodable words. Repeated practice through mechanical drills sounding out words to the point of automaticity, and structured progression in learning phonic rules would consolidate learners' knowledge of the grapho-phonic relationships, and allow for automatic phonetic decoding. The automation would free the cognitive load and allow the learner to concentrate on comprehension. Traditionally, phonics instruction is a systematic, sequential learning of letter sounds and blending them in word formation using visuals like flashcards or letter charts using decodable texts. In phonemic awareness, there is identification and manipulation of phonemes through verbal and non-verbal activities that draw attention to sounds in words like clapping out syllables or use of rhymes, segmenting words into sounds, and blending sounds into words. Traditional phonic programs, however, lack adaptability to learner needs. The advent of AI has ushered in tools like Lalilo that can decide on the sequence of phonic patterns for individual learners based on their performance, and not in a rigid one-size-fits-all characteristic of the traditional phonics instruction approaches. AI tools bring in personalization and adaptation in letter-sound correspondence, blending, and word articulation exercises. The tool Reading Rockets adjusts its instruction to provide targeted practice in areas of learner weaknesses. One widely researched tool is Amira Learning which assesses and coaches learners, with teachers coming in to assist those most in need of support (Mellard & Johnson, 2008). The collaboration of the artificial and the human can happen simultaneously, where the teacher can do whole class or group instruction, and the AI tool personalize instruction for some learners. This addresses time constraints occasioned by learner diversity and large classes characteristic of most developing countries' education systems. The human teachers' capacity to provide emotional support and to ensure a conducive learning context that is culturally and contextually relevant, and to detect whether a learner understands the grapho-phonic correspondence or is merely guessing cannot be sub-contracted to the AI tools. AI tools may fail to provide phonic examples reflective of how language is used locally. AI-powered phonic tools may compare learners' word pronunciation to native speakers' when that is not really the goal in most second language learning contexts. The AI tools are also not endowed with the human intuition (Binu, 2024) for diagnosing either complex or subtle mispronunciations emanating from a speech defect, regional accent, non-standard pronunciations, or dialects. The teacher can moderate that and the combination of the human and the artificial enriches learners' learning experience.

AI tools are notorious for focusing on decontextualised individual sounds and letters at the expense of instruction in a meaningful, integrated context facilitative of skills transfer. There is need for careful choice of AI tools as some tools focus on basic phonics rules at the expense of phonic patterns that are complex or have exceptions, which underprepares learners for reading.

Fluency

Fluency is a multidimensional reading skill comprising interrelated components of accurate and effortless word recognition, rate, and prosody. In reading accuracy, learners should be past word decoding to word recognition on sight and word comprehension.

Traditionally, teachers rely on flashcards to test accurate and effortless word recognition. Contemporary methods for fluency instruction are repetitive in nature to develop automaticity. This can be done through reading and re-reading the same text multiple times, having learners echo the teacher's reading, choral or paired reading of text, as well as timed reading. According to Binu (2024, p.35), "AI enables the development of intelligent chatbots and virtual language tutors, fostering conversational practice and enhancing language fluency." Tools like Read along can now immediately pick up mispronunciations, automate real-time corrective feedback, and identify the word-level errors learners keep making. The teacher can then review such persistent errors. In terms of rate or reading speed, the teacher drills repeated timed reading to automaticity. However, the teacher is hard-pressed for time to capture all the nuances of reading rate when assessing learners' reading speed and ends up capturing only the words per minute (WPM). The AI tools go further to document word hesitations or decoding challenges, individualize learner pacing strategies and targets, and provide useful feedback the teacher can use for future instructional decisions (Wang et al., 2020). Tools like Amira measure learners' WPM, detects the words or phrases that slow down students or cause them to pause, and documents individual, group, or whole-class progress and trends.

Wang et al.'s (2020) study, where students used Amira, reported significant improvement in reading rate. What was noteworthy was that frequency of use and use alongside teacher-led instruction accounted for the significant gains. The same factors of repeated practice and teacher involvement accounted for gains using the Raz-Kids tool.

Prosody seeks to produce, not only fluent readers, but expressive ones as well and comprises the learner's expression, intonation, and rhythm. In the conventional teacher-led approaches are modelled by the teacher through reading aloud or choral reading. The teacher would then give feedback on elements such as pitch, stress, and phrasing. The time-intensity occasioned by several aspects needing to be modelled or assessed simultaneously compromise the accuracy of the teacher's capture of the processes. Another major challenge is the subjectivity on the rating of these elements compromising the teacher's ability to track incremental progress or compare inter-learner performance. AI tools like Amira can objectively score the prosodic features and provide sufficient feedback data on which teachers can base their future instructional decisions.

Automaticity in the traditional classroom is also developed through drills and repeated exposure. With AI tools, the time it takes learners to recognize high-frequency words is tracked and practice activities are set for those who have not developed automaticity. GraphoGame employs rapid, repeated exposure and needs to be used in conjunction with teacher modelling; emotional support; and feedback on pace, expression, and accuracy. The teacher, not the AI tool, can detect emotion in learners' voice modulation, accommodate the diversity of learner speech differences, and make sound pedagogical judgement. Sometimes, the AI tool compares learners' fluency against a model, which may not be contextually relevant.

Wang et al. (2020) reported significant gains in overall oral reading fluency among learners from their regular use of Amira. How well the AI tool was integrated into the broader teacher-led instructional framework determined its success. The AI tool personalized practice, and automated predictable routine assessments; yielding requisite data the teacher interpreted to modify instruction, motivate learners and even give nuanced feedback. The advent of AI redefines the role of the teacher to that of making complex decisions that AI tools cannot automate, thereby leveraging the strengths of the artificial and the human. In modelling fluency, AI tools lack emotional expression as humans, which may affect comprehension. Human teachers are better at detecting decoding challenges, hesitations, and poor phrasing than AI tools.

Vocabulary

In traditional vocabulary instruction, picture-word associations are common, especially for concrete noun vocabulary. There is much use of vocabulary walls with high-frequency or thematic words, and direct teaching through synonyms, antonyms, definitions, illustrations, and contextual examples. For vocabulary development, typical traditional instruction would define and exemplify novel words' use in sentences, and learners practicing the same in diverse contexts. Contextual explanation of words is also common. These are largely standardized, repetitive encouraging rote memorization. They overly focus on decoding and lacking in application of the novel vocabulary in diverse contexts. Time limitation compromise the scope (both breadth and depth) of vocabulary teachers can develop in the learners. The traditional approach, however, is free from cultural biases or contextual inaccuracies characteristic of AI generated word lists and activities.

AI-powered tools like Quizlet use adaptive multimedia approaches that combine images, audio, and text tailored to learners reading levels and interests to automate vocabulary instruction and testing. The tools are adaptive to learners' performance, automatically adjusting the level of test difficulty to align with the learner's proficiency level. "By leveraging data analytics and machine learning algorithms, AI can tailor reading materials and activities to match each student's unique needs and abilities (Jin, 2024, p.29). Some tools like Memrise can recommend vocabulary for learners to practice based on their extant word knowledge, and exercises to practice the vocabulary in context, in a fun and engaging way. Learners get to see and experience novel vocabulary in diverse contexts that enrich their understanding of real-world vocabulary use, and retention of the learnt vocabulary. The tool can use native speaker videos integrating novel words into authentic, real-world contexts and usage. The tool has the capacity to track words likely to be forgotten by a learner and bring them up for review. The spaced repetition is meant to revisit words at intervals that prompt learners to review vocabulary, strengthen neural connections, and interrupt the forgetting curve. To expand the breadth of word knowledge, Memrise can suggest synonyms or antonyms of the novel words.

Chen et al.'s (2021) quasi-experimental study with 120 Grade 4 students in China using an experimental group (using an AI-based vocabulary learning app) and a control group (taught using traditional vocabulary instruction) for eight weeks, revealed significant vocabulary gains ($p < .01$). They attributed the vocabulary knowledge growth to the app's feedback that was adapted to individual learners, spaced repetition, and contextualized word use. Li and Tsai (2020) examined the efficacy of an AI chatbot in the learning of English vocabulary by 90 Grade 5 Taiwan learners. The pre- and post-test compared the gains by a group assisted by chatbot and another taught using conventional methods. There was significant vocabulary retention and application ($p < .05$) by the former. The two studies (Chen et al.'s, 2021; Li & Tsai, 2020) confirmed the efficacy of teacher involvement in guiding learners to interpret feedback from the AI tool, reinforcing word use in diverse tasks and contexts, and encouraging deeper semantic group discussions that link new words to learners' lived experiences. The teacher can check whether vocabulary databases used by AI tools cover the relevant key vocabulary and are free of cultural bias. While AI is shaping and reshaping the vocabulary instruction and assessment landscape, its lack of cultural and contextual insensitivity requires that it complements rather than supplants traditional teaching methods. Despite AI's affordances in vocabulary instruction and development, it has not been able to deal with language's contextual variability manifest in dialect and cultural variations (Mohebb, 2025). AI cannot provide nuanced human-like conversations and meanings, connotations, and context relevance as human teachers can. Koh et al. (2023, p. 202) sees AI tools as limited because of their basis on broad algorithms rather than proven pedagogical approaches concomitant with best practices in teaching and learning.

Comprehension

The traditional teaching of reading comprehension is characterised by teacher modelling and scaffolding, as well as learners practising read-alouds, guided reading, and shared reading of texts through predicting, questioning, summarizing, visualizing, and making inferences. Traditional approaches to teaching reading comprehension include guided reading through questioning, think alouds, retelling or summarising the story, among others. Assessment is largely in the form of question answering (tests), quizzes, cloze tests, story retelling, and comprehension tests. Jin (2024, p. 30) makes the apt observation that "Traditional assessments often provide a one-size-fits-all approach to evaluating students' reading comprehension abilities. AI, however, offers adaptive assessment tools that adjust the difficulty level of questions based on students' responses."

Wang et al. (2020) evaluated the effectiveness of the AI tool, iReadSmart, in enhancing comprehension among 200 Grade 3 students in Singapore. Findings showed that learners who used the tool performed better in comprehension tests than the control group ($p < .01$). Heil et al. (2021) investigated the effectiveness of a voice-activated AI tool (Ello) meant for early readers. The study was administered on 68 kindergarten learners for eight weeks. Findings showed that the learners who interacted with the AI tool registered enhanced oral comprehension. The success of the tool, however, depended on teacher facilitation and guidance aligned with curriculum goals.

In reading comprehension, AI tools like Quizlet can generate comprehension questions based on the text and covering the full range of the cognitive levels, and provide real-time feedback. They then track the kind of comprehension questions specific learners find problematic and propose practice exercises. Their tutoring systems and chatbots scaffold comprehension strategies and provide customized feedback to learner responses. The teacher then provides the nuanced, relational, and pedagogical expertise, and interprets AI-generated data, harnessing the AI affordances to scaffold critical complex thinking, emotional support, and make instructional decisions that deepen learners' reading experiences. Over-reliance on AI tools would deprive learners of the emotional, cultural, and interpersonal aspects of reading instruction that are built on empathy, intuition, and context sensitivity that cannot be replicated by AI tools. They need to be used reflectively to supplement not supplant the teacher efforts. That is why Kılıçkaya and Kic-Drgas (2025, para. 1) see "AI as an enhancer— augmenting and animating learning experiences rather than substituting human instruction."

AI tools are better at assessing comprehension using objective or short-answer items that do not capture the complexity of comprehending texts. The feedback is meant to provide answers to questions without indicating why the answers given were incorrect. Probing and following-up is not part of AI's reading instruction and assessment practices. The emotional, social, cultural and contextual elements of language use are not given any consideration.

AI AND TEACHER INSTRUCTION AND ASSESSMENT WITHIN THE BALANCED LITERACY FRAMEWORK.

In exploring the AI affordances that can be leveraged for teaching reading in English, the chapter also considers the synergy between AI tools and human teachers within the context of a balanced reading or literacy approach comprising reading aloud, shared reading, group guided reading, and independent reading. Used judiciously, AI can transform these modes of reading instruction around the same affordances of personalization, real-time feedback, and targeted interventions.

Read Aloud

In the traditional approach, read aloud has the teacher or more knowledgeable other (to use Vygotsky's term) reading a text aloud to learners to model fluency (rate, accuracy, expression) and proficient reading behaviors. The teacher communicates the focal aspects learners should attend to. Students are then asked to read aloud while the teacher assesses the focal aspects. In most classrooms, only one learner reads to the teacher at a time and for large classes, this can be time consuming, and some learners may only receive vicarious feedback through other learners' feedback.

AI tools like Fluency Tutor can listen to learners read aloud, evaluate their fluency, provide instant feedback and correction, and recommend areas for improvement. Other tools like Google Assistant can do the read aloud and model fluent reading.

In reading texts to learners, AI tools may not have the expressiveness and human intonation responsive to the text and the context, reducing the reading to mechanical, flat, emotionless, unnatural, or robotic reading. The tools cannot replicate teacher voice modulations, teacher light moments here and there, or adaptive non-verbal emphasis. For Mohebb (2025, p.10), the tools cannot capture the "…nuances of spoken language, including accent variation and emotional tone." In the traditional classroom, the teacher reads to the class and decides where to stop and engage the learners before resuming the reading. AI reading may be too neat and too artificial to be motivating.

Shared Reading

In shared reading, which is a form of interactive read-aloud, the teacher and learners read a text together collaboratively, allowing engagement, discussion and comprehension. Focus is placed on decoding, fluency, and comprehension strategies. It is, not only the reading that is interactive, but also the discussions, predictions, questioning, summarizing, and so on. The developing readers get to practise reading behaviors under supportive and non-threatening conditions.

With the use of AI tools like Raz-Kids, e-books with highlighted text, and multimedia integration of voice narrations (replacing the teacher) and auditory cues and visual media, are used. The tools can give additional context or explanations, and make comprehension checks or prompt discussions on particular points as the teacher would do in the traditional classroom. Vargas-Diaz et al.'s (2024) TaleMate system allowed parents and children to do interactive storytelling where they embodied different story characters, thereby developing early reading habits and cognitive development in children.

In shared reading, focus is on peer collaboration, teacher-learner discussion, and critical thinking around a text. AI tools often rob learners of proactive engagement where learners can initiate discussions, or even interrupt the teacher, limiting them to passive and responsive engagement. Texts from AI tools may be too biased to specific cultural and linguistic settings to resonate with learners in opposite contexts. A physical teacher would be abler to match texts with contexts than the AI tools.

Group Guided Reading

In contemporary Group Guided Reading instruction, the teacher works with a small group of learners on texts at their instructional reading levels. The learners should be reading at the same level or having the same instructional needs so that the teacher's intervention can be targeted enough to accelerate reading progress. Normally, the teacher would have several tables with an activity each for learners to rotate tables each day. Although learners are taught within a group, GGR is meant to address each learner's individual needs.

AI tools like i-Ready can provide personalization even within the shared activity. The tool uses technology for generating adaptive texts. "Unlike traditional static texts, adaptive texts are highly flexible, able to adjust in real-time according to the student's evolving learning state, ensuring that the difficulty, depth, and breadth of the content remain synchronized with the learner's current capabilities" (He, 2024, p. 47). The adaptive text system allows for personalized reading pathways by delivering text in formats preferred by learners, whether visual or auditory (He, 2024). Even the allocation of learners to groups according to their needs can be more accurately done by AI tools than by the human teacher. The tracking of progress helps to wean learners from specific groups. My review of literature failed to yield a study that explicitly, comprehensively, and empirically examines the efficacy of AI tools in Group Guided Reading (GGR). The limitations of AI tools are in the facilitation of the interaction that is implicit in the term 'Group' for GGR, and in fully understanding group dynamics and mood, best inferred from the physical group interactions only a physical teacher has access to. The GGR is as good as the richness of the discussions among group members and the complexity of the ideas, questions, thinking, and discourse that ensues. While AI tools need to be applauded for the way they match the text, and sometimes simplify the text in accordance with learner proficiency, that may end up in oversimplification that robs texts of their depth and authenticity. The teacher needs to scaffold the text that is sufficiently challenging to spur progress rather than have learners read at their independent reading level always. The physical teacher can also adapt their reading plan to align it with learner responses and interests, but AI tools follow a preset plan. Teacher presence and input is invaluable when harnessing AI's power in reading instruction and assessment.

Independent Reading

For independent reading, the AI and the traditional approaches converge in that in both, learners self-select and read texts at their pace frequently and for significant durations. In the traditional approach, learners self-select texts at their independent reading levels, read at their own pace, while the teacher conducts minilessons and short personalized conferences with learners to promote further thinking. The conferences provide the teacher an opportunity to advise on strategic actions. Apart from modelling independent reading behaviors, the teacher creates literacy-rich environments with relevant books (relevant to learners' proficiency level and interests), and thoughtfully develops a classroom conducive to the development of independent reading. This entails the comfort and lighting, quiet zones, accessibility to texts, and workstations that promote love for reading. Reading logs or interest surveys can be used to track learner progress and encourage learners to set and track goals.

AI tools like Raz-Kids utilize algorithms to recommend personalized texts to learners aligned to their personal interests, proficiency levels, and learning/ reading pace. While conferences in the traditional classroom can help ensure that learners do not inflate the texts read, AI tools like Reading Plus can accurately track books or even pages read and even give badges or rewards for attaining some milestones. The AI tools can enhance engagement in the reading through quizzes and games.

Hidayat (2024) explored the efficacy of an AI-individualized reading tool on reading comprehension using randomized experimental and control groups for eight weeks. Findings showed more significant improvement in reading comprehension in the experimental group than the control group. Despite independent reading being a solitary enterprise by its nature, a human teacher can guide reflection and deepen comprehension. The learner can read iteratively than reading from an AI tool where reading must follow a strict pattern. Learners can do well in AI generated post-reading quizzes when they have not clearly understood the texts read. Most AI limitations can be mitigated by using them in conjunction with the teacher's guidance.

THE DOWNSIDES OF AI TOOLS IN READING INSTRUCTION AND ASSESSMENT

The potential downsides of AI in reading instruction and assessment include issues of human interaction (or lack of it), accessibility, equity, content quality, privacy, uncertain role of the teacher, and over-reliance on technology.

Effective teaching and learning thrives on the quality of human interactions and the emotional support that comes with such interaction. AI tools lack the capacity to provide social and emotional support and can neither detect nuanced learner emotions, nor empathize with them. The social interaction implicit in literacy activities like shared reading and group guided reading are compromised as AI tools are big on personalization and very little on collaboration and social learning. The automated feedback provided by the AI tools "...cannot provide that sense of community and emotional support" (Binu, 2024, p. 40) rendering them impersonal and demotivating. That explains why AI cannot forge meaningful relationships with learners.

There is also the risk of AI tools aggravating the digital divide (Binu, 2024) by further disadvantaging those with no access to uninterrupted internet services and devices for AI use. Access can further be compromised through a language and cultural barrier where non-English literate users may not find tools in their language or where tools are based on irrelevant western realities. Karatzas and Zogopoulos (2024) advise critically considering the nature of AI tool and the context to ensure that it does not marginalize others.

AI tools often disaggregate language into isolated elements be they language rules or lists of vocabulary, robbing learners of opportunities to visualize language in holistic, integrated, and communicative ways needed for them to use language in context-rich communicative settings (Mohebb, 2025).

Another downside of AI is more in the user than the AI itself and relates to the over-reliance on technology that dehumanises teaching and learning, degrading it to a transactional, mechanical exercise that deskills the teachers. Both teacher and learners forego the rich interactions and critical reflective engagements. It diminishes learners' capacity to think critically creatively, and independently through problem-solving, and critical cognitive higher order processes like analysis, synthesis, and evaluation critical for deep learning are bypassed (Mohebb, 2025). The assessment of complex ways of learner understanding may be missed if the AI tools are not used in conjunction with the human teacher observations. Where the teacher is not creative enough to recognize their role in AI-powered classrooms, their role is greatly diminished and compromised.

The strength of AI tools' collection of voluminous and sensitive learner data (be it reading habits, preferences, progress, behaviors, etc) to personalize feedback and interventions may "...pose serious ethical challenges to data privacy" Binu (2024, p. 34) especially considering the "...absence of a regulatory framework for integrating AI applications into education" (p. 38). The data collected can almost amount to unconsented to surveillance. Again, the teacher is the one who can make decisions about the ethical use of the AI tools and their limited or non-invasiveness.

Far from some people's assumption of AI tools being infallible owing to their sophistication, AI tools are subject to errors or misinterpretations of learners' complex reading performance. The tools use patterns and not nuanced understanding of learners or contextual features like telling when a learner is being ironic. Failure to generate accurate data may then lead to corresponding inaccurate feedback and unwarranted interventions. The failure to pick on the nuanced and idiosyncratic features lead to proposing generic interventions where specific ones are needed. Solutions to these downsides require that the AI tools be used in conjunction with the human teacher.

AI's inflexible rule sets and predefined algorithms may mismatch learners' immediate and unique needs. AI tools cannot forge an emotional connection with learners, when relationships are foundational to any meaningful learning. AI tools cannot make decisions based on learner background or context but on algorithms and superficial data they generate. They make interventions oblivious to both classroom and group dynamics, and are incapable of intuitive responsive decisions. What the AI tools lack is what the human teacher supplies in a synergistic relationship.

NEED FOR SYNERGY BETWEEN THE TEACHER-LED AND AI SUPPORTED INSTRUCTION

To demonstrate the efficacy of AI tools in reading instruction several extant studies (e.g. Wei, 2023) have used the experimental method with the control group being teacher led and the experimental group being AI-assisted. While such studies are instructive, especially on the benefits of AI reading instruction, they present reading instruction in binary terms where it is either the teacher or the AI-powered tool offering instruction. A third group that combines teacher-led and AI-assisted instruction should be added to such experimental designs. The 'teacher-led and AI-assisted' designation I use is deliberate as I see the AI tools' roles as subservient to, dependent on, and supportive of the teacher's role. Even when the teacher relies on AI generated data to make instructional decisions, the teacher is the one who decides on their deployment and the purpose for that deployment. In essence, the teacher, not the AI tool, is the teacher, and the AI tool is the medium despite "making intelligent decisions akin to human decision-making" (Wei, 2023, p.3). The synergy and partnership between the human and the artificial should be evident.

Based on the discussion of how AI can complement teacher-led instruction across key building blocks of learning to read (phonemic awareness, phonics, fluency, vocabulary, and comprehension) within a balanced reading framework, it is important to demonstrate this theoretical discussion practically. The next section presents a practical two-week lessons outline covering all the building blocks of reading situated within the balanced reading framework of reading aloud, shared reading, group guided reading, and independent reading. The lessons outline seeks to show how AI tools can personalize reading and provide real-time feedback, while the teacher remains central in the instructional and assessment process. The aim is to present the AI tools and the teacher in their collaborative and mutually supportive roles.

PRACTICAL 10-DAY GRADE 3 READING LESSON OUTLINE

In the two-week (10-day) lesson outline for a Grade 3 reading block, I integrate phonemic awareness, phonics, fluency, vocabulary, and comprehension within the balanced reading framework (read aloud, shared reading, group guided reading, and independent reading). For each day I try to show how AI tools can complement the teacher's role synergistically. I use the South African Grade 3 English Home

Language curriculum for this exemplification. The lessons are based on the fable 'The Lion and the Mouse' accessible on https://read.gov/aesop/007.html I try to map the AI tools I made reference to in the discussion.

The Department of Basic Education Curriculum Assessment Policy Statement (CAPS) (2011, p. 9) structures the Grade 3 reading per week as collated in Table 1 below.

Table 1. Grade 3 CAPS reading time allocation

Reading component	**Time per day**	**Time per week**	**Mode**
Phonics	15 mins x 5 days	1h 15m	Whole class
Shared Reading/Writing	15 mins x 5 days	1h 15m	Whole class
Group Guided Reading	2 x 15 mins per day	2h 30m	Small groups
Independent Reading & Fluency Practice	Integrated flexibly	Ongoing	Individual

The reading lesson outline in Table 2 below attempts to consider the curriculum stipulations in Table 1 above.

Table 2. Condensed 10-day reading lesson outline

Day	Focus	Teacher role	AI tool role	Reading mode
1. Introduce fables and the story's context	Activating prior knowledge, introducing theme, and introducing key vocabulary	Says key words in the story and have learners identify their initial sound, uses flashcards and gestures, models blending letter sounds, reads aloud a picture book, explains key vocabulary	*Google Read Along* provides interactive read-aloud. *Memrise* introduces key vocabulary using visual/audio cues (digital flashcards and interactive voice recognition), provides spaced repetition. Teacher reviews learner progress and identifies words to emphasise during the read-aloud.	*Shared reading* Teacher reads aloud, learners join in on repeated and key words and phrases. Identify rhyming words, isolate initial and final sounds from key vocabulary This is to motivate learners and activate their background knowledge.
2. Character description using adjectives	Developing precise descriptive language, expanding vocabulary with synonyms and opposites	Models reading aloud, pauses to talk about character descriptions, lists physical and personality traits on a chart. Facilitates vocabulary brainstorming.	*Memrise or Quizlet provides* adjectives related to character traits, uses visuals and audio to reinforce vocabulary, uses spaced repetition games.	*Shared Reading:* Teacher reads the story again, pausing to highlight descriptive words (e.g., "a *big* lion"). Learners read along and identify adjectives.
3. Character traits of the lion and mouse	Developing fluency	Models expressive reading of a nonfiction text with an animal theme	*Fluency Tutor* provides learners opportunity to record their own reading. Teacher listens to the recordings, identifies learners' expression and/or pace challenges to for intervention.	*Read Aloud & Paired Fluency*: Teacher models reading, and learners reread in pairs and record themselves. Learners echo-read selected parts as a class.
4. Exploring character feelings and motivations	Infer characters' feelings and motivations from their actions	Facilitates emotional inference based on the text, uses emotion cards/ wheel and sentence stems to guide learner responses.	*Quizlet or TaleMate allows* learners to record retellings based on vocabulary introduced by the teacher, helps with feeling vocabulary	*Guided Reading* Small groups reread specific sections of the text. Teacher asks guiding questions.
5. The lesson or moral in fables	Cultural context; drawing inferences	Guides discussion based on the illustrations and dialogue; prompts learners to draw inferences	*iReadSmart* yields differentiated comprehension questions. Teacher uses learner answers to have a deep group discussion.	*Guided Reading.* Teacher leads small groups in reading levelled texts from *Raz-Kids*; learners draw inferences using text clues.

continued on following page

Table 2. Continued

Day	Focus	Teacher role	AI tool role	Reading mode
6. Dialogue and expressive reading	Reading dialogue with expression	Models reading with expression reading, highlights punctuation cues, provides feedback.	Learners self- record reading the lion's or mouse's lines on *Amira. Amira* provides playback, scores fluency (prosody & accuracy); gives feedback. Teacher uses scores for further coaching	*Shared Reading & Paired Practice.* Teacher and class practice reading the lion and mouse's lines with emotion; learners do role-play reading in pairs.
7. Sequencing and summarizing	Retelling story in correct order	Provides sequencing graphic organizers; models how to summarize a story using key details.	*i-Ready or Lalilo* Provides story structure or gives sequencing tasks at the right reading level, provides tailored practice which teacher uses to plan small group instruction.	*Group Guided Reading.* Teacher scaffolds summarising to small groups as other learners read independently on *Raz-Kids.*
8. Opinion writing: Was the lion brave or foolish?	Opinion and persuasive writing	Facilitates debate and helps learners plan writing	*TaleMate* makes learners draft oral stories or opinions first. Teacher transcribes and co-revises the written versions.	*Shared Reading & Independent writing.* Learners listen to each other's *TaleMate* stories before writing them down.
9. Review and reflect	Reinforcing vocabulary and fluency	Leads review games and re-reading parts of interest	*GraphoGame* reviews phonemes and blending. Teacher assigns activities based on past learner errors and listens to oral review.	*Shared Reading & Group Reading.* Teacher re-reads with learners key passages; learners take turns to lead the reading in small groups.
10. Comprehension and moral retelling	Monitor progress in fluency and comprehension	Administers oral reading/ comprehension checks	*Amira* conducts diagnostic oral reading. Teacher compares Amira data with class observations and i-Ready reading skill snapshots.	*Independent Reading.* Learners read texts assigned by AI. Teacher rotates and attends to one-on-one conferences.

I deliberately over-employed the AI tools just to demonstrate their use and synergy with the human teacher. In the real classroom, the teacher may not need to have an AI tool for every lesson. My attempt has been to show how the teacher does not relinquish his or her responsibilities but builds on AI affordances. Where AI tools provide data, the teacher acquaints himself or herself with that data to make further informed instructional or assessment decisions. Where the AI tools allow the learners to record themselves, the teacher listens to and makes sense of the recordings to better understand where learners need further emphasis or coaching. Where the AI tools test and score comprehension, the teacher decides targeted interventions informed by the incorrect or incomplete answers. Where the AI tool proposes leveled reading content, the teacher uses it to group learners for GGR. Where the AI tool helps with learners' storytelling, the teacher uses those drafts as a springboard for shared writing activities. In short, the AI tools merely redefine the role of the teacher and, where they are used, the teacher's responsibilities are greater, more intellectual, and less routine than in the traditional classroom. AI-powered tools support and enhance traditional teacher-led activities to increase personalization. The teacher, not the AI tool, provides the social-emotional support and the context within which learners reading skills develop holistically. Acknowledging the importance of a partnership between the human teacher and the AI tools in reading instruction, there is need to develop a framework to theorize such synergy.

NEED FOR A UNIFIED THEORETICAL FRAMEWORK FOR TEACHER-LED AI EMPOWERED READING INSTRUCTION

The synergy between AI enhanced and teacher-led instruction can only currently be inferred from disparate and fragmented theoretical lens such as sociocultural theory, constructivism, multiliteracies theory, and universal design for learning. There is need for an integrated theoretical framework that draws on these and other theories to inform teachers' design of meaningful, responsive reading instruction, informed by AI tools' capacity to extend and personalize instruction, automate low-level tasks, offer real-time feedback, and facilitate multimodal engagement. This fusion of human expertise and technological adaptability positions AI as a mediator of teacher-led reading instruction. In this section, I discuss, not the much-needed unified theoretical framework, but the disparate theoretical positions further studies can coalesce and converge into a unified framework. This synthesis of multiple theoretical frameworks seeks to inform the optimization of reading instruction and assessment through human-led teaching and AI practice in complementary ways.

Sociocultural Theory

Sociocultural theory is attributed to Vygotsky (1978) and posits that learning emanates from social interaction and the use of mediating tools to scaffold learning within a learner's 'Zone of Proximal Development (ZPD)'. Teachers, as the 'more knowledgeable other' (another of Vygotsky's term) have long been the sole experts in the scaffolding of instruction. The AI tools now complement the teacher's role through determining the learners' ZPD, and providing automated, individualized scaffolding, to extend the teacher's reach and mediate instruction. Reading under the sociocultural theory is not merely an individual cognitive skill but a socially constructed activity. Learners should engage in discussions, collaborative reading, and shared literacy experiences and the teacher comes in handy to create such social interaction activities.

Constructivism

The leading luminaries of constructivist theory are Piaget and Bruner, who see learning as stemming from exploration, interaction, and reflection. Allen (2022) cites Tomljenovic and Tatalovic Vorkapic (2020, p.1-2), who "contrast the "transmissive" or "traditional" approach to learning, which involves students passively receiving facts presented by their teacher, with "transformational" learning built on cognitivist and constructivist theories, which promote "the student's active participation through exploratory, problem-based learning" (p. 13)." AI-powered tools help with exploratory learning and facilitate learners' choice of appropriate level texts, provide immediate personalized feedback, and allow learners some measure of self-direction in meaning-making. In line with constructivist ideals, teachers further facilitate discussions, and employ intellectually engaging questioning and group reflections.

Multiliteracies Theory

The multiliteracies theory is credited to the New London Group (1996) and requires learners' exposure to literacy across multiple modalities be they text, audio, video, or interactive digital platforms. Hong and Tan (2020, p. 42) observe that under multiliteracies theory "... literacy pedagogy should embody the growing linguistic and cultural diversities of today's globalised world and reflect the new ways of textual interaction that have emerged due to new information and multimedia technologies." AI reading instruction and assessment tools use multimodal and diverse formats like animations, audio-visual models, voice modulation, among other modalities. The teacher then frames the multimodal experiences with critical relevant questions facilitative of deeper engagement, comprehension and reflection.

Universal Design for Learning (UDL)

Universal Design for Learning (UDL) also informs teacher-led and AI-supported reading instruction through its emphasis of the need for multiple means of engagement, representation, and expression. Dalton (2017, p. 17) defines UDL as "... a framework for designing instruction to address the wide range of learner variation in today's inclusive classrooms..." characterized by "... diverse, multiple, and accessible learning opportunities." It goes beyond the one-size-fits-all instruction targeted at the typical, average, regular, standard, and normal student, as such designations do not reflect the reality of classroom learner variability. Dalton (2017) identifies UDL as reflected in multiple means of representation, expression and engagement. AI tools align with UDL principles through tailoring reading levels to learners' proficiency levels, providing audio-visual support, and providing adaptive feedback while the teacher uses AI-generated data to foster inclusion, differentiation, and equity.

Cognitive Load Theory

Cognitive Load Theory by Sweller (1994) underscores the need to reduce the cognitive load of learners to optimize learning. Reading requires that several processes occur simultaneously, and that can strain learners' mental reserves. AI tools ease the load by automating repetitive, mundane, and low-level tasks to free learners' cognitive load so that sufficient cognitive reserves are channelled towards more demanding tasks. The teacher can then capitalize on the cognitive reserves made available to guide learners to higher-order thinking. The teacher is central to deciding what AI will deal with and what the teacher will deal with.

TPACK Framework

The Technological Pedagogical Content Knowledge (TPACK) framework posits the need for an intersection in three knowledges for effective instruction. These are content knowledge (the individual reading skills), pedagogical knowledge (how to teach reading), and technological knowledge (how to effectively incorporate AI tools effectively). Following the TPACK framework, AI tools should instruct and guide learners to a better and more robust understanding reading. Teachers are knowledgeable about the content and the pedagogy that they can make decisions about which AI tools are context sensitive and responsive for a particular task. The AI tools should be merged into teachers' pedagogically sound practices. The content, pedagogy, and technology should be so seamless that learning is enhanced and guaranteed.

What can be distilled from these frameworks is that AI enhances, extends, and enriches human interaction; that learners construct meaning through interactive, personalized engagement through the guidance of both AI and teachers; that while AI provides multimodal access to information, teachers encourage critical thinking and ensure and cultural relevance; that technology offers diverse ways of representing information and keeping learners involved, but teachers design inclusive lessons that are equity driven; that AI helps reduces the reading cognitive load, making focus on higher order thinking possible; that teachers help learners deepen their processing from the nature of interactions they facilitate; and that real synergy occurs when teachers make thoughtful, context sensitive decisions that combine AI tools with proven teaching practices. As Mohebb (2025, p.13) observes, "A balanced approach, where AI is used as a supplement to teacher-led learning, ensures that students benefit from technological innovation while still receiving the personalised attention and engagement that only human instructors can provide." For Kılıçkaya and Kic-Drgas (2025),

> *... AI should be implemented as an aid rather than a crutch, ensuring that learners remain active participants in the learning process rather than passive recipients of automated guidance. ... While AI can provide instant feedback and scaffold learning experiences, the irreplaceable human capacity for empathy, mentorship, and nuanced contextual understanding ensures that educators will continue to play a vital role in fostering intellectual and emotional growth. A well-designed hybrid learning model should integrate AI in ways that enhance, rather than diminish, the role of human teachers.*

CONCLUSION

This chapter demonstrated the richness that emanates from the synergy between AI tools and human teachers when both are utilized strategically and purposefully in reading instruction. The two-week lesson outline shows that AI is not an add-on to the human teacher's cocktail of pedagogical strategies, but an integrated scaffold the teacher actively designs instruction around, and judiciously responds to so as to best develop reading across all five pillars of reading development, and within the balanced reading framework. The synthesis of disparate theoretical positions further reinforced the potency of the teacher-led and AI-supported collaborative reading instruction, and how the collaboration fosters learner-centred design. The teacher retains a central role in reading instruction as AI-powered technology continues unabated. The time of traditional sole teacher-led instruction is past, and the teacher has an ally in AI that he or she can leverage to co-plan, co-teach, and co-assess, so that reading instruction and assessment draws on the strengths of the human and the artificial.

Recommendations

Seeing that AI cannot be wished away from the classroom, this chapter recommends ongoing training and professional development to enable teachers to understand, evaluate, and purposefully integrate AI tools in reading instruction. In the use of AI tools, focus should be on ensuring their use is embedded in curriculum goals and research based best practices. Care should be taken to ensure ethical use of AI tools, particularly with regard to learner data privacy. Future studies could explore the gains from AI–teacher synergy on reading instruction.

REFERENCES

Allen, A. (2022). An introduction to constructivism: Its theoretical roots and impact on contemporary education. *Journal of Learning Design and Leadership*, *1*(1), 1–11.

Binu, P. M. (2024). Affordances and challenges of integrating artificial intelligence into English language education: A critical analysis. *English Scholarship Beyond Borders, 10*(1), 34–51. https://esbbjournal.org/volume-10-issue-1-2024/

Bora, D., Patel, P., Psyridou, M., Ruotsalainen, J., Richardson, U., & Torppa, M. (2025). Foundational English literacy development in India: A randomised-control trial using phonics instruction and GraphoLearn. *Reading and Writing*, *38*(5), 1309–1335. DOI: 10.1007/s11145-024-10551-6

Chen, M., Zhang, Y., & Liu, X. (2021). AI-supported vocabulary learning in elementary school: Effects on vocabulary knowledge and reading comprehension. *Journal of Educational Computing Research*, *59*(3), 543–562. DOI: 10.1177/0735633120966558

Dalton, E. M. (2017). Beyond Universal Design for Learning: Guiding Principles to Reduce Barriers to Digital & Media Literacy Competence. *The Journal of Media Literacy Education*, *9*(2), 17–29. DOI: 10.23860/JMLE-2019-09-02-02

Duggan, S. (2020). *AI in education: Change at the speed of learning*. UNESCO Institute for Information Technologies in Education.

Ecochard, J. (2015). The role of adult support in educational games: Insights from Ecochard (2015). *Journal of Educational Technology*, *12*(3), 45–59. DOI: 10.1234/jet.2015.012345

He, X. (2024). Enhancing reading comprehension with AI-generated adaptive texts. *International Journal of New Developments in Education*, *6*(7), 46–52. DOI: 10.25236/IJNDE.2024.060708

Heil, C. R., Wu, J. S., Lee, J., & Schmidt, T. (2021). Exploring the impact of AI voice assistants on early childhood literacy development. *Computers & Education*, *167*, 104172. DOI: 10.1016/j.compedu.2021.104172

Hidayat, M. T. (2024). Effectiveness of AI-based personalised reading platforms in enhancing reading comprehension. *Journal of Learning for Development*, *11*(1), 117–124. https://jl4d.org/index.php/ejl4d/article/view/955

Hong, A. L., & Tan, K. H. (2020, November 1). A review of theories and practices of multiliteracies in classroom: Issues and trends. *International Journal of Learning. Teaching and Educational Research*, *19*(11), 41–52. DOI: 10.26803/ijlter.19.11.3

Jin, M. (2024). Leveraging artificial intelligence for enhanced English reading instruction in senior high school. *Academic Journal of Management and Social Sciences*, *7*(3), 29–32. DOI: 10.54097/pekwxc50

Karatzas, A., & Zogopoulos, K. (2024). Literacy and artificial intelligence: Applications and concerns. *IOSR Journal of Humanities and Social Science, 29*(9, Series 7), 12–23. https://doi.org/DOI: 10.9790/0837-2909071223

Kılıçkaya, F., & Kic-Drgas, J. S. (2025). The future of tutoring: AI as an augmenting force. *AI & Society*, *40*(4). Advance online publication. DOI: 10.1007/s00146-025-02356-0

Koh, J., Cowling, M., Jha, M., & Sim, K. N. (2023). The human teacher, the AI teacher and the AIed-teacher relationship. *Journal of Higher Education Theory and Practice*, *23*(17). Advance online publication. DOI: 10.33423/jhetp.v23i17.6543

Kurzeja, O., Flynn, S., Grindle, C. F., Sutherland, D., & Hastings, R. P. (2024). Teaching reading skills to individuals with autism and/or intellectual disabilities using computer-assisted instruction: A systematic review. *Review Journal of Autism and Developmental Disorders*. Advance online publication. DOI: 10.1007/s40489-024-00465-y

Li, H., & Tsai, C. C. (2020). The effectiveness of a chatbot-assisted vocabulary learning tool for young EFL learners. *Computers & Education*, *158*, 103983. DOI: 10.1016/j.compedu.2020.103983

McTigue, E. M., Solheim, O. J., Zimmer, W. K., & Uppstad, P. H. (2019). Critically reviewing GraphoGame across the world: Recommendations and cautions for research and implementation of computer-assisted instruction for word-reading acquisition. *Reading Research Quarterly*, *55*(4), 435–458. DOI: 10.1002/rrq.256

Mellard, D. F., & Johnson, E. (2008). *RTI: A practitioner's guide to implementing response to intervention*. Corwin Press.

Miller, R. T. (2019). *English Orthography and Reading*. The TESOL Encyclopedia of English Language Teaching.

New London Group. (1996). A pedagogy of multiliteracies: Designing social futures. *Harvard Educational Review*, *66*(1), 60–92.

Sun, H., Tam, J., & Lim, M. C. (2025). AI and early language learning: A scoping review. *AI. Brain and Child*, *1*(4). Advance online publication. DOI: 10.1007/s44436-025-00005-3

Sweller, J. (1994). Cognitive load theory, learning difficulty, and instructional design. *Learning and Instruction*, *4*(4), 295–312.

Vargas-Díaz, D., Kim, J., Karunaratna, S., Reinhardt, M., Hornburg, C., Choi, K., & Lee, S. W. (2024). *TaleMate: Exploring the use of voice agents for parent-child joint reading experiences*. arXiv. https://doi.org//arXiv.2405.13968DOI: 10.48550

Vygotsky, L. S. (1978). *Mind in society: The development of higher psychological processes*. Harvard University Press.

Wang, Y., Ong, Y. S., & Kankanhalli, A. (2020). Enhancing reading comprehension with AI-supported intelligent tutoring systems: A classroom study. *British Journal of Educational Technology*, *51*(6), 2150–2165. DOI: 10.1111/bjet.12999

Wei, L. (2023). Artificial intelligence in language instruction: Impact on English learning achievement, L2 motivation, and self-regulated learning. *Frontiers in Psychology*, *14*, 1261955. DOI: 10.3389/fpsyg.2023.1261955 PMID: 38023040

Chapter 8
Student Teacher Enhancement Program for Cross-Cultural Communication Skills Development Integrating Collaborative Learning With STEP Buddies +AI:
Student Teacher Enhancement Program (STEP)

Joseph Malaluan Velarde
https://orcid.org/0000-0003-0292-0129
Taylor's University, Malaysia

Vinothini Vasodavan
https://orcid.org/0000-0002-9672-5326
Taylor's University, Malaysia

ABSTRACT

The pedagogical use of artificial intelligence (AI) tools in the classroom has been the buzzword for educators since the popularization of generative AI, ChatGPT, in the early 2020's. However, behaviorists and pragmatists argue that technology is only a tool especially in developing communication skills, as it requires regular human interaction in a real setting. Hence, this paper presents STEP Buddies+AI

DOI: 10.4018/979-8-3373-3755-5.ch008

or Student Teacher Enhancement Program (STEP), a 5-week workshop series designed to improve cross-cultural communication skills of pre-service teachers by developing collaborative learning approaches with AI tools. As an action research, the conception of this program started with literature review and needs analysis. Before the implementation of the program, students underwent a diagnostics test (Pre-test) on cross-cultural communication. During the implementation, participants were interviewed, and documentary evidence was collected. After the implementation phase, students took the Post-Test and shared their reflective journal. The paired sample t-test analysis of the pre-test and post-test scores show a significant difference on their cross-cultural communication competencies. For the interviews and documentary evidence, the data analysed using ATLAS.ti rendered the following themes: cultural awareness development; cross-cultural communication techniques; benefits and challenges of using AI; and benefits and challenges of working in pairs. With the results of this study, developers of programs for student teachers and for the development of cross-cultural communication skills may propose the need to integrate a buddy system and AI tools in collaborative activities like Think-Pair-Share.

INTRODUCTION

For pre-service teachers in multicultural schools, cross-cultural communication skills are fundamental in delivering instruction and in promoting a conducive learning and working environment. Cultural biases and stereotypes are embedded in the mindset of any pre-service teacher due to their upbringing and environment, and if managed improperly, this could manifest negatively in miscommunication and misunderstanding (Shannon-Baker, 2020). Hence, cross-cultural communication skills development has been integrated in teacher education; however, it is noted that a theoretical approach in developing such skills should be coupled with a more practical and informal approach through co-curricular programs and activities (Jin, Cooper, & Golding, 2020). In response to this, we developed STEP Buddies+AI (Student Teacher Enhancement Program) as a co-curricular program designed to provide pre-service teachers from a private university in Malaysia opportunities to acquire and apply knowledge and skills in cross-cultural communication in a school setting.

STEP Buddies+AI is a five-week workshop series, which aims to develop students' cultural awareness, as well as cross-cultural communication competencies and character by employing a buddy system using the Think-Pair-Share learning strategy and by integrating generative artificial intelligence (AI), particularly ChatGPT. Following Deardoff's (2006) model of cross-cultural competency development, the topics and activities in STEP ensure to equip students with the knowledge and comprehension of cultural concepts and information (i.e., meaning of culture, identity, multiculturalism, etc.), skills (i.e., listening, observing, communicating, etc.), and attitudes (i.e., empathy, respect, etc.) through four 60-minute interactive sessions. In addition, students are encouraged to complete weekly asynchronous tasks (i.e., dialogues, presentation, self-reflection) on Google classroom for further practice. With the use of "Think Pair Share" As an effective strategy in developing communication skills (Apriyanti & Ayu, 2020), the students in this program were strategically paired to form their "STEP Buddies" so that they accomplish the synchronous and asynchronous tasks together (i.e., brainstorming, discussions, presentations, vlogs, etc.). Furthermore, students were given prompts on when and instructions on how to use AI in their brainstorming and planning for their synchronous and asynchronous tasks. Although several studies have noted the benefits of integrating technological tools, the use of AI tools such as ChatGPT in developing cross-cultural communication skills of pre-service teachers requires further exploration (Sehlaoui, 2001; Deng, Shen, & Chan, 2021).

Hence, this action research investigates the integration of a buddy system and generative AI tools could improve the cross-cultural communication skills of pre-service teachers. Especially in the context of the students of the private university in this study, preparing them as student teachers for their internship and as future teachers in schools require the development of essential soft skills, such as cross-cultural communication. Moreover, similar cases have been reported by other teacher-training institutions and other studies that call for further development of programs aimed at cross-cultural communication (Barrow, 2023; Shannon-Baker, 2020; Widati & Hayati, 2019). In line with this, although pair-learning and the use of AI have been identified as advantageous in separate studies, it is yet to be fully explained how the integration of these two strategies could be beneficial in the improvement of cross-cultural communication skills of pre-service teachers.

LITERATURE REVIEW

Cross Cultural Communication Competencies

Cross-cultural experiences are helpful in preparing pre-service teachers to work with diverse students in multicultural classroom teaching in private and international schools. As a result, as a future teacher, ST must develop the skills and knowledge necessary to adapt to various worldview, new cultural situations by gaining confidence, a better appreciation and respect for the differences of others and other cultures, and awareness, all of which are important professional skills that must be understood and applied in today's complex and changing world (Jin, Cooper &

Golding, 2016; Chinnappan, McKenzie & Fitzimmons, 2013). It was evidenced by a number of studies showing that ST are not well-prepared to integrate cross-cultural communication in the classroom (Choi, 2016; Widiati &Hayati, 2019; Nindya, Landa,Stephens, 2017; Nindya, Widiati &Khoiri, 2022). Most of the literature focuses on ST perspectives and growth during the international teaching practices however in this study looking at developing the ST skills and knowledge in cultural communication competencies even before the actual teaching practices take place in the school settings (Jin, Cooper & Golding, 2016).

According to Deardorff's model of cultural competence which has been widely accepted by scholars across various disciplines and specifically grounded in higher education emphasized knowledge, skills, and behaviors needed for ST to successfully interact in an intercultural setting (Deardorff, 2006; Barrow, 2023; Barnatt et. al, 2020). Deardorff identifies three types of cultural competence: knowledge and skills, as well as ST attitude toward comprehending and conceiving cross-cultural relationships with others (Barrow, 2023; Barnatt et. al, 2020). He conceptualizes that cultural understanding and positive attitudes towards all cultural groups serve as the foundation for other components (Landa & Stephens, 2017;Deardorff, 2006).

Some research discovered that ST who successfully connect with people from different cultures enhance cross-cultural communication with their students and have the power to influence teaching and learning approaches in the classroom (Barrow, 2023; Cushner, 2008 & Merryfield, 1997). To successfully prepare ST to be culturally responsive teachers,the STEP Buddies+AI enable ST to prepare them to become reflective practitioners.Such program could foster well-rounded classroom leaders who can teach diverse populations of students successfully

Figure 1. Deardorff's model of cultural competence: Adapted from (Deardorff, 2006;Barrow, 2023)

Integration of AI Tools in Teacher Training and Communication Skills Development

Studies have attempted to explain how technology could be incorporated into teaching. To effectively integrate technology into instruction, there is a need to have a good understanding of how technology can be incorporated together with pedagogy and content knowledge (Hughes, 2005; Margerum-Leys & Marx, 2002; Niess, 2005; Zhao, 2003). Mishra and Koehler (2006) proposed a technology pedagogical content knowledge (TPACK) as a body of knowledge that is required to integrate technology into teaching and to learn in a meaningful way as shown in

Figure 1.2. With this integration, TPACK serves as a set of knowledge in applying emerging technologies into supporting specific pedagogical strategies, with the aim of enhancing students learning in particular subject matter (Koehler & Mishra, 2008; Mishra & Koehler, 2006; Saudelli & Ciampa, 2016).

Figure 2. Technological Pedagogical Content Knowledge (TPCK) Framework. Reprinted from TPACK ORG, by Mishra & Koehler, 2006, from http://www.tpack .org/. Copyright 2012 by Mishra & Koehler. Reprinted with permission.

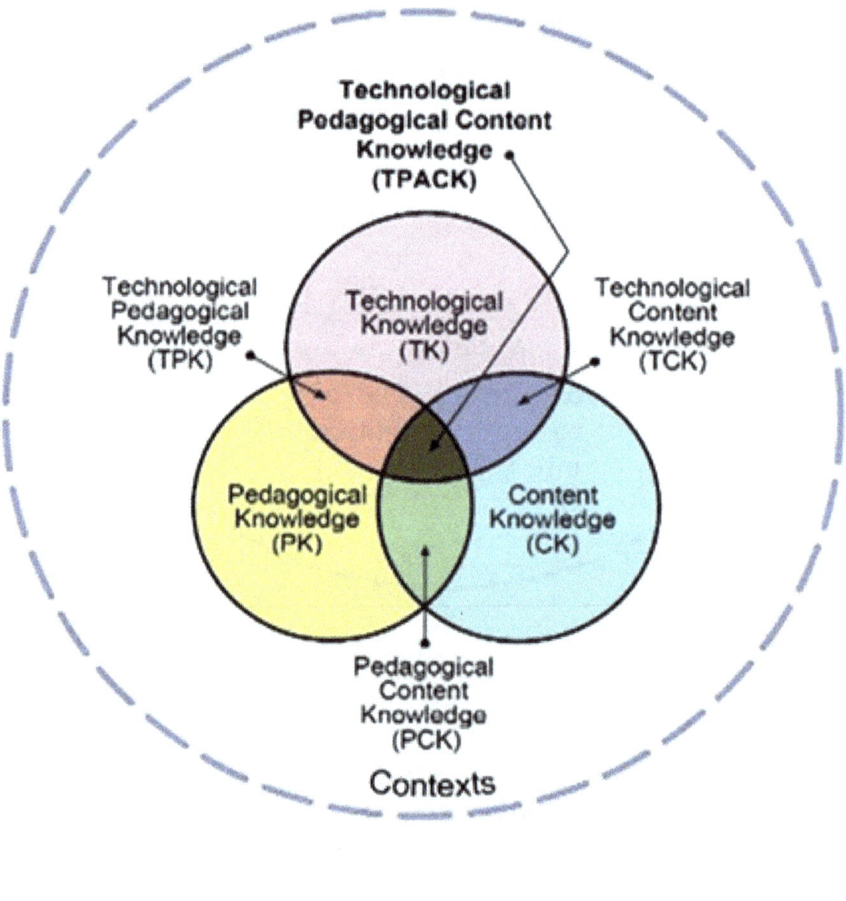

One of the emerging technologies supporting teaching and learning is artificial intelligence (AI), which is being used in education at a very rapid rate, and this is drastically altering the way that lessons are taught in classrooms, especially ChatGPT (Chat Generative Pre-trained Transformer) and other similar AI technologies (Zhang & Aslan, 2021, Zhang et.al, 2023). Some research seems to agree with the potential of AI in education to create fairness and equality for students, however some students indicate fears that AI might replace teachers in the classroom (Reiss, 2021; Zhang et.al, 2023). Major studies indicate that AI is mainly used for decision making on learning content, intervention plan, lesson planning and intervention (Celik et. al 2022;Tammets & Ley, 2023). However the use of AI such as ChatGPT on professional development, training, and support for ST remains limited in discussions. Therefore in this study ChatGPT was used in order to support ST in developing communication skills as this is vital skills ST need to acquire to build effective teacher-parent-student communication in the future (Kana, 2015).ChatGPT could provide a rapid and easy review of the essentials about a specific issue at the expense of a tolerable amount of inaccuracy (Menichetti et. al, 2023). In addition, ST could prompt ChatGPT to create roleplay scenarios, which could assist ST in practicing communication skills through Think-Pair Share.

Student-Teacher Development Programs

Student-teacher (ST) development programme focus on the ST longer-term goal of expansion of skills which can lead them to become good professionals who have the desire to grow and succeed as a long life endeavor (Richards,2015;Peña, 2020). In recent years, most of the ST development programme are focusing in developing ST pedagogy skills technical skills, fine arts or shape ST professional vision (Santos, 2019; Cheng & Zhao, 2023;Rosenbluh & Power, 2023; Khasawneh, 2023). In addition to that,communication skills are regarded as crucial, especially for ST, because they are at the center of the teaching and learning process and these skills are not easily demonstrated through resumes or teaching certificates and can only be evaluated by experts (Ağçam & Doğan, 2021). Many skills need to be improved to produce strong and quality ST. Among the skills identified are communication ability in English, as ST will be working in private and international schools where the medium of instruction is English. Communication skills are basic skills which are supposedly cultivated in education curricula because teachers with strong communication skills that create an interesting and entertaining learning environment will affect students' interest and conduct in learning (Naibaho, 2022). Furthermore, effective communication can assist teachers in implementing good ideas to help students enhance their social and emotional abilities (Naibaho, 2022). However, due to critical issues such as lacking language skills, not interpreting the messages accurately and appropriately have been some obstacles preventing ST from communicating with others and expressing themselves.(Kana, 2015; Naibaho, 2022). It is becoming more apparent that not all pre-service teacher training programs fully address the intricate requirements of communication skills that lead to failure in soft skills development (Ağçam&Doğan, 2021). The current ST development programs usually conducted in larger class sizes, being too academically focused, and insufficient period of training lead to failure in communication skills development (Ağçam&Doğan, 2021; Ngang & Chan, 2015). However, little research has focused on improving communication skills of ST development programs focusing on improving cross-cultural communication skills of ST by developing collaborative learning approaches with AI tools.

METHODOLOGY

In response to the call to improve the cross-cultural communication skills of student teachers in a private university in Malaysia, this action research follows the practical design (Creswell & Guetterman, 2019) and the dialectic action research spiral by Mills (2011). Following this action research framework, an area of focus in terms of addressing the need to improve student teachers' cross-cultural communication competencies was identified to develop STEP (Student-Teacher Enhancement Program) as an action plan. For the purpose of enquiring for the teacher-researchers in this study, the data collected and analyzed from the pre- and post-tests, interviews, and documents serve as reflection points in the discussion section to ensure that the student teachers in the university are better equipped with the skills they need prior to joining any academic institution for their practicum.

Sampling

The participants of STEP are composed of 103 first year Bachelor of Education students from a private university in Malaysia. A week before the start of the program, the students were given a briefing about the objectives, structure, and expectations of STEP as to how this program could help them improve their cross-cultural communication skills. All 103 students took the diagnostic test before the program began, while 71 took the post-test in the final week of the program. Hence, only 71 samples were considered for the pre- and post-test analysis.

Of the 71 students who took the pre- and post-tests, 16 students were purposefully selected to participate in interviews. These were the students who showed a significant improvement in their pre- and post-test scores, who were present in all sessions, and who submitted all the asynchronous tasks on Google Classroom.

Instrumentation and Data Collection

For having a baseline understanding of the students' cross-cultural competencies and to monitor students' outcomes at the end of this program, this action research employed pre and posttests to make direct comparisons in students' competencies. The cross-cultural competency test given to the students during the diagnostic and post tests were adapted from the Intercultural Knowledge and Competence Value test by the Association of American Colleges and Universities (2017). The test questions and procedures were validated by experts in sociolinguistics from the private university. The students are given three-five minutes to give a presentation in front of an audience based on culture-related prompts (i.e., Describe the culture of your country.). Before the diagnostic test (pre-test) on the orientation day (Week 0), the rubrics were explained to the students. For the post-test on the final week (Week 4), the students were reminded of the rubrics and were given the same amount of time with a similar range of questions.

To further shed light on the results of the pre- and post-tests, interviews were conducted with student participants. The interview questions were designed to enquire on the experiences and perceptions of the students on STEP and how this program enabled them to develop their cross-cultural communication competencies. For triangulation, documents were collected from the facilitators (i.e., STEP plan, slides, students' attendance) and from the students' notes and works submitted on Google Classroom (i.e., pair introduction, cultural presentation, reflective sharing, etc.).

Data Analysis

In analyzing the results from the pre and posttest, SPSS v19 was used to calculate for the mean, mean differences, and paired samples *t Test* following the assumptions of Pallant (2020). To further explain the test results and potential differences, the interviews and documents were organized and coded using ATLAS.ti for thematic analysis. The analysis of the results from the quantitative and qualitative data serves as reflection points in gauging the extent of effectiveness of STEP and in suggesting future actions in developing the cross-cultural communication skills of student teachers.

FINDINGS

The findings of this action research are divided into two sections. The first section presents the quantitative findings based on the comparison of the pre- and post-tests. In explaining the difference between the pre- and post-tests, the second section reports the experiences and views of the students who took part in the program to show the extent STEP has helped them improve their cross-cultural communication competencies.

Quantitative Results: Pre- and Post-Test

As shown in Table 1, the results show positive differences in the mean scores of the pre- and post-test of all the subscales of Cross-cultural Communication Competency Assessment. The paired samples *T*-test rendered *P-values of <0.005,* which indicate significant differences in the subscales Cultural Awareness, Empathy & Openness, and Verbal & Nonverbal Communication. Hence, it could be inferred that the four-week STEP initiative has a positive effect on the development of the cross-cultural communication competencies of student teachers from this private university.

Table 1. Pre- and Post-test Results of the Cross-cultural Communication Competency Assessment

Variables	Pre-test Mean	Post-test Mean	Mean Differences	T-value
Knowledge of cultural worldviews	2.58	3.16	0.58	2.96
Cultural Self-awareness	2.55	3.03	0.48	0.0007
Empathy & Openness	2.34	2.81	0.47	0.002
Verbal & Non-verbal Communication	2.37	2.85	0.48	0.001
TOTAL	9.84	11.85	2.01	0.000125

Qualitative Results: Experiences and Perspectives of Student Teachers on the Development of their Cross-cultural Communication Competencies in STEP

Throughout the four-week program, the students were involved in interactive activities and pair tasks that enabled them to develop their cross-cultural communication skills. The sessions and tasks also directed them to make use of technological tools, especially Artificial Intelligence (AI) platforms such as ChatGPT. As shown in the results of the pre- and post-tests, there has been a marked improvement in the cultural awareness, empathy and openness, and communication skills of the students, and the students shared their experiences and perspectives to explain this improvement. The interviews with the student participants of the STEP workshops, as well as the documents collected (i.e., reflections, journals, tasks) rendered the following themes: cultural awareness development; cross-cultural communication techniques; benefits and challenges of using AI; and, benefits and challenges of working in pairs.

Cultural awareness development

In developing their cultural awareness through STEP, the student participants reported how the sessions allowed them to understand their own identities, personalities, strengths, and weaknesses. One of the students noted:

"This is a great opportunity for me to understand my strengths and weaknesses. It would be through the process of learning ourselves and knowing our strengths and how we can use it to our best advantage." (9:4 p 3 in STEP Interview_S9)

Aside from understanding oneself, some students highlighted that they were able to get a deeper understanding of others' cultures. Considering that most of the participants of this program were from China, some of them shared that being able to study in Malaysia and interact with Malaysian students and those from other countries gave them new perspectives of culture outside of China. One of the students from China remarked:

"Dr V explained very well so I know about the culture. Besides, the group task about culture has also helped me a lot in knowing the culture. I can say that this programme created opportunities for us to know more people from other countries . In the past four weeks, we learned how to use appropriate language as a student teacher in multicultural schools. We also learned how to adapt in different cultural settings. I think it have the section where we introduce our buddies' culture which help me to introduce to some others culture that really interesting and unique which also I know that we should accept the diverse culture in the worlds and having diversity and inclusion, it's really important for a multicultural school especially we have to respect on them ." (1:6 p 4 in STEP Interview_S1)

Because of their awareness of their own culture and others through STEP, the student teachers were able to develop respect towards others' cultures and gain the mindset of adapting to different cultural settings, as reported by one participant:

"STEP taught us a lot about respecting different cultures and being more confident in ourselves. The learning experience was not bad at all because we made new friends which is from other countries, know more about the good teaching method and the way to improve myself, feel grateful on the opportunity to learn the useful information which can benefit me and develop my critical thinking skill, and also help me to build my confidence and adapt in any situation by learning how to diversify my approaches in communicating to others and seeking to cope with my inability to express myself thoroughly." (16:6 p 4 in STEP Interview_S16)

From the journals and reflective tasks submitted by the students, students shared their newly acquired knowledge and perspectives on culture. Likewise, in their presentations, the students were also able to integrate cultural ideas when they explain their personal experiences or share their thoughts on a particular topic.

Cross-cultural communication techniques

Aside from developing their cultural awareness, the student teachers also shared ways STEP helped them develop their communication skills in a cross-cultural situation. Most of the students interviewed highlighted how the STEP sessions allowed them to build their confidence especially when communicating with other people from different cultures or when they are asked to speak in front of an audience. One interviewee shared:

"STEP helped me to improve my communication skills by giving me the opportunities to talk in front of the class with any fears as no answer is right or wrong. It makes me more confident in communicating. I speak more bravely and confidently on the stage and will not care about other people's eyes because of the cross-cultural communication techniques I learnt here. Now, I am more confident in speaking in front of other people in a classroom setting." (1:1 p 3 in STEP Interview_S1)

The students acknowledged that this confidence stemmed from the number of activities they had to do in and out of the STEP classroom. The interaction they had with their "buddies" and with the other students in the classroom through the brainstorming and speaking activities made them more confident in communicating with each other, as shared by one of the interviewees:

"Through STEP, I learned about the teacher's expression about 101 teacher talk, some helpful words and methods of communication with others.. STEP requires us to do a new task with our peers and it helps us communicate with others and provides an opportunity to practice how to communicate effectively with people. By the weekly tasks, we are needed to work with the pair assigned. This is where I need to step out of my own zone to communicate and work together with my pair. Additionally, the tasks that Dr T requires us to prepare and speak in front of the class during every session meant a lot as this would lead us to think as well as arrange our words in order to present what we want to share." (4:4 p 4 in STEP Interview_S4)

STEP did not only develop cross-cultural communication skills of the students but also their organization and presentation skills. Some students expressed how their facilitators reminded them of organizing their ideas before speaking for clarity in communicating with others and in presenting in front of the class. Tips were also given to the students before the task to ensure that they could be able to structure their ideas well, which was further explained by one student:

"The constant need to speak up in front definitely helped me formulate my thoughts better and able to talk smoother than before. Because of the guidance of my facilitator and also the activities, I speak more clearer and I also slow

down when I speak so people can understand me because I know speak with more sense and order." (9:2 p 3 in STEP Interview_S9)

The videos submitted by the students on Google Classroom showed how most of them were able to follow the guidelines or cross-cultural communication techniques provided by their facilitators in terms of structuring their ideas and communicating their thoughts. Students also produced notes and outlines to show how they brainstormed and organized their ideas prior to delivering their presentation tasks.

Benefits and challenges of using AI

Following the theories and frameworks in technology integration in instruction, STEP systematically integrated the use of technological tools, especially artificial intelligence generative tools such as Chat GPT throughout the sessions. Based on slides obtained from the facilitators, students were instructed and encouraged to use ChatGPT during the brainstorming and discussion activities where students are asked questions and may refer to online tools to extend or verify their understanding. Hence, this comes with some benefits for the student in terms of making research more convenient for them and for giving them bitesize information they can use in their tasks. One of the students shared:

"The AI or tech tools helped us in all our tasks. For example, the first task given was to learn the 101 teacher talk which AI was implied in the slides, leading us to the right way to pronounce and practice expressions. Using AI or tech tools such as ChatGPT makes it easier to find things that we do not understand. Also, it helps synthesize information for our analysis." 5:4 p 4 in STEP Interview_S5 (14:7 p 4 in STEP Interview_S14)

On the other hand, one of the challenges of allowing students to use ChatGPT during the sessions would be over-reliance on the tool, especially in generating ideas. Although the use of ChatGPT in STEP is in a controlled manner, this should still be done in moderation as described by a student teacher:

"I think I can learn more information, but I still need to rely on myself. I think we should use artificial intelligence tools in moderation, but more of it requires us to think and summarize ourselves. Sometimes we are tempted to just follow everything and use everything from it. I appreciate that our facilitators tell us only when to use it and when not to. But I think some of my classmates are tempted to use it all the time and get all their ideas from it without consideration, which could look like plagiarism." (13:7 p 4 in STEP Interview_S13)

Benefits and challenges of working in pairs

Another critical aspect of the STEP sessions is the implementation of the buddy system through the adaptation of Think-Pair-Share structure in all the sessions, as well as in accomplishing asynchronous tasks. Evidently, students felt that through this buddy system and the Think-Pair-Share system, they were able to know the content and other students better based on an interview with one student teacher:

"The pair activities and tasks have given me a better understanding of how to be a better teacher. The interaction process with my buddy is pleasant, because I can share a lot of ideas and learn from other people's experiences. Also, it allowed me to get to know my buddy better and make friends with them, while completing the given tasks." (8:4 p 3 in STEP Interview_S8)

Because of the buddy system and the activities in the Think-Pair-Share, the students reported that they had more opportunities to talk during the workshop session. As the session is only for an hour, the students are given 40 minutes to engage with each other through guided activities and discussion points. One student relayed:

"STEP really provides a lot of opportunities for us to talk and just share our thoughts in-front of people which we rarely have the opportunity to practice in our own life. We don't feel like a very formal class to attend. It's more learner centered and lets us interact with people." (11:4 p 3 in STEP Interview_S11)

Another interviewee shared:

"At first, I was reluctant to join the programme as it was just an extra class. The reason to feel that is because I was not aware of the purpose of having this programme. Yet, throughout the sessions I joined in the past few weeks, I have understood the purpose of this programme and started to actively participate in it. It is a very student-centered learning approach as Dr. T gave all students the most opportunity to stand out and share their opinions with the help of our buddies. Nevertheless, my buddy would help me out if Ido not have any ideas and encourage me to speak." (14:9 p 4 in STEP Interview_S14)

On the other hand, time constraint was also considered as a challenge in doing pair work in a 60-minute session. A lot of the students interviewed mentioned the need for more time especially when they are engaged in discussion with their partner. An interviewee explained:

"I think that 1 hour is too short. If we have longer time in the class, then we may have time to discuss our task in the class directly as our peers are from different specialties. We have different classes which make us have a hard time deciding on a time that both of us are okay with. I think more interactions and activities can be increased, and more time, because an hour is too short for many people to share more ideas." (1:5 p 4 in STEP Interview_S1)

Another issue highlighted was the lack of participation or motivation of some students due to language barrier and attitude towards learning. Since this is a buddy system, the success of the pair relies on shared contributions and attitudes. One student reported:

"The classes are good but not all of us contribute to the session, which makes it a bit awkward. Honestly, maybe this programme would be much more enjoyable if it wasn't our task to teach others English. I personally believe that we should be equal before we came to University, thus I'm going to mention how in the requirements, we need to be fluent in English reading/writing/speaking. So, having to use our time teaching basic English when we could have done assignments does feel somewhat heavy on us. This is not a rant about hating to teach, rather I believe many of us prefer equality, and many would agree with me. Other than that, the class may be effective to some of my peers who aren't fluent in English because they got the chance to practice more. As a mentor, it is quite overwhelming to guide our mentees as we ourselves are struggling to cope with ourselves and the work at hand.

(9:5 p 4 in STEP Interview_S9)

Overall, most of the asynchronous tasks submitted on Google classroom showed collaborative efforts of the buddies. Since the tasks are designed to be completed by students in pairs, the output (i.e., dialogues, cultural presentation, reflective sharing) reflected the contributions of the students in pairs.

DISCUSSION

The overall findings from this study reveal that there are sIgnificant difference in cross cultural competencies as per pre and post test for students who took the STEP Buddies+AI from the aspect of cultural awareness development; cross-cultural communication techniques; benefits and challenges of using AI; and, benefits and challenges of working in pairs. This is in line with the study conducted by Jin et al. (2016) and Kana (2015) that the ability of pre-service teachers to adapt to new cultural situations and to teach using different approaches such as AI in this context of study are important professional skills that they need to understand and be able to enact in today's complex and changing world. To present the discussion, we have organized it into four specific themes:

Theme 1. STEP provided opportunities for cultural awareness development

Effective cross-cultural communication is crucial for pre-service teachers as to be able to see things from another person's point of view and comprehend diverse cultures. In line with this, STEP provided the opportunity for ST to develop cultural awareness. To achieve authentic cross-cultural communication, STEP used two methods: learning with AI and Buddy System. The findings also in line with Jin et al. (2016) that ST broadened their global perspectives and ideas of global citizenship between two different countries as part of mutual benefits of cross-cultural teacher education professional experiences. Furthermore, the results of STEP showed that each the student teachers' path toward developing cultural awareness is distinct, and that as they engage in various cross-cultural exchanges, they do so with the ability and perspective to interact, communicate, and understand many cultural contexts (Barrow, 2023; Deardorff, 2006). ST must understand how their attitudes, emotional responses, and empathy can impact their relationships with future students eventually affecting their success or failure. Therefore Integrating cultural awareness into STEP fosters social consciousness, understanding of the relationship between teaching and social equity, and equips pre-service teachers to be change agents and advocates for social equity (Siwatu & Starker, 2010; Landa & Stephens, 2017)

Theme 2. STEP enabled students to improve their cross-cultural communication techniques

Student teachers needs STEP to help them develop cross-cultural communication skills, particularly in confidence building, to provide them an international viewpoint and to empower them to engage students in learning effectively in multicultural classroom environments. This findings also supported by several study that pre-service teachers likely to benefit from acquiring skills and knowledge of cross cultural communication such being more flexibility, tolerance, patience, self-confidence, self-criticism, politeness, independence and ability to adapt in a different culture (Chinnappan, McKenzie & Fitzsimmons, 2013; Willard-Holt, 2001; Jin et.al., 2016). During STEP sessions, students gain confidence in speaking with peers from diverse cultural backgrounds and in front of class, demonstrating their strong desire to engage with their peers from various cultural backgrounds. Despite their strong desire to engage with individuals from diverse cultural backgrounds, ST frequently exhibit low self-confidence, as seen by their actions. (Ang & Van Dyne, 2015; Barnatt et al., 2020). In the future, pre-service teachers may need to use several techniques including managing cross-cultural conflict, communicating with peers in an effective manner, being aware of the beliefs, values, and communication styles of diverse cultures, and being aware of potential barriers to cross-cultural communication to build successful professional relationships across cultures (Tseng, 2017; Catana, 2014). Not only that, instructors also witnessed increased cross-cultural communication when students were able to work collaboratively, give constructive feedback, use technology more effectively, and deliver professional presentations (Vozza, 2014; Tseng, 2017).

Theme 3. Benefits and challenges of using AI

AI is used in education in different ways. For instance, AI is integrated into STEP as chatbots called ChatGPT to support students' learning by engaging to answer their questions, and keep them motivated in learning (Trust & Whalen, 2013). ChatGPT can immediately detect areas where students are suffering and provide further assistance to help them overcome these obstacles. This rapid feedback can help learners stay motivated and engaged throughout their learning journey (Rueda et al., 2023; Trust & Whalen, 2013. ChatGPT can also be used as a "teachable agent," encouraging students to learn by teaching it a topic via text-based interaction (Tate et al., 2023, p. 11). In order to do so, pre-service teachers need to have the skills and knowledge of asking the right questions. This is where ChatGPT enabled STEP participants to improve their reading comprehension skills, writing skills, language skills as ChatGPT can seemingly write anything however it does have limitations as it was trained on data pulled from the Internet prior to 2021(Kasneci et al., 2023;OpenAI, n.d.).In addition, ChatGPT can be misused in various ways, including as copying an author's material, spreading misinformation, or creating damaging or prejudiced content. ChatGPT, an advanced chatbot with a vast language model, can produce text that is nearly identical to human language.

Theme 4. Benefits and challenges of working in in Buddy System (I changed this from peer)

A buddy system pairs students in the classroom and asks them to help each other with certain tasks or skills. Buddy systems are proven to improve student performance because student teachers could comprehend and grasping relatively complex subjects among numerous persons, who then exchange their expertise in their own language (Roychowdhury et. al, 2020; Brame & Biel, 2015). Compared to other teaching and learning methods, buddy systems have the advantage of having a large potential to foster critical reflection, collaborative learning can be an effective tool for creating knowledge jointly, and they can foster critical thinking and "deep" learning as opposed to rote learning (Cranfield, 2016; Hakkarainen et al.2013).Additionally, by using this buddy system, students were able to view their communication assignment from a different angle, which was very helpful to them because their buddy could be patient and helpful in starting conversations and giving information thus developing a sense of belonging. (Cruz & Kwinta, 2013; Naidooi, Bylesii & Kwenaite, 2021). The buddy method did, however, have certain drawbacks. For example, when companions were unresponsive, unable to focus on the assigned activity, or exerted little effort, it implied that pre-service teachers were not motivated to participate in group task (Naidooi, Bylesii & Kwenaite, 2021; Roychowdhury et. al, 2020).

CONCLUSION

The implementation of STEP Buddies+AI and the results of this action research led to the conclusion that a structured workshop series integrating pair learning and the use of technological tools could improve the cross-cultural communication skills of pre-service teachers. This could be explained by the opportunities in the program in which students can develop their cultural awareness and acquire cross-cultural communication skills. Despite the challenges of working in pairs like inadequate participation and unequal commitment, the students in this program shared how this buddy system enabled them to know each other better and practice more together. Similarly in the use of AI, the benefits outweigh the consequences as the students felt that using ChatGPT made it easier for them to brainstorm and synthesize ideas for their tasks. Thus, as a point for reflection, pre-service teachers can maximize their learning experience in a cross-cultural communication skills development program if they are strategically paired up and if the use of AI is regulated.

As this action research was designed for pre-service teachers from a private university in Malaysia, questions of transferability may arise. Aside from the targeted setting and population of this study, the restricting nature of action research contributes to this concern. Hence, it would be of great interest to further examine and explore the potentials of integrating a buddy system and AI use in developing cross-cultural communication skills of pre-service teachers in a different setting, such as government institutions. Furthermore, conducting a larger scale quantitative research or a rigorous qualitative study could render more reliable or credible results on the effectiveness of such programs. Despite these limitations, future cross-cultural communication skills development programs for pre-service teachers can still be patterned after STEP Buddies+AI to further test its applicability in various settings.

REFERENCES

Ağçam, R., & Doğan, A. (2021). A Study on The Soft Skills of Pre-Service Teachers. *International Journal of Progressive Education, 17*(4), 35–48. DOI: 10.29329/ijpe.2021.366.3

Ang, S., & Van Dyne, L. (2015). *Handbook of cultural intelligence*. Routledge.

Apriyanti, D., & Ayu, M. (2020). Think-Pair-Share: Engaging Students in Speaking Activities in Classroom. *Journal of English Language Teaching and Learning, 1*(1), 13–19.

Association of American Colleges and Universities (2017). Intercultural Knowledge and Competence Value Rubric.

Barnatt, J., Andries D'Souza, L., Gleeson, A. M., Mitchell Viesca, K., & Wery, J. (2020). Intercultural Competence in Pre-Service Teacher Candidates. *International Journal of Educational Reform, 29*(3), 211–235. DOI: 10.1177/1056787919896866

Barrow, E. C. (2023). Defining intercultural competence: How four pre-service teachers developed a more complex understanding of ICC. *Journal of Global Education and Research, 7*(1), 1–17. https://www.doi.org/10.5038/2577-509X.7.1.1210

Brame, & Biel. (2015). *CFT HOME PAGE*. Vanderbilt University. http://cft.vanderbilt.edu/

Catana, S. E. (2014). Teaching Cross-cultural Communication Issues – A Way of Successfully Integrating into the Multicultural Knowledge Society. *Procedia: Social and Behavioral Sciences, 128*, 343–348. DOI: 10.1016/j.sbspro.2014.03.168

Celik, I., Dindar, M., Muukkonen, H., & Järvelä, S. (2022). The Promises and Challenges of Artificial Intelligence for Teachers: a Systematic Review of Research. *TechTrends, 66*(4). Springer. https://doi.org/DOI: 10.1007/s11528-022-00715-y

Cheng, C., & Zhao, J. (2023). The impact of professional learning communities on pre-service teachers' professional commitment. *Frontiers in Psychology, 14*, 1153016. DOI: 10.3389/fpsyg.2023.1153016 PMID: 37448713

Chinnappan, M., McKenzie, B., & Fitzsimmons, P. (2013). Pre-service teachers' attitudes towards overseas professional experience: Implications for professional practice. *The Australian Journal of Teacher Education, 38*(12), 36–53. DOI: 10.14221/ajte.2013v38n12.5

Cranfield, S. (2016) Enhancing Teaching Practice in Higher Education (Chapter 3), Sage, London – Edited by Pokorny, H & Warren, D.

Creswell, J. W., & Guetterman, T. C. (2019). *Educational research: Planning, conducting, and evaluating quantitative and Qualitative Research* (6th ed.). Pearson.

Cruz, M., & Kwinta, A. (2013). "Buddy System": A Pedagogical Innovation to Promote Online Interaction. *Profile Issues in Teachers'. Professional Development (Philadelphia, Pa.), 15*(1), 207–221.

Cushner, K. (2008). International socialization of young people: Obstacles and opportunities. *International Journal of Intercultural Relations, 32*(2), 164–173. DOI: 10.1016/j.ijintrel.2007.09.004

Deardorff, D. K. (2006). Identification and assessment of intercultural competence as student outcome of internationalization. *Journal of Studies in International Education, 10*(3), 241–266. DOI: 10.1177/1028315306287002

Deng, L., Shen, Y. W., & Chan, J. W. (2021). Supporting cross-cultural pedagogy with online tools: Pedagogical design and student perceptions. *TechTrends, 65*, 760–770.

Hakkarainen, K., Paavola, S., Kangas, K., & Seitamaa-Hakkarainen, P. (2013). Sociocultural perspectives on collaborative learning: Toward collaborative knowledge creation. In C. E. Hmelo-Silver, C.A. Chinn, C. K. K. Chan & A. M. O"Donnell (Eds.), *The international handbook of collaborative learning* (57-73). New York, NY: Routledge/Taylor & Francis.

Hughes, J. (2005). The role of teacher knowledge and learning experiences in forming technology- integrated pedagogy. *Journal of Technology and Teacher Education, 13*(2), 277–302.

Jin, A., Cooper, M., & Golding, B. (2016). Cross-Cultural Communication in Teacher Education. *The Australian Journal of Teacher Education, 41*(6). Advance online publication. DOI: 10.14221/ajte.2016v41n6.2

Kairit Tammets, & Ley, T. (2023). Integrating AI tools in teacher professional learning: A conceptual model and illustrative case. *Frontiers in Artificial Intelligence, 6*. Advance online publication. DOI: 10.3389/frai.2023.1255089 PMID: 38130325

Kana, F. (2015). Investigation of Pre-service Teachers' Communication Skills. *International Journal of Educational Research, 6*(3). https://eric.ed.gov/?id=ED571507

Kasneci, E., Seßler, K., Küchemann, S., Bannert, M., Dementieva, D., Fischer, F., Gasser, U., Groh, G., Günnemann, S., Hüllermeier, E., Krusche, S., Kutyniok, G., Michaeli, T., Nerdel, C., Pfeffer, J., Poquet, O., Sailer, M., Schmidt, A., Seidel, T., & Stadler, M. (2023). ChatGPT for Good? On Opportunities and Challenges of Large Language Models for Education. *Chatgpt for Good? On Opportunities and Challenges of Large Language Models for Education*. https://doi.org/DOI: 10.35542/osf.io/5er8f

Khasawneh. (2023). An Investigation of Pre-Service Teacher Preparation Programs in Teacher Education and Co-Teaching Models. *Information Sciences Letters (Online), 12*(7), 2849–2857. https://doi.org/DOI: 10.18576/isl/120714

Koehler, M., & Mishra, P. (2008). Introducing TPCK. In AACTE Committee on Innovation and Technology (Ed.) (Ed.), *Handbook oftechnological pedagogical content knowledge (TPCK) for educator* (pp. 3–29). New York, NY: Routledge.

Landa, M. S., & Stephens, G. (2017). Promoting Cultural Competence in Preservice Teacher Education through Children's Literature: An Exemplary Case Study. *Issues in Children Education, 26*, 53–71.

Margerum-Leys, J., & Marx, R. (2002). Teacher knowledge of educational technology: A study of student teacher/mentor teacher pairs. *Journal of Educational Computing Research, 26*(4), 427–462.

Menichetti, J., Hillen, M. A., Papageorgiou, A., & Pieterse, A. H. (2023). How can ChatGPT be used to support healthcare communication research? *Patient Education and Counseling, 115*, 107947. DOI: 10.1016/j.pec.2023.107947

Merryfield, M. M. (1997). A framework for teacher education in global perspectives. In Merryfield, M. M., Jarchow, E., & Pickert, S. (Eds.), *Preparing teachers to teach global perspectives* (pp. 1–24). Corwin.

Mills, G. E. (2011). *Action research: A guide for the teacher researcher* (6th ed.). Pearson.

Mishra, P., & Koehler, M. (2006). Technological Pedagogical Content Knowledge: A Framework for Teacher Knowledge. *Teachers College Record, 108*(6), 1017–1054.

Naibaho. (2022). The pre-service teachers' communication ability analysis at teacher training and education faculty. *Indonesian EFL Journal, 8*(2), 237-246. https://doi.org/.DOI: 10.25134/ieflj.v8i2.6474

Naidoo, A., Byles, H., & Kwenaite, S. (2021). Student Support and Transition Through a Buddy Programme to Foster Social Integration. *Journal for Students Affairs in Africa, 9*(2), 47–63. DOI: 10.24085/jsaa.v9i2.3698

Ngang, T. K., & Chan, T. C. (2015). Critical issues of soft skills development in teaching professional training: Educators' perspectives. *Procedia: Social and Behavioral Sciences, 205*, 128–133.

Ngang, T. K., & Chan, T. C. (2015). Critical issues of soft skills development in teaching professional training: Educators' perspectives. *Procedia: Social and Behavioral Sciences, 205*, 128–133.

Niess, M. L. (2005). Preparing teachers to teach science and mathematics with technology: Developing a technology pedagogical content knowledge. *Teaching and Teacher Education*, *21*, 509–523.

Nindya, M. A., Widiati, U., & El Khoiri, N. (2022). Pre-service Teachers' Perceived Understandings and Practices of Intercultural Communicative Competence in EFL Teaching. *International Journal of Language Education*, *6*(3), 297. DOI: 10.26858/ijole.v6i3.22747

Open, A. I. (n.d.). *Educator considerations for ChatGPT*. https://platform.openai.com/docs/chatgpt-education [https://platform.openai.com/docs/chatgpt-education]

Peña, M. (2020). *Working With Pre-service Teachers Towards Professional Development*. June 2020. https://www.hltmag.co.uk/june2020/working-with-pre-service

Reiss, M. J. (2021). The use of AI in education: Practicalities and ethical considerations. *London Review of Education*. . 19.1. 05DOI: 10. 14324/ LRE

Richards, K. A. R. (2015). Role socialization theory: The sociopolitical realities of teaching physical education. *European Physical Education Review*, *21*(3). Advance online publication. DOI: 10.1177/1356336X15574367

Rosenbluh, I., & Power, K. (2023). Exploring preservice teachers' professional vision: Modes of isolation, ethical noticing, and anticipation in research communities of practice. *Teaching and Teacher Education*, *132*, 104245. DOI: 10.1016/j.tate.2023.104245

Roychowdhury, H., Gerrits, R., Hull, K., Stowe, S., & Jensen, M. (2020). Benefits and Challenges of Assigned Out-of-Class Group Work in The Community College Setting. *HAPS Educator*, *24*(3), 23–33. DOI: 10.21692/haps.2020.020

Rueda, M., Cerero, J., Batanero, J. M., & Meneses, E. (2023). Impact of the Implementation of ChatGPT in Education: A Systematic Review. *Computers*, *12*(8), 153. DOI: 10.3390/computers12080153

Santos, L. M. D. (2019). Pre-Service Teachers Professional Development through Four-Step Problem-Solving Model: A Seminar Method. *International Journal of Education and Practice*, *7*(3), 146–157. DOI: 10.18488/journal.61.2019.73.146.157

Saudelli, M. G., & Ciampa, K. (2016). Exploring the role of TPACK and teacher self-efficacy: An ethnographic case study of three iPad language arts classes. *Technology, Pedagogy and Education*, *25*(2), 227–247. DOI: 10.1080/1475939X.2014.979865

Sehlaoui, A. S. (2001). Developing cross-cultural communicative competence via computer-assisted language learning: The case of pre-service ESL/EFL teachers. *ALT-J, 9*(3), 53–64.

Shannon-Baker, P. (2020). "Those who can't hear must feel": Confronting racism, privilege, and self with pre-service teachers. *Theory into Practice, 59*(3), 300–309.

Siwatu, K. O. (2007). Pre-service teachers' culturally responsive teaching self-efficacy and outcome expectancy beliefs. *Teaching and Teacher Education, 23*(7), 1086–1101. DOI: 10.1016/j.tate.2006.07.011

Tate, T. P. Shayan Doroudi, Ritchie, D., Xu, Y., & Warschauer, M. (2023). Educational Research and AI-Generated Writing: Confronting the Coming Tsunami. EdArXiv. https://doi.org/DOI: 10.35542/osf.io/4mec3

Trust, T., Whalen, J., & Mouza, C. (2023). Editorial: ChatGPT: Challenges, opportunities, and implications for teacher education. *Contemporary Issues in Technology and Teacher Education, 23*(1). https://citejournal.org/volume-23/issue-1-23/editorial/editorialchatgpt- challenges-opportunities-and-implications-for-teacher-education

Tseng, C.-T. H. (2017). Teaching "Cross-cultural Communication" through Content Based Instruction: Curriculum Design and Learning Outcome from EFL Learners' Perspectives. *English Language Teaching, 10*(4), 22. DOI: 10.5539/elt.v10n4p22

Vozza. (2014). Using Professional Presentations to Improve Cross-Cultural Communication. *The CATESOL Journal*, 26(1), 17–22.

Widiati, U., & Hayati, N. (2019). *Teacher Education for English as a Lingua Franca: How well prepared are Indonesian pre-service teachers to develop their future students' intercultural communicative competence? A study of English as a lingua franca*. Routledge., DOI: 10.4324/9780203730522-5

Willard-Holt, C. (2001). The impact of short-term international experience for pre-service teachers. *Teaching and Teacher Education, 17*(4), 505–517. DOI: 10.1016/S0742-051X(01)00009-9

Zhang, C., Schießl, J., Plößl, L., Hofmann, F., & Gläser-Zikuda, M. (2023). Acceptance of artificial intelligence among pre-service teachers: A multigroup analysis. *International Journal of Educational Technology in Higher Education, 20*(1). Advance online publication. DOI: 10.1186/s41239-023-00420-7 PMID: 36743849

Zhang, K., & Aslan, A. B. (2021). AI technologies for education: Recent research & future directions. *Computers and Education Artificial Intelligence, 2*, 100025. . caeai. 2021. 100025DOI: 10. 1016/j

Zhao, Y. (2003). *What teachers should know about technology: Perspectives and practices*. Information Age Publishing.

KEY TERMS AND DEFINITIONS

Collaboration: students working together with others to achieve a goal or complete a task.

Communication Skills: The ability to clearly share your own thoughts and understand others, whether by speaking, writing, or listening.

Generative AI: A type of computer tool (like ChatGPT) that can create text, images, or ideas based on what you ask it.

Higher education: Education that happens after high school, like at universities

Learning Buddy: An AI that helps students' study and learn more easily by guiding or supporting them

Teacher education: The training and preparation someone gets to become a teacher.

TPACK: A way for teachers to think about using the right mix of technology, teaching methods, and subject knowledge to help students learn better.

Chapter 9
Teaching English to Digital Natives in Rural Societies:
Why Project-Based Learning Is Key to Optimizing Instruction

Katrina Broughman
https://orcid.org/0009-0000-6913-0979
Mary Baldwin University, USA

ABSTRACT

As digital natives evolve alongside innovation, educators must stay open-minded with tools like AI technology to enhance instruction and develop curriculum. In secondary English Language Arts (ELA) classrooms and other areas, AI use is becoming more common among teachers and students alike in daily writing, reading, research, and communication tasks. Globally, AI is finding its way into all of these pedagogical elements, yet access is not always reliable in more rural societies due to poverty, polarization, and isolation. Furthermore, ongoing AI interactions can lead to negative effects like suicidal ideation and depression (Hill, 2025). Project-based learning (PBL) counteracts this issue for digital native learners by encouraging interaction, responsibility, and experimentation (Santamaria, 2020). Current research fails to connect PBL to ELA instruction, regardless of AI technology interacting with digital natives. ELA-centric stakeholders in rural communities should seriously reduce AI consumption and increase the use of environment-based methodologies like PBL.

DOI: 10.4018/979-8-3373-3755-5.ch009

INTRODUCTION

In an age of rising AI technology, digital natives are often the first to navigate and adapt to the ever-evolving twists and turns of applying a multitude of fresh innovations to daily life. For educators, staying open-minded is a core element of being a lifelong learner. Across subject areas, schoolteachers are now using various tools, devices, and equipment in order to enhance instruction and develop curriculum around the globe. Why not make more effort to understand each other through effective communication skills and interdisciplinary instruction?

Particularly in secondary English Language Arts (ELA) classrooms, AI is becoming a common resource used by teachers and students alike to optimize written and verbal communication skills which are ultimately incorporated not just in the ELA curriculum but virtually in every classroom. For instance, daily writing allows self-expression when formulating formative and summative responses. Reading is an essential way that learners are able to comprehend myriads of informative texts. Furthermore, cultivating research skills identify reliable sources, avoid plagiarism, and make discoveries. Presentation, collaboration, and communication skills allow deeper comprehension and stronger connections; learners recognizing their potential yield great power through the written word by persuading, explaining concepts, reflecting, and discussing ideas. Without a doubt, AI is finding its way into all of these elements of secondary ELA curriculum worldwide.

Since the onslaught of the coronavirus pandemic (more commonly known as Covid-19), access to computers and the worldwide web has become a non-negotiable for everyone involved in the pedagogical realm. However, for those living in rural societies, this is an ongoing challenge. Accessibility to up-to-date technology and reliable broadband continues to be an issue due to intergenerational poverty, institutionalized polarization, and geographical isolation. Furthermore, recent studies reveal that ongoing interactions with AI technology and digital media can lead to negative effects on digital natives such as increased isolation, suicidal ideation, anxiety, and depression (Hill 2025).

Educators teaching digital natives in rural societies are often left with no choice other than to approach these problems with creative solutions. According to qualitative participatory research, one of the most effective methodologies for pedagogical-centered stakeholders is project-based learning (PBL) because it encourages healthy amounts of active interaction, social responsibility, and autonomous experimentation for learners while engaged in learning experiences that take place in the natural world (Santamaria 2020).

Nature-based learning (NBL), a cross-curricular model that can be successful in informal, formal, or non-formal ELA settings by supporting interdisciplinary learning (Jordan & Chawla 2019). Defined as using the outdoors and elements of landscapes, NBL connects learners with real-world opportunities (Newman 2020). When used in education to increase positive attitudes and ensure its permanence, NBL helps learners value elements of nature and have positive attitudes towards it (Sevin 2020). This significantly benefits environmental attitudes and consciousness (Nkoana 2020), guiding leaders to think holistically and sustainably and care more about the world around them.

However, current research has failed to connect PBL and NBL to ELA instruction. This is regardless of whether or not innovations such as AI technology have been incorporated. Therefore, this chapter recommends that those interacting regularly with digital natives, particularly stakeholders like parents, educators, and ELA curriculum developers in rural communities, seriously reduce the consumption of AI technology and increase the application of environment-based methodologies such as PBL.

AN OVERVIEW OF THE SOCIOLOGY OF EDUCATION

The sociology of education, also known as educational sociology, is an element within the field of sociology that has been historically challenging to develop as an academic discipline (Aslan 2020). Its history is rooted in the United States (US), the United Kingdom (UK), Canada, and even as far as Taiwan and China (Aslan 2020; Dworkin et al 2013; Robson 2019). Theoretical terminology used within the field is vast and includes microsocial, macrosocial, mesosocial, and other theories from its inception with Emile Durkheim to the present day with ecological systems theory and other modern discourse. Methodologies used within the field have been qualitative and quantitative as well as a mix of both.

Ultimately, more attention and collaboration is needed on the sociology of education specifically within the academic fields of sociology and education to conduct research and provide insight with a sociological lens for emerging issues in education regarding topics such as globalization, stratification, inequalities, multiculturalism politics, assessment and accountability, effects of peer groups on learning, teacher supply and demand, teacher status and morale, teacher burnout, and social control (Aslan 2020). Additionally, more attention should be brought to nature-based learning within the arena of the sociology of education through the ecological systems theory due to its unique opportunities for bringing learners, educators, sociologists, and other stakeholders together with the natural environment.

The History of The Sociology Of Education

The history of educational sociology, or the sociology of education, is a global phenomenon. There have been several discourses on whether to use "educational sociology" or "the sociology of education" terminology when describing the field (Aslan 2020). Overall, the sociology of education is now being used by those who see the discipline as an objective science, where "educational sociology" is used by ones who think of it as a policy (2020).

While the sectors of education and sociology used to collaborate academically in the US and the UK, nowadays this is seen less often, despite it being seen by some as a key field in solving human problems and issues within the field of education (2020).

According to Aslan (2020), educational sociologists in the early days were predominantly and basically educated to be sociologists, whereas today's educational sociologists from the 1960s onwards have essentially been primarily trained to become educators in the arena of education. This has led to a disconnect between the two fields which nowadays is an institutional issue, and there is unfortunately not a plethora of universities that offer sociology of education courses in neither the UK nor the US (2020).

Of course, the sociology of education field is not limited to the US and the UK. In Canada, the sociology of education field has had its own progression. In particular, Canadian sociologists have been looking at the importance of anti-racist pedagogy within the field of education (Robson 2019). Other countries that have been focusing on the sociology of education include China, Taiwan, and Latin America. China has been deeply focused on the effects of industrialization, outsourcing, and credentialism on its educational system (Dworkin et al 2013).

In addition, Taiwan has recently been looking at the hidden curriculum and ideology within education. Both China and Taiwan have also hosted international education of sociology events and conferences in the past (2013). Additionally, countries in Latin America such as Brazil have been spending a significant amount of time looking at political sociology as it relates to the field of education (2013).

Until about 50 years ago, the sociology of education was not only seen weakly as an acknowledged subdivision of the sociological field, but it was also thought to be a contested and controversial field (Aslan 2020). Sometimes it was interrupted or disturbed by outsiders, and occasionally it was debated highly internally. Nevertheless, the sociology of education has begun to pave the way for changes in the focal points of methodology and research for the fields of education and sociology as well as within direct sociology in particular (2020).

Theoretical Approaches within the Sociology of Education

Theoretical approaches to the sociology of education include: agency/structure, microsocial theory, macro-social theory (structural functionalism), mesosocial theory, institution theory, middle range theory, epistemology and ontology, poststructuralism (cultural reproduction theory), rational action theory, theory of practice/praxis, social exclusion, social capital, theory of language codes, and modern and postmodern theories such as ecological systems theory, the hidden curriculum, political approaches, feminist approaches, critical race theory, and cultural hegemony. This chapter will focus on the major theories and concepts found within them (macrosocial, microsocial, mesosocial) as well as ecological systems theory. Macrosocial theory focuses more on the structure surrounding one's experience, whereas microsocial theory looks at the agency of individuals; alternatively, mesosocial theory attempts to bridge agency and structure (Robson 2019).

The theoretical elements of the sociology of education are originally rooted in macrosocial theory which sees society as an objective living organism (Robson 2019). *Macrosocial theory* looks at the structures of people's actions using mostly quantitative and positivist methods (2019). This idea originates from Emile Durkheim, the father of *Structural Functionalism* and of the sociology of education (2019). Durkheim saw society, and the educational processes within it, as a large-scale system of working parts, and focused on *moral education and regulation* (2019).

In the 1800s, the society of Durkheim and his contemporary, Parsons, was transforming from being religiously homogeneous (Catholic collectivism) to individualistically valuing trust within societal members (2019). Both saw schools as educational systems (Aslan 2020) existing within society to socialize students and prepare them for adult roles through a focus on common values and moral codes (Robson 2019). While helpful for seeing how norms and morality are dispersed across society, this perspective fails to account for gender, race, socioeconomic backgrounds, and life outcomes as it mutually depends on the individual and society (2019).

Another important macrosocial classical theory from the 1800s is Marxism and later neo-marxism with the development of critical pedagogy (Robson 2019). Originating from Karl Marx, Marxism is founded in his *Communist Manifesto*. Marx was interested in theories about conflict and change as well as social reproduction (Aslan 2020; Robson 2019; Dworkin et al 2013). He saw school systems as being created to benefit the elite as students become socialized into subordinate classes (Robson, 2019).

This *ideological role* of the state in education meant that the capitalist system (Dworkin et al 2013) is reinforced within class statuses by the educational system alongside media, regulations, etc. (Robson 2019). Marx pointed out the differences in achievement between different classes of students rather than level of intelligence, revealing that "schools reflect the needs of the powerful, dominant groups in society and serve to perpetuate the capitalist system" (Aslan 2020, p. 189).

Arguing that the ruling class dominates with the *state ideological apparatus* by utilizing a *hidden curriculum*, Marxism claims that children are taught to cooperate within society where economic and educational systems work together to keep them from having any control over their place in it (Robson 2019). Similarly, the *correspondence principle* reveals that the educational system has been organized to serve the system through ongoing, intergenerational class reproduction so elites can maintain their positions (2019). While this analysis ignores race, gender, and other elements, Marxism, as well as Weberian theory which will be discussed next, does recognize that neither students nor teachers are passive participants (Aslan 2020).

The third classic theorist that dealt with the sociology of education is *Max Weber* in the late 1800s and early 1900s. Unlike Marx, Weber took a multidimensional approach when inspecting human agency, the material, and the normative elements of structure (Dworkin et al 2013). He is considered the father of *microsocial theory* (Robson 2019) which focuses on the individual subjective experience within social life mainly through qualitative methods and includes theories about interactions between students and teachers, students and teachers, students and students, etc. (Aslan 2020).

Weber's ideas about rationalism, bureaucracy, status, social groups, credentialism, credit inflation, intensified positional competition of labor market differentiation, educational stratification, and stigmatization all support his thesis that people are simultaneously constrained by and construct society, especially as regulations continue to disadvantage people without specific qualifications or credentials (Robson 2019).

From here, microsocial theory moved to Mead and Cooley's theory of *symbolic interactionism* and the overarching field of social psychology in the early 1900s (Robson 2019). An action-based theory, this symbolic interaction focuses on the self-development of an individual (Aslan 2020), asserting that the world is built through meanings that a person attaches to his or her social interactions (Robson 2019).

There is the "Me" stage of the social self, followed by the "I" stage which is who we are when we interact with and respond to others (2019). According to Robson (2019), there is the *play stage* (a child picks between two limiting roles), the *game stage* (where a child learns how to take on another's attitude and has fully self-developed), the *generalized other* (a comprehension of collected attitudes), and significant symbols (imbedded in deep meaning through the use of vocal language).

Blumer extended this theory to include meaning, language, and thought in the 1960s, claiming that one's behavior towards an object is based on the meaning that object has for him or her, and different points of view are necessary to create this meaning (Robson 2019). This also connects to labeling theory, rational choice or exchange theory, and the role of language as well as having assumptions (Aslan 2020).

There are several contemporary theories specifically stemming from the Weberian microsocial approach. One is *social exclusion theory*, the idea that some people are intentionally left out of educational experiences within society, which has fundamentally impacted the modern sociology of education (Aslan 2020). *Phenomenology,* based on work by Austrian social scientist Alfred Schütz, focused on analyzing life-world meanings and concentrating on studying consciousness and direct experience objects (2019). Additionally, Vygotsky's *sociocultural approach to cognition*, argued that learning depends on interactions between the learner and his or her social environment, including peers, parents, teachers, etc. (Dworkin et al 2013).

Similarly, Demanet and Van Houtte's *oppositional culture theory* adds to this analysis of interaction by discussing various misconduct in schools and causes of feelings of futility in students in/out of school (Dworkin et al 2013). Meyer's *institutional theory* argues that worldwide educational expansion has not been due to workforce or institutional requirements, but instead has been based off of a more vast democratic dedication to the good of widening education related to legitimizing institutional ceremonies and rituals instead of real workplace-based practices that necessitate different levels of training (Robson 2019). Furthermore, Mickelson's work reveals various gender differences when interacting in classrooms for girls and boys and shows how this affects their experiences (Dworkin et al 2013).

Within the sociology of education, these various theories related symbolic interactionist perspectives are certainly useful for examining how meaning is attributed to language in various social settings (2019). While microsocial theories had a limited development of theories concerning schooling, these have helped to improve the field of educational sociology as a whole by providing an increase in theoretical models for schooling processes (Aslan 2020).

Mesosocial theory is the final category of theoretical approaches within the sociology of education. This theory attempts to bridge microsocial and macrosocial theories together. It recognizes that within the *micro-social*, people have their own connections and networks, and within the *macro-social,* the property of societies has individual effects to serve the public group (Robson 2019). Together, this was evidence of a micro–macro linkage, or the *mesosocial,* which is the idea of bridging capital and connecting groups to each other (2019). Mesosocial theory includes poststructuralism (cultural reproduction theory) and ecological systems theory. Other theories that will not be discussed in great detail in this paper but are important to mention within mesosocial theory include feminist approaches, critical race theory, and cultural hegemony.

Poststructuralism and *cultural reproduction theory* are most closely associated with the work of French sociologist Pierre Bourdieu in the mid to late 1900s. There is a large collection of theories whose main agreement was that Durkheimian structuralism was flawed (Robson 2019). In their reactions to structural functionalism, these theories tend to favor the importance of social structures in explaining social life over the actions of individuals (2019). While influenced by Marxism, Bourdieu disagreed with the notion of class, arguing that social stratification processes have emerged from different sources, like *forms of capital* (2019). These include cultural capital, economic capital, social capital, and cultural reproduction (2019).

Bourdiu's solution to the problem between structure and agency was the *habitus*, best understood as an embodied social structure that internally self-regulates actions, guides behaviors, and determines dispositions (2019). In other words, one's decisions are hugely restricted and guided by social structures existing within us (2019). This also connects to conflict theory and the theory of praxis or practice (1984) as well as Basil Bernstein's (1996) theory of language codes and Randall Collins's (1979) Weberian theory of social exclusion (Aslan 2020).

Ecological systems theory, coined by American psychologist Bronfenbrenner in the 1960s and founder of the Head Start program, looks at the ways that a child interacts with his or her environment (Robson 2019). The theory concurs that youth outcomes result from various reciprocated effects between the environment and the child; for instance, how one is treated by a parent or peers strongly influences one's development (2019).

Elements of both microsocial and macrosocial theory echo in Bronfenbrenner's breakdown of this theory when he defines the five interconnecting layers of the individual and society: *microsystem* (the immediate place in which one lives and her or his interactions with family, friends, caregivers, teachers, etc.), *mesosystem* (the relation between microsystems; for instance: a child's interactions with parents may reflect in interactions with teachers), *exosystem* (contains places and people where a youth may not be involved directly but still somehow impacted), *macrosystem* (the greater environment where individuals live: underdeveloped or developed, rural or urban, multicultural or not, non-democratic or democratic, etc.) and *chronosystem* (major events and socio-historical changes that are globally influential) (2019).

The different elements of these systems move together to mold a child's development, and many of these are beyond a parent's control (Robson 2019). Additionally, this theory points out that parents may have an essential role in shaping their children's lives, but these larger forces that exist have just as much of an impact on the development of a child, and parents are unable to control that (2019). Ecological systems theory also connects to nature-based learning, an up-and-coming concept within educational research (Jordan & Chawla 2019, Newman 2020).

Methodologies Used in the Sociology of Education

There have been a variety of methodologies used within the field of the sociology of education. Specifically, these include qualitative and quantitative studies as well as a mix of both. According to Dworkin et al (2013), the standardized 'method of the day' is what ultimately characterizes research in the educational world. Researching students within schools, however, can be more complicated than the availability of methods for research (2013). While many do recognize contextual effects, there are often no efficient methods available for studying those effects (2013). Nevertheless, the Wisconsin model is one that uses a multivariate causal model and has opened up a new era for quantitative research.

There has also been an expansion recently of statistical techniques such as PLSPath and LISREL (from Sweden) which support latent variables and measured variables in a causal model, and HLM (USA) which lets researchers account for nesting data (2013). There have also been qualitative advances such as the evolution towards enhancing the validity of researching educational processes. This includes participant observation, observational processes, and studying contents of documents which has expanded to incorporate both narrative and biological methods. As these evolutions in sociological methods continue to respond to various challenges in educational research, the sociology of education remains the leader in research method and statistical technique development (2013).

The following section of the chapter focuses on some of the current connections present between the sociology of education and environmental sociology. While not comprehensive, this section covers a variety of perspectives within the topic that have been discovered in various sociological articles. Specifically, it looks at the sociological significance of environmental education (EE) and nature-based learning (NBL). It also explores what makes a well-designed EE or NBL focused program from a sociological perspective based on available literature.

When possible, this section also touches on the limitations of the research explored. Overall, this section of the chapter has found that these articles reveal how sociology of education connects with environmental sociology by developing NBL research; analyzing relationships between dirt and the child; observing the role of family in a child's educational experience; exploring the management, perception, and performance of risk amongst educators; examining the maintenance of control; and considering the concept of being nature smart.

A COORDINATED RESEARCH AGENDA FOR NATURE-BASED LEARNING (NBL)

Researching NBL within multiple fields, this article includes a literature review, recommendations for improvement regarding research questions and methodologies, and ways to increase rigor and relevance (Jordan & Chawla, 2019). Questions focus on seeking out understanding how one is affected by learning in nature and how that varies based on socioeconomic status, age, ethnic background, gender, individual differences, and special needs (J&C, 2019). Outcomes of greatest interest include practical skills, academic performance, personal development, and environmental stewardship, as well as causal explanations for outcomes that have been observed (J&C, 2019).

Sociologically, this research takes a look at both qualitative and quantitative methods that could be used to dig deeper into this topic in order to create optimal conditions for NBL. Specifically, it includes practical questions about getting teachers ready for successfully working in nature and ways to support their adoption of the NBL approach (J&C, 2019). Furthermore, the research asks whether or not learning in nature can touch on major societal issues through moderation of socioeconomic disadvantages and their effects on a child's personal development, well-being, and academic achievement, and how benefits may be gained affordably (J&C, 2019).

The sociological significance of this article is that NBL can and should be accessible regardless of one's position within society. However, more research is needed to continue supporting this thesis. This is why a deeper comprehension of why, how, and for whom various forms of contact with nature enhance development and learning is required to guide policy decision-making and practice (J&C, 2019). Conclusively, this article argues that a well-designed nature-based program should be accessible to all learners regardless of that child's background or various forms of identification within his or her society. So, a deeper understanding of NBL is needed within the field of education and sociology alike.

DIRT AND THE CHILD

This paper explores, documents, and examines the roles of dirt and child, further bridging the gap between the sociology of education and environmental sociology. First of all, it looks at the taxonomy of space and spacial destiny in the nineteenth century as adults attempted to 'save' children from their own geography, directly connecting the educational experience of a child at that time period as well as his or her interactions with the environment (Grosvenor & Myers, 2020). This exploration is done with a variety of descriptive vocabulary (G&M, 2020). Secondly, it connects education and the environment by documenting how dirt is dually seen as both risky and pastoral within society (G&M, 2020). It reveals how middle class privatized spaces contrast highly with impoverished inner city slums, which is too often stigmatized by an unfair association with danger and destruction (G&M, 2020).

Additionally, activists in a city proved neglect for nature in urban environments while centralizing its role (ie, fertile rural soil) for the sustainability of life (G&M, 2020). Furthermore, it exposes the cultural divide that has existed for centuries between people and their surrounding environments (G&M, 2020). Since not all children have access to the same kind of nature-based learning (NBL) experiences, how do we successfully provide equitable NBL for all children in the United States and beyond to learn outside? This topic is in need of further investigation by both environmental and educational sociologists.

The sociological significance of educational programs taking place outdoors is that the middle class and slum environments are highly contrasted to make a point: the twentieth century divide between rich and poor (G&M, 2020). This obviously had an effect on one's relationship with the environment as well, since urban environments were being neglected while rural ones were being industrially nurtured to make space for more fertile soil (G&M, 2020). If one grew up near a privatized outdoor space in an urban environment, he or she was more likely to develop a positive relationship with nature than those living in inner city neighborhoods with little to no access to more than concrete and broken glass (G&M, 2020).

For those coming from deprecated delinquency, dirt, and disease, there were less opportunities to be exposed to fertile soil due to societal neglect (G&M, 2020). Nevertheless, activists in one city sought to change this by exploring ways to bridge the gap between those in upper-class versus slum-like housing (G&M, 2020). In conclusion, it would be significant for sociologists to dig deeper into this idea in the modern Amcrican city.

FAMILIES, EXPERIMENTS, AND NATURE

Fortunately, learning communities based in more rural areas have a greater opportunity to access the natural world than those in highly populated areas. This allows for educators and parents to collaborate in order to address ongoing challenges that digital natives are too often experiencing such as isolation and mental health challenges. For instance, research done by Santamaria (2020) addresses the use of project-based learning (PBL) in science education within a rural learning community. PBL is an active methodology for learning meant to teach issues in a social context through projects (Santamaria 2020). It is based on John Dewey's idea that learners need to be involved in the environment around them so they can be socialized into active citizens (Santamaria 2020). In other words, participation is the key element of PBL because it encourages responsibility and autonomy as students' roles are centralized in the learning process.

Essentially, Santamaria (2020) identifies PBL as an effective tool for adapting to natural area resources through outings, activities, and family participation during lessons about plants for first and second graders. This is demonstrated in a Spanish school system whose surrounding families have an intermediate socio-economic status. From a sociological perspective, this connection between education and the environment is revealed through PBL teaching methods to learn science in a rural location. It engages the learner with his or her natural world at the microsocial level through individual agency (Robson 2019).

Santamaria (2020) used qualitative methodology, specifically participatory research, to test how effective PBL is for science education. This was done while maintaining high validity and credibility through categorical data collection in research that took place in a rural community, so different results could be obtained from an urban learning setting (2020). One could infer, for instance, that families in lower socioeconomic classes may have less access to these kinds of learning opportunities. For instance, digital natives from more isolated regions of Virginia's Appalachian mountains struggled during the Covid-19 pandemic to connect to reliable broadband and therefore experienced less opportunities for online learning than their peers logging in virtually from more urban locations like Roanoke City.

In some places, measures are being taken to increase the perceived usefulness of science in daily life (Santamaria 2020). However, traditional perspectives frame students as protagonists in their own learning while solely transmitting content without applying active learning strategies (2020). Thus, PBL is didactically effective in learning science, which is revealed through this research's use of qualitative methods and field note analysis of participation (2020).

During outings, experimental activities, and the encouragement of family participation, Santamaria (2020) analyzed data on content acquisition, reinforcement sessions, experiments, and educational excursions. Santamaria (2020) also noted that parents were informed of and supported the lack of a textbook during these lessons and out-of-class assignments since students were considered digital natives and accessed information about their environment online; this relationship between parents and schools is key to a successful learning experience for the child, especially in rural areas.

From the lens of ecological systems theory, involving the family in learning experiences more greatly supports the healthy development of a child within his or her greater social and natural environments alike (Robson 2019). Furthermore, a Marxist macrosocial perspective would reiterate the importance of the student as an active participant in his or her society of fellow learners (Robson 2019), which is supported by Santamaria's (2020) advocacy for family-school relationships.

Santamaria (2020) reveals that science teaching should be more inclined toward educational methodologies like PBL that are more innovative because they are well-received by students and their families and have various positive effects for the learners (more motivated, more attentive, etc.) Therefore, both informal and formal education-based stakeholders should consider incorporating PBL into EE and related NBL programs (Santamaria 2020). Furthermore, it is important to teach science because of its relevance in modern society (Santamaria 2020).

Well-designed programs incorporating science and PBL should encourage questions and investigation as technology continues to advance (Santamaria 2020). This will help awaken a student's scientific spirit that is increasingly latent in schools today, motivating them to participate more than what is currently typical in the classroom (Santamaria 2020). From a symbolic interactionist perspective, the world is built through meaning that a person attaches to his or her social interactions, so a well-designed program should encourage self-development and include language and different points of view (Robson 2019).

Unfortunately, this research, while touching deeply on science learning, fails to take into account how other subjects areas can benefit from PBL and nature-based settings. Certainly, ELA instructors can also utilize PBL in lesson plans and incorporate NBL opportunities while reinforcing concepts learned and skills transferable (writing, reading comprehension, vocabulary, etc.) to the science classroom. In other words, PBL has positive coexisting relationships in various ways, like when parents, neighborhood gardeners, and other local experts become actively involved in the learning process alongside digital natives.

Santamaria's (2020) research models the ability to enhance nature-based educational opportunities through interdisciplinary connections regardless of rural or urban setting. PBL-incorporated objectives centered around constructive inquiry and investigation are effective in the entire learning process regardless of subject area (not just science) because they involve relevant issues, are goal oriented, remain flexible, and are context-specific (Santamaria 2020). The main idea, after all, is to stimulate interest in learning and understand the importance of asking questions (Santamaria 2020), so those questions can be scientific or otherwise. When students are able to engage in this process organically, rather than overutilizing AI technology, even more opportunities for social engagement and active learning can take place. According to qualitative analysis, this also facilitates a greater sense of community and global responsibility.

THE PERCEPTION, MANAGEMENT AND PERFORMANCE OF RISK AMONGST FOREST SCHOOL EDUCATORS

Connolly & Haughton (2017) attach the sociology of education and environmental sociology in their use of the social constructionist perspective for theorizing risk and childhood experiences in an outdoor setting. Basically, the sociological connection between education and the environment here is the performance, management, and perception of risk by educators teaching within an outdoor education context. This is analyzed in three categories: students' childhood, a teacher's professional identity, and pedagogy (C&H 2017).

The article argues that concerns about a child's vulnerability, which are contemporary and hyper-sensitized, emanate from not just one's fear of the modern world, but also the proclivity towards too much protection, from which these fears have precipitated (C&H 2017). This paper avoids treating this hyper-sensitivity as paranoid or irrational and instead draws on qualitative research methods and socio-cultural theories in order to interrogate how risk is performed, perceived, and managed by teachers (C&H 2017). Specifically, this interrogation is done within an initiative that has aimed to reintroduce risk into the life of the young learner (C&H 2017).

The sociological significance of environmental education according to this article is the tensions created by institutional risks and hegemonic cultural aversions surrounding an educator at a Forest School (C&H 2017). Educators motivated by outdoor learning are faced by tensions created by these aversions to risk (C&H 2017). This happens in how they attempt to both manage and perform risk, and these tensions militate against this school's full realization of its pedagogy (C&H 2017).

Based on the research presented, a well-designed environmental education (EE) or related NBL program should incorporate some level of risk-taking outdoors for kids (C&H 2017). This can be coupled with training for teachers about the effects of tensions created by institutional risks and hegemonic cultural aversions surrounding them so that they may recognize these and be prepared to handle them in the future as they attempt to counter these by teaching in the outdoors (C&H 2017). In this way, educators will be more prepared for supporting their professional identity, their students' childhood, and their overall pedagogy (C&H 2017).

CONTROL MUST BE MAINTAINED

This study uses qualitative research methods and data to analyze teachers' practices and expectations in relation to teaching and learning outdoors (Glackin 2018). Connecting to both the sociology of education and environmental sociology, the theories used within this method about 'space', set practices, and routines (Glackin 2018).

Glackin's (2018) research used the theories presented by Foucault's and Bernstein to find that teachers fear losing control of their students during outdoor learning or outside of the classroom in general. This fear was constructed due to boundaries (or lack of), disturbances, and familiarity (Glackin 2018). Glackin (2018) claims that this fear felt by teachers ignites the use of technologies that are regulatory. Therefore, teachers became more authoritative in their teaching approaches (Glackin 2018). However, when technologies were developed for outdoor use specifically, teachers were able to translate these and apply them to lessons in a way that was much like their normal dialogic classroom-based teaching approaches (Glackin 2018).

According to this article, sociologists can identify (through the points of view provided by Foucault's and Bernstein's theories) that an increase in student self-regulation through the use of collaborative group work will allow for a well-designed EE or related program model (Glackin 2018). In this way, teachers incorporating the outdoors in their classroom curriculums can resolve tensions between instruction in new contexts and dialogic pedagogy (Glackin 2018).

NATURE SMART

This article covers the clear importance of nature-based education which bridges the sociology of education and the environment. Essentially, schools who provide nature-based learning experiences allow opportunities for their students to have a variety of benefits: they become healthier, happier, smarter, and more prone to practice conservation (Louv 2016). Specifically, youth exposed to outdoor learning opportunities have greater physical and mental health; have less issues with bullying, obesity, and troublesome behavior; and experience higher academic performance (Louv 2016).

Because nature learning transcends political and religious barriers, providing more Vitamin N (nature) represents a powerful and significant counter-trend to the digital age and increasing use of technology in schools by returning to the real (Louv 2016). For instance, greening schools is a cost effective way to raise test scores and get kids outside (Louv 2016).

A major point that Louv (2016) makes which greatly echoes the previous research mentioned is teachers being hesitant or uncomfortable with going outdoors: a common theme seen on a national level. This is sociologically significant because it is part of a greater cultural phenomenon centered around fear (Louv 2016). Louv (2016) also points out that school systems and educators need to move beyond programmatic thinking and start creating deep and sustainable cultural and environmental change instead because all kids need nature; not just those whose parents appreciate it. This requires moving towards a nature-rich civilization that builds upon ethnic and cultural diversity (Louv 2016).

In order to make this possible, there needs to be social and cultural infrastructure in place to support the movement (Louv 2016). Teachers, administrators, students, and parents alike need to find ways to become more comfortable with learning outdoors in nature and learn how to be more mindful of irrational fears that society may have instilled upon them(Louv 2016). This can be as micro-social as one teacher or administrator starting a trend within a school by developing outdoor learning spaces (gardens, parks, playscapes, etc.), or as macro-social as including nature-based learning elements in No Child Left Behind legislation (Louv 2016).

Adults who have a strong environmental ethic have almost always had some kind of transcendent experience in nature during childhood (Louv 2016). Therefore, a well-designed outdoor program would include opportunities for a nature-rich civilization that reinforces ethnic and cultural diversity (Louv 2016). Sociologically, this needs to incorporate leaders from various walks of life: politicians (mayors, city council members, etc.) leading outdoor efforts; healthcare professionals (doctors, nurses, etc.) prescribing outdoor time for sensory experiences that will combat dysfunctional childhoods; community organizations using available resources like the National Wildlife Federation's Playscapes guides to create outdoor play areas for local youth; parents, grandparents, and/or guardians forming family nature clubs; and nearby parks making their facilities available for free to neighboring families and their children (Louv, 2016).

Nevertheless, the ultimate idea is this: if a society works together for nature access to everyone involved, then these programs can be reinforced and, as a direct result, more consistently available (Louv 2016).

The Biophilia Hypothesis

One important concept connecting people to nature that educators may not be aware of is the biophilia hypothesis. The *biophilia hypothesis* is the idea that nature is beneficial for not just children, but for all humans. In other words, having a relationship with nature is vital for the sustainable health of individuals and their surrounding communities (Annerstedt & Wahrborg 2011; Weinstein et al 2015; Louv 2005). Despite its slightly intimidating title, this hypothesis is quite sensible when one truly thinks about it. There are even those who would consider the earth itself to be a sacred organism from which all life develops (Ruether, 1995). By acknowledging that nature is good for us, English teachers can connect students to the outdoors and let everyone get a chance to reap the benefits that the biophilia hypothesis proclaims.

In direct relation to literacy, great writers and thinkers such as Henry David Thoreau, Ralph Waldo Emmerson, Rachel Carson, Ingrid Waldron, John Muir, and Aldo Leopold often reflected this hypothesis in their books and essays. These writers not only contributed to American literature but to the environmental movement and consequently NBL, which continues to expand as a part of EE and the greater field of education. Therefore, the biophilia hypothesis within the scope of NBL is of interest for not just educators, but also environmental sociologists and educational sociologists looking for ways to help society.

The biophilia hypothesis and its relationship with NBL is all a part of the environmental movement, a social movement that includes ecological conceptions and the cultivation of knowledge as a whole (Bell &Ashwood 2016). Because sociologists have been looking at the relationship between society and education since Emile Durkheim at the start of the 20th century investigated the social nature of humans (Aslan 2020), this makes the added consideration of nature even more relevant. Specifically, the field of educational sociology ranges from interactions between students and teachers to different international systems of education (Aslan 2020). Environmental sociologists point out that what is hard on families and communities (such as conventional farming methods), is also hard on the environment, but a healthy planet supports a healthy human (Bell & Ashwood 2016). However, the movement towards nature as a way to facilitate positive social change (Charles 2009) currently lacks significant research in educational sociology. More studies are needed to support the connection between the biophilia hypothesis, nature-based learning (NBL), and educational sociology.

CONCLUSION

The sociology of education is a field that needs more collaboration between the disciplines of education and sociology, especially when considering the biophilia hypothesis. In addition, more academics in these fields need to be paying attention to the thoughtful insights and calculated research that educational sociologists can offer. There are emerging issues in education when sociology is included: globalization, stratification, inequalities, multiculturalism, politics, assessment and accountability, effects of peer groups on learning, teacher supply and demand, teacher status and morale, teacher burnout, and social control.

Emerging ideas within mesosocial theories like ecological systems theory as well as additional research in microsocial and macrosocial theories are needed to continue this collaborative process between sociologists and educational professionals. One recommendation I make as an environmental sociologist and educator is to incorporate nature-based learning in this increased collaborative effort, since a plethora of research supports the benefits of outdoor exploration for the learner. The field of sociology would greatly benefit from being involved in this powerful pedagogical movement.

Overall, the sociology of education can be connected with environmental sociology. This is possible through a variety of topics: developing more NBL research; analyzing the relationship between dirt and the child; observing the role of the family in a child's educational experience; exploring the management, perception, and performance of risk amongst educators; examining the maintenance of control; and considering the concept of being nature smart. Further investigation is needed within both environmental sociology and sociology of education, specifically when it connects with teaching language arts to digital natives attempting to use AI and other technological innovations in rural societies.

REFERENCES

Annerstedt, M., & Wahrborg, P. (2011). Nature-assisted therapy: Systematic review of controlled and observational studies. *Scandinavian Journal of Public Health, 39*(4), 371–388. Retrieved May 4, 2020, from www.jstor.org/stable/45150415

Aslan, C. (2020). An analysis on the development of sociology of education in USA and England. *African Educational Research Journal, 8*(2), S186–S195.

Bell, M., & Ashwood, L. (2016). *An Invitation to Environmental Sociology. Fifth Addition*. Sage Publications, Inc.

Charles, C. (2009, October 2). The Ecology of Hope: Natural Guides to Building a Children and Nature Movement. Journal of Science Education and Technology. https://link.springer.com/article/10.1007/s10956-009-9193-z?error=cookies_not _supporte d&code=e548e227-9255-4ed1-979f-25a6849262ea

Connolly, M., & Haughton, C. (2017). The perception, management and performance of risk amongst Forest School educators. *British Journal of Sociology of Education, 38*(2), 105–124.

Dworkin, A. G., Ballantine, J., Antikainen, A., Barbosa, M. L., Konstantinovskiy, D., Saha, L. J., ... & Teodoro, A. (2013). The sociology of education. Sociopedia. isa, 1, 16.

Glackin, M. (2018). 'Control must be maintained': Exploring teachers' pedagogical practice outside the classroom. *British Journal of Sociology of Education, 39*(1), 61–76. DOI: 10.1080/01425692.2017.1304204

Grosvenor, I., & Myers, K. (2020). "Dirt and the child": A textual and visual exploration of children's physical engagement with the urban and the natural world. *History of Education, 49*(4), 517–535. https://proxy.marybaldwin.edu:2238/10.1080/0046760X.2019.1701097

Hill, K. (2025). "A Teen Was Suicidal. ChatGPT Was the Friend He Confided In." The New York Times. Accessed 29 August 2025. https://www.nytimes.com/2025/08/26/technology/chatgpt-openai-suicide.html

Jordan, C., & Chawla, L. (2019). A Coordinated Research Agenda for Nature-Based Learning. *Frontiers in Psychology, 10*, 766. DOI: 10.3389/fpsyg.2019.00766

Louv, R. (2005). *Last Child in the Woods: Saving Our Children from Nature Deficit Disorder*. Algonquian Books of Chapel Hill.

Louv, R. (2016). Nature Smart. National Wildlife (World Ed.); 54(2):40-43. Accessed August 2025. proxy.marybaldwin.edu:2060/login.aspx?direct=true&db=a9h&AN=112738502&site=ehost-live

Newman, G. (2020). Nature-based-learning for students with disabilities.

Nkoana, E. M. (2020). Exploring the effects of an environmental education course on the awareness and perceptions of climate change risks among seventh and eighth grade learners in South Africa. *International Research in Geographical and Environmental Education*, *29*, 1, 7–22. DOI: 10.1080/10382046.2019.1661126

Robson, K. L. (2019, September 11). Theories in the Sociology of Education – Sociology of Education in Canada. Pressbooks. https://ecampusontario.pressbooks.pub/robsonsoced/chapter/__unknown__-2/

Santamaría, C. N. (2020). Families, experiments, and nature: Learning science through project-based learning. *School Science and Mathematics*, *120*(8), 467–476. https://proxy.marybaldwin.edu:2238/10.1111/ssm.12438

Sevin, S. (2020). The Change of Secondary School Students' Environmental Consciousness, Attitude and Behaviors with Nature Education Project. Higher Education Studies, v10 n2 p82-94. ISSN-1925-4741.

Weinstein, N., Balmford, A., DeHaan, C. R., Gladwell, V., Bradbury, R. B., & Aman, T. (2015). Seeing the Community for the Trees: The Links Among. *Contact (Thousand Oaks, Ventura County, Calif.).*

Chapter 10
The Future of AI in English Language Education:
Opportunities, Challenges, and Ethical Pathways

Mohammed H. Alaqad
https://orcid.org/0000-0002-9953-5763
University of Malaya, Malaysia

Mohammad Ali Al-Saggaf
https://orcid.org/0000-0001-7401-0509
Xiamen University Malaysia, Malaysia

Sajed S. Ingilan
https://orcid.org/0000-0002-4466-2028
University of Southeastern Philippines, Philippines

ABSTRACT

The rapid advancement of artificial intelligence (AI) is transforming nearly every sector of society, and English language education is no exception. From adaptive learning systems to AI-powered chatbots, these technologies promise to revolutionize how English is taught, learned, and assessed. Yet, while AI offers new opportunities for personalization, accessibility, and engagement, it also raises profound challenges related to equity, ethics, cultural diversity, and the evolving role of educators. As scholars increasingly recognize, the integration of AI into education must be guided not merely by technological possibility but by pedagogical, ethical, and sociocultural considerations (Niemi, 2024; Williamson & Eynon, 2020).

DOI: 10.4018/979-8-3373-3755-5.ch010

1. INTRODUCTION

The rapid advancement of artificial intelligence (AI) is transforming nearly every sector of society, and English language education is no exception. From adaptive learning systems to AI-powered chatbots, these technologies promise to revolutionize how English is taught, learned, and assessed. Yet, while AI offers new opportunities for personalization, accessibility, and engagement, it also raises profound challenges related to equity, ethics, cultural diversity, and the evolving role of educators. As scholars increasingly recognize, the integration of AI into education must be guided not merely by technological possibility but by pedagogical, ethical, and sociocultural considerations (Niemi, 2024; Williamson & Eynon, 2020).

This chapter aims to critically examine the future directions of AI in English language education, highlighting both its transformative potential and its inherent risks. It explores how AI can personalize learning experiences, expand access to quality education, and foster learner autonomy, while also addressing concerns about bias, over-reliance on technology, and the exacerbation of existing educational inequalities. Moreover, the chapter argues that the future of English language education will depend not simply on technological innovation, but on the active reshaping of the teacher's role, the development of responsible AI policies, and the cultivation of ethical, culturally sensitive AI tools (Tapalova et al., 2022).

Drawing on recent research and examples, the expected findings suggest that while AI will increasingly augment English language teaching and learning, it cannot replace the human elements essential to linguistic and intercultural competence. Instead, successful integration will require a balanced approach that empowers teachers as facilitators of critical inquiry and ethical engagement with AI, rather than relegating them to passive users of technology. Ultimately, the chapter argues that if developed and deployed thoughtfully, AI can help build a more inclusive, personalized, and empowering future for English language learners worldwide but only if human agency, ethical responsibility, and cultural diversity remain at the center of this technological evolution.

A Day in the Life: English Class, 2035

Adam, a 16-year-old student from a small village in Gaza Strip, wakes up to the soft chime of his personalized AI learning assistant, *Lula*. After breakfast, he puts on his lightweight AR glasses and joins his English class - a virtual classroom where students from twenty countries interact in real time.

Today's lesson: mastering persuasive writing in English. *Lula* has already analyzed Adam's recent essays, identifying his struggles with argument organization and tone. As the class begins, Adam's AI recommends a custom set of micro-lessons tailored to his needs, drawing examples from his favorite topics - climate change activism and Arabic literature. Meanwhile, Adam's teacher, Ms. Fatimah, reviews a dashboard showing the students' progress - not just raw scores, but their emotional engagement, speaking fluency, and collaboration patterns, all analyzed by the AI. Instead of lecturing, Ms. Fatimah moves between groups, facilitating discussions, encouraging debate, and helping students reflect critically on the AI's feedback.

In this classroom, AI is not the teacher - it is the silent architect, building bridges between students' ambitions and the English language they need to express them. As Adam crafts his speech draft, the AI nudges him gently: *"Would you like to strengthen your argument by citing a real-world example from today's news?"* With a smile, Adam accepts - knowing he's not learning English just for a grade, but to change the world.

This imagined classroom of 2035 offers a glimpse into the extraordinary possibilities AI holds for English language education: hyper-personalized learning, global connectivity, and the seamless integration of technology and pedagogy. Yet, it also raises critical questions about the future of education - about equity, authenticity, human agency, and ethical responsibility. As AI becomes more sophisticated, its role in shaping how English is taught, learned, and experienced will only grow. This evolution is not without tensions: while AI promises unprecedented opportunities for language acquisition, it also introduces risks of depersonalization, cultural bias, and educational inequality.

This chapter argues that the future of AI in English language education must be approached with a balanced, human-centered vision - one that leverages AI's transformative potential while safeguarding the core values of equity, creativity, critical thinking, and human connection.

2. OPPORTUNITIES: REDEFINING LANGUAGE LEARNING THROUGH AI

The integration of artificial intelligence into English language education offers a profound opportunity to personalize learning experiences on a scale never before possible. Traditional "one-size-fits-all" approaches often fail to address the diverse needs, backgrounds, and learning styles of students. In contrast, AI-driven platforms can adapt content, pacing, and feedback based on individual performance and preferences. Research has shown that adaptive learning systems, such as intelligent tutoring platforms, can significantly improve student outcomes by identifying specific areas of weakness and tailoring instruction accordingly (Zawacki-Richter et al., 2019). For English language learners, this means more targeted grammar exercises, pronunciation correction based on real-time speech analysis, and writing feedback customized to their cultural and linguistic backgrounds.

Another major advantage AI brings is expanding access to high-quality English education across geographical and socio-economic barriers. In regions where skilled English teachers are scarce, AI tools like conversational chatbots, automated assessment systems, and virtual reality simulations can provide immersive learning experiences previously available only in well-resourced environments (Luckin & Holmes, 2016). This technological leap could help democratize language learning, empowering students from marginalized communities to acquire English skills essential for global participation. However, it is essential that developers and educators work collaboratively to ensure these AI systems are culturally sensitive and linguistically inclusive, rather than reinforcing dominant linguistic norms that marginalize local dialects and world Englishes (Pennycook, 2010).

Moreover, AI has the potential to foster more engaged and autonomous learners. Gamified learning apps, AI-assisted storytelling, and interactive platforms powered by natural language processing allow students to practice English in authentic, meaningful contexts, rather than rote drills. Scholars argue that when learners are active participants rather than passive recipients, motivation and long-term retention significantly increase (Dörnyei, 2001). Through AI, English learning can become a dynamic process where students not only master linguistic structures but also cultivate critical thinking, intercultural communication skills, and creative expression - competencies vital for success in the 21st century.

The challenges surrounding AI integration in English language education highlight a crucial reality: technology alone cannot resolve the complex, human-centered nature of learning. While AI can offer tools, resources, and efficiencies, it is educators who must guide, interpret, and humanize the learning experience. As AI systems take on more instructional and administrative functions, the role of teachers is not diminished but profoundly reshaped. In the emerging educational landscape, teachers are poised to become not just conveyors of knowledge, but facilitators of critical inquiry, ethical guardians of AI use, and cultural mediators who ensure that language learning remains deeply human, creative, and socially relevant.

3. CHALLENGES AND RISKS: NAVIGATING THE DARK SIDE OF AI

While the promises of artificial intelligence in English language education are substantial, navigating the dark side of AI reveals a landscape fraught with critical challenges that demand urgent attention. Among the most pressing concerns is the risk of bias embedded within AI systems. Numerous studies have demonstrated that language models and educational algorithms often reflect and reinforce existing social, racial, and linguistic inequalities (Mehrabi et al., 2021). When AI tools standardize a narrow conception of English often favoring native-speaker norms from the Global North they inadvertently marginalize diverse linguistic expressions and cultural identities, thereby perpetuating a hidden form of linguistic imperialism (Floridi, 2023). This bias not only threatens linguistic diversity but also risks demotivating learners who find their own varieties of English devalued. Another significant danger in navigating the dark side of AI is the over-reliance on automated feedback and machine-led instruction. As AI becomes more sophisticated, there is a growing temptation to substitute human judgment with algorithmic assessments of writing quality, speech proficiency, and comprehension (Kooli, 2023). However, such mechanistic evaluations often fail to capture the nuanced, context-sensitive aspects of language use such as irony, creativity, and intercultural pragmatics which are critical to true communicative competence. If educational institutions become overly dependent on AI, there is a real risk that English language education will shift towards a technocratic model that prioritizes efficiency over depth, and standardization over critical thinking.

Ethical concerns also loom large in this evolving landscape. AI systems in education often collect massive amounts of learner data, raising questions about surveillance, consent, and data privacy (Williamson & Eynon, 2020). In many cases, students and educators have little transparency or control over how their data is used, exacerbating asymmetries of power between technology providers and end-users. Moreover, recent research warns that unchecked deployment of AI in educational contexts may exacerbate the digital divide, benefiting those with access to cutting-edge technology while further marginalizing under-resourced communities (Göçmez & Okur, 2023). Thus, navigating the dark side of AI in English language education is not merely a technical challenge; it is a profoundly ethical, social, and political project that demands collaborative vigilance from educators, technologists, and policymakers alike.

The problem of algorithmic opacity adds another dimension to the risks posed by AI in English language education. Many AI-based systems function as "black boxes," making decisions about learner progress, content recommendations, and even grading, without offering transparent explanations of how these conclusions are reached (Burrell, 2016). When educational stakeholders teachers, students, administrators cannot understand or challenge the logic behind AI-driven decisions, they lose agency in the learning process. This opacity can lead to serious consequences, especially when errors occur in high-stakes assessments or when marginalized learners are systematically disadvantaged. To truly navigate the dark side of AI, the field must prioritize the development of explainable AI (XAI) models that uphold transparency, fairness, and accountability in pedagogical contexts.

Additionally, the psychological and emotional impact of AI on learners remains an underexplored yet crucial risk. Emerging research suggests that frequent interaction with AI-driven language tutors, chatbots, and assessment tools may inadvertently create feelings of isolation, anxiety, or diminished self-efficacy among students (Xiao et al., 2024). Unlike human teachers, AI systems lack genuine empathy, contextual sensitivity, and the ability to adapt dynamically to the emotional needs of learners. This absence can lead to a depersonalized educational experience where learners are treated as data points rather than complex, holistic individuals. Thus, while AI can support certain aspects of language acquisition, it cannot and should not attempt to replace the inherently relational dimensions of teaching and learning.

Finally, ethical dilemmas surrounding intellectual property and authorship have intensified with the rise of generative AI tools such as ChatGPT and automated writing assistants. In English language education, questions arise about the originality of student work, the authenticity of learning outcomes, and the fairness of using AI-generated texts in assessments (Kasneci et al., 2023). Without clear guidelines, students may either unintentionally plagiarize or come to rely excessively on AI outputs, undermining the development of their critical thinking and creative language skills. Educators face the challenge of fostering AI literacy the ability to critically engage with, rather than passively consume, AI tools so that students use these technologies ethically and responsibly. In this way, navigating the dark side of AI requires not only technical safeguards but also a reimagining of pedagogical ethics for the AI era.

4. THE EVOLVING ROLE OF TEACHERS IN AN AI-INTEGRATED FUTURE

As AI technologies become increasingly embedded in English language education, the role of teachers is undergoing a profound transformation. Far from rendering educators obsolete, AI necessitates a redefinition of their responsibilities as facilitators of critical thinking, ethical stewards of technology, and cultural mediators. Recent studies emphasize that human teachers remain irreplaceable for nurturing higher-order cognitive skills such as creativity, empathy, and intercultural competence, areas where AI still falls significantly short (Luckin et al., 2022; Holmes et al., 2019). Teachers must therefore not only adapt to new technological tools but also guide learners in questioning, critiquing, and ethically engaging with AI outputs. In navigating an AI-enhanced future, the educator's role is elevated, not diminished.

Moreover, English language teachers will increasingly need to develop AI literacy alongside their pedagogical skills. AI literacy goes beyond basic operational knowledge; it involves understanding how AI systems work, recognizing potential biases, evaluating the credibility of AI-generated content, and modeling responsible use for students (Long & Magerko, 2020). Without this critical expertise, teachers risk becoming passive implementers of opaque technologies rather than active shapers of meaningful educational experiences. Recent research advocates for the inclusion of AI literacy training in teacher education programs, arguing that empowering teachers with such competencies is essential for ensuring that AI serves human-centered educational goals rather than commercial or technocratic interests (Zawacki-Richter et al., 2025).

In addition, the emotional and relational dimensions of teaching are expected to gain even greater importance in an AI-mediated classroom. While AI can offer rapid feedback and personalized practice, it cannot replicate the mentorship, encouragement, and moral guidance that human teachers provide. In fact, as learners interact more frequently with impersonal AI systems, the human presence of a teacher will become a critical anchor for maintaining emotional engagement and motivation (Popenici & Kerr, 2017). Teachers will be called upon to cultivate classroom cultures that prioritize human connection, ethical inquiry, and critical engagement with AI-generated materials. Thus, the future of English language education lies not in a competition between humans and machines, but in a thoughtful partnership where teachers lead the way in ensuring that technological innovation enhances, rather than erodes, the humanistic core of education.

4.1 From Knowledge Transmitters to Critical Thinking Facilitators

Traditionally, teachers have been viewed as primary sources of knowledge and linguistic models. However, with AI providing immediate access to language rules, vocabulary explanations, and personalized practice, the teacher's function must shift toward facilitating critical thinking and metacognition. Research by Holmes et al. (2019) highlights that AI can efficiently deliver factual content but lacks the capacity to challenge students to think critically, question assumptions, and engage in reflective dialogue. In this new landscape, teachers must design learning experiences that encourage students to critically evaluate AI-generated outputs, interrogate linguistic norms, and explore multiple perspectives on language and culture. By doing so, educators ensure that students are not passive recipients of machine-produced content, but active, questioning learners.

Furthermore, fostering critical thinking in AI-mediated classrooms requires a deliberate emphasis on process over product. Instead of valuing only the correctness or fluency of AI-generated language outputs, teachers must help students develop skills such as questioning the source of information, identifying embedded biases, and proposing alternative interpretations. For example, when students use AI to generate essays or translations, teachers can require them to annotate these outputs critically, reflecting on what the AI might have missed or misunderstood. This meta-cognitive engagement transforms AI tools from mere answer generators into catalysts for deeper learning, helping students see language not as static knowledge but as a socially and culturally dynamic practice (Luckin et al., 2022).

Moreover, teachers must actively create spaces for dialogic learning, where students collaboratively engage in discussions about AI-generated materials. Such dialogues encourage learners to voice disagreements, build on each other's ideas, and develop a sense of intellectual agency. In contexts where AI provides individualized feedback, group discussions led by teachers can help reintroduce the social, interpretive dimensions of language use that machines alone cannot foster. As Popenici and Kerr (2017) argue, preserving these social elements of learning is essential for resisting the dehumanization risks posed by over-automation. Thus, the shift from knowledge transmission to critical facilitation is not merely an instructional adjustment but a philosophical commitment to human-centered education.

4.2 Developing AI Literacy Among Educators and Learners

A second critical transformation is the imperative for teachers to develop and model AI literacy. Long and Magerko (2020) define AI literacy as the ability to understand how AI systems work, assess their limitations, detect bias, and use them ethically and responsibly. Without this literacy, teachers risk either rejecting AI tools entirely, thereby missing opportunities, or adopting them uncritically, exposing students to hidden biases and ethical pitfalls. Recent work by Zawacki-Richter et al. (2025) stresses the need for formal AI education modules in teacher training programs. Through targeted professional development, teachers can be empowered to guide learners not only in using AI tools effectively but also in understanding when and why to question their outputs. In a world where students may increasingly rely on AI for writing assistance, pronunciation practice, and even conversation simulations, teachers must ensure that learners maintain a critical distance, nurturing autonomy rather than dependence.

In addition to teacher training, curriculum reforms must embed AI literacy explicitly within language learning objectives. English language education should not treat AI tools as mere supplementary aids; instead, students must be taught to critically evaluate machine translations, chatbot conversations, and automated writing feedback. For instance, instructors can design tasks where learners compare human and AI-produced texts, identify errors or cultural insensitivity, and discuss why such discrepancies matter (Holmes et al., 2019). By incorporating such critical exercises, educators prepare students for real-world encounters with AI, where uncritical reliance could perpetuate stereotypes, misinformation, or linguistic inaccuracies.

Moreover, promoting AI literacy aligns closely with broader educational goals of fostering digital citizenship and ethical responsibility. As students increasingly interact with AI outside academic contexts, from social media algorithms to automated customer service, their ability to recognize manipulation, bias, and ethical dilemmas becomes crucial for democratic participation. Teachers, therefore, play a foundational role in cultivating a generation of critically aware citizens who can navigate AI-mediated environments with discernment and integrity. Rather than seeing AI as a threat, English language educators must seize this opportunity to strengthen learners' critical faculties and ethical awareness, positioning them for success in an increasingly AI-saturated world (Zawacki-Richter et al., 2025).

4.3 Prioritizing Human Connection in an Automated Environment

As AI assumes more administrative and instructional functions, the emotional and relational work of teaching becomes even more vital. AI systems, no matter how advanced, cannot provide genuine empathy, encouragement, or mentorship. Popenici and Kerr (2017) argue that as classrooms become more technologically mediated, students will crave authentic human connection and guidance more than ever. Teachers must intentionally foster inclusive, supportive learning environments where emotional well-being, cultural identity, and ethical inquiry are prioritized alongside linguistic proficiency. They must act as mediators between students and machines, ensuring that AI serves human flourishing rather than subordinating it. This new emphasis on relational pedagogy is not ancillary but central to the future of English language education in the AI era (Muñoz-Basols, et al., 2024).

Moreover, human connection is essential for building resilience and motivation, both of which are critical for language acquisition. Research shows that emotional factors such as anxiety, confidence, and motivation significantly affect second language learning outcomes (Dewaele & Li, 2020). While AI can provide corrective feedback and personalized practice, it cannot genuinely celebrate student successes, nurture perseverance after failures, or inspire a love for language and culture. Teachers, by contrast, can tailor emotional and motivational support to individual learner needs, creating an environment where students feel safe to take risks and grow. In this sense, the teacher's role as an emotional guide becomes even more significant in an AI-enhanced classroom.

Finally, relational pedagogy fosters intercultural understanding and critical skills in a globalized world. AI systems tend to standardize interactions based on dominant cultural norms encoded in their training data (Blodgett et al., 2020). Teachers must counterbalance this homogenizing effect by promoting diverse linguistic models, culturally sensitive materials, and opportunities for authentic intercultural communication. By doing so, educators ensure that language learning remains a deeply human, socially situated endeavor rather than a sterile technical exercise. In short, human connection is not a luxury in AI-mediated language education; it is a necessity for maintaining the soul of the learning experience.

4.4 Ethical Guardianship and the Reassertion of Human Values

Finally, teachers must embrace a new role as ethical guardians in an AI-integrated educational environment. The growing influence of AI in assessments, curriculum design, and learner feedback carries the risk of narrowing educational aims to what is easily measurable by machines. Holmes et al. (2019) warn that without critical human oversight, educational practices could become overly technocratic, neglecting essential values such as justice, equity, creativity, and intercultural understanding. Teachers must therefore advocate for educational practices that prioritize human dignity, cultural diversity, and democratic participation. This involves challenging algorithmic biases, resisting harmful standardizations, and continually asking: *Whose interests are served by this AI system, and whose are marginalized?* In short, teachers are no longer merely implementers of curriculum; they are ethical leaders who must safeguard the soul of education in a digital age.

One key ethical challenge is addressing biases embedded within AI tools used for English language learning. Numerous studies have documented how AI language models reflect and perpetuate societal biases, particularly against non-standard English varieties, minority dialects, and marginalized cultures (Blodgett et al., 2020; Mehrabi et al., 2021). Teachers must therefore critically examine the AI applications they introduce into the classroom, question the assumptions embedded within their design, and teach students to do the same. Simply relying on AI without this critical lens risks reinforcing linguistic hierarchies and cultural prejudices, contrary to the inclusive goals of modern language education.

Moreover, teachers must advocate for transparency, accountability, and student agency in the use of AI. This includes informing students about how AI systems make decisions, what data they are trained on, and what limitations they possess (Zawacki-Richter et al., 2025). Empowering students to question and critique AI fosters not only ethical literacy but also a more equitable educational environment. In this light, ethical guardianship is not a passive responsibility but an active, ongoing practice of resistance, vigilance, and advocacy. Teachers, by reasserting human values at the core of English language education, ensure that technology remains a servant of pedagogy, never its master.

Toward a Human-AI Partnership in Education

The evolving role of teachers in English language education signals not an obsolescence, but a renaissance of human-centered pedagogy. In navigating the integration of AI, educators must embrace new responsibilities as facilitators of critical inquiry, developers of AI literacy, relational anchors, and ethical stewards (Muñoz-Basols, et al., 2024).

Only by reasserting human values at the heart of educational practice can we ensure that AI technologies serve as tools for empowerment rather than instruments of control. The future of English language education, therefore, lies in a dynamic human-AI partnership, one in which teachers lead the way.

5. ETHICS AND EQUITY: FOUNDATIONS FOR RESPONSIBLE INNOVATION

As Artificial Intelligence (AI) becomes increasingly embedded within English language education, the call for ethical and equitable practices has grown urgent. Recent scholarship emphasizes that innovation without ethical grounding risks exacerbating social inequalities and undermining the transformative potential of education itself (Jobin, Ienca, & Vayena, 2019). Teachers, policymakers, and developers must prioritize ethical considerations from the outset, ensuring that AI tools do not merely serve efficiency or profitability but advance inclusivity, justice, and human dignity. Responsible innovation must therefore be guided by a commitment to minimizing bias, promoting cultural sensitivity, and safeguarding the rights and autonomy of all learners. Without these foundations, technological progress risks becoming a tool of exclusion rather than empowerment.

One major ethical concern is the reproduction of systemic biases within AI language applications. Studies have shown that AI models trained on large corpora often inherit biases reflecting dominant linguistic, racial, and cultural norms, thereby marginalizing minority voices (Blodgett et al., 2020; Mehrabi et al., 2021). In the context of English language education, this could result in the privileging of standardized "inner circle" English varieties (e.g., American or British English) at the expense of World Englishes, thus reinforcing linguistic hierarchies. Educators must therefore advocate for the development and adoption of AI systems that recognize and respect linguistic diversity. A truly ethical AI-enhanced classroom would celebrate the multiplicity of Englishes, not erase them in favor of a monolithic norm, ensuring that all learners see their identities reflected and valued in the learning process.

Equity must also be a guiding principle in access to AI-enhanced educational tools. The "digital divide" the unequal access to technology based on socio-economic status, geography, or disability risks widening if AI innovations cater only to privileged populations (UNESCO, 2021). In English language learning, AI-driven personalization and adaptive feedback systems offer great promise, but only for those who can afford or access them. Without conscious efforts to ensure accessibility and affordability, AI risks deepening educational inequalities. Therefore, responsible innovation requires partnerships between governments, educational institutions, and the tech industry to make AI resources publicly available, customizable for local contexts, and usable by learners with diverse needs, including those with disabilities.

Moreover, ethical innovation demands transparency and explainability in AI systems used in education. Learners and educators must be able to understand how AI tools generate recommendations, corrections, or assessments. Black-box algorithms, systems whose internal logic is opaque, undermine trust and disempower users (Zawacki-Richter et al., 2025). For instance, if an AI-powered writing assistant consistently downgrades non-standard but grammatically correct constructions, students must have the tools to question and critique those decisions. Transparency is not just a technical requirement; it is a pedagogical necessity that empowers learners to remain critical thinkers rather than passive consumers of AI judgments.

Finally, embedding ethics and equity into AI-enhanced English education is not a static task but a continuous, participatory process. It demands ongoing dialogue between developers, educators, learners, and communities about evolving challenges and emerging harms. Ethics codes, fairness audits, and participatory design models must be institutionalized within educational technology development (Al Aqad, 2022). Most importantly, learners themselves must be positioned not just as users of AI but as co-creators of ethical educational futures. Through critical engagement, students can help shape AI systems that align with human values of justice, dignity, and collective flourishing. Thus, responsible innovation is not only about preventing harm; it is about actively building a better, more equitable educational landscape.

5.1 Confronting Biases and Ensuring Linguistic Justice

One major ethical concern is the reproduction of systemic biases within AI language applications. Studies have shown that AI models trained on large corpora often inherit biases reflecting dominant linguistic, racial, and cultural norms, thereby marginalizing minority voices (Blodgett et al., 2020; Al Aqad, Al-Saggaf, & Muthmainnah, 2021). In the context of English language education, this could result in the privileging of standardized "inner circle" English varieties (e.g., American or British English) at the expense of World Englishes, thus reinforcing linguistic hierarchies. Educators must therefore advocate for the development and adoption of AI systems that recognize and respect linguistic diversity. A truly ethical AI-enhanced classroom would celebrate the multiplicity of Englishes, not erase them in favor of a monolithic norm, ensuring that all learners see their identities reflected and valued in the learning process.

Equity must also be a guiding principle in access to AI-enhanced educational tools. The "digital divide" the unequal access to technology based on socio-economic status, geography, or disability risks widening if AI innovations cater only to privileged populations (UNESCO, 2021). In English language learning, AI-driven personalization and adaptive feedback systems offer great promise, but only for those who can afford or access them. Without conscious efforts to ensure accessibility and affordability, AI risks deepening educational inequalities. Therefore, responsible innovation requires partnerships between governments, educational institutions, and the tech industry to make AI resources publicly available, customizable for local contexts, and usable by learners with diverse needs, including those with disabilities.

5.2 Promoting Transparency, Accountability, and Student Agency

Moreover, ethical innovation demands transparency and explainability in AI systems used in education. Learners and educators must be able to understand how AI tools generate recommendations, corrections, or assessments. Black-box algorithms systems whose internal logic is opaque undermine trust and disempower users (Zawacki-Richter et al., 2019). For instance, if an AI-powered writing assistant consistently downgrades non-standard but grammatically correct constructions, students must have the tools to question and critique those decisions. Transparency is not just a technical requirement; it is a pedagogical necessity that empowers learners to remain critical thinkers rather than passive consumers of AI judgments.

Finally, embedding ethics and equity into AI-enhanced English education is not a static task but a continuous, participatory process. It demands ongoing dialogue between developers, educators, learners, and communities about evolving challenges and emerging harms. Ethics codes, fairness audits, and participatory design models must be institutionalized within educational technology development (Floridi, 2023). Most importantly, learners themselves must be positioned not just as users of AI but as co-creators of ethical educational futures. Through critical engagement, students can help shape AI systems that align with human values of justice, dignity, and collective flourishing. Thus, responsible innovation is not only about preventing harm; it is about actively building a better, more equitable educational landscape.

6. FUTURE MODELS OF LANGUAGE EDUCATION: HYBRID, AI-FIRST, AND BEYOND

The future of English language education is poised to be shaped by dynamic, AI-driven models that transcend traditional pedagogies. Hybrid models, combining human instruction with AI support, are rapidly gaining traction as the most balanced approach. Research highlights that while AI can provide personalized practice and instant feedback, human teachers remain essential for fostering critical thinking, cultural nuance, and emotional intelligence (Luckin et al., 2022). Rather than displacing teachers, AI augments their capacities, allowing them to focus on higher-order instructional tasks. Future classrooms may thus increasingly operate as "co-teaching environments," where AI handles routine tasks such as grammar correction and vocabulary drilling, freeing teachers to guide interpretation, creativity, and collaborative learning (Muñoz-Basols, et al., 2024).

Meanwhile, "AI-first" models of education are beginning to emerge, where the structure of learning is fundamentally designed around AI capabilities rather than traditional curricular frameworks. In such models, students might interact primarily with AI tutors that adapt lessons instantaneously based on performance data, emotional engagement, and learning preferences (Holmes & Tuomi, 2019). Although this approach promises radical personalization, it also raises concerns about dehumanization and over-reliance on algorithmic authority. As researchers have warned, unchecked AI-first education risks narrowing learners' intellectual horizons by optimizing efficiency at the expense of exploration and deep critical inquiry (Williamson & Eynon, 2020). Therefore, educational stakeholders must design AI-first models with strong safeguards that protect learner agency, promote intellectual diversity, and maintain spaces for human connection.

Beyond hybrid and AI-first frameworks, future models may evolve toward even more integrative and participatory ecosystems. The rise of generative AI tools, such as advanced language models and virtual reality language immersion environments, enables learners to become active co-creators of knowledge rather than passive recipients (Popenici & Kerr, 2017). For instance, students could collaboratively "train" their own language-learning AIs tailored to specific cultural contexts or personal goals, fostering metacognitive skills and deeper engagement. Such participatory models not only democratize education but also prepare learners for future workplaces where AI-human collaboration will be the norm. As educational futures scholars suggest, truly transformative models will blend technology with human-centered pedagogies, promoting adaptability, resilience, and ethical responsibility among learners (Facer, 2011).

Nevertheless, realizing these future models requires a profound shift in educational policy, teacher training, and curriculum design. Teachers must be equipped not only with digital skills but also with critical AI literacy to navigate, question, and ethically deploy AI tools in the classroom (Zawacki-Richter et al., 2025). Institutions must invest in infrastructure that ensures equitable access to AI technologies, particularly in under-resourced settings. Curricula must evolve from fixed content delivery toward fostering AI co-navigation skills, teaching students how to collaborate with, critique, and ethically leverage AI agents. If these shifts are undertaken thoughtfully, future models of English language education could fulfill the promise of a more personalized, inclusive, and dynamic learning experience for all.

6.1 Hybrid Learning Models: The Best of Both Worlds

Hybrid learning models, blending AI-driven resources with traditional instruction, represent a pragmatic and promising vision for the near future. AI tools can personalize learning experiences by adjusting content difficulty, offering instant feedback, and catering to individual learner profiles (Holmes & Tuomi, 2019). Meanwhile, human educators can provide socio-emotional support, foster deeper discussions, and develop critical literacies that AI cannot replicate. This dual approach recognizes the irreplaceable human dimensions of language learning-such as empathy, ethical reasoning, and cultural negotiation while leveraging AI's strengths in adaptability and scalability. Research indicates that when AI is integrated thoughtfully into human-led instruction, student engagement and achievement both improve significantly (Luckin et al., 2022).

Furthermore, hybrid learning models can accommodate diverse learner needs in ways traditional models often cannot. For instance, multilingual learners, students with disabilities, and learners from varied socio-economic backgrounds can benefit from AI's ability to tailor interventions at scale (Popenici & Kerr, 2017). In a hybrid model, AI can detect subtle learning gaps or difficulties that may not be immediately visible to a teacher and suggest micro-adaptations in instruction. This ensures that learning is not only more inclusive but also more efficient, thereby fostering greater educational equity.

However, the successful implementation of hybrid models requires careful design and ongoing evaluation. As Holmes and Tuomi (2019) argue, merely placing AI tools into classrooms without integrating them meaningfully into pedagogy can lead to superficial use and eventual abandonment. Teachers must be actively involved in co-creating hybrid learning experiences, ensuring that AI complements rather than dictates pedagogical goals. Hybrid models must prioritize teacher agency, continuous feedback loops, and ethical transparency to avoid inadvertently reinforcing educational inequalities.

6.2 AI-First Classrooms: Opportunities and Limitations

Meanwhile, "AI-first" models of education are beginning to emerge, where the structure of learning is fundamentally designed around AI capabilities rather than traditional curricular frameworks. In such models, students might interact primarily with AI tutors that adapt lessons instantaneously based on performance data, emotional engagement, and learning preferences (Holmes & Tuomi, 2019). Although this approach promises radical personalization, it also raises concerns about dehumanization and over-reliance on algorithmic authority. As researchers have warned, unchecked AI-first education risks narrowing learners' intellectual horizons by optimizing efficiency at the expense of exploration and deep critical inquiry (Williamson & Eynon, 2020). Therefore, educational stakeholders must design AI-first models with strong safeguards that protect learner agency, promote intellectual diversity, and maintain spaces for human connection.

Nonetheless, an AI-first approach also presents profound pedagogical and ethical challenges. One major concern is the risk of algorithmic determinism, where AI systems predetermine educational trajectories based on incomplete or biased data (Blodgett et al., 2020). In such environments, students may lose agency over their learning, simply following recommendations without critical reflection. Additionally, the absence of human mentorship could impair the development of essential soft skills, such as empathy, negotiation, and critical intercultural communication all crucial for language learners operating in globalized contexts.

To address these risks, researchers emphasize the need for "human-in-the-loop" AI-first models, where human educators oversee and mediate AI interactions (Zawacki-Richter et al., 2025). In this way, AI can support mass personalization without sacrificing human judgment, empathy, and adaptability. Ethical frameworks must also guide AI-first classrooms, ensuring that students' data rights, cognitive autonomy, and well-being remain protected. A purely AI-dominated learning environment is unlikely to produce the resilient, critical, and socially responsible citizens that 21st-century societies need.

6.3 Participatory Models: Co-Creating the Future of Language Learning

Beyond hybrid and AI-first frameworks, future models may evolve toward even more integrative and participatory ecosystems. The rise of generative AI tools, such as advanced language models and virtual reality language immersion environments, enables learners to become active co-creators of knowledge rather than passive recipients (Popenici & Kerr, 2017). For instance, students could collaboratively build language bots tailored to specific social contexts such as business English, academic discourse, or intercultural negotiation thereby gaining both language skills and critical technological literacies. Such participatory models not only democratize education but also prepare learners for future workplaces where AI-human collaboration will be the norm. As educational futures scholars suggest, truly transformative models will blend technology with human-centered pedagogies, promoting adaptability, resilience, and ethical responsibility among learners (Facer, 2011).

Such participatory approaches also foster deeper engagement and intrinsic motivation among learners. When students are empowered to co-create their learning tools, they are more likely to take ownership of their progress, reflect metacognitively on their strategies, and develop agency (Facer, 2011). Moreover, participatory models encourage ethical thinking, as students must confront questions about bias, representation, and inclusivity when designing language models. In this sense, language education becomes not only a technical exercise but also a platform for cultivating responsible digital citizens.

Nevertheless, participatory models require significant scaffolding and support to be effective. Not all learners possess the technical skills or critical literacies needed to design or critique AI tools independently. Educators must therefore integrate AI literacy, design thinking, and ethical reasoning explicitly into the language curriculum (Luckin et al., 2022). Institutions must also ensure equitable access to the technologies necessary for participatory learning, preventing further digital divides. If these challenges are met, participatory models could redefine language education as a dynamic, democratic, and socially transformative endeavor.

6.4 Policy, Training, and Curriculum: Preparing for the AI-Enhanced Future

Nevertheless, realizing these future models requires a profound shift in educational policy, teacher training, and curriculum design. Teachers must be equipped not only with digital skills but also with critical AI literacy to navigate, question, and ethically deploy AI tools in the classroom (Zawacki-Richter et al., 2025). Institutions must invest in infrastructure that ensures equitable access to AI technologies, particularly in under-resourced settings. Curricula must evolve from fixed content delivery toward fostering AI co-navigation skills-teaching students how to collaborate with, critique, and ethically leverage AI agents. If these shifts are undertaken thoughtfully, future models of English language education could fulfill the promise of a more personalized, inclusive, and dynamic learning experience for all.

Teacher training programs must be radically updated to include AI pedagogy, ethical AI use, and interdisciplinary collaboration skills (Zawacki-Richter et al., 2019). Teachers should not only know how to operate AI tools but also critically evaluate their implications, question their outputs, and adapt them creatively for diverse learning needs. Professional development must be ongoing, collaborative, and aligned with rapidly evolving AI technologies, preventing teachers from being marginalized in increasingly AI-mediated classrooms.

At the curricular level, English language education must move beyond traditional four-skills models (listening, speaking, reading, writing) to include AI co-navigation skills. Students must learn how to interact critically with AI-generated content, discern bias, manage information overload, and leverage AI responsibly to enhance their communication capabilities. Curricula should also prioritize cross-cultural competencies, ethics, and adaptability, preparing learners not just for language exams but for lifelong learning in a world where AI will be ubiquitous. If education systems embrace these reforms, the future of English language learning can be one of empowerment, inclusion, and innovation.

7. POLICY, RESEARCH, AND THE ROAD AHEAD

As AI technologies rapidly permeate English language education, policy and research must move just as swiftly to shape responsible, equitable, and innovative futures. Without robust, forward-thinking policy frameworks, the risk of exacerbating existing inequalities and introducing new forms of harm becomes alarmingly high (Holmes & Tuomi, 2019). Governments, educational institutions, and international organizations must collaboratively define ethical standards for AI use in education, including data governance, algorithmic transparency, and learner rights. Recent work by Zawacki-Richter et al. (2025) emphasizes that leaving AI integration to commercial tech companies without public oversight risks educational systems becoming driven by profit motives rather than pedagogical or societal goals. Policies must prioritize the public good, safeguarding education as a fundamental human right, even amidst disruptive technological change.

In tandem with policymaking, educational research must evolve to address the profound complexities introduced by AI. Traditional paradigms focused solely on instructional outcomes are no longer sufficient. Researchers must now investigate the socio-cultural, ethical, and emotional dimensions of AI-mediated learning (Williamson & Eynon, 2020). For example, studies are needed on how algorithmic personalization affects learner identity formation, motivation, and critical thinking capacities. Furthermore, interdisciplinary approaches are essential, bringing together expertise from linguistics, computer science, education, psychology, and ethics to holistically evaluate AI's impacts. Without sustained, critical research, language education risks being swept along by technological novelty without understanding its long-term consequences. An urgent area for policy and research is addressing bias and inequity in AI systems used in language education. AI models trained predominantly on Western, English-centric datasets may reinforce linguistic imperialism and marginalize non-standard varieties of English and non-Western cultures (Blodgett et al., 2020). Policies must mandate inclusive dataset practices, multilingual AI development, and culturally responsive design. Researchers must also critically interrogate how AI's "neutrality" is often a myth, masking deep-seated biases embedded in data and design decisions. As Popenici and Kerr (2017) argue, ethical AI in education is not just about protecting privacy but actively fostering diversity, representation, and justice in learning environments. Another key consideration for the road ahead is ensuring that teachers are central to AI policy and research discussions. Teachers are not merely implementers of AI tools; they are critical agents who must shape how technology is used in classrooms (Luckin et al., 2022). Therefore, policies should fund teacher-led AI innovation projects, include teacher voices in regulatory bodies, and prioritize research into teacher experiences with AI integration. Ignoring the perspectives of educator's risks creating solutions that are technologically impressive but pedagogically hollow. By positioning teachers as partners rather than passive recipients, education systems can harness AI to genuinely enhance, rather than replace the craft of teaching.

Finally, international collaboration is vital to crafting a coherent and equitable future for AI in language education. The challenges of bias, equity, ethical use, and access are global in nature and require shared solutions (Jobin, Ienca, & Vayena, 2019). International organizations such as UNESCO and OECD are already working toward global AI education guidelines, but greater participation from the Global South is necessary to avoid replicating colonial hierarchies in digital form (UNESCO, 2021). Policies and research agendas must thus be globally informed but locally responsive, balancing universal human rights with the contextual realities of diverse communities. The road ahead is fraught with complexities, but with collaborative governance, critical scholarship, and ethical vigilance, the integration of AI into language education can become a force for global empowerment rather than division.

8. CONCLUSION

As AI continues to transform English language education, the ultimate challenge is ensuring that technological innovation serves human flourishing, not the other way around. A human-centered AI future demands that learners' dignity, agency, and diversity are placed at the forefront of technological design and deployment. Scholars like Luckin (2022) stress that AI should augment rather than automate human intelligence, supporting teachers and students rather than sidelining them. If left unchecked, AI risks reducing education to a data-driven process, stripping away the relational and ethical dimensions that are fundamental to meaningful learning. Therefore, shaping AI's role in education must start with an unwavering commitment to human values.

Secondly, a human-centered AI future must actively confront and correct existing inequities rather than exacerbate them. Research has shown that AI systems often replicate and even deepen social, racial, and linguistic biases (Blodgett et al., 2020; UNESCO, 2021). In language education, this could marginalize non-native English speakers and entrench Western-centric worldviews. It is not enough for AI tools to be efficient; they must also be equitable. Policymakers and developers must adopt ethical design principles, inclusive data practices, and rigorous bias auditing processes to ensure that all learners, regardless of background, can benefit from AI-enhanced education.

Moreover, achieving a human-centered AI future necessitates empowering educators as critical designers and decision-makers. Teachers are uniquely positioned to interpret learners' needs, contextualize AI outputs, and foster critical engagement with technology (Holmes & Tuomi, 2019). Rather than treating AI tools as fixed systems to be blindly adopted, educators must be equipped with the skills and authority to adapt, critique, and even reject AI interventions that do not align with pedagogical goals. Supporting teacher agency is not merely a technical issue but a political one it is about who holds power over the educational process in an AI-driven era (Muñoz-Basols, et al., 2024).

Finally, international collaboration is essential to ensure that AI developments reflect the diverse realities of global learners rather than reinforcing digital colonialism. As Jobin, Ienca, and Vayena (2019) argue, current AI ethics guidelines are still disproportionately shaped by Western institutions. Creating a truly human-centered AI future requires centering voices from the Global South, indigenous communities, and marginalized groups who have historically been excluded from technological governance. Language education, rooted as it is in cultural identity and communication, must be especially attentive to ensuring AI systems celebrate and sustain linguistic and cultural diversity rather than erasing it. Only through inclusive, participatory, and justice-oriented approaches can we ensure that AI becomes a tool for human empowerment rather than domination.

8.1 Prioritizing Human Dignity and Educational Equity

As AI continues to transform English language education, the ultimate challenge is ensuring that technological innovation serves human flourishing, not the other way around. A human-centered AI future demands that learners' dignity, agency, and diversity are placed at the forefront of technological design and deployment. Scholars like Luckin (2022) stress that AI should augment rather than automate human intelligence, supporting teachers and students rather than sidelining them.

If left unchecked, AI risks reducing education to a data-driven process, stripping away the relational and ethical dimensions that are fundamental to meaningful learning. Therefore, shaping AI's role in education must start with an unwavering commitment to human values. Secondly, a human-centered AI future must actively confront and correct existing inequities rather than exacerbate them. Research has shown that AI systems often replicate and even deepen social, racial, and linguistic biases (Blodgett et al., 2020; UNESCO, 2021). In language education, this could marginalize non-native English speakers and entrench Western-centric worldviews. It is not enough for AI tools to be efficient; they must also be equitable. Policymakers and developers must adopt ethical design principles, inclusive data practices, and rigorous bias auditing processes to ensure that all learners, regardless of background, can benefit from AI-enhanced education.

8.2 Empowering Educators and Expanding Global Participation

Moreover, achieving a human-centered AI future necessitates empowering educators as critical designers and decision-makers. Teachers are uniquely positioned to interpret learners' needs, contextualize AI outputs, and foster critical engagement with technology (Holmes & Tuomi, 2019). Rather than treating AI tools as fixed systems to be blindly adopted, educators must be equipped with the skills and authority to adapt, critique, and even reject AI interventions that do not align with pedagogical goals. Supporting teacher agency is not merely a technical issue but a political one it is about who holds power over the educational process in an AI-driven era. Finally, international collaboration is essential to ensure that AI developments reflect the diverse realities of global learners rather than reinforcing digital colonialism. As Jobin, Ienca, and Vayena (2019) argue, current AI ethics guidelines are still disproportionately shaped by Western institutions. Creating a truly human-centered AI future requires centering voices from the Global South, indigenous communities, and marginalized groups who have historically been excluded from technological governance. Language education, rooted as it is in cultural identity and communication, must be especially attentive to ensuring AI systems celebrate and sustain linguistic and cultural diversity rather than erasing it. Only through inclusive, participatory, and justice-oriented approaches can we ensure that AI becomes a tool for human empowerment rather than domination.

In shaping the future of AI-driven English language education, the responsibility rests not merely in technological advancement but in reaffirming education's humanistic core a future where innovation, ethics, and inclusivity walk hand in hand. As we move forward, let us remain committed to ensuring that AI serves as a bridge to greater empowerment, understanding, and equity for all learners across the globe.

REFERENCES

Al Aqad, M. H., Al-Saggaf, M. A., & Muthmainnah, M. (2021). The impact of audio-visual aids on learning English among MSU third-year students. ENGLISH FRANCA: Academic Journal of English Language and Education, 5(2 November), 201-214.</unknown>

Al Aqad, M. H. (2022). Multilingualism and Personal Health Benefits: Connecting the. Multilingualism: Interdisciplinary Topics, 123.

Blodgett, S. L., Barocas, S., Daumé, H., III, & Wallach, H. (2020). Language (technology) is power: A critical survey of" bias" in nlp. *arXiv preprint arXiv:2005.14050.*

Burrell, J. (2016). How the machine 'thinks': Understanding opacity in machine learning algorithms. *Big Data & Society*, *3*(1), 2053951715622512.

Dewaele, J. M., & Li, C. (2020). Emotions in second language acquisition: A critical review and research agenda. *Foreign language world, 196*(1), 34-49.

Dörnyei, Z. (2001). *Motivational strategies in the language classroom* (Vol. 10). Cambridge University Press.

Facer, K. (2011). *Learning futures: Education, technology and social change*. Routledge.

Floridi, L. (2023). *The Ethics of Artificial Intelligence: Principles, Challenges, and Opportunities*. Oxford University Press.

Göçmez, L., & Okur, M. R. (2023). Artificial intelligence applications in open and distance education: A systematic review of the articles (2007-2021). *Asian Journal of Distance Education*, *18*(1).

Holmes, W., Bialik, M., & Fadel, C. (2019). *Artificial intelligence in education promises and implications for teaching and learning*. Center for Curriculum Redesign.

Jobin, A., Ienca, M., & Vayena, E. (2019). The global landscape of AI ethics guidelines. *Nature Machine Intelligence*, *1*(9), 389–399.

Kasneci, E., Sessler, K., Betsch, P., & Kasneci, G. (2023). ChatGPT for Good? On Opportunities and Challenges of Large Language Models for Education. *Learning and Individual Differences*, *103*, 102274.

Kooli, C. (2023). Chatbots in education and research: A critical examination of ethical implications and solutions. *Sustainability*, *15*(7), 5614.

Long, D., & Magerko, B. (2020, April). What is AI literacy? Competencies and design considerations. In *Proceedings of the 2020 CHI conference on human factors in computing systems* (pp. 1-16).

Luckin, R., & Holmes, W. (2016). Intelligence unleashed: An argument for AI in education.

Luckin, R., Cukurova, M., Kent, C., & Du Boulay, B. (2022). Empowering educators to be AI-ready. *Computers and Education: Artificial Intelligence*, *3*, 100076.

Mehrabi, N., Morstatter, F., Saxena, N., Lerman, K., & Galstyan, A. (2021). A survey on bias and fairness in machine learning. *ACM Computing Surveys*, *54*(6), 1–35.

Mehrabi, N., Morstatter, F., Saxena, N., Lerman, K., & Galstyan, A. (2021). A Survey on Bias and Fairness in Machine Learning. *ACM Computing Surveys*.

Muñoz-Basols, J., & Gutiérrez, M. F. (2024). 13 Opportunities for Artificial Intelligence (AI) in Language Teaching and Learning. *Technology-Mediated Language Teaching*, 297.

Niemi, H. (2024). AI in Education and Learning: Perspectives on the Education Ecosystem. In *New Frontiers in Science in the Era of AI* (pp. 169–194). Springer Nature Switzerland.

Pennycook, A. (2010). *Language as a local practice*. Routledge.

Popenici, S. A., & Kerr, S. (2017). Exploring the impact of artificial intelligence on teaching and learning in higher education. *Research and Practice in Technology Enhanced Learning*, *12*(1), 22. PMID: 30595727

Tapalova, O., & Zhiyenbayeva, N. (2022). Artificial intelligence in education: AIEd for personalised learning pathways. *Electronic Journal of e-Learning*, *20*(5), 639–653.

UNESCO. (2021). AI and education: Guidance for policymakers. United Nations Educational, Scientific and Cultural Organization (UNESCO). https://unesdoc.unesco.org/ark:/48223/pf0000377071

Williamson, B., & Eynon, R. (2020). Historical Threads, Missing Links, and Future Directions in AI in Education. *Learning, Media and Technology*, *45*(3), 223–235.

Xiao, Y., Zhang, T., & He, J. (2024). A review of promises and challenges of AI-based chatbots in language education through the lens of learner emotions. *Heliyon*.

Zawacki-Richter, O., Cefa, B., & Bai, J. Y. (2025). Towards reproducible systematic reviews in Open, Distance, and Digital Education An umbrella mapping review. *Review of Education*, *13*(1), e70031.

Zawacki-Richter, O., Marín, V. I., Bond, M., & Gouverneur, F. (2019). Systematic review of research on artificial intelligence applications in higher education – where are the educators? *International Journal of Educational Technology in Higher Education, 16*(1), 39.

Zawacki-Richter, O., Marín, V. I., Bond, M., & Gouverneur, F. (2019). Systematic review of research on artificial intelligence applications in higher education–where are the educators? *International Journal of Educational Technology in Higher Education, 16*(1), 1–27.

Chapter 11
The Integration of Artificial Intelligence in English Language Education:
Revolutionizing Teaching and Learning Methodologies

Sanjeev Kumar
https://orcid.org/0000-0002-7375-7341
Lovely Professional University, India

ABSTRACT

Artificial Intelligence (AI) has emerged as a transformative force in various fields. The implications of the integration of English language Education into the English language are radically transforming the teaching and the learning processes. This abstract addresses the challenges of bringing AI technologies to English language teaching and the benefits of such use of technologies to language acquisition, individualized learning, and overall student gains. English Language Education is increasingly taking advantage of AI-powered tools and applications to bring creative solutions to long-standing issues. These technologies include intelligent tutoring systems, chats, automated writing evaluation and speech-recognition software. With machine learning algorithms and natural language processing AI can give feedback to learners about all things, and provide them with adaptive content and constructive practice. The English Language Education such as heightened interaction of the learners with the lessons, better availability, and much faster evaluation strategies.

DOI: 10.4018/979-8-3373-3755-5.ch011

INTRODUCTION

The 21st century is witnessing a lot of change in the world of education because of modern technological changes. Artificial Intelligence (AI) has become one of the strongest tools that have changed the nature of knowledge delivery and learning. AI does not only serve as an auxiliary tool in ELE but is a discontinuity that challenges current teaching methods, learning activities, and classroom management. AI is the term used to refer to those computer systems (intelligent systems) that have the capability to imitate human intelligence procedures like the solution of problems, recognition of speech, and decision-making. When deployed in an English Language Teaching (ELT) context, the use of artificial intelligence technologies such as Natural Language Processing (NLP), speech recognition and adaptive learning platforms, as well as chatbots, introduces innovations in instruction and learning (Anwar et al., 2025). It is delivered in contrast to traditional approaches, which are more rigid with a fixed curriculum and human instructor-oriented teaching and AI brings flexibility, customization, and access to a new level. Personalization of learning experiences is one of the main insights that artificial intelligence brings to English language learning. AI-based systems use the strengths and weaknesses of a learner and the progress he or she makes to develop a personalized learning program. As an example, learning apps like Duolingo or Lingvist auto-adjust the difficulty based on a user performance, making the experience neither too challenging, nor too easy. This individualized feedback system motivates and helps learners stay focused. It also facilitates automated assessment and feedback, which is an absolute requirement in languages. Grammar checkers such as Grammarly or Quillbot use AI-powered algorithms to immediately recognize grammatical mistakes, suggest an alternative word choice, and enhance sentence structure. Equally, automated scoring systems used in essays give comprehensive feedback, and they save the teacher's time even as the students get instant corrections (Boborakhim Kanayev, 2024). This lessens the intensity of work done by the teacher, and enables him/her to concentrate on creative and interactive activities, and in higher order tasks.

The use of AI-powered conversational agents and chatbots is another way to be transformative. These virtual assistants are interactive simulators that help students train their speaking and listening skills without the pressure that real life has when beginning to learn a new language. Unlike human teachers, the artificial intelligence chatbots will be available all the time, offering a person constant training and learning experiences. Speech recognition software can also be used to supplement pronunciation practice because it can correct mistakes and teach the student to get it right (Yadav, 2025). AI introduces immersive learning experiences via the Virtual Reality (VR) and Augmented Reality (AR). Think of a student drilling in an airport / restaurant virtual environment. The application of artificial intelligence is a unique attribute of such language learning scenarios since it gives learners a chance to be exposed to vocabulary that feels like the real world and lets them practice these real-life communications, thus being able to significantly develop fluency and confidence. The use of artificial intelligence through gamification also engages learners with the help of points, prizes, and challenges (Talukder, Khan, et al., 2025). There are still various challenges involved in the implementation of artificial intelligence in English language education. The issues related to the data privacy, algorithmic discrimination, and the resistance of teachers tends to appear. Also, the availability of AI-based learning resources can be scarce in disadvantaged populations because of the excessive expenses and the absence of information technology. Thus, artificial intelligence has big potential but it cannot be seen as a substitute to human teachers. Rather, it must be viewed as an assistant in the classroom-satellite rather than replacement of the teacher (Talukder, Mia, et al., 2025).

The future of English language education is in the hybrid model where an AI and a human teacher harmoniously co-exist. Teachers will remain focal in nurturing creativity, critical thinking, and cultural awareness, and artificial intelligence will do repetitive tasks, personalized feedback, and insights based on data. It allows breaking educational inequalities, and the English language learning process can become more inclusive and productive. The introduction of Artificial Intelligence in the teaching English language education practice is transforming the teaching and learning practices (Khang et al., 2023). AI allows delivering such advantages as personalization, automation, immersion, and accessibility to learners and teachers alike. The ethical concerns, equally, need to be dealt with, and fair access should be provided to those in need, as well as educators need to be train to change in regards to AI-driven tools. With the future development of AI, there is the potential of seeing English language education be turned into a more interactive, efficient, and accessible practice across the world.

SIGNIFICANCE OF AI IN MODERN EDUCATION AND RATIONALE FOR INTEGRATING AI IN ENGLISH LANGUAGE TEACHING

The booming of Artificial Intelligence (AI) has introduced tremendous dynamics within the scope of various sectors, education being one of them. Contemporary education no longer operates within the settings of conventional classrooms with text-books and blackboard, but has transformed into a dynamic learning process that incorporate use of technology in improving the learning experiences. Amongst them, the role of artificial intelligence is particularly high because it can process data, individualize learning, and give smart feedback (Kumar et al., 2025). It is palpable in every field, including learning and teaching of English- a worldwide language of communication, academia, and professional growth.

Significance of AI in Modern Education

AI is revolutionizing education in several ways. One of its most important contributions is personalized learning. Conventional educational models tend to be one-size-fits-all; using a uniform pace in which all students are supposed to progress identically. The AI-based platforms though, examine the strengths, weaknesses and learning patterns of the learners and fashion a personalized learning experience. This will guarantee that students get content according to their needs which will enhance efficiency and motivation. The other important implication of AI is automated scoring and evaluation. Intelligent systems are capable of marking multiple choice exams, the grading of essays, and instant corrections on grammar and composition. This relieves teachers of workload since they now deliver immediate and constructive readers to the students (Anwar & Kumar, 2025). It also allows real-time tracking of the progress, so both teachers and learners can track the improvement and make sure that some aspects need to be attended to. Additionally, artificial intelligence promotes an inclusive and accessible education. Students with disabilities have an advantage of using artificial intelligence tools like speech-to-text, screen reader, and translator tools. Such innovations lead to equitability in the learning environment as no learners with various needs are left behind.

Rationale for Integrating AI in English Language Teaching (ELT)

English is now a global lingua franca, an international language necessary to communicate study and stay at the top in the labor market. Nevertheless, learning the English language is not usually easy to learners, especially non-native speakers. Here, artificial intelligence can have a big role in enabling teaching and learning alike. To begin with, AI allows an interactive and interesting language learning process. Using chatbots and voice assistants as well as AI-based conversation simulators, students can train their speaking and listening to avoid feeling judged and misjudged. The technology of speech recognition also aids in the enhancement of good pronunciation and fluency by providing instantaneous corrective feedback (Kumar, 2024).

Secondly, artificial intelligence promotes individual and self-directed learning in ELT. Such tools include adaptive vocabulary builders or reading platforms that are AI-powered and offer individual exercises designed to the level of learners. This kind of personalization will make sure that beginner learners can get simplified contents and advanced learners can get complex materials. Thirdly, artificial intelligence can help teachers by eliminating repetition. Grading, structural corrections, and practice questions preparation can be fulfilled with the help of artificial intelligence software, giving a teacher additional time to focus on more creative teaching, critical thinking, and cultural English learning. artificial intelligence also introduces immersive learning options to ELT (Karki & Karki, 2025). Language training in collaboration with artificial intelligence can be supported by VR and AR, which simulates real-life properties including Airport check-ins, business meetings, or social conversations, so language practice is authentic and compelling. Lastly, the incorporation of artificial intelligence in the process of teaching English is in line with the general idea of preparing children who are yet to live in the digital age. The ability to fluently speak in English and be literate in artificial intelligence will ensure students have all the needed skills to become global citizens and future professionals (Kumar & Bayram, 2025). The importance of artificial intelligence to contemporary education is reasonable individualization, greater accessibility, less burden on teachers, and lifelong learning. In particular, AI plays the role of a language learning companion and a language study assistant in the context of the English language education as it facilitates more interactive, dynamic, and efficient learning. Explaining why artificial intelligence is being integrated is straightforward in regards to the fact that not only will learners become proficient in language skills but also will be more prepared in a world where technology and communication go hand in hand. The use of artificial intelligence in English Language Teaching is not only an innovation but a need to have education ready to embrace the present and future trends (Crompton et al., 2024).

Research Methodology: Secondary data refers to the information that has already been collected, processed, and published by someone else. It is not collected directly by the researcher but is obtained from existing sources which includes; Books and textbooks, Government reports, Newspapers and magazines, Research papers and journals, Online databases and websites and Census reports and surveys

LITERATURE REVIEW

Historical Overview of English Language Teaching (ELT) Methods

The pedagogy of English as a second language or foreign language has been changing throughout the ages. All the methods have been based on the philosophies of education and the societal cultures existing during these periods and found their way into current English education. The Grammar-Translation Method is one of the oldest methods that prevailed in the 18th and19th centuries. Based on the classical education, it focused on the rules of grammar, learning vocabulary and translating texts. Although it enhanced reading and writing, it did not encourage speaking and listening much, a situation which left most learners very sound in theory and weak in practice speech and listening skills. The Direct Method surfaced in the late 19th century (Howatt & Smith, 2014). This procedure put off translation and emphasized the teaching of English by the use of English. It encouraged immersion in terms of real life objects, dialogues and conversation practice. The learners were pushed toward thinking in English instead of on their first language, so this resulted in better oral fluency. In 20th century witnessed the emergence of Audio-Lingual Method that was informed by behaviorist psychology. It was based on repetition, drilling and formation of habits and focused on listening and speaking. It was successful in rote learning, but critics said that it resulted in mechanical responses that did not necessarily result in acquisition of communication skills (Cheng & Wang, 2012). Thereafter, the Communicative Language Teaching (CLT) approach became popular in the 1970s. It replaced the importance laid on grammatical correctness by communicative competence. Role plays and group tasks prompted learners to take advantage of authentic materials and use English in real-life situations (Huda et al., 2024). This method is still highly influential now because it is both fluency-focused and accuracy-based. In modern decades, ELT was further developed due to the Task-Based Language Teaching (TBLT) and Content and Language Integrated Learning (CLIL) approaches. TBLT focuses on accomplishment of real world tasks, whereas CLIL involves practice of language together with learning of a subject. Both can be explained with a learner-centered philosophy that is putting more emphasis on practical application than on abstract knowledge. Generally, the development of ELT techniques shows that there was a gradual transition in instruction to gradually allow learner-centered instruction with respect to communication. This historical excursion predetermined the past and present process of the incorporation of modern technologies including Artificial Intelligence into English language education (Saito, 2019).

Emergence of Artificial Intelligence in Education

Artificial Intelligence (AI) is one of the most disruptive entities in learning. The origin of AI dates back to the middle of the XX century when the first computing and machine research was conducted and the emphasis was made on solving problems and thinking symbolically. In the 1960s, the concept of Intelligent Tutoring Systems (ITS) was created, and it has been oriented in creating an individualized instruction that a tutor would do. With the development of technology AI applications in education are now considerably higher. Advancement of Natural Language Processing

(NLP) gave computers the ability to comprehend human language and process it, which made it possible to come up with technologies like the automatic marking of essays, grammatical analyzers, and engaged chatbots. In the 2000s, starting to analyze student data to provide personalized pathways, adaptive learning platforms were considered an important step of individualized education. Over the last years, artificial intelligence has moved into the classroom and online environments of learning. The tools such as speech recognition software can be used to work on the pronunciation, and the machine learning algorithms can be used to have the individual feedback and the progress tracking. VR and AR, sometimes combined with artificial intelligence, have now provided immersive learning experiences that allow simulating real-life communication situations. The rise of AI in education is hence in line with the world changes towards digitalization and lifetime learning (Dewangan et al., 2024). It provides convenience to the teachers in that they do not have to manually grade tests, attendance and so much more; it also gives students a sense of freedom with regards to pace and flexibility of the learning process. Notably, artificial intelligence does not only complement the traditional teaching model but also reinvents the tasks of teachers and learners so that human knowledge and machine intelligence can cooperate.

Key AI Tools and Technologies for Language Learning:

The implementation of AI in teaching languages has offered a considerable variety of tools and technologies which contribute to teaching/learning procedures. These solutions not only make the learning of languages efficient, but also more interesting and individualistic. Natural Language Processing (NLP) is one of the most popular technologies because its application enables machines to comprehend, parse and generate human language. NLP is the force behind applications, like grammar checkers, automated translation, and writing assistants. Grammarly and Quillbot tools allow students to edit and perfect their writing right away with advanced assistance with words, grammar, and style. Another significant artificial intelligence application is speech recognition and synthesis. The tools help learners in pronunciation and in listening comprehension. As an example, tools such as Google Speech-to-Text or ELSA Speak analyze the pronunciation accuracy and give corrective feedback to facilitate the acquisition of oral fluency (Kumar, 2023). Conversational length practice is being increasingly used with chatbots and virtual assistants. ChatBot uses Artificial Intelligence to mimic a human-like conversation where the learner is free to talk without the fear of being judged. These devices (tools) promote practicing practice of speaking, which is the key to the language mastering. Adaptive learning platforms are another innovation of language learning. See, such systems as Duolingo or Lingvist detect the progress of a learner, adapting the course to his/her level. By assessing the learning trends, they can develop the individualized strata that are not frustrating and can keep motivation up. Not only that, gamification aided by artificial intelligence has made language learning more fun. Using AI algorithms, the design of quizzes, challenges, and reward systems will be adaptive and keep the motivation up. Virtual Reality (VR) and Augmented Reality (AR), coupled with artificial intelligence, offers a learning experience that gets immersed and allows learners to practice English in scenarios where they would be undergoing that experience in the real world, e.g. placing a food order at a restaurant or attending a business meeting.

THEORETICAL FRAMEWORKS IN AI-DRIVEN EDUCATION

There are a number of theoretical frameworks to support the use of artificial intelligence in education as technologies can improve learning outcomes. The most applicable is Constructivism i.e. learners develop knowledge as a result of an interaction and involvement. Chatbots along with VR platforms facilitate the constructivist approach to learning, allowing students to learn through experimentation, communication, and problem-solving in realistic (or simulated) situations. AI-driven learning also uses the Socio-Cultural Theory put forward by Vygotsky (Kumar, 2023). It emphasises the significance of social interaction and the zone of proximal development (ZPD). The AI applications are in line with this theory because they provide scaffolds, i.e., they provide aid when the student needs it and less assistance as skill improves. As an example, an adaptive system adapts difficulty to the learner and directs her or him within the ZPD. Behaviorist learning theory is also involved in the design of artificial intelligence. The reinforcement method is used by many AI-based applications with an immediate feedback, scores, and rewards to propel the formation of habit in language learning. Gamified platforms display this to the learners by encouraging them to perform tasks by using positive reinforcements. Learning analytical tools which provide real-time insights on the content being processed by the student can assist them in better balancing cognitive demand, memorization, and transferring the acquired information into novel situations (Dhiraj & Kumar, 2023). Finally, the Connectives Theory, based on the understanding of learning as a kind of network construction with the help of technologies and collaboration, complies with the AI-driven education. Online services, learning management systems, smart tutoring systems and other technologies combine to offer learners a broader variety of chances to communicate with authenticity whether they are interacting with resources, teachers or peers across the globe.

Artificial Intelligence in Language Learning

Artificial intelligence (AI) has taken the sphere of language acquisition to a new revolution. In contrast to traditional approaches that are based on using textbooks and traditional classroom instruction, AI brings new interactive, dynamic and personified learning experiences. The possibility to analyze a great variety of data, adjusting to preferences, and miming the communication process in the real world make it a great companion in learning languages. Personalization is one of the best opportunities of AI in language learning. AIs enable on-demand learning, with learning platforms monitoring learner progress and adjusting the complexity of the tasks. As a more specific example, apps that aid vocabulary development focus on words that a learner needs to know, or needs to know better, to help him/her improve continuously without getting large amounts of information at once. Self-checking online tools like Grammarly, or a pronunciation tool like ELSA Speak, provide instant feedback on student performance, suggest and display the answer and possible ways to fix an error. The immediacy has the benefit of not only increasing the accuracy, but it has the effect of increasing confidence amongst the learners because they do not have to worry about whether their mistake might become a habitual action already (Singh & Kumar, 2021). Artificial Intelligence facilitates immersive and interesting learning. Through Natural Language Processing (NLP), AI-related tools can interpret and respond to human text that makes practice sessions more realistic. There are also Augmented and Virtual Reality applications that make the process even more appealing as learners can be put in real life situations, i.e. they need to buy something in a foreign country or attend a business-related meeting, where they need to be able to use the language to communicate adequately. According to another significant role of artificial intelligence, it is in accessibility (Talukder et al., 2024). Students with disabilities including hearing or visual disability take advantage of the artificial intelligence technologies that convert the sound to written text, offer audio description, or modify the way the content is presented. By so doing, AI allows free access and equal power to language learners with different backgrounds.

AI-Powered Chatbots and Virtual Assistants for Conversational Practice

Chatbots and virtual assistants are among the many artificial intelligence uses in language learning that are particularly effective to help train communication. There is a need to know words and grammar but also the capability of communicating in substantive ways. Chatbots can be used to simulate conversation between learners and artificial intelligence chatbots that are able to offer a safe and non-judgmental way to practice. Learners can also have context-specific conversation due to the use of AI-powered chatbots. An example would be a chatbot that mimics a restaurant conversation and helps a learner to order food, as well as asks questions and answers staff members. The mentioned practice will help learners to use acquired knowledge in realistic conditions and increase fluency and confidence (Nithya et al., 2024). Virtual assistants, such as Siri, Alexa, or Google Assistant also present a possibility of conversational practice. Children are able to ask questions, issue commands or even engage in simple conversation, and this enhances listening and talking skills. These assistants are accessible around the clock which makes it easier to practice the language on a regular basis. The other advantage of chatbots is their adaptive learning nature. Through the analysis of the answers the learners provide, chatbots are capable of modifying the complexity of questions as well as to introduce some new vocabulary or even to correct grammatical errors right in real-time (Tu, 2020). This feedback system is a loop that enables a learner to develop a personal learning journey that is specific to his proficiency level. Significantly, chatbots brings about a reduction in the fear of error. Most learners fear practicing speaking because they are anxious or embarrassed to do it in front of teachers or their peers. Chatbots provide an environment free of judgment: learning mistakes will be a learning experience, and learners are encouraged to use the language freely. Moreover, AI-based conversation devices can be useful in lectures with many students or an online course since the teacher will not have time to talk to every student directly. Chatbots can serve as auxiliary tutors, so that each learner will have a chance to practice at least no matter how many students are in the classroom (Balakrishnan & Dwivedi, 2024). AI has completely transformed the way language learning is done offering personalize, immersive, and highly accessible experiences. Among this wider shift, the chatbots and virtual assistants with AI mechanism can be considered a great tool of conversational practice. They mimic real-life situations, are easier to receive feedback, and lessen the anxiety of the learners, making the process of achieving communication skill more efficient. With the further development of the technologies, these tools will only help closer the gap between the academic language and its use in practice (Nguyen & Pham, 2024).

Virtual Reality (VR) and Augmented Reality (AR) for Immersive English Learning

Within the past couple of years, both Virtual Reality (VR) and Augmented Reality (AR) have become effective learning tools in English language studies and provide students with more memorable experiences than traditional classrooms. Such technologies, coupled with Artificial Intelligence, produce immersive spaces where users practice English in contextual and meaningful real-life settings. Virtual Reality (VR) immerses learners in the entire simulated environments where they can interact using the English language as a means of communication. Die example is they can have conversations performed in a virtual airport, restaurant, or business meeting and apply vocabulary and grammar in real-life situations (Dilobarkhon Azimova & Dilyorjon Solidjonov, 2023). This experience-based method will improve fluency, confidence, and cultural awareness, and they are not memorizing words but using them in real life situations. AR, conversely, superimposes digital content on the real one with the help of such devices as smart-phones or AR glasses. In language acquisition, AR can be used to make a textbook interactive by showing 3-D objects, being able to talk to the textbook or labels of unfamiliar words, when the book is scanned. Such as, a look on a phone at a picture of fruit could be the push that defined its English name, pronunciation and sentences. These characteristics promote the active study and facilitate the learning of vocabulary. Gamification Both VR and AR advance learner motivation and engagement through gamification (Beck, 2019). Other fun activities, like treasure hunts, role plays, or interactive storytelling help make practicing English memorable and fun. They also accommodate various types of learning people with a combination of visual, audio, and kinesthetic elements. In addition, VR and AR will allow filling the gap between theory and practice. Rather than memorizing the grammar rules, the students interact with the English language and this enhances the communication process. Once these technologies become more affordable, they will likely serve a bigger purpose towards ensuring English language education is more immersive, effective, and accessible to more people in different parts of the world.

Benefits of AI Integration in English Language Teaching (ELT)

Artificial Intelligence (AI) in English Language Teaching (ELT) has altered the traditional classrooms by making them dynamic and leaner-centered classrooms. AI has a great potential to transform education by tapping into data-driven insights, automation, and interactive technologies to provide multiple benefits to the efficiency of the teaching process and learning results. Among the greatest advantages are individualized learning. Ordinary classrooms do not succeed in incorporating individual differences in students. The use of AI-powered platform tracks the progress of each learner, identifies weak points and strengths, and adjusts relevant content. To take one example, vocabulary apps such as Lingvist adapt exercises according to student errors so that learners get personalized training that is appropriate to their degree of proficiency (Kovalenko & Baranivska, 2024). Learners will be motivated and this personalization can guard them against feeling frustration. Fast feedback and evaluation is yet another key advantage. Software such as Grammarly, Turnitin, or auto-scoring essay tests correct and make suggestions instantly. As compared to manual grading that is time-consuming; artificial intelligence allows real-time checking of grammar, vocabulary, coherence, and pronunciation. This is faster than learning and less demanding to the teachers since they get to concentrate on the creative and communicative side of teaching. AI increases student engagement and motivation as well. Gamification of language learning via chatbots, voice-interactive assistants, gamified learning platforms, etc. will make the process much more pleasant (Rukiati et al., 2023). Students are able to chat with AI-powered conversational agents any time and overcome the shyness or fear to make mistakes. The elements of gamification, including points, levels, and rewards can also serve to foster good practice and keep the information at hand, longer. The other advantage is inclusivity and accessibility. Computer programs like voice recognition and automatic text-based support, audio-based support, and translating software help students with disabilities, as well as students with non-English-speaking backgrounds. By reducing the linguistic and physical barriers, AI makes the English learning less unequal and more accommodating.

Moreover, artificial intelligence leads to the support of teachers and professional improvement. Intelligent systems to analyze the data - in the classroom, make predictions, and provide teaching recommendations. This enables teachers to take information-based choices and improve their course of action. It also eliminates routine kind of work such as attendance, test correction and generating practice thus providing educators more time to develop high creativity and critical thinking. Finally, artificial intelligence facilitates worldwide learning. Using virtual learning environments and online tuition services, together with AI-assisted community networks, students can apply to learn with other students and educators across the globe (Chung & Jeong, 2024). This mixing of different cultures and accents enhances communication skills and opens minds to different things by the learners. The gains of AI integration in ELT are extensive and include one-on-one learning and feedback in real-time, as well as better accessibility and global connectivity. Although artificial intelligence will never be able to substitute the work of teachers as teaching humans is quite different, it is a powerful ally and brings efficiency, inclusiveness, and interest to language teaching. artificial intelligence can be carefully incorporated in the world of education and transform learning English in the future (Kristiawan et al., 2024).

CASE STUDY 1: DUOLINGO – USING AI TO PERSONALIZE ENGLISH LANGUAGE LEARNING

Overview: Duolingo, one of the world's most popular language learning apps, has effectively integrated Artificial Intelligence to make English learning adaptive, engaging, and data-driven.

Key Points

- **Adaptive Learning:** AI analyzes learners' strengths and weaknesses, then customizes lessons to fit their individual progress.
- **Speech Recognition Technology:** AI-based pronunciation evaluation gives instant feedback to improve speaking accuracy.
- **Gamification Powered by AI:** Intelligent reward systems (like streaks and XP) encourage consistent practice.
- **Impact:** Studies show up to a 30% increase in retention rates and significant improvement in pronunciation accuracy among English learners.

Learning Outcome: AI helps create personalized learning paths and provides real-time feedback, making English learning more effective and enjoyable.

CASE STUDY 2: CHINA'S AI ENGLISH CLASSROOMS – THE "AI ENGLISH TEACHER" INITIATIVE

Overview: In China, many schools have introduced "AI English Teacher" systems to enhance English language education through smart classrooms and intelligent tutoring tools.

Key Points

- **AI-driven Assessment:** Automated systems analyze grammar, vocabulary, and pronunciation errors instantly.
- **Emotion & Engagement Tracking:** AI cameras monitor students' engagement levels and alert teachers if attention drops.
- **Personalized Tutoring:** Students receive tailored exercises and feedback based on their performance data.
- **Impact:** Teachers' workload decreased, while students' speaking fluency improved by 25–40%.

Learning Outcome: AI integration created a more interactive, responsive, and student-centered English learning environment.

CHALLENGES AND ETHICAL CONSIDERATIONS IN AI INTEGRATION FOR ENGLISH LANGUAGE TEACHING (ELT)

Although Artificial Intelligence (AI) holds great potential of enhancing English Language Teaching (ELT), it brings challenges and ethical issues with it. These are some of the main concerns that need to be considered to make sure that AI tools will improve the educational process without lowering equity, privacy, or quality. Data privacy and security is one of the greatest challenges (Babanoğlu et al., 2025).

The use of personal information: Artificial intelligence systems hinge on gathering and interpreting the personal data of their learners such as performance statistics, recordings of voices, and examples of writing. Otherwise, this data can be misused or otherwise exposed to cyber-threats. Remaining compliant with the rules of data protection and being transparent regarding the use of learner information are urgent needs. The next problem is algorithm bias Such I models can be biased based on the cultural/linguistic biases in the large datasets on which they are fed. As an example, speech recognition application fail to read non-native accents, and it makes their verdicts inaccurate (Bekou, 2024). Likewise, computer-assisted grading will discriminate against imaginative writing or in ways that might favor particular language forms. Without being addressed, such biases may be reaffirming inequalities and disadvantaging learners. Another risk is the overreliance on technologies.

Although AI tools are valuable assistants, overutilization of them can decrease problem-solving, thinking, and communication among people in language acquisition. Learners are more likely to pursue obtaining the right answer as quickly as possible with the use of AI instead of attaining problem-solving skills. There is also a possibility that teachers can over-depend on automated evaluation procedures and forget about human factors of language learning, such as empathy, cultural awareness and motivation. There are the problems with the teacher resistance and training as well. Most educators are new to artificial intelligence technologies or are afraid that AI will make their jobs redundant due to the erroneous belief that artificial intelligence can take their place. Lack of appropriate training and professional development will mean that the teachers will not easily incorporate artificial intelligence in their teaching, thus, failing to realize the maximum out of it (Saud, 2025). Lastly, the economic factors pose as a relevant constraint in terms of cost and infrastructure especially in the developing regions. AP powered tools are usually significant in the availability of steady internet connection, state-of-the-art equipment and funding which are not readily available in deprived schools. This erects a digital divide in which only privileged learners can enjoy AI-driven learning. The possibilities of AI used in ELT are exciting, they also encounter pitfalls of privacy concerns, bias, over reliance, teacher readiness, and affordability. Ethical considerations should act as the focal point in integrating artificial intelligence technologies because they will promote fairness, inclusness, and ethical use of the technology. I believe that IA should not be regarded as the substitute to teachers, but rather as the complementary method of interaction with humans in the classroom. Seriously tackling these issues will help make AI a positive force in English language teaching and learning that is more equitable and meaningful.

CASE STUDIES AND PRACTICAL APPLICATIONS OF AI IN ENGLISH LANGUAGE TEACHING (ELT)

Blending Artificial Intelligence (AI) with English Language Teaching (ELT) is no longer a farfetched idea, but an actively developing tendency that is changing classrooms and online learning spaces all over the world. Case study examples and practical applications illustrate how AI can help make teaching more efficient, lead to increased engagement of learners and language acquisition. A good example is Duolingo, an artificially intelligent language learning program that boasts more than 500 million users. Duolingo has adaptive learning algorithms to customize the lessons based on the performance of its users. In case a learner is weak in aspects of verb conjugation, the app ensures he/she is subjected to consistent exposure until he/she masters the process. With an AI-driven gamified design, it also encourages learners by giving them rewards, monitoring their progress, and setting them specific challenges.

A more popular use is Grammarly a writing companion that applies naturally Language Processing (NLP) and machine learning to give immediate feedbacks on mistakes in grammar, vocabulary, and style. Academic and work environments are the areas where learners of English can use the immediate corrections that enhance the error-free writing and writing confidence. Educators equally deploy Grammarly to cut on the marking load of a piece of work. Artificial intelligence virtual tutors and chatbots are becoming more common in the classroom. Or, to take a more concrete example, Andy English Bot and Replika allow learners to exercise conversational English as they interact in text and voice. The artificial intelligence tutors adjust to the learner level, with corrective interventions to near- errors and vocabulary recommendations, flowing in the natural conversation style. This aids students to train in communication outside classroom in a non-judgmental and secure setting.

THE FUTURE OF AI IN ENGLISH LANGUAGE EDUCATION

Artificial Intelligence (AI) has already started transforming English Language Education, but its future portends even higher change. In response to the development of technology, AI is going to not only enhance the efficiency and accessibility but also transform the teacher-learner dynamic in the classroom. The future awaits artificial intelligence to enter even further into the field of personalized learning, immersion, and communication worldwide, thus turning English education more universal, engaging, and successful. When it comes to the future of AI in English language education, one of the essential trends is augmented personalized learning channels. Adaptive or customized learning platforms, such as Duolingo and Lingvist, already adapt learning materials according to learner performance, but in the future these platforms are likely to be more nuanced. Due to the analysis of the emotional state of the learner, the level of motivation, and the way of studying, I will be able to offer individual lessons adjusted not only to mistakes but also to emotions and interest to the material. This will provide a more whole-person, human-like learning.

The other significant progress will be in immersive technologies like Virtual Reality (VR) and Augmented Reality (AR). AI integration will be used to model those tools in real world scenarios, with user-like advertising partners. As an example, students may take part in a virtual international conference or negotiate during a business meeting and practice English in realistic ways. Such immersive learning experiences shall offer learners experiences that can be difficult to simulate in the classroom setting. It will also have a major hand in real-time translation and multilingual communication. Although English has been and is the lingua franca of the global community, AI-powered translation services will help make the language easier to learn since language learners will be able to compare their native language with English in real-time, which will increase their knowledge of the grammar, vocabulary, and cultural background of the language. These tools will enhance cross-cultural competence, which is a skill that is becoming rather critical in the globalized world.

The future of the artificial intelligence provides powerful teaching assistants to teachers. The intelligent systems will take care of administrative work like grading and attendance as well as achievement tracking relieving the teachers to be able to concentrate on creative teaching and individual coaching. Its use will also equip teachers with information about the performance in the classes and what problems they may expect to occur in learning and how they can overcome them. This change will not substitute teachers but will enable them to become facilitators, mentors, and cultural mediators. But there are some ethical and equity issues with the future of artificial intelligence in English education. It is critical to ensure that AI-powered tools become available to learners of all backgrounds in order to avoid the further digitization of the divide. Similarly, developers should minimize algorithm bias especially in speech recognition systems that have been known to fail to understand non native accents. It will also be essential to have clear data utilization and enhanced privacy controls. In the future, the combination of human tutoring and artificial intelligence is probably the most successful one. Although artificial intelligence will be able to provide immediate feedback, adaptive material, and practice in a realistic setting, teachers will still have to focus on teaching not only critical thinking, creativity, and empathy but also promoting it in students. Such a balance will bring the scenario in the classroom where we have a balance between technology and human interaction, where the technology supplements the human interaction rather than supplementing the technology.

CONCLUSION

The combination of Artificial Intelligence (AI) in English Language Education (ELE) is one of the most important changes in the contemporary pedagogy. The analysis carried out in this paper has demonstrated that AI is not just a technological improvement but a game-changer that alters the teaching and learning environment of English as well as its experiences. With the ability to provide personalized learning and adaptive feedback, as well as immerse users in real-life situations and make language learning more accessible than ever, artificial intelligence can fill historical gaps in language learning and make it a safer, more inclusive, and far more effective experience. The description of the chronology of the English Language Teaching (ELT) methodology shows that there was a slow rise in the use of communicative and more learner-centered methods. The next step of this evolution is the move to put learners in the centre of the process, customizing the training to the student needs, whilst giving the teachers effective instruments to improve the teaching activities. Some real-world examples of AI technology can be seen in the form of chatbots, writing assistants, speech recognition software, and virtual reality/augmented reality applications to illustrate how theory is being advanced into practice and make English learning as interactive and context-driven as possible.

Nevertheless, there are several challenges and ethical considerations revealed in the study. Certain problems, like data privacy, algorithmic bias, overreliance on technology, and unequal access to digital resources need to be mitigated to make the use of AI safe and equitable. Roles of teachers remain unaltered except that they have been re-established; they become important as explanators, coaches and even cultural leaders who can introduce the element of empathy and human-like connectivity to the educational experience- all of which computers will be unable to deliver. In the future, a more efficient way is the hybrid models that take the best of worlds, artificial intelligence efficiency and teacher creativity and human understanding. It is possible that AI will continue to advance to an even more sophisticated level in which it will not only teach linguistic capabilities but also cross-cultural communications, critical thinking, and the capabilities of working across the globe. The use of artificial intelligence in English language education is not only something inevitable but also the opportunity. It has the potential of transforming the way teaching and learning is conducted and as long as it is done in a considered, ethical and inclusive way it can do exactly that. By accepting artificial intelligence as a collaborator instead of a competitor, teachers and students can use the concept to innovate education that is more accessible and engaging with the English language to learners in the new world filled with opportunities to connect.

REFERENCES

Anwar, A., & Kumar, S. (2025). Leveraging AI to Achieve Sustainability Goals in TVET: A Multifaceted Approach. In Sorayyaei Azar, A., Kant Gupta, S., Taherdoost, H., & Alhamaty, F. (Eds.), (pp. 33–60). Advances in Computational Intelligence and Robotics. IGI Global., DOI: 10.4018/979-8-3373-1142-5.ch002

Anwar, A., Kumar, S., & Manoharan, G. (2025). Revolutionizing the Hospitality Industry: The Impact and Challenges of Smart Operations. In Talukder, M. B., & Chowdhury, H. H. K. (Eds.), *Smart Operations and Enhancing Guest Experience in the Hospitality Industry* (pp. 271–296). IGI Global., DOI: 10.4018/979-8-3373-2145-5.ch010

Azimova, D., & Solidjonov, D. (2023). LEARNING ENGLISH LANGUAGE AS A SECOND LANGUAGE WITH AUGMENTED REALITY. *QO'QON UNIVERSITETI XABARNOMASI*, *6*, 112–115. DOI: 10.54613/ku.v6i6.264

Babanoğlu, M. P., Karataş, T. Ö., & Dündar, E. (2025). Ethical considerations of AI through a socio-technical lens: Insights from ELT context as a higher education system. *Cogent Education*, *12*(1), 2488546. DOI: 10.1080/2331186X.2025.2488546

Balakrishnan, J., & Dwivedi, Y. K. (2024). Conversational commerce: Entering the next stage of AI-powered digital assistants. *Annals of Operations Research*, *333*(2–3), 653–687. DOI: 10.1007/s10479-021-04049-5

Beck, D. (2019). Special Issue: Augmented and Virtual Reality in Education: Immersive Learning Research. *Journal of Educational Computing Research*, *57*(7), 1619–1625. DOI: 10.1177/0735633119854035

Bekou, A. (2024). Exploring opportunities and challenges of using ChatGPT in English language teaching (ELT) in Morocco. *Focus on ELT Journal*, 87–106. https://doi.org/DOI: 10.14744/felt.6.1.7

Cheng, A., & Wang, Q. (2012). English Language Teaching in Higher Education in China: A Historical and Social Overview. In Ruan, J., & Leung, C. B. (Eds.), *Perspectives on Teaching and Learning English Literacy in China* (Vol. 3, pp. 19–33). Springer Netherlands., DOI: 10.1007/978-94-007-4994-8_2

Chung, J. Y., & Jeong, S.-H. (2024). Exploring the perceptions of Chinese pre-service teachers on the integration of generative AI in English language teaching: Benefits, challenges, and educational implications. *Online Journal of Communication and Media Technologies*, *14*(4), e202457. DOI: 10.30935/ojcmt/15266

Crompton, H., Edmett, A., Ichaporia, N., & Burke, D. (2024). AI and English language teaching: Affordances and challenges. *British Journal of Educational Technology*, *55*(6), 2503–2529. DOI: 10.1111/bjet.13460

Dewangan, S., Manoharan, G., Sharma, A. K., Kumar, S., & Talukder, M. B. (2024). Leveraging Blockchain Technology for Enhanced Government Services, Transparency, and Administrative Efficiency. *2024 Second International Conference on Advanced Computing & Communication Technologies (ICACCTech)*, 202–207. https://doi.org/DOI: 10.1109/ICACCTech65084.2024.00042

Dhiraj, A., & Kumar, S. (2023). Impact of E-learning on the Higher Education Sector during the COVID-19 pandemic through Pedagogy tools: An observational Study. *Revista de Educación y Derecho*, *27*. Advance online publication. DOI: 10.1344/REYD2023.27.40935

Howatt, A. P. R., & Smith, R. (2014). The History of Teaching English as a Foreign Language, from a British and European Perspective. *Language & History*, *57*(1), 75–95. DOI: 10.1179/1759753614Z.00000000028

Huda, Md. N., Talukder, M. B., & Kumar, S. (2024). Securing Healthcare AI: Applied Federal Learning. In P. Bhattacharya, H. Liu, P. K. Dutta, J. J. P. C. Rodrigues, & G. Sethi (Eds.), *Revolutionizing Healthcare 5.0: The Power of Generative AI* (Vol. 571, pp. 255–272). Springer Nature Switzerland. https://doi.org/DOI: 10.1007/978-3-031-75771-6_17

Kanayev, B. (2024). *REVOLUTIONIZING LANGUAGE LEARNING: THE ROLE OF ARTIFICIAL INTELLIGENCE IN TEACHING FOREIGN LANGUAGES*. https://doi.org/DOI: 10.5281/ZENODO.14200461

Karki, B., & Karki, T. M. (2025). Integrating AI in English Language Teaching: Challenges and Opportunities. *Dristikon: A Multidisciplinary Journal*, *15*(1), 13–28. https://doi.org/DOI: 10.3126/dristikon.v15i1.77118

Khang, A., Abdullayev, V., Jadhav, B., Gupta, S., & Morris, G. (2023). *AI-Centric Modeling and Analytics: Concepts, Technologies, and Applications* (1st ed.). CRC Press., DOI: 10.1201/9781003400110

Kovalenko, I., & Baranivska, N. (2024). INTEGRATING ARTIFICIAL INTELLIGENCE IN ENGLISH LANGUAGE TEACHING: EXPLORING THE POTENTIAL AND CHALLENGES OF AI TOOLS IN ENHANCING LANGUAGE LEARNING OUTCOMES AND PERSONALIZED EDUCATION. *European Socio-Legal & Humanitarian Studies*, *1*, 86–95. DOI: 10.61345/2734-8873.2024.1.9

Kristiawan, D., Bashar, K., & Pradana, D. A. (2024). Artificial Intelligence in English Language Learning: A Systematic Review of AI Tools, Applications, and Pedagogical Outcomes. [TATEFL]. *The Art of Teaching English as a Foreign Language, 5*(2), 207–218. DOI: 10.36663/tatefl.v5i2.912

Kumar, S. (2023). Impact of Digitalization in Higher Education and Smart Learning Techniques. In Nadda, V., Tyagi, P. K., Moniz Vieira, R., & Tyagi, P. (Eds.), *Advances in Hospitality, Tourism, and the Services Industry* (pp. 198–207). IGI Global., DOI: 10.4018/979-8-3693-0650-5.ch013

Kumar, S. (2024). Impact of Assessment on Childhood Education Theories and Practice. In Badea, M., & Suditu, M. (Eds.), *Advances in Early Childhood and K-12 Education* (pp. 84–101). IGI Global., DOI: 10.4018/979-8-3693-0956-8.ch004

Kumar, S., & Bayram, G. E. (2025). The effect on education and training. In *Greening Our Economy for a Sustainable Future* (pp. 177–185). Elsevier., DOI: 10.1016/B978-0-443-23603-7.00014-5

Kumar, S., Talukder, M. B., & Tyagi, P. K. (2025). The Impact of Virtual Reality and Augmented Reality in TNE Learning. In Crawford, C. M., & Gee, T. T. (Eds.), *Motivating Engagement, Belonging, and Success in Higher Education Student Experience* (pp. 359–382). IGI Global., DOI: 10.4018/979-8-3693-8089-5.ch013

Nguyen, N. H. V., & Pham, V. P. H. (2024). AI Chatbots for Language Practices. *International Journal of AI in Language Education, 1*(1), 56–67. DOI: 10.54855/ijaile.24115

Nithya, M., S, Sakthi., S, Lingadurai., & B, Mohamedarsath. (2024). Revolutionizing Customer Experience with AI-Powered Chat bots and Virtual Assistants. *2024 International Conference on Innovative Computing, Intelligent Communication and Smart Electrical Systems (ICSES)*, 1–7. https://doi.org/DOI: 10.1109/ICSES63760.2024.10910297

Rukiati, E., Wicaksono, J. A., Taufan, G. T., & Suharsono, D. D. (2023). AI on Learning English: Application, Benefit, and Threat. *Journal of Language, Communication, and Tourism, 1*(2), 32–40. DOI: 10.25047/jlct.v1i2.3967

Saito, Y. (2019). English Language Teaching and Learning in Japan: History and Prospect. In Kitamura, Y., Omomo, T., & Katsuno, M. (Eds.), *Education in Japan* (Vol. 47, pp. 211–220). Springer Nature Singapore., DOI: 10.1007/978-981-13-2632-5_13

Saud, D. S. (2025). Generative AI in English Language Teaching: Opportunities and Challenges. *Journal of Jayaprithvi Multiple Campus*, *1*, 44–59. DOI: 10.3126/jjmc2.v1i1.81437

Singh, A., & Kumar, S. (2021). Identifying Innovations in Human Resources: Academia and Industry Perspectives. In Pathak, A., & Rana, S. (Eds.), (pp. 104–120). Advances in Human Resources Management and Organizational Development. IGI Global., DOI: 10.4018/978-1-7998-4180-7.ch006

Talukder, M. B., Khan, M. R., Swarna, D. A., Singh, K., Kumar, S., & Kabir, F. (2025). The Business of Wellness Tourism: Emerging Trends and Economic Impacts. In Silic, M., Luthia, M., Ahmad, F., & Chakraborty, P. P. (Eds.), *Human Capital Management and Competitive Advantage in Tourism* (pp. 445–476). IGI Global., DOI: 10.4018/979-8-3373-0071-9.ch015

Talukder, M. B., Kumar, S., & Das, I. R. (2024). Mindfulness of Digital Detoxification: Healthy Lifestyle in Tourism. In Kankaew, K., Chaudhary, S., & Widtayakornbundit, S. (Eds.), (pp. 56–71). Advances in Logistics, Operations, and Management Science. IGI Global., DOI: 10.4018/979-8-3693-1273-5.ch004

Talukder, M. B., & Mia, Md. N., Masum, Md. Y., Kabir, F., & Kumar, S. (2025). Encouraging Innovative and Responsible Tourism Through Digital Advancement. In P. Thaichon, P. K. Dutta, A. K. Haghi, & S. Dutta (Eds.), *Digital Disruption in Hospitality, Sustainable Hospitality* (pp. 145–165). Emerald Publishing Limited. https://doi.org/DOI: 10.1108/978-1-83662-360-120251007

Tu, J. (2020). Learn to Speak Like A Native: AI-powered Chatbot Simulating Natural Conversation for Language Tutoring. *Journal of Physics: Conference Series*, *1693*(1), 012216. DOI: 10.1088/1742-6596/1693/1/012216

Yadav, S. (2025). Leveraging AI to Enhance Teaching and Learning in Education: The Role of Artificial Intelligence in Modernizing Classroom Practices. In Basha, J. S., Alade, T. O., Al Khazimi, M. O. A., Vasudevan, R., & Khan, J. B. (Eds.), *Optimizing Research Techniques and Learning Strategies With Digital Technologies* (pp. 211–238). IGI Global., DOI: 10.4018/979-8-3693-7863-2.ch008

Chapter 12
The Position of English in Algeria: English Language Learning in a Multilingual Society

Malika Gheraissa
https://orcid.org/0009-0008-9886-3176
International Islamic University Malaysia, Malaysia

ABSTRACT

In a country with rich linguistic diversity like Algeria, where Arabic, Berber, and French interact in both daily life and education, the role of English is gradually shifting. This chapter explores Algeria's complex multilingual landscape, tracing the historical and cultural influences shaping current language practices. Although English remains a foreign language in the national curriculum, its rising relevance—driven by globalization and the aspirations of younger generations—signals a changing educational focus. The chapter addresses challenges in English language education, such as limited exposure, outdated methods, and insufficient teacher training. In response to global digital transformation, special attention is given to the potential of Artificial Intelligence (AI) in supporting English learning. Drawing on recent studies, this chapter highlights how AI can deliver personalized, accessible, and effective learning in Algeria's multilingual context.

1. INTRODUCTION

Algeria is a society with multiple languages, where Arabic, Berber, and French exist together in a complex sociolinguistic context. It is the most linguistically diverse society in the Arab world. This chapter's sociolinguistic analysis of Algeria

DOI: 10.4018/979-8-3373-3755-5.ch012

establishes the basis for discussing the incorporation of English language acquisition within a multilingual context. Algeria features a variety of languages, with Arabic and Tamazight as the official tongues and French as a prevalent language. This variety of languages stems from historical, political, and sociocultural influences that have molded the country's sociolinguistic landscape. The educational landscape in Algeria is intricately linked to this complex linguistic environment. A major development in recent years is the increasing significance of English as a worldwide language in Algeria. While English is positioned as a foreign language in the national curriculum, its presence and relevance are increasingly felt in society. Many young people are showing interest in English and actively using it, particularly in social contexts and online platforms. Overcoming Challenges in Language Learning Exclusively Integrating English Language Learning in Algeria The integration of English as a core component of Algeria's educational system is neither a simple process nor a guaranteed solution to linguistic challenges. The language ecosystem in Algeria is already marked by a preference for French and an indifference or even hostility toward English. Thus, the essential factor is to apply educational strategies that are both effective and well-received by students, teachers, parents, and educators in Algeria. By doing so, we can address a myriad of specific linguistic issues that Algerian students face, such as gaps in linguistic proficiency and difficulties with key topics. The use of Information Agents (IA) in learning English can be a game-changer in this regard. These AI-driven tools can change the learning experience by providing customized and prompt feedback. This is particularly valuable in the Algerian context, where students may encounter diverse linguistic challenges and have varying levels of exposure to English outside the classroom (Hamadi, 2025). The interactive nature of IA can also foster greater engagement and motivation among students, which is crucial for language learning success (Febriani, 2024). It is crucial to note that the effective integration of IA in the learning process is not about replacing teachers but rather empowering them. Teachers can focus on guiding the learning process, facilitating discussions, and addressing complex linguistic nuances while leaving the task of routine feedback and practice to AI (Hamadi, 2025). However, the accessibility and practicality of implementing AI have only recently become feasible (Febriani, 2024). AI is the culmination of a long journey of development, where the lines between science and myth, fiction and reality, and literature and life have been blurred (Febriani, 2024). This concept should not be seen as static or bound by traditional constraints. Instead, AI is a dynamic and evolving technology that can significantly benefit Algeria's educational and linguistic landscape. In a multilingual Algerian context, where English often struggles to find a foothold, the use of IA can be a strategic tool. By leveraging AI, teachers and students can address the linguistic needs of Algerian learners in a targeted and effective manner (Febriani, 2024). The integration of AI in the English learning process has the potential to provide precise and immediate feedback, which is invaluable in overcoming specific language challenges (Hamadi, 2025). This might result in enhanced language abilities and, therefore, a successful incorporation of English into the Algerian education system. The incorporation of AI into the learning of English, from our perspective, should be a part of Algeria's educational advancement process. A system that remains static in today's fast-paced world will, in time, lag behind. Therefore, the introduction of AI in English learning is not just an option but a strategic step towards empowering a new generation of Algerian learners.

2. ALGERIA'S LINGUISTIC LANDSCAPE

Understanding Algeria's linguistic landscape requires an appreciation of its complex historical background. The linguistic diversity in Algeria has deep historical roots. As Belmihoub (2016) notes, this complexity is a product of centuries of foreign rule and cultural exchange. Benrabah (2014) traces Algeria's historical layering through invasions and settlements by the Romans, Vandals, Byzantines, Arab-Berber dynasties, the Ottoman Turks, and finally the French. Each era left behind linguistic and cultural traces that are still evident in modern Algerian society.

Among these, French colonialism had the most lasting impact. According to Benrabah and Maamri (2014), the French occupation did not merely dominate the territory but also sought to reshape Algerian identity by imposing French language and culture. French was portrayed as the language of modernity and power, and it quickly became embedded in education, governance, and public life. As Le Roux (2016) explains, schools were used as a primary tool for this cultural transformation. Through educational reforms led by the French Ministry of Education, Arabic and Tamazight were pushed aside, and French became the primary language of instruction. Moreover, French has had a greater impact on Algerians compared to other languages, largely due to several factors. One key reason is the lengthy period of French colonization in Algeria, which spanned over 130 years. During this time, Algerians were compelled to use French in their daily lives. Additionally, French became the primary language used in education, while the public use of Arabic was prohibited. (Sadouki, 2023).

This linguistic imposition was met with strong resistance from Algerian nationalists. Following independence in 1962, a campaign for Arabisation emerged, aiming to revive Arabic as the core language of education and governance (Sharkey, 2014). However, decades of colonial influence could not be easily reversed. French remained deeply rooted in institutions and continued to function as a language of prestige and opportunity.

Today, Algerian society is often divided linguistically into three broad categories: Arabophones, Berberophones, and Francophones (Benrabah, 2014). In practice, many Algerians move fluidly between these languages depending on context. This multilingualism is both a cultural asset and a policy challenge, especially as the country navigates the introduction and expansion of English as an additional foreign language. Therefore, balancing this rich linguistic diversity while fostering effective communication and national unity remains a key priority for Algeria's future development.

3.MULTILINGUALISM IN ALGERIA

Algeria's linguistic landscape is a fascinating reflection of its rich and complex history. To truly understand the country's multilingual reality, it is important to explore how historical influences, and social dynamics have shaped the languages spoken today. Algeria has historically been a multilingual country due to its long history of colonization by many colonizers, including the Romans, Phoenicians, French, and others (Sahraoui, 2020). This rich history has left a lasting imprint on the country's linguistic landscape, making it a melting pot of languages and cultures. Because of the reasons described above, Algeria's language situation has become highly complex (Sahraoui, 2020). Such complexity is not surprising given the layers of historical influence and the coexistence of multiple languages within society.

The use of several languages in Algeria displays linguistic diversity and explains how society has evolved into a multilingual community (Sadouki, 2023). This diversity is more than just a collection of languages; it reflects the social and cultural fabric that shapes everyday life in Algeria. To comprehend the linguistic background of a multilingual community, we must first identify certain multilingualism terminology that can be used to describe the phenomenon of language interaction, such as bilingualism and multilingualism. Bilingualism and multilingualism are both concepts that refer to the capacity to use two or more languages proficiently (Sadouki, 2023). Understanding these terms helps clarify how individuals and communities navigate their linguistic realities.

This implies that bilinguals and multilinguals can use two or more languages with the same level of proficiency, as Myers-Scotton (2006, p. 3, as cited in Sadouki, 2023) claims that bilinguals have "acquired or learnt to speak or understand - as a minimum - some phrases that show internal structural relations in a second language". Such proficiency highlights the cognitive and social skills involved in managing multiple languages effectively. Similarly, in Algeria, the majority of participants supported multilingualism in higher education and public life, seeing it as an empowering method to understand one another and strengthen the Algerian identity (Rouabah, 2022). This positive attitude towards multilingualism suggests that language diversity is viewed as a source of national strength rather than division.

English is the second foreign language taught in the early stages of education. It is also a language that is steadily expanding throughout the country, particularly among the younger generation, and some people believe it will eventually compete with the French language. The impact of this spread may be unknown; nonetheless, intellectuals believe that it will require more than simply the fact that young people are interested in learning it to pose a danger to a language that has been spoken and taught for years and has strong historical linkages to the country. The reality is that French is widely spoken in both professional and casual situations throughout the country, as well as in many spoken dialects. However, English is gradually gaining popularity, and it may only be a matter of time before it supplants French. Many factors, including the global status that the English language has gained over the years, have led Algerians, like many other countries, to recognise its importance and are becoming increasingly interested in learning it, much to the chagrin of the country's Francophone population. Furthermore, certain individuals in control of the existing system are capitalising on the growing acceptance of English in the globe and in the country, and they want to reignite the old discussion about replacing French with English (Sahraoui, 2020). This ongoing linguistic shift reveals the dynamic nature of language use in Algeria and the tensions that arise when historical ties confront global trends.

4.THE POSITION OF ENGLISH IN ALGERIA

The status and spread of the English language in Algeria have become more and more interesting to academics and the general public in recent years. In Algeria, English was first taught in schools in the late 1970s and early 1990s (Belmihoub, 2018). After Algeria became independent in 1962, the country's language policy went through a number of changes in an effort to make Arabic the main language of instruction instead of French. As time went on, other foreign languages were added to the school system to give Algerians more access to global languages. For example, English was added in 1989, and more recently, German, Italian, and Spanish were added (Sadouki, 2023).

As more and more people around the world became interested in English, Algerian policymakers wanted to make English the main foreign language taught in schools instead of French. At first, French was the only foreign language taught in primary school, but by 1993, the Ministry of Education let students choose between French and English as their first required foreign language. Even though this was done, only 1.28% of the two million schoolchildren who chose English between 1993 and

1997 showed that French was still the most popular language. So, to understand how English is used and spread in Algeria, we need to know how Algerians feel about foreign languages in general, especially English. Even though conditions are good for its growth, many people think that French is the main reason why English isn't growing as fast as it could be (Sahraoui, 2020). This means that English has promise, but historical and sociolinguistic variables still affect its progress.

People in Algeria see English as a new language that doesn't have the political baggage that comes with languages like French and Arabic (Jacob, 2019). People who think this way see English more as a useful tool than as a sign of political or cultural identity. Jacob (2019) cites Ager (2001, p. 21) as saying that English is an outside language that is "neutral" and is sometimes used by supporters of Standard Arabic to make French seem less important. These kinds of changes show how language, politics, and identity all affect each other in Algeria's multilingual environment.

In recent years, the use of English has increased significantly among the younger generation in Algeria, indicating its importance as a language to learn (Sahraoui, 2020). Youth are increasingly seeing English as a gateway to new opportunities, which reflects changing attitudes. Many Algerian youths are becoming more aware of the value of English for employment opportunities both at home and abroad, leading them to learn and use it instead of or in addition to French (Sahraoui, 2020). The growing interest in English is thus driven largely by economic factors. Most Algerians who study English for personal or career reasons live in major cities like Algiers or coastal cities (Benrabah, 2009). Increasingly globalized and foreign-invested urban areas are the centers of this shift in linguistics.

Currently, Algerians learn English to improve their careers, where they need it for work in countries that do not speak French, which has typically been the young people's preferred place (Sahraoui, 2020). This places an international perspective on language learning within Algeria's changing socio-economic landscape. Algeria attracts a lot of foreign investment with many establishments located in the uninhabited Sahara—this is formless part of the country (Sahraoui, 2020). That foreign company presence further motivates English acquisition particularly in the technical fields.

English is the language of science and technology, according to proponents of replacing French with it, and this is crucial for Algeria's advancement (Miliani, 2001). This strategic value placed on English is thus tied to the modernization of Algeria's economy and education system. On the other hand, linguistic diversification has been skyrocketing with the increased use of English because more languages are now being learned such as Spanish and German (Sadouki, 2023). Increasing multilingual repertoires signals more global languages beyond this traditional French-Arabic binarism. However, some argue that the dominance of French in Algeria impedes assimilation of English by a wider population (Sahraoui, 2020). This tension depicts exactly what a country would face balancing old ties with France and new trends in world linguistics.

5. ENGLISH LANGUAGE EDUCATION IN ALGERIA

In 1993, French was replaced by English as the first foreign language in many elementary schools. English instruction was standardized nationwide by the government in 1995. However, this policy soon changed, as the government decided to reintroduce French in the fourth grade of primary schools and postpone English instruction until middle school. These changes were driven by Algerians' reluctance to fully abandon French in favor of another language. French remained widely spoken and was the preferred language of choice for parents, largely because it is essential for employment and considered easier to learn, having been in use since 1830 (Sahraoui, 2020). This shift reflected a broader desire to redefine national identity by prioritizing Arabic while adopting English as a fresh foreign language, distancing the country from its colonial legacy tied to French. Bellalem (2014) states that French was replaced by English, which began to be taught in schools from an early age. By making Arabic the first national language and English the primary foreign language, the country aimed to turn a new page in its history, abandoning its colonial past and embracing a foreign language with no historical colonial ties to Algeria.

However, despite these policy changes favoring English, both languages face limited use outside the classroom, with English gradually gaining more positive recognition and support among Algerians. Rouabah (2022) emphasized that despite the fact that English and French are taught at school, their usage is extremely limited outside of classes; students and teachers reportedly have a negative attitude towards French, while English is perceived more positively, with the majority of Algerians (52 percent) anticipating that English will dominate the future in Algeria. This limited presence and recognition of English in everyday Algerian society is echoed by educators' experiences, as illustrated by a lecturer's surprise and the recurring concerns raised during discussions with teachers and inspectors. One lecturer from Algiers once said, "But there's no English here!" illustrating how Algerian scholars outside of English departments often expressed amazement or even incredulity at my research topic. During a focus group with teachers from the Algiers area, as well as in informal discussions with secondary school teachers and inspectors at a teacher conference and a series of continuous professional development workshops attended by participants from across the country, the lack of visibility of English outside the classroom and the perceived absence of English speakers in Algerian society were repeatedly highlighted (Jacob, 2019).

Furthermore, although France remains the most popular destination for Algerian students studying abroad, it is now clear that an increasing number of young people are choosing to learn English in order to pursue education in countries other than France. What excites them even more is that they are not limited to visiting English-speaking countries, which can be costly and challenging. Many non-English-speaking countries offer programs taught exclusively in English. Since 2004, the number of children choosing to learn English has significantly increased, reflecting Algerians' growing awareness of its global importance (Sahraoui, 2020). These shifting attitudes and policy changes reflect a growing national awareness that mastering English is no longer a bonus but a strategic necessity for Algerians seeking to participate more fully in global academic, professional, and cultural spheres.

In response to the rapid globalization of English, Algeria has been compelled to reconsider the role of this language within its educational and socio-economic frameworks. Due to English's dominant position in most fields worldwide, it is now imperative that students learn the language and receive early instruction in Algerian schools. This will help the country improve its economy by enabling negotiations with powerful governments and by providing access to various technologies that are dominated by English-speaking nations (Sahraoui, 2020). There is, therefore, a need for a radical change in Algeria's educational system and English Language Education to undergo a metamorphosis (Bemmoussat & Bouyakoub, 2019). At the same time, the government recognized that introducing English early in schools was crucial to equip students with the skills needed to engage effectively in the global economy and technological fields. Sahraoui (2020) states that Algeria was likewise affected by the globalization of English. Using the fact that English has become a worldwide language and is the language of science and technology as justification, the government began to explore the potential of including it in the curriculum of mandatory schools. Policymakers asserted that it ought to be taught alongside Standard Arabic in schools as part of the curriculum, along with French as a foreign language. To turn this vision into reality, the government implemented a targeted strategy to introduce English early in the education system, aiming to build strong language skills from the start. Benadla (2013) points out that in light of this significance, the government chose to promote English through a unique acquisition approach that begins in the first year of middle school, aiming to develop proficient English speakers and open up new markets worldwide. However, in practice, the shortage of qualified teachers for the English as a Foreign Language (EFL) acquisition process meant that more effort was needed to achieve successful results. Algerian schools and universities (even military, security, economic, and cultural institutions) require students to study English (Slimani, 2016).

To ensure these early instructional efforts are effective, the Algerian official syllabuses clearly define the main goals of teaching and learning English as a foreign language. According to the Algerian official English syllabuses from June 1999, the main goals of teaching and learning English as a foreign language are to help students communicate effectively in all its forms, aspects, and dimensions. These goals are grouped into four main categories: socio-cultural, humanistic, educational, and academic (Negadi, 2015). While the official syllabuses outline broad educational goals for English learning, real-world insights from informants highlight the critical role of English proficiency, specifically in advancing scientific research and global communication. Mokdad (2023) states that based on the responses of our two informants, it is clear that they both emphasize the importance of the English language in science and scientific research. Consequently, proficiency in English is essential for writing articles in prestigious international journals and for participating in international conferences or colloquia, especially in scientific fields such as physics, chemistry, natural sciences, and medicine. The first informant, A, further highlighted English's role as a "lingua franca," a global language that facilitates broad and effective communication among people from diverse linguistic backgrounds. Given the growing importance of English in academic and scientific contexts, it makes practical sense to leverage French as a supportive tool to help learners more effectively acquire English proficiency. Mokdad (2023) argues that with the appointment of the new Minister, who has issued operational instructions for the dissemination and teaching of English at universities, we suggest using French favorably as a bridge language to master English. English has recently begun to attract serious interest in Algerian society, especially in university centers for intensive language teaching.

Although English teaching in Algeria has historically evolved slowly and remained largely a foreign language, recent governmental initiatives and growing interest in higher education signal a shift toward greater emphasis on English proficiency. Algerian English teaching has undergone a series of transformations, often without urgency or strong social demand. Throughout history, English has remained a foreign language in the country. Despite efforts by some political and educational authorities to reshape its role, its place and status continue to be largely determined by society (Miliani, 2001). In sum, while English has long held a complex and evolving position in Algeria, recent efforts and growing awareness highlight its vital role in opening doors to global communication, education, and scientific advancement.

Furthermore, English is increasingly used for practical and professional purposes. According to Abid-Houcine (2007), while French remains widely spoken, English is gaining substantial favour. This trend is further supported by Algeria's diplomatic and educational collaboration with English-speaking countries, such as the UK and the United States. Fox and Mazzouzi (2019) highlight a significant shift: four major ministries—National Education, Higher Education and Scientific Research, Vocational Training, and Employment—have officially replaced French with English in various functions, garnering public support as high as 94.3%. The Ministry of Vocational Training and Employment emphasizes integrating English into technical education to help trainees adapt to international technological standards. Anes (2018) reports that around 7% of Algerians—approximately 2.59 million people—use English regularly for communication.

Foreign governments have also played a key role. The UK, via the British Council, has offered Chevening Scholarships to Algerians pursuing master's degrees in areas like economics, politics, and engineering. Between 2015 and 2020, the UK supported 500 Algerian PhD students in British universities. Simultaneously, the US has sponsored 13 academic, cultural, and professional programs designed to create local expertise, economic stability, and social development. Private English language centers across Algeria have been encouraged by both the British Council and the US Embassy (Belmihoub, 2018), resulting in a reported 5% increase in English fluency. In 2012, the Algerian government even enlisted Indian teachers to meet the growing demand for qualified English instructors. The expansion of English extends beyond the classroom. Belmihoub (2018) notes that several institutions—such as Radio Television Algérienne, the Ministry of Defense, and the Institute of Petroleum Studies—train employees in English to enable communication with international partners. Notably, the oil and gas industry accounts for 96.5% of English language use in the professional sphere, making it a central domain for applied English proficiency. Media and digital platforms have also facilitated the rise of English. Platforms like Facebook and YouTube offer Algerians new spaces to learn and express themselves in English. While French still dominates many areas of public life, English continues to gain popularity and utility, especially among younger generations.

6. CHALLENGES IN ENGLISH LANGUAGE LEARNING

Certainly, in Algeria, where French ranks as the second most spoken language, the need to learn English as a third language is increasingly perceived as essential in various areas of personal life (Negadi, 2015). Nevertheless, English usage remains uneven across Algeria, limited to certain regions, sectors, and social groups. Formal training is necessary to improve fluency among professionals, particularly in the south, where the oil and gas industries dominate. As Belmihoub (2018) points out, the promotion of English not only supports economic and technological development but also symbolizes a potential political alignment with the wider Arab world and global powers like the US. To support these efforts and address the existing challenges, the official syllabuses for English in Algeria (June 1999) outline comprehensive objectives aimed at developing learners' communicative competence across multiple dimensions. Slimani (2016) states that based on the official syllabuses for English in Algeria, June 1999, the general objectives of teaching and learning English as a foreign language are to enable learners to communicate effectively in all its forms, aspects, and dimensions; there are four main categories of objectives: - socio-cultural objectives, - humanistic objectives, -educational objectives, -academic objectives.

Moreover, although the English language has faced many challenges, Algerian political and educational authorities have succeeded in rehabilitating its status. As Algeria has developed technical and economic connections around the world, English has gained greater prominence in the Algerian educational system. Consequently, Algerian students and parents are becoming increasingly aware of its importance as an international language 'par excellence' (Slimani, 2016). Nevertheless, despite this growing awareness, challenges in the implementation of English language programs and teacher training have limited students' ability to achieve sufficient proficiency. Benadla (2013) reports that the Algerian Ministry of Education promoted a program that differed from that of foreign teachers trained. Despite these efforts, they also had difficulty spreading the language due to a number of problems. Due to this situation, Algerian students were not able to benefit from high-quality English preparation, and their proficiency level in English was insufficient for them to apply their skills outside of the classroom. According to official documents and directives from the Algerian government (June 1999), the English language curricula are designed to equip Algerian students with the skills necessary to communicate effectively in both written and spoken forms across everyday social and professional contexts. At the same time, the curricula aim to enhance the abilities of students pursuing higher education—particularly in fields such as English language, translation, or journalism—to use English as a tool for expanding their academic knowledge. Additionally, they prepare those entering the workforce to independently comprehend professional materials such as documents, flyers, and notices relevant to their occupations (Slimani, 2016).

Furthermore, Algerian students are not accustomed to communicating in English, which results in the language being largely absent from their daily lives, except for the limited exposure they have through listening, speaking, reading, or writing in the classroom (Slimani, 2016). While English continues to gain importance, the enduring presence and widespread use of French in Algerian society significantly influence how English is learned and perceived. Mokdad (2023) argues that regardless of the interest in English, whose sociolinguistic and political demand is very strong today in Algerian society to prove the international market, the two informants' responses demonstrate that French is a foreign language whose use is ubiquitous, and which cannot be disregarded or stigmatized. In this regard, it is evident that learning English in French can be effective, particularly for Algerians who are already somewhat fluent in French. French is therefore expected to be used as a useful tool for language transfer to grasp English, if formal, if needed. Benmekki and Lama (2018) conclude that French no longer holds official status, though it remains embedded in administration and public discourse. Growing calls advocate for elevating English to co-official status, reflecting a national desire to align with global trends and reduce reliance on colonial linguistic legacies.

7. ENGLISH IN ALGERIA AND GLOBALIZATION

In the Algerian context, the growing prominence of English in education and society has become a significant focus of scholarly attention, reflecting broader shifts in language policy and global engagement. Specifically, the rise in interest in English has been interpreted as a component of the global process of what is known as the "spread of English" (Crystal, 2003; Graddol, 2006; Kachru, 1992; Schneider, 2011). In this context, it's no surprise that English is often seen as the defining language of our era, shaping how people connect and communicate around the world. As a result, it is often considered the century's distinctive language for global communication (Slimani, 2016). This growing recognition reflects how English is becoming more than just a language—it's turning into a vital tool that connects people across the globe every day. Moreover, as previously said, the number of people using English as a second or foreign language is rising annually due to the language's increasing significance as a lingua franca and an international language (Slimani, 2016). This trend is further highlighted by English's prominent role in major international organizations like the United Nations, underscoring its status as a truly global language. Sahraoui (2020) confirms that another illustration of the English language's globalization is its dominance in international organizations such as the United Nations, which is regarded as a global community of 193 sovereign states. Correspondingly, this global prominence of English is mirrored in Algeria, where its integration into the education system reflects the country's efforts to align with international trends and prepare students for a more interconnected world.

Benmoussat (2015) discusses how English has become a global language in Algerian education, and he asserts that, in the context of globalization, English has become the linguistic tool by which the desire not to lag and remain isolated is expressed. In terms of national identity, Algeria's designation as a unimodal or Multi-modal nation is determined by the group concerned. Nevertheless, linguistic decisions are decided based on nationalism rather than nationism, and in addition to the educational aims of the Algerian School, the curriculum as a whole has been moulded to instill and promote feelings of nationalism as a counter to ethnicity. Furthermore, in multilingual situations, language policies (whether explicit or implicit) frequently reflect a power dynamic and serve an ideology. In this regard, the school is an important component of overall policy since it promotes the state's values, attitudes, and policies. Yet, given the globalization movement and the need to fully participate in the economic, professional, scientific, and technical arenas, a decent working understanding of the English language is de facto required (Benmoussat, 2015). Simultaneously, the colonial legacy was not the only factor influencing language choice under the umbrella of globalization effects (Beddiaf & Safi, 2018). This nuanced situation is reflected in how Arabic and English are portrayed as agents of decolonization and globalization, and French is considered tied to cruel colonialism (Benrabah 2013). Ultimately, this contrast in perception lays the groundwork for understanding why, in the Algerian context, English is increasingly seen as a liberating force, while French continues to carry the weight of its colonial past.

Beddiaf & Safi (2018) state that while serving as an international delegate for global welfare, English acquired empathy with progressive momentum. Moreover, from a socio-political perspective, English in Algeria is more warmly received in public opinion than obnoxious French. This growing preference for English is further confirmed by empirical findings, which highlight how it holds a more dominant and favorable position among bilingual and multilingual speakers in professional settings. Beddiaf & Safi (2018) argue that, in fact, the linguistic diversity panel does not rank the importance of all languages equally among workers in the current study. The respondents also claim to be either bilingual or multilingual, but French does not seem to be a significant language. The English language dominates when compared to the French language. Consequently, this suggests that, despite its widespread use, French holds limited practical value in the eyes of many, particularly in multilingual contexts where English appears more relevant and advantageous. According to Beddiaf and Safi (2018), while French has a significant number of speakers, it is not a desirable language to be widely used in the study's setting. Likewise, this is also true in Algeria, where most people have qualifications in two or three languages rather than just one. This ongoing shift in preference becomes even more striking when considering how French, despite its prevalence, is increasingly sidelined in favor of English across Algerian contexts. It is startling to learn that French is marginally placed aside in the Algerian environment, far behind English (Beddiaf & Safi, 2018).

According to Informant A, there exists an increasing enthusiasm for foreign languages within Algeria, primarily attributable to their recognized function in facilitating the nation's advancement and affluence. In particular, she emphasizes that the acquisition of additional languages promotes receptiveness to diverse cultures and historical narratives, as well as grants access to global scientific progress. Furthermore, in agreement with Informant B, she views English as essential for academic research, global communication, and participation in tourism and international affairs.

English, they argue, serves as the language of universal commercial transactions and academic publication domains, and Algerian universities must actively engage with. Notably, informant A, who also holds an additional degree, demonstrates innovative teaching practices at CEIL, where she effectively incorporates English in the classroom (Sahraoui, 2020).

In conclusion, the increasing use of English in Algeria represents not only a change in language but also the nation's strong desire to engage with the rest of the world. Indeed, Algerians, particularly students and educators, are increasingly adopting English as a tool for international communication and advancement as globalization continues to influence the academic, cultural, and economic domains. Thus, the adoption of English demonstrates a deliberate shift towards decolonization, inclusivity, and progressive advancement, even though the influence of French is still noticeable. Ultimately, English is now recognized not only as a foreign language but also as an essential tool for navigating the opportunities and complexities presented by a globally interconnected world.

8. HOW CAN THE AI BE USED IN LEARNING ENGLISH AS A SECOND LANGUAGE?

The prevalence of the English language within non-native communities has experienced a substantial increase; however, the insufficiency of meaningful interactions with proficient and knowledgeable English speakers constitutes a significant obstacle for novice English language learners. Learners of English in a foreign context possess a heightened opportunity for engagement with native speakers, thereby facilitating more effective acquisition of the language. Nevertheless, educational institutions that support English language instruction in non-native communities are often constrained by inadequate resources and encounter additional challenges, such as insufficient instructional materials. This study proposes a framework aimed at enhancing the English language learning experience for non-native students by offering unrestricted access to conversational practice opportunities. The process of acquiring proficiency in English as a secondary language not only serves to facilitate the comprehensive development of the individual but also plays a pivotal role in significantly boosting one's self-assurance and confidence in various social contexts. Furthermore, this linguistic acquisition serves to deepen intercultural awareness, allowing individuals to cultivate a genuine appreciation for, and demonstrate profound respect towards, the myriads of diverse perspectives, cultural practices, and belief systems that exist within our global society, while simultaneously presenting individuals with a plethora of opportunities in both the educational sphere and the professional job market. Attaining a high level of fluency in the English language can dramatically expand one's professional prospects, thereby empowering individuals to gain unfettered access to an extensive array of information and invaluable resources that are readily available on the vast expanse of the internet.

English language education has been significantly transformed by Artificial Intelligence (AI), which provides innovative solutions and enhances various aspects of the learning process. The integration of this approach to ESL teaching offers a number of benefits, including more personalized learning opportunities, enhanced assessments, and more effective teaching methods (CA , 2024). According to Pang & Heng (2025), the use of artificial intelligence (AI) in English as a Second Language (ESL) learning is increasingly influential, offering various benefits and functions, but also posing some concerns. Moreover, as Artificial Intelligence (AI) plays an increasingly important role in English Language Teaching (ELT), it offers many benefits while simultaneously presenting certain challenges (Pang & Heng, 2025). AI has also been shown to be a significant facilitator of the learning of English as a Second Language (ESL) by creating a more engaging, personalized, and effective learning environment. Consequently, learners as well as educators can benefit from numerous practical applications (Fitria, 2021). In addition, non-native speakers can become more confident and less stressed by teaching their English with artificial intelligence (AI) without being detected as imitating. It is further demonstrated that the proposed AI-based framework leads to a considerable reduction in the cost of teaching the English language correctly (Almutairi et.al, 2020).

Language learning platforms powered by artificial intelligence offer personalized, interactive experiences tailored to the individual needs of each learner (AbuSahyon et al., 2023). Moreover, a wide range of intelligent tools and immersive experiences are available to learners thanks to AI-driven technologies. Among the most commonly used AI-driven language learning methods are chatbots, virtual tutors, speech recognition systems, and language learning applications (AbuSahyon et al., 2023). By offering individualized instruction, interactive practice, and real-time feedback, AI-driven solutions have revolutionized language acquisition. These cutting-edge resources encourage engagement and motivation, and they hold great promise for the future of language learners everywhere (AbuSahyon et al., 2023). The application of artificial intelligence (AI) to English as a foreign language provides effective and varied educational service programs that improve student motivation, process flexibility, and opportunities for a customised learning environment (AbuSahyon and others, 2023). According to the presented research, AI can enhance language speaking, reading, and learning, as well as the overall learning process (AbuSahyon et al, 2023). Finally, the use of artificial intelligence (AI) in language teaching is one of the most promising advancements (Fitria, 2021).

First, AI helps create a positive learning environment for English by allowing students to practise their English skills using their senses at the same time, depending on their hobbies, needs for a job, or present English proficiency. It also establishes a customised setting where adult learners can practise their English language abilities using all of their senses. AI further improves practical abilities like written communication by offering a real-life simulated dialogue platform, like spoken English. In addition, it maximizes the teaching impact of English and expands students' practice capacity. By offering continuous, personalized training, plenty of feedback, and scaffolding tasks in a low stakes setting, AI can reduce the time needed to learn language skills. Furthermore, compared to human teachers alone, AI solutions for spoken English learning are more successful and accessible options that can benefit a greater number of students. They can be accessed at any time, from any location, and occasionally even without internet connectivity. Thus, AI-powered educational software transcends time and location barriers to provide amazing worldwide connectedness. Moreover, AI makes it possible to produce excellent teaching-learning resources that cover all language proficiency levels, including speaking, listening, reading, and writing. Additionally, it serves as an additional resource for teachers and students, providing targeted support at any time and location Fitria (2021). English language teaching (ELT) has also benefited greatly from recent developments in generative artificial intelligence. Specifically, generative artificial intelligence (AI) has transformed English language instruction, making it more efficient, interesting, and motivating. First, AI can help EFL students create personalised learning plans by greatly increasing their intrinsic drive and self-efficacy. In fact, it has been discovered that ChatGPT in particular enhances students' motivation to learn and their language proficiency. Second, by immersing users in simulated discussions, adapting responses according to learners' ability levels, and offering real-time feedback, AI can assist in improving speaking abilities. For voice-driven interactions and learning conversational English, tools such as ChatGPT-4o are perfect since they provide improved multimodal capabilities, such as text, audio, and visual inputs. Third, AI-powered tools can help students write more fluently and with more syntactic complexity. They also assist with brainstorming, structuring, refining, and delivering grammatical criticism in real time. Additionally, in language learning settings, ChatGPT has been shown to lessen learning anxiety. Finally, generative AI may modify challenging texts according to students' proficiency levels, adding questions and annotations to the text to boost comprehension and engagement (Pang and Heng, 2025). Artificial intelligence (AI) systems like ChatGPT and Gemini can serve as personal tutors, tailoring educational experiences to each student's needs (Pang & Heng, 2025). Moreover, English language teaching (ELT) and AI technology interact, examining how language education is changing in the digital era (CA , 2024). The benefits of using Artificial Intelligence (AI) into English as a Second Language (ESL) instruction are numerous and significant. First of all, AI technologies make it easier to provide dynamic and captivating content, which is essential for sustaining student interest. AI-powered technologies can use gamification, simulations, and multimedia to build immersive learning environments. Additionally, by automating administrative duties like class planning, attendance monitoring, and grading, AI greatly increases teacher effectiveness by freeing up teachers' time for more meaningful pursuits like individualized education. Furthermore, with translation tools driven by cutting-edge machine learning algorithms, AI can assist in expanding access to ESL instruction for a wide variety of learners. Particularly in multicultural classrooms, these resources help non-native speakers comprehend instructions and interact with students and teachers. In addition, by offering personalised learning resources and accessibility capabilities like text-to-speech and speech-to-text technologies, AI can also help students with special needs. Lastly, AI gives students the ability to take charge of their education by providing them with autonomous learning platforms that provide a variety of resources, such as multimedia content, interactive exercises, and language games (CAK, 2024). As a result, learners can now progress through English classes without being constrained by typical class hours thanks to AI tools like chatbots and intelligent tutoring systems, which suggests that ESL instruction will become more accessible and flexible (Yuniari, 2024).

According to studies, chatbots are being used in a variety of contexts to improve English language acquisition, including virtual conversation partners, vocabulary and grammar drills, and engaging real-world scenarios. Additionally, chatbots can offer tailored suggestions for extra resources and techniques to further quicken the learning process of the English language (AbuSahyon et al., 2023). By offering an interactive and captivating language practice environment, prompt feedback and appropriate language instruction, tracking learners' progress, and delivering data-driven insights to identify areas for improvement, chatbots have the potential to completely transform the way English language learners practice and advance their language proficiency. Through the provision of individualized, interactive, and thorough language tasks and practice opportunities, chatbots have completely transformed language learning. Moreover, they may be adjusted to accommodate different learning styles and preferences and offer timely feedback and corrections, which improves the language learning process by making it more individualised and engaging (AbuSahyon et al., 2023).

As stated by Tiwari et al. (2024), there is growing scientific evidence of the advantages and effects of AI in English language acquisition. First, research shows that, in comparison to conventional teaching techniques, AI-assisted instruction greatly enhances the writing abilities and motivation of English as a Foreign Language (EFL) students, underscoring the transformative potential of AI. AI-powered resources are thought to be beneficial for ESL (English as a Second Language) learners. Furthermore, by enhancing language processing and comprehension for learners, artificial intelligence (AI) innovations like ChatGPT and Convolutional

Neural Network (CNN) models improve English listening abilities, which are essential for efficient communication. Equally significant is the Fluency Mentor app, which provides interactive exercises, tailored instruction, and immediate feedback by utilizing generative AI technologies such as ChatGPT and Gemini API (Tiwari et al., 2024). Overall, English language learning is being profoundly changed by artificial intelligence (AI), which provides interactive experiences, tailored feedback, and dynamic information. The goal of this integration is to improve language fluency and communication abilities (Tiwari et al., 2024).

Numerous researches have explored learners' impressions of AI approaches used in English Language Teaching (ELT), with many demonstrating students' positive attitudes towards AI incorporation in language learning (Yuniari, 2024). According to the research, ESL students have a generally positive opinion of AI-based technologies, particularly in terms of English acquisition. This optimistic vision is critical for the successful integration of AI in language teaching (Yuniari, 2024). Additionally, EFL instructors have also demonstrated a generally positive attitude towards AI-based language learning technology, acknowledging AI's potential to improve EFL sessions. This instructor's perspective is critical for the successful deployment of AI solutions (Yuniari 2024).

In summary, AI is revolutionizing English language learning by providing smart, tailored, and readily available resources that improve multiple facets of language acquisition, including pronunciation, grammar, conversational abilities, and overall fluency. These technologies enhance conventional teaching strategies, increasing efficiency and engagement for a wide variety of learners. Moreover, generative AI offers personalised, adaptable, and engaging tutoring experiences across a wide range of linguistic skills. However, its implementation necessitates careful consideration of ethical issues, accessibility, and the need for balanced integration to preserve human interaction and critical thinking at the core of the learning process. Overall, the incorporation of AI into English language learning marks a radical shift, delivering innovative solutions that enhance the experience for both ESL students and educators. This technology not only addresses long-standing challenges but also paves the way for more successful and accessible language acquisition. While challenges remain, ongoing research and development continue to refine AI applications, making English learning increasingly effective and inclusive for learners worldwide.

9. THE USE OF AI IN LEARNING ENGLISH IN ALGERIAN EDUCATION

Artificial Intelligence (AI) is increasingly acknowledged for its potential in numerous educational systems around the world, including its use in learning English as a Foreign Language (EFL). In the context of Algerian higher education, AI is becoming more recognised for its ability to significantly enhance English language learning, driven by the urgent need to move beyond conventional teaching approaches and adopt innovative strategies suited for a globalized society. A large number of Algerian EFL university students have already begun to incorporate AI-driven tools into their learning processes to a certain degree. This study examines the views and difficulties faced by Algerian university educators regarding AI usage, offering insights relevant to ongoing discussions on AI integration in English as a Second Language (ESL) education in Algeria. As highlighted by Boukhelkhal (2025), universities should provide workshops and strategic guidance on integrating AI into higher education. In addition, the Ministry of Higher Education is encouraged to invest in AI literacy initiatives targeting students, researchers, and educators to support successful implementation. To ensure meaningful progress, policymakers and educational leaders must also prioritise the connection between AI systems and EFL teaching and learning practices in Algerian universities (Boukhelkhal, 2025).

In recent years, academics and researchers have expressed great enthusiasm about the limitless potential of artificial intelligence, highlighting its broad implications for education (Zitouni, 2022). AI has also emerged as a prominent phenomenon in recent years, with particular interest in teaching and learning foreign languages. As Sehlaoui (2024) observes, the growing demand for foreign language instruction necessitates AI-powered support and the incorporation of AI tools to promote student autonomy. Moreover, it has become increasingly evident in the 21st century that artificial intelligence technology and applications are becoming more widely used in educational settings as essential means of enhancing the learning and teaching process, especially by offering learners individualized guidance and support (Zitouni, 2022).

With artificial intelligence, foreign language learning can be facilitated by a variety of opportunities and supports, congenial to both the needs of teachers, who are imparting knowledge, as well as students, who are seeking information and knowledge retrieval (Zitouni, 2022). In fact, there is a multitude of programs and applications that can be integrated into education particularly when it comes to foreign language learning each with specific functions, such as addressing learners' writing, reading, speaking, listening, and communication skills (Zitouni, 2022). With the assistance of artificial intelligence applications, teachers and students can learn foreign languages more effectively by enhancing speech transcription, checking pronunciation, and using voice commands, as noted by Zitouni (2022). Bensaber and Mebarki (2025) observed that ChatGPT has demonstrated tremendous potential for assisting learners in language learning, particularly in improving writing skills. It improves pupils' writing skills, particularly in grammar, vocabulary, and coherence. According to Algerian students, it has led to noticeable improvements in writing quality, while teachers recognised its value in promoting classroom learning and learner autonomy. Moreover, AI-powered feedback tools such as ChatGPT can analyse Algerian students' work and make targeted suggestions to improve word use and sentence construction (Bensaber & Mebarki, 2025). ChatGPT is also capable of generating a large amount of text in various genres including samples, exercises, and assignments and tailoring it to different language ability levels. It may even generate tailored vocabulary lists or grammar-focused activities to help improve linguistic accuracy (Bensaber & Mebarki, 2025). In addition, ChatGPT can serve as a brainstorming tool, helping users understand unfamiliar topics and structure their ideas. Student feedback gathered by Bensaber and Mebarki (2025) highlighted the tool's usefulness in concept generation and organization. In particular, AI technologies have surpassed traditional teaching techniques in improving grammar and communication skills, with a mean grammar improvement score of 2.7 compared to a neutral score of 2, a finding reported by Merazi (2025).

The use of artificial intelligence is increasingly being investigated in Western countries; however, little research has been conducted specifically in Algeria. A notable gap in studies on AI applications within Algerian EFL contexts was highlighted by Aliouche and Mezghich (2022). Their research, which surveyed 41 third-year English students at Barika University Centre, suggested that AI could enhance educational outcomes by offering practice opportunities, improving linguistic skills, and personalizing the teaching and learning process. Numerous studies have emphasized the importance of AI in improving English language proficiency. It is regarded as a key component of the digital revolution, particularly in enhancing speaking abilities in English as a foreign language, as well as contributing to improvements in writing skills and pronunciation. Moreover, a study involving 41 instructors of literature, linguistics, and translation from 11 Algerian universities found that AI was primarily used to improve educational activities (41.5%) and conduct scientific research (51.2%). Additionally, 26.8% of the professors reported using AI in translation, highlighting its value in facilitating language transitions, especially in academic contexts and communication (Achili & Zerrouki, 2024).

While a sizable majority of teachers (61%) believe that AI can enhance educational quality, and 73.2% of respondents generally support the integration of AI in education, with varying degrees of caution, significant hurdles remain. Notably, 87.8% of teachers reported having received no specific training on how to integrate AI into their instruction. This lack of professional development, coupled with inadequate infrastructure, further complicates the implementation of AI in educational contexts (Achili & Zerrouki, 2024). In addition, ethical concerns remain prevalent among educators. According to the same study, 85.4% of teachers expressed doubts about the ethical implications of AI, with 70.7% worried it might stifle creativity and critical thinking. Furthermore, concerns such as increased assignment cheating, over-reliance on technology, and rising student passivity, each cited by approximately 68.3% of respondents, have discouraged nearly half of the participants (48.8%) from adopting AI tools in the classroom. Despite its potential, the full integration of AI technologies and virtual platforms into Algerian education is hindered by persistent constraints, including inadequate digital infrastructure, limited technical competencies among students, and poor internet access (Merazi, 2025). Nevertheless, AI shows promise in supporting online learning. As Zitouni (2022) explains, 80% of learners believe AI can simplify the online learning process, and 87% think it can improve overall quality. His study suggests that combining AI tools with teacher guidance and creativity is a powerful method for enhancing EFL learners' experiences, particularly in vocabulary, writing, speaking, listening, and communication skills. Students also demonstrate clear usage patterns in AI adoption. Boukhelkhal (2025) found that most learners use AI primarily to enhance writing, grammar, and vocabulary, while placing less emphasis on speaking and listening skills. This avoidance may be attributed to limited awareness or a continued preference for human interaction during oral practice.

Students learning English as a foreign language in Algeria generally hold favorable perceptions of AI-driven tools in their English education. As Boukhelkhal (2025) reports, these learners regard AI technologies as effective in optimizing the learning process, providing instant feedback, improving language proficiency, and enabling personalized learning experiences. Among the perceived advantages, the ability of AI tools to save time and energy stands out as the most widely accepted benefit. Furthermore, AI-powered instruments are recognized for offering tailored and flexible educational experiences, particularly beneficial in Algeria's multilingual context. Research in the Algerian setting also underscores the role of AI in reducing learners' anxiety, fostering fluency, and supporting self-directed learning (Boukhelkhal, 2025). However, despite these advantages, many students encounter challenges in using AI tools efficiently. There remains a lack of structured guidance on how to engage with AI thoughtfully and responsibly. Key barriers include limited access to advanced AI functionalities, persistent reliance on traditional learning methods by some students, and concerns related to data privacy and security. Moreover, doubts have been raised regarding the reliability of AI-generated content, as well as the potential for academic dishonesty and plagiarism (Boukhelkhal, 2025).

The techniques used for teaching English in Algerian universities are frequently viewed as outdated and inadequate for tackling the challenges of contemporary language learning. Conventional approaches, which depend significantly on textbooks, lectures, and classrooms, restrict individualized support and engaging learning experiences (Hamadi, 2025). However, the increasing availability of technology such as smartphones and tablets, alongside improved internet connectivity, has expanded access to AI-driven language learning apps for Algerian students. This development enables learning beyond conventional classroom settings, offering both flexibility and convenience (Hamadi, 2025). Furthermore, global educational trends and the growing acknowledgment of English as a vital skill for academic and professional success in Algeria are strong motivators for universities to adopt AI tools. These platforms offer customized and adaptive learning experiences that conventional methods often fail to provide, addressing learners' needs in grammar, vocabulary, pronunciation, and fluency (Hamadi, 2025). As a result, Algerian universities are beginning to integrate AI-driven applications into their instructional practices, recognizing their potential to improve teaching effectiveness, enhance student outcomes, and foster more personalized language learning environments. According to recent institutional findings, the regular use of Grammarly significantly improves students' writing accuracy and bolsters their confidence. This allows educators to shift their focus toward more complex writing elements such as argumentation and content development (Hamadi, 2025). In addition, showcasing the benefits of AI in education through success stories and pilot programs can help dispel misconceptions and encourage broader adoption among stakeholders. To ensure sustainable implementation, Hamadi (2025) also emphasizes the importance of supportive policies, investments in AI research, financial incentives for AI-based educational initiatives, and collaborations among universities, technology developers, and educational organizations.

In summary, although AI holds considerable potential to enhance English language acquisition in Algeria—particularly in areas such as speaking, pronunciation, and writing—its widespread and effective integration faces significant challenges. These include a lack of targeted research within the Algerian EFL context, insufficient teacher training, limited technological infrastructure, and ethical concerns regarding AI's impact on student learning and academic integrity. Addressing these issues through comprehensive training and robust infrastructure is crucial for successful AI adoption in ESL education. Ultimately, while AI offers promising opportunities to personalize and advance English language education, its effective implementation requires overcoming infrastructural, cultural, and pedagogical barriers. A balanced approach that blends traditional methods with AI-enhanced strategies supported by strategic investment, teacher development, and culturally responsive adaptations is vital to preparing Algerian learners for success in a globally connected world.

10. CONCLUSION

In conclusion, the role of English in Algeria is a reflection of the intricate relationship between national identity, historical influences, and international aspirations. English has steadily gained ground, especially in academic and scientific circles, while French continues to echo colonial history and Arabic remains central to official and cultural life. Both policymakers and learners must negotiate these intersecting linguistic landscapes, balancing social and political factors against pragmatic advantages. Future generations' educational opportunities and choices will probably be influenced by the changing status of English as Algeria continues to interact with the outside world. A strategic move towards increased academic competition and global integration is reflected in recent initiatives that have made English the medium of instruction in a few universities. This changing educational approach demonstrates the growing awareness of English ability as a key asset in international cooperation and economic development. Furthermore, the growing prominence of English in the digital media and technological industries has boosted its popularity among Algerian young people seeking global participation. This trend is fuelled by companies' increasing preference for English fluency in international business and research collaborations.

REFERENCES

Abid-Houcine, S. (2007). *La langue anglaise en Algérie: Attitudes et usages*. Office des Publications Universitaires.

AbuSahyon, A. S. A. E., Alzyoud, A., Alshorman, O., & Al-Absi, B. (2023). AI-driven technology and chatbots as tools for enhancing English language learning in the context of second language acquisition: A review study. *International Journal of Membrane Science and Technology*, *10*(1), 1209–1223.

Achili, N., & Zerrouki, N. (2024). Using Artificial Intelligence in Algerian Higher Education: Opportunities and Challenges from TeachersPerspectives. أطراس, 5(3), 541-556.

Almutairi, A. F., Gegov, A., Adda, M., & Arabikhan, F. (2020). Conceptual artificial intelligence framework to improving English as second language. *WSEAS Transactions on Advances in Engineering Education*, *17*, 87–91.

Anes, M. (2018). *English language status in Algeria: Current trends and future prospects*. National Institute of Education Research.

Beddiaf, A., & Safi, Z. B. (2018). The position of English in the workplace in Algeria: An economic-oriented perspective. *Traduction et Langues*, *17*(1), 122–133.

Belmihoub, K. (2018). English in Algeria: A historical and contemporary overview. *World Englishes*, *37*(2), 207–227. DOI: 10.1111/weng.12312

Bemmoussat, N. D., & Bouyakoub, N. (2019). English Language Education in Algeria: Hostage of an Exam-Centric Education System. *Arab World English Journal*, *10*(3), 202–219.

Benadla, L. (2013). The Competency Based Language Teaching in the Algerian Middle School: From EFL Acquisition Planning to its Practical Teaching/Learning. Arab World English Journal, 4(1). URL: https://bit.ly/2ASf5gt (Visited on 15/05/2016)

Benmekki, F., & Lama, A. (2018). The status of English in Algeria: Between rejection and desire. *Algerian Journal of Language Policy and Planning*, *5*(1), 15–29.

Benmoussat, S. (2015). Globalization, language planning, and the future prospect of English in Algeria. *Traduction et Langues*, *14*(1), 7–13.

Benrabah, M. (2013). *Language Conflict in Algeria: From Colonialism to Post-Independence* (1st ed.). Multilingual Matters.

BENSABER. M., & MEBARKI, A. (2025). Exploring ChatGPT as a Writing Assistant in Algerian EFL Classrooms: Opportunities, Challenges and Perceptions: The Case Study of First Year University Students of Ain Temouchent (Doctoral dissertation, UNIVERSITY OF AIN TEMOUCHENT).

Boukhelkhal, O. (2025). ALGERIAN EFL STUDENTS'PERSPECTIVES AND PRACTICES ON AI-ENABLED LEARNING AT THE UNIVERSITY OF MEDEA. Journal of Studies in Language [JSLCS]. *Cultura e Scuola*, *8*(1), 93–110.

Crystal, D. (2003). *English as a Global Language*. Cambridge University Press.

Febriani, H. (2024). Navigating English learning with AI: A qualitative study of university students experiences. *PPSDP International Journal of Education*, *3*, 220–232.

Fitria, T. N. (2021). The use technology based on artificial intelligence in English teaching and learning. ELT Echo. *The Journal of English Language Teaching in Foreign Language Context*, *6*(2), 213–223.

Fox, J., & Mazzouzi, M. (2019). The shifting language policies in Algerian ministries: From French to English. *Policy and Language in North Africa*, *12*(3), 88–105.

Graddol, D. (2006). *English Next: Why global English may mean the end of 'English as a Foreign Language*. British Council.

Hamadi, N. A. (2025). Enhancing english proficiency with intelligent assistants in Algerian universities. *Studies in Education Sciences*, *6*(2), e16062–e16062.

Jacob, C. (2019). 'Back to the "futur"': Mobility and immobility through English in Algeria. *Language & Communication*, *68*, 6–16.

Kachru, B. B. (1992). World Englishes: Approaches, issues and resources. *Language Teaching*, *25*, 1. DOI: 10.1017/S0261444800006583

Merazi, N. (2025). The Role of Artificial Intelligence in Language Learning: Enhancing Communities of Practice Among Algerian University Students. *Revue Algérienne des Sciences du Langage*, *10*(1), 465–478.

Miliani, M. (2001). Teaching English in a multilingual context: The Algerian case.

MOKDAD, A. P. P. D. N. (2023). French as a"spoil of war"and a springboard for accelerated teaching/learning and effective mastery of other foreign languages, especially English in Algeria in the era of globalization. [IJHS]. *International Journal of Humanities and Social Science*, (1), 29–36.

Negadi, M. N. (2015). Learning English in Algeria through French-based background proficiency. *Procedia: Social and Behavioral Sciences*, *199*, 496–500.

Pang, S., Nol, E., & Heng, K. (2025). Generative AI as a personal tutor for English language learning: A review of benefits and concerns. International Journal of Changes in Education.

Rouabah, S. (2022). Multilingualism in Algeria: Educational policies, language practices and challenges. *Journal of the British Academy*, *10*(4), 21–40.

Sadouki, F. (2023). Language contact in Algeria: A sociolinguistic study. *Argumentum*, *19*, 70–87.

Sahraoui, S. (2020). English and the languages of Algeria: Suggestions towards a new language policy.

Schneider, E. W. (2011). *English Around the World: An Introduction.* Cambridge University Press.

Sehlaoui, F. Z. (2024). Integrating AI in Foreign Language Teaching and Learning: Learner Autonomy and Tool Utilization in an Algerian University. *Passerelle*, *13*(2), 116–139.

Slimani, S. (2016). Teaching English as a foreign language in Algeria. مجلة العلوم الانسانية, 16(2), 33-44.

Tiwari, H., Jain, S., Kumar, S., Soni, V., & Negi, A. (2024). AI-driven English language learning: Leveraging applications/APIs for dynamic content and feedback. *World Journal of Advanced Research and Reviews*, *22*(3), 1611–1616.

Yuniari, N. M. (2024). Students' Perception toward Chat PDF AI Applied in Critical Reading Course. *Indonesian Journal of Foreign Language Studies*, *1*(1), 35–44.

Zitouni, K. S. (2022). New trends in EFL online learning and teaching through the lens of artificial intelligence. مجلة المقدمة للدراسات الانسانية و الاجتماعية, 7(1), 1065-1080.

Compilation of References

Abid-Houcine, S. (2007). *La langue anglaise en Algérie: Attitudes et usages*. Office des Publications Universitaires.

Abiero, D. (2024). Ethical AI development in Africa: Integrating cultural values and addressing global disparities. Strathmore University CIPIT. https://cipit.strathmore.edu/ethical-ai-development-in-africa-integratingcultural-values-and-addressing-global-disparities/

AbuSahyon, A. S. A. E., Alzyoud, A., Alshorman, O., & Al-Absi, B. (2023). AI-driven technology and chatbots as tools for enhancing English language learning in the context of second language acquisition: A review study. *International Journal of Membrane Science and Technology*, *10*(1), 1209–1223.

Achili, N., & Zerrouki, N. (2024). Using Artificial Intelligence in Algerian Higher Education: Opportunities and Challenges from TeachersPerspectives. , 5(3), 541-556.

Afitska, O. (2014). Formative Use of Language Assessment: Supporting Learning through the Medium of a Second Language. *US-China Education Review A*, *4*(8), 517–535.

Ağçam, R., & Doğan, A. (2021). A Study on The Soft Skills of Pre-Service Teachers. *International Journal of Progressive Education*, *17*(4), 35–48. DOI: 10.29329/ijpe.2021.366.3

Ahmed, M. (2023). ChatGPT and the EFL classroom: Supplement or substitute in Saudi Arabia's eastern region. *Information Sciences Letters*, *12*(7), 2727–2734. DOI: 10.18576/isl/120704

Ahmed, S. T. S., & Qasem, B. T. A. (2019). Problems of Teaching and Learning English as a Foreign Language in South Yemen: A Case Study of Lahj Governorate. *ELS Journal on Interdisciplinary Studies in Humanities*, *2*(4), 485–492. DOI: 10.34050/els-jish.v2i4.7458

Akkerman, S. F., & Bakker, A. (2011). Boundary crossing and boundary objects. *Review of Educational Research, 81*(2), 132–169. DOI: 10.3102/0034654311404435

Al Aqad, M. H. (2022). Multilingualism and Personal Health Benefits: Connecting the. Multilingualism: Interdisciplinary Topics, 123.

Al Aqad, M. H., Al-Saggaf, M. A., & Muthmainnah, M. (2021). The impact of audio-visual aids on learning English among MSU third-year students. ENGLISH FRANCA: Academic Journal of English Language and Education, 5(2 November), 201-214.</unknown>

Albiladi, W. S. (2019). Teaching English Pronunciation Revisited: The Challenges of Teaching EFL in Non-English-Speaking Countries. European Journal of Foreign Language Teaching.

Alhusaiyan, E. (2025). A systematic review of current trends in artificial intelligence in foreign language learning. *Saudi Journal of Language Studies, 5*(1), 1–16. DOI: 10.1108/SJLS-07-2024-0039

Allen, A. (2022). An introduction to constructivism: Its theoretical roots and impact on contemporary education. *Journal of Learning Design and Leadership, 1*(1), 1–11.

Almutairi, A. F., Gegov, A., Adda, M., & Arabikhan, F. (2020). Conceptual artificial intelligence framework to improving English as second language. *WSEAS Transactions on Advances in Engineering Education, 17*, 87–91.

Al-Saggaf, M. A. (2024). Freedom and Responsibility in Education 5.0. In Preconceptions of Policies, Strategies, and Challenges in Education 5.0 (pp. 275-283). IGI Global.

Al-Saggaf, M. A. (2024). Freedom and Responsibility in Education 5.0. In *Preconceptions of Policies, Strategies, and Challenges in Education 5.0* (pp. 275-283). IGI Global. https://doi.org/DOI: 10.4018/979-8-3693-3041-8.ch016

Al-Saggaf, M. A. (2025). NLP in Action: Enhancing Translation and Interpretation. In Role of AI in Translation and Interpretation (pp. 175-204). IGI Global Scientific Publishing.

Al-Saggaf, M. A. (2025). NLP in Action: Enhancing Translation and Interpretation. In *Role of AI in Translation and Interpretation* (pp. 175-204). IGI Global Scientific Publishing. https://doi.org/DOI: 10.4018/979-8-3373-0060-3.ch007

Al-Saggaf, M. A. (2020). Investigating the types of motivation of TESL students in a higher education institute in Malaysia. *TESOL and Technology Studies, 1*(1), 55–69. DOI: 10.48185/tts.v1i1.105

Al-Sofi, B. B. M. A. (2024). Artificial intelligence-powered tools and academic writing: To use or not to use ChatGPT. *Saudi Journal of Language Studies*, *4*(3), 145–161. DOI: 10.1108/SJLS-06-2024-0029

Alsofyani, A. H., & Barzanji, A. M. (2025). The effects of ChatGPT-generated feedback on Saudi EFL learners' writing skills and perception at the tertiary level: A mixed-methods study. *Journal of Educational Computing Research*, *63*(2), 431–463. DOI: 10.1177/07356331241307297

Altukhi, Z. M., & Pradhan, S. (2024). "Systematic Literature Review: Explainable AI Definitions and Challenges in Education" *ICIS 2024 Proceedings*. 11. https://aisel.aisnet.org/icis2024/lit_review/lit_review/11

Amin, M. Y. M. (2023). AI and ChatGPT in language teaching: Enhancing EFL classroom support and transforming assessment techniques. *International Journal of Higher Education Pedagogies*, *4*(4), 1–15. DOI: 10.33422/ijhep.v4i4.554

Amiri, E., & El Karfa, A. (2021). The Impact of Learning Environment on EFL Students' Academic Achievement: A Study of Sociocultural Factors Affecting Academic Achievement. *Arab World English Journal*, *12*(4), 387–400.

Anes, M. (2018). *English language status in Algeria: Current trends and future prospects*. National Institute of Education Research.

Ang, S., & Van Dyne, L. (2015). *Handbook of cultural intelligence*. Routledge.

Annerstedt, M., & Wahrborg, P. (2011). Nature-assisted therapy: Systematic review of controlled and observational studies. *Scandinavian Journal of Public Health*, *39*(4), 371–388. Retrieved May 4, 2020, from www.jstor.org/stable/45150415

Anwar, A., & Kumar, S. (2025). Leveraging AI to Achieve Sustainability Goals in TVET: A Multifaceted Approach. In Sorayyaei Azar, A., Kant Gupta, S., Taherdoost, H., & Alhamaty, F. (Eds.), (pp. 33–60). Advances in Computational Intelligence and Robotics. IGI Global., DOI: 10.4018/979-8-3373-1142-5.ch002

Anwar, A., Kumar, S., & Manoharan, G. (2025). Revolutionizing the Hospitality Industry: The Impact and Challenges of Smart Operations. In Talukder, M. B., & Chowdhury, H. H. K. (Eds.), *Smart Operations and Enhancing Guest Experience in the Hospitality Industry* (pp. 271–296). IGI Global., DOI: 10.4018/979-8-3373-2145-5.ch010

Apriyanti, D., & Ayu, M. (2020). Think-Pair-Share: Engaging Students in Speaking Activities in Classroom. *Journal of English Language Teaching and Learning*, *1*(1), 13–19.

Ardito, C. G. (2025). Generative AI detection in higher education assessments. *New Directions for Teaching and Learning, 2025*, 11–28. DOI: 10.1002/tl.20624

Aslan, C. (2020). An analysis on the development of sociology of education in USA and England. *African Educational Research Journal*, *8*(2), S186–S195.

Assalihee, M., Boonsuk, Y., Bakoh, N., & Sano, I. L. (2019). Reconceptualizing the 21st Century English Pedagogies for Islamic School Teachers in Asean. *Journal of Nusantara Studies*, *4*(1), 401–421.

Association of American Colleges and Universities (2017). Intercultural Knowledge and Competence Value Rubric.

Azimova, D., & Solidjonov, D. (2023). LEARNING ENGLISH LANGUAGE AS A SECOND LANGUAGE WITH AUGMENTED REALITY. *QO'QON UNIVERSITETI XABARNOMASI*, *6*, 112–115. DOI: 10.54613/ku.v6i6.264

Babanoğlu, M. P., Karataş, T. Ö., & Dündar, E. (2025). Ethical considerations of AI through a socio-technical lens: Insights from ELT context as a higher education system. *Cogent Education*, *12*(1), 2488546. DOI: 10.1080/2331186X.2025.2488546

Babiker, A. (2018). Improving Speaking Skills in EFL Classes through Collaborative Learning. [ASRJETS]. *American Scientific Research Journal for Engineering, Technology, and Sciences*, *44*(1), 137–154.

Badwan, K. M. (2017). "Did We Learn English or What?"A Study Abroad Student in the UK Carrying and Crossing Boundaries in Out-of-Class Communication. *Studies in Second Language Learning and Teaching*, *7*(2), 193–210.

Bahrani, T., Qadery, S., & Bahrani, D. (2023). The impact of artificial intelligence-based chatbots on (EFL) learners' speaking and listening skills: A review of recent studies. *International Journal of English Language and Literature Studies*, *12*(2), 89–102. DOI: 10.18488/ijels.v12i2.3385

Baker, R. S., & Hawn, A. (2022). Algorithmic bias in education. *International Journal of Artificial Intelligence in Education*, *32*(4), 1052–1092. DOI: 10.1007/s40593-021-00285-9

Bakri, M., & Pongpalilu, F. (2025). Reclaiming the argument: Students' perceptions of ChatGPT's role in constructing argumentative texts in the age of AI. *International Journal of Multidisciplinary Research and Analysis*, *8*(5), 2531–2538. DOI: 10.47191/ijmra/v8-i05-29

Balakrishnan, J., & Dwivedi, Y. K. (2024). Conversational commerce: Entering the next stage of AI-powered digital assistants. *Annals of Operations Research, 333*(2–3), 653–687. DOI: 10.1007/s10479-021-04049-5

Baldauf, R. B., Kaplan, R. B., Kamwangamalu, N., & Bryant, P. (2013). Success or Failure of Primary Second/Foreign Language Programmes in Asia: What Do the Data Tell Us? Language Planning in Primary Schools in Asia, 205-219.

Barnatt, J., Andries D'Souza, L., Gleeson, A. M., Mitchell Viesca, K., & Wery, J. (2020). Intercultural Competence in Pre-Service Teacher Candidates. *International Journal of Educational Reform, 29*(3), 211–235. DOI: 10.1177/1056787919896866

Barrow, E. C. (2023). Defining intercultural competence: How four pre-service teachers developed a more complex understanding of ICC. *Journal of Global Education and Research, 7*(1), 1–17. https://www.doi.org/10.5038/2577-509X.7.1.1210

Beck, D. (2019). Special Issue: Augmented and Virtual Reality in Education: Immersive Learning Research. *Journal of Educational Computing Research, 57*(7), 1619–1625. DOI: 10.1177/0735633119854035

Beddiaf, A., & Safi, Z. B. (2018). The position of English in the workplace in Algeria: An economic-oriented perspective. *Traduction et Langues, 17*(1), 122–133.

Bekou, A. (2024). Exploring opportunities and challenges of using ChatGPT in English language teaching (ELT) in Morocco. *Focus on ELT Journal*, 87–106. https://doi.org/DOI: 10.14744/felt.6.1.7

Bell, M., & Ashwood, L. (2016). *An Invitation to Environmental Sociology. Fifth Addition*. Sage Publications, Inc.

Belloula, S. (2025). Empowering Educators: Leveraging AI to Revolutionize Lesson Planning. *International Journal of Research in Education and Science, 11*(2), 264–280. https://files.eric.ed.gov/fulltext/EJ1475735.pdf

Belmihoub, K. (2018). English in Algeria: A historical and contemporary overview. *World Englishes, 37*(2), 207–227. DOI: 10.1111/weng.12312

Bemmoussat, N. D., & Bouyakoub, N. (2019). English Language Education in Algeria: Hostage of an Exam-Centric Education System. *Arab World English Journal, 10*(3), 202–219.

Ben Hammou, S., & Kesbi, A. (2024). Exploring Multilingual Education in Morocco: Official Documents and Teachers' Perceptions. *International Journal of Multilingualism, 21*(4), 1906–1927.

Benadla, L. (2013). The Competency Based Language Teaching in the Algerian Middle School: From EFL Acquisition Planning to its Practical Teaching/Learning. Arab World English Journal, 4(1). URL: https://bit.ly/2ASf5gt (Visited on 15/05/2016)

Benmekki, F., & Lama, A. (2018). The status of English in Algeria: Between rejection and desire. *Algerian Journal of Language Policy and Planning*, *5*(1), 15–29.

Benmoussat, S. (2015). Globalization, language planning, and the future prospect of English in Algeria. *Traduction et Langues*, *14*(1), 7–13.

Benrabah, M. (2013). *Language Conflict in Algeria: From Colonialism to Post-Independence* (1st ed.). Multilingual Matters.

BENSABER. M., & MEBARKI, A. (2025). Exploring ChatGPT as a Writing Assistant in Algerian EFL Classrooms: Opportunities, Challenges and Perceptions: The Case Study of First Year University Students of Ain Temouchent (Doctoral dissertation, UNIVERSITY OF AIN TEMOUCHENT).

Bertino, E., Kundu, A., & Sura, Z. (2019). Data transparency with blockchain and AI ethics. [JDIQ]. *Journal of Data and Information Quality*, *11*(4), 1–8. DOI: 10.1145/3312750

Bicknell, K., & Brust, C. (2020, October 7). *Learning how to help you learn: Introducing Birdbrain!* Duolingo Blog. https://blog.duolingo.com/learning-how-to-help-you-learn-introducing-birdbrain/

Bimpong, W. K. (2020). Teaching purposefully: Considering the perspectives of foreign language learners in language skill development. *Educational Resources Information Center*. https://eric.ed.gov/?id=ED598551

Binu, P. M. (2024). Affordances and challenges of integrating artificial intelligence into English language education: A critical analysis. *English Scholarship Beyond Borders, 10*(1), 34–51. https://esbbjournal.org/volume-10-issue-1-2024/

Blodgett, S. L., Barocas, S., Daumé, H., III, & Wallach, H. (2020). Language (technology) is power: A critical survey of" bias" in nlp. *arXiv preprint arXiv:2005.14050.*

Blodgett, S. L., Barocas, S., Daumé, H.III, & Wallach, H. (2020). Language (technology) is power: A critical survey of "bias" in NLP. *Proceedings of the 58th Annual Meeting of the Association for Computational Linguistics*, 5454–5476. https://doi.org/DOI: 10.18653/v1/2020.acl-main.485

Bloom, B. S. (1984). The 2 sigma problem: The search for methods of group instruction as effective as one-to-one tutoring. *Educational Researcher*, *13*(6), 4–16. DOI: 10.3102/0013189X013006004

Blyth, C. (2022). Immersive technologies and language learning. In *The Routledge handbook of second language acquisition and technology* (pp. 377–390). Routledge.

Bora, D., Patel, P., Psyridou, M., Ruotsalainen, J., Richardson, U., & Torppa, M. (2025). Foundational English literacy development in India: A randomised-control trial using phonics instruction and GraphoLearn. *Reading and Writing, 38*(5), 1309–1335. DOI: 10.1007/s11145-024-10551-6

Boudouaia, A., Mouas, S., & Kouider, B. (2024). A study on ChatGPT-4 as an innovative approach to enhancing English as a foreign language writing learning. *Journal of Educational Computing Research, 62*(6), 1289–1317. DOI: 10.1177/07356331241247465

Boukhelkhal, O. (2025). ALGERIAN EFL STUDENTS'PERSPECTIVES AND PRACTICES ON AI-ENABLED LEARNING AT THE UNIVERSITY OF MEDEA. Journal of Studies in Language [JSLCS]. *Cultura e Scuola, 8*(1), 93–110.

Boumediene, H. (2025). The AI Evolution in Higher Education: Enhancing Teaching with ChatGPT. *Journal of Studies in Language* [JSLCS]. *Cultura e Scuola, 8*(1), 15–29.

Boumediene, H., & Bouakkaz, M. (2025). Artificial Intelligence in Education: Emerging Trends, Ethical Considerations, and Future Directions. In Cela, E., Vajjhala, N., & Fonkam, M. (Eds.), *Next-Generation AI Methodologies in Education* (pp. 407–438). IGI Global Scientific Publishing., DOI: 10.4018/979-8-3693-7220-3.ch014

Boumediene, H., & Hamadi, N. A. (2024). Integrating artificial intelligence into language learning to enhance proficiency through adaptive and ethical AI solutions. *Akofena, 4*(14), Article 32. https://doi.org/DOI: 10.48734/akofena.n014.vol.4.32.2024

Boumediene, H., Ouarniki, O., & Supran, A. (2025). Exploring the Effectiveness of Problem-Based Learning in Improving English for Specific Purposes (ESP) Proficiency: The Case of EAP Students. *Revue Algérienne des Sciences du Langage, 10*(1), 116–134.

Brame, & Biel. (2015). *CFT HOME PAGE*. Vanderbilt University. http://cft.vanderbilt.edu/

British Council. (2024). *Artificial intelligence and English language teaching: Preparing for the future*. https://www.teachingenglish.org.uk/sites/teacheng/files/2024-08/AI_and_ELT_Jul_2024.pdf

Bruner, J. S. (1996). *The culture of education*. Harvard University Press.

Buolamwini, J., & Gebru, T. (2018). Gender shades: Intersectional accuracy disparities in commercial gender classification. *Proceedings of Machine Learning Research, 81*, 1–15. https://proceedings.mlr.press/v81/buolamwini18a/buolamwini18a.pdf

Burrell, J. (2016). How the machine 'thinks': Understanding opacity in machine learning algorithms. *Big Data & Society*, *3*(1), 2053951715622512.

Case, R., Liu, L., & Mintz, J. (2025). Integrating AI technology into language teacher education: Challenges, potentials, and assumptions. *Computers in the Schools*, *42*(2), 93–99. DOI: 10.1080/07380569.2025.2458950

Catana, S. E. (2014). Teaching Cross-cultural Communication Issues – A Way of Successfully Integrating into the Multicultural Knowledge Society. *Procedia: Social and Behavioral Sciences*, *128*, 343–348. DOI: 10.1016/j.sbspro.2014.03.168

Celik, I., Dindar, M., Muukkonen, H., & Järvelä, S. (2022). The Promises and Challenges of Artificial Intelligence for Teachers: a Systematic Review of Research. *TechTrends, 66*(4). Springer. https://doi.org/DOI: 10.1007/s11528-022-00715-y

Chan, C. K. Y., & Hu, W. (2023). Students' voices on generative AI: Perceptions, benefits, and challenges in higher education. *International Journal of Educational Technology in Higher Education*, *20*(43). Advance online publication. DOI: 10.1186/s41239-023-00411-8

Chapelle, C. A. (2021). The role of applied linguistics in the age of AI. *Applied Linguistics*, *42*(5), 957–963. DOI: 10.1093/applin/amab040

Chapelle, C. A., & Sauro, S. (Eds.). (2017). *The handbook of technology and second language teaching and learning*. Wiley-Blackwell.

Charles, C. (2009, October 2). The Ecology of Hope: Natural Guides to Building a Children and Nature Movement. Journal of Science Education and Technology. https://link.springer.com/article/10.1007/s10956-009-9193-z?error=cookies_not_supporte d&code=e548e227-9255-4ed1-979f-25a6849262ea

Cheng, A., & Wang, Q. (2012). English Language Teaching in Higher Education in China: A Historical and Social Overview. In Ruan, J., & Leung, C. B. (Eds.), *Perspectives on Teaching and Learning English Literacy in China* (Vol. 3, pp. 19–33). Springer Netherlands., DOI: 10.1007/978-94-007-4994-8_2

Cheng, C., & Zhao, J. (2023). The impact of professional learning communities on pre-service teachers' professional commitment. *Frontiers in Psychology*, *14*, 1153016. DOI: 10.3389/fpsyg.2023.1153016 PMID: 37448713

Chen, M., Zhang, Y., & Liu, X. (2021). AI-supported vocabulary learning in elementary school: Effects on vocabulary knowledge and reading comprehension. *Journal of Educational Computing Research, 59*(3), 543–562. DOI: 10.1177/0735633120966558

Chenoweth, N. H. (2014). *Cultural and Linguistic Obstacles for ELLs*. Beyond Words, 2(2), 91–120.

Chimpololo, A. (2010). Assessing Pupils ' Language Proficiency in a Bilingual Education Programme: Insights from Two Primary Schools in Malawi. *The Buckingham Journal of Language and Linguistics, 3*, 1–10.

Chinnappan, M., McKenzie, B., & Fitzsimmons, P. (2013). Pre-service teachers' attitudes towards overseas professional experience: Implications for professional practice. *The Australian Journal of Teacher Education, 38*(12), 36–53. DOI: 10.14221/ajte.2013v38n12.5

Chiu, T. K. F. (2022). Teachers' professional development and AI integration in education: A systematic review. *Computers & Education: Artificial Intelligence, 3*, 100066. DOI: 10.1016/j.caeai.2022.100066

Chung, J. Y., & Jeong, S.-H. (2024). Exploring the perceptions of Chinese pre-service teachers on the integration of generative AI in English language teaching: Benefits, challenges, and educational implications. *Online Journal of Communication and Media Technologies, 14*(4), e202457. DOI: 10.30935/ojcmt/15266

CNBC. (2020, August 21). *How a computer algorithm caused a grading crisis in British schools*. https://www.cnbc.com/2020/08/21/computer-algorithm-caused-a-grading-crisis-in-british-schools.html

Colonna, L. (2024). Human oversight in AI-based educational assessments: A GDPR perspective. *European Journal of Law and Technology, 15*(1), 1–18.

Connolly, M., & Haughton, C. (2017). The perception, management and performance of risk amongst Forest School educators. *British Journal of Sociology of Education, 38*(2), 105–124.

Council of Europe. (2024, Jan. 31). *AI and deeper learning in language education: Unlocking opportunities for sign languages users – The European Centre for Modern Languages launches new projects for 2024–2027*. https://www.coe.int/en/web/portal/-/ai-and-deeper-learning-in-language-education-unlocking-opportunities-for-sign-languages-users-the-european-centre-for-modern-languages-launches-new-projects-for-2024-2027

Cranfield, S. (2016) Enhancing Teaching Practice in Higher Education (Chapter 3), Sage, London – Edited by Pokorny, H & Warren, D.

Creswell, J. W., & Guetterman, T. C. (2019). *Educational research: Planning, conducting, and evaluating quantitative and Qualitative Research* (6th ed.). Pearson.

Crompton, H., Edmett, A., Ichaporia, N., & Burke, D. (2024). AI and English language teaching: Affordances and challenges. *British Journal of Educational Technology, 55*(6), 2503–2529. DOI: 10.1111/bjet.13460

Cruz, M., & Kwinta, A. (2013). "Buddy System": A Pedagogical Innovation to Promote Online Interaction. *Profile Issues in Teachers'. Professional Development (Philadelphia, Pa.), 15*(1), 207–221.

Crystal, D. (2003). *English as a Global Language*. Cambridge University Press.

Cukurova, M., Luckin, R., & Kent, C. (2020). *Artificial intelligence and the future of learning: Expert panel report*. UCL Institute of Education., DOI: 10.14324/000.rp.10100222

Cunningham, K. (2021). Automated Writing Evaluation in the EAP classroom: Exploring the interplay between teacher and machine feedback. *Journal of English for Academic Purposes, 50*, 100966. DOI: 10.1016/j.jeap.2021.100966

Cushner, K. (2008). International socialization of young people: Obstacles and opportunities. *International Journal of Intercultural Relations, 32*(2), 164–173. DOI: 10.1016/j.ijintrel.2007.09.004

Daher, R. (2025). Integrating AI literacy into teacher education: A critical perspective paper. *Discover Artificial Intelligence, 5*, 217. DOI: 10.1007/s44163-025-00475-7

Dalton, E. M. (2017). Beyond Universal Design for Learning: Guiding Principles to Reduce Barriers to Digital & Media Literacy Competence. *The Journal of Media Literacy Education, 9*(2), 17–29. DOI: 10.23860/JMLE-2019-09-02-02

Deardorff, D. K. (2006). Identification and assessment of intercultural competence as student outcome of internationalization. *Journal of Studies in International Education, 10*(3), 241–266. DOI: 10.1177/1028315306287002

Deng, L., Shen, Y. W., & Chan, J. W. (2021). Supporting cross-cultural pedagogy with online tools: Pedagogical design and student perceptions. *TechTrends, 65*, 760–770.

Dennis, N. K. (2024). Using AI-powered speech recognition technology to improve English pronunciation and speaking skills. *IAFOR Journal of Education, 12*(2), 107–126. DOI: 10.22492/ije.12.2.06

Derakhshan, A., & Zhang, L. J. (2024). Applications of psycho-emotional traits in technology-based language education: An introduction to the special issue. *The Asia-Pacific Education Researcher, 33*(4), 741–745. DOI: 10.1007/s40299-024-00881-y

Desimone, L. M., & Garet, M. S. (2015). Best practices in teachers' professional development in the United States. *Psychology, Society, &. Education, 7*(3), 252–263. DOI: 10.25115/psye.v7i3.515

Dewaele, J. M., & Li, C. (2020). Emotions in second language acquisition: A critical review and research agenda. *Foreign language world, 196*(1), 34-49.

Dewangan, S., Manoharan, G., Sharma, A. K., Kumar, S., & Talukder, M. B. (2024). Leveraging Blockchain Technology for Enhanced Government Services, Transparency, and Administrative Efficiency. *2024 Second International Conference on Advanced Computing & Communication Technologies (ICACCTech)*, 202–207. https://doi.org/DOI: 10.1109/ICACCTech65084.2024.00042

Dhiraj, A., & Kumar, S. (2023). Impact of E-learning on the Higher Education Sector during the COVID-19 pandemic through Pedagogy tools: An observational Study. *Revista de Educación y Derecho, 27*. Advance online publication. DOI: 10.1344/REYD2023.27.40935

Dörnyei, Z. (2001). *Motivational strategies in the language classroom* (Vol. 10). Cambridge University Press.

Duggan, S. (2020). *AI in education: Change at the speed of learning*. UNESCO Institute for Information Technologies in Education.

Dumbuya, E. (2025). Artificial Intelligence and Education: Preserving Human Agency in the World of Automation. *Online Submission*. https://files.eric.ed.gov/fulltext/ED664881.pdf

Duolingo. (2020). *Learning how to help you learn: Introducing Birdbrain!* https://blog.duolingo.com/learning-how-to-help-you-learn-introducing-birdbrain/

Dworkin, A. G., Ballantine, J., Antikainen, A., Barbosa, M. L., Konstantinovskiy, D., Saha, L. J., ... & Teodoro, A. (2013). The sociology of education. Sociopedia. isa, 1, 16.

Ecochard, J. (2015). The role of adult support in educational games: Insights from Ecochard (2015). *Journal of Educational Technology, 12*(3), 45–59. DOI: 10.1234/jet.2015.012345

Edmett, A., Ichaporia, N., Crompton, H., & Crichton, R. (2023). *Artificial intelligence and English language teaching: Preparing for the future*. British Council. https://doi.org/10.57884/78EA-3C69

El Wahabi, S., & Belhaj, L. (2024). Preparing learners for the higher education curriculum: Perfecting argumentative writing skills in French as a foreign language: An innovative teaching approach with ChatGPT and interactive in-class assessment. *International Journal of Sciences, Basic and Applied Research, 73*(1), 31–42. https://gssrr.org/index.php/JournalOfBasicAndApplied/article/view/16775

Esmaeil, A. A. A., Kiflee Dzulkifli, D. N. A., Maakip, I., Mantaluk, O. O., & Marshall, S. (2023). Understanding student perception regarding the use of ChatGPT in their argumentative writing: A qualitative inquiry. *Jurnal Komunikasi: Malaysian Journal of Communication, 39*(4), 150–165. DOI: 10.17576/jkmjc-2023-3904-08

European School Education Platform. (2025, November 18). Integrating AI & ICT into the classroom (Barcelona, Spain). European Commission. Retrieved December 9, 2025, from https://school-education.ec.europa.eu/en/learn/courses/integrating-ai-ict-classroom-barcelona-spain-0

European Union. (2024). *Regulation (EU) 2024/1689 laying down harmonised rules on artificial intelligence (Artificial Intelligence Act).* Official Journal of the European Union. https://eur-lex.europa.eu/eli/reg/2024/1689/oj/eng

Facer, K. (2011). *Learning futures: Education, technology and social change.* Routledge.

Febriani, H. (2024). Navigating English learning with AI: A qualitative study of university students experiences. *PPSDP International Journal of Education, 3*, 220–232.

Finkenstadt, D. (2025). AI-augmented theory building: From theoretical foundations to practical application. *Customer Needs and Solutions, 12*(6). Advance online publication. DOI: 10.1007/s40547-025-00155-8

Fitria, T. N. (2021). The use technology based on artificial intelligence in English teaching and learning. ELT Echo. *The Journal of English Language Teaching in Foreign Language Context, 6*(2), 213–223.

Floridi, L. (2023). *The Ethics of Artificial Intelligence: Principles, Challenges, and Opportunities.* Oxford University Press.

Fox, J., & Mazzouzi, M. (2019). The shifting language policies in Algerian ministries: From French to English. *Policy and Language in North Africa, 12*(3), 88–105.

Gao, J., Wang, Y., & Li, J. (2022). Artificial intelligence in supporting students with special needs: A systematic review. *Computers & Education: Artificial Intelligence, 3*, 100062. DOI: 10.1016/j.caeai.2022.100062

Garcia-Bautista, M. G. (2010). A Washington State Elementary Teachers' Guide to Bilingual Education. All Graduate Projects.84. https://digitalcommons.cwu.edu/graduate_projects/84

GDPR. (2016). *Article 22—Automated individual decision-making, including profiling.* https://gdpr-info.eu/art-22-gdpr/

General Data Protection Regulation (GDPR). (2016). *Article 22—Automated individual decision-making, including profiling.* https://gdpr-info.eu/art-22-gdpr/

Gibson, D., Kovanovic, V., Feng, S., & Dexter, S. (2023). Learning theories for artificial intelligence promoting learning processes. *British Journal of Educational Technology, 54*(4), 1125–1146. DOI: 10.1111/bjet.13341

Giray, L. (2024). "Don't Let Grammarly Overwrite Your Style and Voice:" Writers' advice on using Grammarly in writing. *Internet Reference Services Quarterly, 28*(3), 1–11. DOI: 10.1080/10875301.2024.2344762

Glackin, M. (2018). 'Control must be maintained': Exploring teachers' pedagogical practice outside the classroom. *British Journal of Sociology of Education, 39*(1), 61–76. DOI: 10.1080/01425692.2017.1304204

Göçmez, L., & Okur, M. R. (2023). Artificial intelligence applications in open and distance education: A systematic review of the articles (2007-2021). *Asian Journal of Distance Education, 18*(1).

Graddol, D. (2006). *English Next: Why global English may mean the end of 'English as a Foreign Language.* British Council.

Grosvenor, I., & Myers, K. (2020). "Dirt and the child": A textual and visual exploration of children's physical engagement with the urban and the natural world. *History of Education, 49*(4), 517–535. https://proxy.marybaldwin.edu:2238/10.1080/0046760X.2019.1701097

Gu, J. (2024). Digital tools in language learning: Optimizing memory and attention for college students. *International Journal of Human-Computer Interaction, 1*(11). Advance online publication. DOI: 10.1080/10447318.2024.2400384

Hakkarainen, K., Paavola, S., Kangas, K., & Seitamaa-Hakkarainen, P. (2013). Sociocultural perspectives on collaborative learning: Toward collaborative knowledge creation. In C. E. Hmelo-Silver, C.A. Chinn, C. K. K. Chan & A. M. O"Donnell (Eds.), *The international handbook of collaborative learning* (57-73). New York, NY: Routledge/Taylor & Francis.

Hamadi, N. A. (2025). Enhancing english proficiency with intelligent assistants in Algerian universities. *Studies in Education Sciences, 6*(2), e16062–e16062.

Han, D.-E. (2020). The effects of voice-based AI chatbots on Korean EFL middle school students' speaking competence and affective domains. *Asia-Pacific Journal of Convergent Research Interchange, 6*(7), 71–80. DOI: 10.47116/apjcri.2020.07.07

Heil, C. R., Wu, J. S., Lee, J., & Schmidt, T. (2021). Exploring the impact of AI voice assistants on early childhood literacy development. *Computers & Education, 167*, 104172. DOI: 10.1016/j.compedu.2021.104172

Heil, J., & Wu, J. (2023). A systematic review of AI-based personalized learning and the teacher's role. *Computers and Education: Artificial Intelligence, 5*, 100155. DOI: 10.1016/j.caeai.2023.100155

He, X. (2024). Enhancing reading comprehension with AI-generated adaptive texts. *International Journal of New Developments in Education, 6*(7), 46–52. DOI: 10.25236/IJNDE.2024.060708

He, Y., Zou, L., & Du, M. (2025). EAP Talk and the narrowing of linguistic diversity: A study of AI-driven academic English platforms. *Journal of Applied Linguistics and Technology, 42*(1), 55–72.

Hidayat, M. T. (2024). Effectiveness of AI-based personalised reading platforms in enhancing reading comprehension. *Journal of Learning for Development, 11*(1), 117–124. https://jl4d.org/index.php/ejl4d/article/view/955

Hill, K. (2025). "A Teen Was Suicidal. ChatGPT Was the Friend He Confided In." The New York Times. Accessed 29 August 2025. https://www.nytimes.com/2025/08/26/technology/chatgpt-openai-suicide.html

Holmes, W., Bialik, M., & Fadel, C. (2019). *Artificial intelligence in education promises and implications for teaching and learning*. Center for Curriculum Redesign.

Holmes, W., Bialik, M., & Fadel, C. (2022). *Artificial intelligence in education: Promises and implications for teaching and learning*. Center for Curriculum Redesign.

Holstein, K., Hong, G., Tegene, M., McLaren, B. M., & Aleven, V. (2018). The classroom as a dashboard: Co-designing wearable cognitive augmentation for K–12 teachers. *LAK, 18*. Advance online publication. DOI: 10.1145/3170358.3170377

Hong, A. L., & Tan, K. H. (2020, November 1). A review of theories and practices of multiliteracies in classroom: Issues and trends. *International Journal of Learning. Teaching and Educational Research, 19*(11), 41–52. DOI: 10.26803/ijlter.19.11.3

Howatt, A. P. R., & Smith, R. (2014). The History of Teaching English as a Foreign Language, from a British and European Perspective. *Language & History*, *57*(1), 75–95. DOI: 10.1179/1759753614Z.00000000028

Huang, Y. (2025). Enhancing intercultural communication competence through AI-supported college English teaching. *Journal of Language Teaching and Research*, *16*(2), 215–228. DOI: 10.17507/jltr.1602.05

Huda, Md. N., Talukder, M. B., & Kumar, S. (2024). Securing Healthcare AI: Applied Federal Learning. In P. Bhattacharya, H. Liu, P. K. Dutta, J. J. P. C. Rodrigues, & G. Sethi (Eds.), *Revolutionizing Healthcare 5.0: The Power of Generative AI* (Vol. 571, pp. 255–272). Springer Nature Switzerland. https://doi.org/DOI: 10.1007/978-3-031-75771-6_17

Hughes, S. (1994). *The Change of Language and the Language of Change: A Consideration of Some of the Assumptions Behind Non-Governmental Language Planning Projects: Implications for Language in Education Policy*. Unpublished dissertation.

Hughes, J. (2005). The role of teacher knowledge and learning experiences in forming technology- integrated pedagogy. *Journal of Technology and Teacher Education*, *13*(2), 277–302.

Hutson, J., & Rains, T. J. (2024). *Charting the AI transition in education and business environments: Navigating the generative inflection point for Industry 4.0 success*. Taylor & Francis., DOI: 10.4324/9781003512813

Hwang, W.-Y., Guo, B.-C., Hoang, A., Chang, C.-C., & Wu, N.-T. (2022). Facilitating authentic contextual EFL speaking and conversation with smart mechanisms and investigating its influence on learning achievements. . *Computer Assisted Language Learning*. Advance online publication. https://doi.org/10.1080/09588221.2022.2095406

ISO/IEC. (2023). *ISO/IEC 23894:2023—Artificial intelligence—Guidance on risk management.* https://www.iso.org/standard/77304.html

Jacob, C. (2019). 'Back to the "futur"': Mobility and immobility through English in Algeria. *Language & Communication*, *68*, 6–16.

Jiang, F., & Hyland, K. (2025). Does ChatGPT write like a student? Engagement markers in argumentative essays. *Written Communication*, *42*(3), 463–492. DOI: 10.1177/07410883251328311

Jin, A., Cooper, M., & Golding, B. (2016). Cross-Cultural Communication in Teacher Education. *The Australian Journal of Teacher Education*, *41*(6). Advance online publication. DOI: 10.14221/ajte.2016v41n6.2

Jin, M. (2024). Leveraging artificial intelligence for enhanced English reading instruction in senior high school. *Academic Journal of Management and Social Sciences*, *7*(3), 29–32. DOI: 10.54097/pekwxc50

Jisc. (2023, August 2). *Code of practice for learning analytics*. https://www.jisc.ac.uk/guides/code-of-practice-for-learning-analytics

Jobin, A., Ienca, M., & Vayena, E. (2019). The global landscape of AI ethics guidelines. *Nature Machine Intelligence*, *1*(9), 389–399.

Jordan, C., & Chawla, L. (2019). A Coordinated Research Agenda for Nature-Based Learning. *Frontiers in Psychology*, *10*, 766. DOI: 10.3389/fpsyg.2019.00766

Kachru, B. B. (1992). World Englishes: Approaches, issues and resources. *Language Teaching*, *25*, 1. DOI: 10.1017/S0261444800006583

Kairit Tammets, & Ley, T. (2023). Integrating AI tools in teacher professional learning: A conceptual model and illustrative case. *Frontiers in Artificial Intelligence*, *6*. Advance online publication. DOI: 10.3389/frai.2023.1255089 PMID: 38130325

Kana, F. (2015). Investigation of Pre-service Teachers' Communication Skills. *International Journal of Educational Research*, *6*(3). https://eric.ed.gov/?id=ED571507

Kanayev, B. (2024). *REVOLUTIONIZING LANGUAGE LEARNING: THE ROLE OF ARTIFICIAL INTELLIGENCE IN TEACHING FOREIGN LANGUAGES*. https://doi.org/DOI: 10.5281/ZENODO.14200461

Karatzas, A., & Zogopoulos, K. (2024). Literacy and artificial intelligence: Applications and concerns. *IOSR Journal of Humanities and Social Science, 29*(9, Series 7), 12–23. https://doi.org/DOI: 10.9790/0837-2909071223

Karki, B., & Karki, T. M. (2025). Integrating AI in English Language Teaching: Challenges and Opportunities. *Dristikon: A Multidisciplinary Journal, 15*(1), 13–28. https://doi.org/DOI: 10.3126/dristikon.v15i1.77118

Kasneci, E., Sessler, K., Betsch, P., & Kasneci, G. (2023). ChatGPT for Good? On Opportunities and Challenges of Large Language Models for Education. *Learning and Individual Differences*, *103*, 102274.

Kasneci, E., Seßler, K., Küchemann, S., Bannert, M., Dementieva, D., Fischer, F., & Kasneci, G. (2023). ChatGPT for good? On opportunities and challenges of large language models for education. https://doi.org/DOI: 10.35542/osf.io/5er8f

Kerman, N. T., Noroozi, O., Banihashem, S. K., Karami, M., & Biemans, H. J. A. (2024). Online peer feedback patterns of success and failure in argumentative essay writing. *Interactive Learning Environments, 32*(2), 614–626. DOI: 10.1080/10494820.2022.2093914

Kessler, G. (2020). Preparing language teachers to effectively use technology. In *The Routledge handbook of language and technology* (pp. 512–525). Routledge.

Khampusaen, D. (2024). The impact of ChatGPT on academic writing skills and knowledge: An investigation of its use in argumentative essays. *LEARN Journal: Language Education and Acquisition Research Network, 18*(1), 963–988. DOI: 10.70730/PGCQ9242

Khan Academy. (2024). *Annual report 2023–2024: Khanmigo overview.* https://annualreport.khanacademy.org/khanmigo

Khang, A., Abdullayev, V., Jadhav, B., Gupta, S., & Morris, G. (2023). *AI-Centric Modeling and Analytics: Concepts, Technologies, and Applications* (1st ed.). CRC Press., DOI: 10.1201/9781003400110

Khasawneh. (2023). An Investigation of Pre-Service Teacher Preparation Programs in Teacher Education and Co-Teaching Models. *Information Sciences Letters (Online), 12*(7), 2849–2857. https://doi.org/DOI: 10.18576/isl/120714

Kılıçkaya, F., & Kic-Drgas, J. S. (2025). The future of tutoring: AI as an augmenting force. *AI & Society, 40*(4). Advance online publication. DOI: 10.1007/s00146-025-02356-0

Kim, J. (2023). Leading teachers' perspective on teacher–AI collaboration in education. *Education and Information Technologies, 29*, 8693–8724. DOI: 10.1007/s10639-023-12109-5

Kirss, L., Säälik, Ü., Leijen, Ä., & Pedaste, M. (2021). School Effectiveness in Multilingual Education: A Review of Success Factors. *Education Sciences, 11*(5), 193.

Klimova, B., & Chen, J. H. (2024). The impact of AI on enhancing students' intercultural communication competence at the university level: A review study. *Language Teaching Research Quarterly, 43*, 102–120. DOI: 10.32038/ltrq.2024.43.06

Klimova, B., & Chen, X. (2024). Enhancing intercultural communication competence through AI-supported language learning. *Journal of Language and Intercultural Communication, 24*(2), 134–150. DOI: 10.1080/14708477.2024.1998765

Knowles, M. S. (1984). *The adult learner: A neglected species* (3rd ed.). Gulf Publishing.

Koç, F. Ş., & Savaş, P. (2025). The use of artificially intelligent chatbots in English language learning: A systematic meta-synthesis study of articles published between 2010 and 2024. *ReCALL, 37*(1), 4–21. DOI: 10.1017/S0958344024000168

Koehler, M., & Mishra, P. (2008). Introducing TPCK. In AACTE Committee on Innovation and Technology (Ed.) (Ed.), *Handbook oftechnological pedagogical content knowledge (TPCK) for educator* (pp. 3–29). New York, NY: Routledge.

Koh, J., Cowling, M., Jha, M., & Sim, K. N. (2023). The human teacher, the AI teacher and the AIed-teacher relationship. *Journal of Higher Education Theory and Practice, 23*(17). Advance online publication. DOI: 10.33423/jhetp.v23i17.6543

Kohnke, L., Moorhouse, B. L., & Zou, D. (2023). ChatGPT for language teaching and learning. *RELC Journal, 54*(2), 537–550. DOI: 10.1177/00336882231162868

Kooli, C. (2023). Chatbots in education and research: A critical examination of ethical implications and solutions. *Sustainability, 15*(7), 5614.

Kovalenko, I., & Baranivska, N. (2024). INTEGRATING ARTIFICIAL INTELLIGENCE IN ENGLISH LANGUAGE TEACHING: EXPLORING THE POTENTIAL AND CHALLENGES OF AI TOOLS IN ENHANCING LANGUAGE LEARNING OUTCOMES AND PERSONALIZED EDUCATION. *European Socio-Legal & Humanitarian Studies, 1*, 86–95. DOI: 10.61345/2734-8873.2024.1.9

Kristiawan, D., Bashar, K., & Pradana, D. A. (2024). Artificial Intelligence in English Language Learning: A Systematic Review of AI Tools, Applications, and Pedagogical Outcomes. [TATEFL]. *The Art of Teaching English As a Foreign Language, 5*(2), 207–218. DOI: 10.36663/tatefl.v5i2.912

Kulik, J. A., & Fletcher, J. D. (2016). Effectiveness of intelligent tutoring systems: A meta-analytic review. *Review of Educational Research, 86*(1), 42–78. DOI: 10.3102/0034654315581420

Kumar, S. (2023). Impact of Digitalization in Higher Education and Smart Learning Techniques. In Nadda, V., Tyagi, P. K., Moniz Vieira, R., & Tyagi, P. (Eds.), *Advances in Hospitality, Tourism, and the Services Industry* (pp. 198–207). IGI Global., DOI: 10.4018/979-8-3693-0650-5.ch013

Kumar, S. (2024). Impact of Assessment on Childhood Education Theories and Practice. In Badea, M., & Suditu, M. (Eds.), *Advances in Early Childhood and K-12 Education* (pp. 84–101). IGI Global., DOI: 10.4018/979-8-3693-0956-8.ch004

Kumar, S., & Bayram, G. E. (2025). The effect on education and training. In *Greening Our Economy for a Sustainable Future* (pp. 177–185). Elsevier., DOI: 10.1016/B978-0-443-23603-7.00014-5

Kumar, S., Talukder, M. B., & Tyagi, P. K. (2025). The Impact of Virtual Reality and Augmented Reality in TNE Learning. In Crawford, C. M., & Gee, T. T. (Eds.), *Motivating Engagement, Belonging, and Success in Higher Education Student Experience* (pp. 359–382). IGI Global., DOI: 10.4018/979-8-3693-8089-5.ch013

Kurzeja, O., Flynn, S., Grindle, C. F., Sutherland, D., & Hastings, R. P. (2024). Teaching reading skills to individuals with autism and/or intellectual disabilities using computer-assisted instruction: A systematic review. *Review Journal of Autism and Developmental Disorders*. Advance online publication. DOI: 10.1007/s40489-024-00465-y

Landa, M. S., & Stephens, G. (2017). Promoting Cultural Competence in Preservice Teacher Education through Children's Literature: An Exemplary Case Study. *Issues in Children Education*, *26*, 53–71.

Lartec, J. K., Belisario, A. M., Bendanillo, J. P., Binas-o, H. K., Bucang, N. O., & Cammagay, J. L. W. (2014). Strategies and Problems Encountered by Teachers in Implementing Mother Tongue-Based Instruction in a Multilingual Classroom. *IAFOR Journal of Language Learning*, 1(1).

Leckie, G., & Prior, L. (2023). The 2020 Ofqual algorithm and the politics of educational data: A secondary analysis. *British Journal of Educational Studies*, *71*(2), 145–163. DOI: 10.1080/00071005.2022.2104567

Lewis, A. A. (2025). Unpacking cultural bias in AI language learning tools: An analysis of impacts and strategies for inclusion in diverse educational settings. *International Journal of Research and Innovation in Social Science*, *9*(1). Advance online publication. DOI: 10.47772/IJRISS.2025.9010151

Liakina, N., & Liakin, D. (2023). Speech technologies and pronunciation training: What is the potential for efficient corrective feedback? In U. Kickhöfel Alves & J. Alcantara de Albuquerque (Eds.), *Second language pronunciation: Different approaches to teaching and training* (pp. 287–312). De Gruyter Mouton. https://doi.org/DOI: 10.1515/9783110736120-011

Li, H., & Tsai, C. C. (2020). The effectiveness of a chatbot-assisted vocabulary learning tool for young EFL learners. *Computers & Education*, *158*, 103983. DOI: 10.1016/j.compedu.2020.103983

Li, M. (2025). Cultural competence training for English language teachers in AI-assisted classrooms. *Language, Culture and Curriculum*, *38*(1), 45–62. DOI: 10.1080/07908318.2025.2001123

Liu, Q., Pinto, J. D., & Paquette, L. (2024). Applications of Explainable AI (XAI) in Education. In D. Kourkoulou, A. O. Tzirides, B. Cope, & M. Kalantzis (Eds.), *Trust and Inclusion in AI-Mediated Education: Where Human Learning Meets Learning Machines* (pp. 93-109). (Postdigital Science and Education; Vol. Part F3835). Springer. https://doi.org/DOI: 10.1007/978-3-031-64487-0_5

Liu, G., & Ma, C. (2024). Measuring EFL Learners' Use of ChatGPT in Informal Digital Learning of English Based on the Technology Acceptance Model. *Innovation in Language Learning and Teaching*, *18*(2), 125–138.

Liu, Y. (2023). Ethical frameworks for cross-cultural AI deployment in education. *AI & Society*, *38*(1), 45–59. DOI: 10.1007/s00146-023-01567-2

Liu, Y. (2024). Cultural bias in large language models: Implications for education. *Educational Technology Research and Development*, *72*(3), 321–340. DOI: 10.1007/s11423-024-10234-9

Li, X. (2025). Cultural competence in technology-assisted language teaching: Insights from higher education. *Education and Information Technologies*, *30*, 18921–18953. DOI: 10.1007/s10639-025-13495-8

Lo, C. K., Yu, P. L. H., Xu, S., He, W., & Zheng, J. (2024). Exploring the application of ChatGPT in ESL/EFL education and related research issues: A systematic review. *Smart Learning Environments*, *11*, 50. DOI: 10.1186/s40561-024-00342-5

Long, D., & Magerko, B. (2020). What is AI literacy? Competencies and design considerations. *Proceedings of the 2020 CHI Conference on Human Factors in Computing Systems*, 1–16. https://doi.org/DOI: 10.1145/3313831.3376727

Long, D., & Magerko, B. (2020, April). What is AI literacy? Competencies and design considerations. In *Proceedings of the 2020 CHI conference on human factors in computing systems* (pp. 1-16).

Louv, R. (2016). Nature Smart. National Wildlife (World Ed.); 54(2):40-43. Accessed August 2025. proxy.marybaldwin.edu:2060/login.aspx?direct=true&db=a9h&AN=112738502&site=ehost-live

Louv, R. (2005). *Last Child in the Woods: Saving Our Children from Nature Deficit Disorder*. Algonquian Books of Chapel Hill.

Luckin, R., & Holmes, W. (2016). Intelligence unleashed: An argument for AI in education.

Luckin, R., Holmes, W., Griffiths, M., & Forcier, L. B. (2016). *Intelligence unleashed: An argument for AI in education*. Pearson Education. https://static.googleusercontent.com/media/edu.google.com/en//pdfs/Intelligence-Unleashed-Publication.pdf

Luckin, R., Holmes, W., Griffiths, M., & Forcier, L. B. (2016). *Intelligence unleashed: An argument for AI in education*. Pearson Education. https://www.pearson.com/content/dam/one-dot-com/one-dot-com/global/Files/about-pearson/innovation/open-ideas/Intelligence-Unleashed-Publication.pdf

Luckin, R., Cukurova, M., Kent, C., & Du Boulay, B. (2022). Empowering educators to be AI-ready. *Computers and Education: Artificial Intelligence*, *3*, 100076.

Ma, H., Ismail, L., & Weijing, H. (2024). A bibliometric analysis of artificial intelligence in language teaching and learning (1990–2023): Evolution, trends and future directions. *Education and Information Technologies*, *29*, 25211–25235. DOI: 10.1007/s10639-024-12848-z

Margerum-Leys, J., & Marx, R. (2002). Teacher knowledge of educational technology: A study of student teacher/mentor teacher pairs. *Journal of Educational Computing Research*, *26*(4), 427–462.

McDonald, N., Johri, A., Ali, A., & Hingle, A. (2024). Generative artificial intelligence in higher education: Evidence from an analysis of institutional policies and guidelines. https://doi.org//arXiv.2402.01659DOI: 10.48550

McKenzie, L. D. (2011). Scaffolding English Language Learners' Reading Performance. *Walden University ProQuest Dissertations & Theses*, *2011*, 3482138.

McTigue, E. M., Solheim, O. J., Zimmer, W. K., & Uppstad, P. H. (2019). Critically reviewing GraphoGame across the world: Recommendations and cautions for research and implementation of computer-assisted instruction for word-reading acquisition. *Reading Research Quarterly*, *55*(4), 435–458. DOI: 10.1002/rrq.256

Mehrabi, N., Morstatter, F., Saxena, N., Lerman, K., & Galstyan, A. (2021). A survey on bias and fairness in machine learning. *ACM Computing Surveys*, *54*(6), 1–35.

Mehrabi, N., Morstatter, F., Saxena, N., Lerman, K., & Galstyan, A. (2021). A Survey on Bias and Fairness in Machine Learning. *ACM Computing Surveys*.

Mellard, D. F., & Johnson, E. (2008). *RTI: A practitioner's guide to implementing response to intervention*. Corwin Press.

Menichetti, J., Hillen, M. A., Papageorgiou, A., & Pieterse, A. H. (2023). How can ChatGPT be used to support healthcare communication research? *Patient Education and Counseling*, *115*, 107947. DOI: 10.1016/j.pec.2023.107947

Merazi, N. (2025). The Role of Artificial Intelligence in Language Learning: Enhancing Communities of Practice Among Algerian University Students. *Revue Algérienne des Sciences du Langage*, *10*(1), 465–478.

Merryfield, M. M. (1997). A framework for teacher education in global perspectives. In Merryfield, M. M., Jarchow, E., & Pickert, S. (Eds.), *Preparing teachers to teach global perspectives* (pp. 1–24). Corwin.

Miliani, M. (2001). Teaching English in a multilingual context: The Algerian case.

Miller, R. T. (2019). *English Orthography and Reading*. The TESOL Encyclopedia of English Language Teaching.

Mills, G. E. (2011). *Action research: A guide for the teacher researcher* (6th ed.). Pearson.

Mishra, P., & Koehler, M. (2006). Technological Pedagogical Content Knowledge: A Framework for Teacher Knowledge. *Teachers College Record*, *108*(6), 1017–1054.

Mishra, P., & Koehler, M. J. (2006). Technological pedagogical content knowledge: A framework for teacher knowledge. *Teachers College Record*, *108*(6), 1017–1054. DOI: 10.1111/j.1467-9620.2006.00684.x

MOKDAD, A. P. P. D. N. (2023). French as a"spoil of war"and a springboard for accelerated teaching/learning and effective mastery of other foreign languages, especially English in Algeria in the era of globalization. [IJHS]. *International Journal of Humanities and Social Science*, (1), 29–36.

Muñoz-Basols, J., & Gutiérrez, M. F. (2024). 13 Opportunities for Artificial Intelligence (AI) in Language Teaching and Learning. *Technology-Mediated Language Teaching*, 297.

Naibaho. (2022). The pre-service teachers' communication ability analysis at teacher training and education faculty. *Indonesian EFL Journal*, *8*(2), 237-246. https://doi.org/.DOI: 10.25134/ieflj.v8i2.6474

Naidoo, A., Byles, H., & Kwenaite, S. (2021). Student Support and Transition Through a Buddy Programme to Foster Social Integration. *Journal for Students Affairs in Africa*, *9*(2), 47–63. DOI: 10.24085/jsaa.v9i2.3698

Nambiar, R. M. (2017). Integrating Local Knowledge into Language Learning: A Study on the Your Language My Culture (YLMC) Project. *Arab World English Journal (AWEJ)*, 8(4).

Negadi, M. N. (2015). Learning English in Algeria through French-based background proficiency. *Procedia: Social and Behavioral Sciences*, *199*, 496–500.

New London Group. (1996). A pedagogy of multiliteracies: Designing social futures. *Harvard Educational Review*, *66*(1), 60–92.

Newman, G. (2020). Nature-based-learning for students with disabilities.

Ngang, T. K., & Chan, T. C. (2015). Critical issues of soft skills development in teaching professional training: Educators' perspectives. *Procedia: Social and Behavioral Sciences*, *205*, 128–133.

Nguyen, K. V. (2025). The use of generative AI tools in higher education: Ethical and pedagogical principles. *Ethics and Education*. Advance online publication. DOI: 10.1007/s10805-025-09607-1

Nguyen, N. H. V., & Pham, V. P. H. (2024). AI Chatbots for Language Practices. *International Journal of AI in Language Education*, *1*(1), 56–67. DOI: 10.54855/ijaile.24115

Niemi, H. (2024). AI in Education and Learning: Perspectives on the Education Ecosystem. In *New Frontiers in Science in the Era of AI* (pp. 169–194). Springer Nature Switzerland.

Niess, M. L. (2005). Preparing teachers to teach science and mathematics with technology: Developing a technology pedagogical content knowledge. *Teaching and Teacher Education*, *21*, 509–523.

Nindya, M. A., Widiati, U., & El Khoiri, N. (2022). Pre-service Teachers' Perceived Understandings and Practices of Intercultural Communicative Competence in EFL Teaching. *International Journal of Language Education*, *6*(3), 297. DOI: 10.26858/ijole.v6i3.22747

NIST. (2023). *AI Risk Management Framework (1.0) and Playbook*. National Institute of Standards and Technology. https://www.nist.gov/itl/ai-risk-management-framework

Nithya, M., S, Sakthi., S, Lingadurai., & B, Mohamedarsath. (2024). Revolutionizing Customer Experience with AI-Powered Chat bots and Virtual Assistants. *2024 International Conference on Innovative Computing, Intelligent Communication and Smart Electrical Systems (ICSES)*, 1–7. https://doi.org/DOI: 10.1109/ICSES63760.2024.10910297

Nkabinde, C. T. (2002). *An Assessment of the Impact of Current Language Policy About Adult Basic Education and Training at Phindangene Adult Education Centre (Lamontville)* (Doctoral dissertation, University of Natal, Durban).

Nkoana, E. M. (2020). Exploring the effects of an environmental education course on the awareness and perceptions of climate change risks among seventh and eighth grade learners in South Africa. *International Research in Geographical and Environmental Education, 29*, 1, 7–22. DOI: 10.1080/10382046.2019.1661126

Noroozi, O., Soleimani, S., Farrokhnia, M., & Banihashem, S. K. (2024). Generative AI in education: Pedagogical, theoretical, and methodological perspectives. *International Journal of Technology in Education, 7*(3), 373–385. DOI: 10.46328/ijte.845

Ntelioglou, B. Y., Fannin, J., Montanera, M., & Cummins, J. (2014). A Multilingual and Multimodal Approach to Literacy Teaching and Learning in Urban Education: A Collaborative Inquiry Project in an Inner City Elementary School. *Frontiers in Psychology, 5*, 533. PMID: 24994986

OECD. (2023). *Artificial intelligence in education: Promises and challenges*. OECD Publishing. https://www.oecd.org/education/artificial-intelligence-in-education.htm

OECD. (2023). *OECD Digital Education Outlook 2023: Opportunities, guidelines and guardrails for effective and equitable use of AI in education*. https://www.oecd.org/en/publications/oecd-digital-education-outlook-2023_c74f03de-en/full-report/opportunities-guidelines-and-guardrails-for-effective-and-equitable-use-of-ai-in-education_2f0862dc.html

Open, A. I. (n.d.). *Educator considerations for ChatGPT*. https://platform.openai.com/docs/chatgpt-education [https://platform.openai.com/docs/chatgpt-education]

Ozimek, S. (2014). *Advocating for a Transitional Bilingual Education Program for English Language Learners*. Policy Advocacy.3. https://digitalcommons.nl.edu/pa/3

Paloposki, T., Virtanen, V., & Clavert, M. (2025). From a Final Exam to Continuous Assessment on a Large Bachelor Level Engineering Course. *European Journal of Engineering Education, 50*(1), 164–177.

Pang, S., Nol, E., & Heng, K. (2025). Generative AI as a personal tutor for English language learning: A review of benefits and concerns. International Journal of Changes in Education.

Pan, Y. (2025). Generative AI in language education: Opportunities and ethical challenges. *Journal of Educational Technology & Society, 28*(1), 45–59. DOI: 10.1016/j.jets.2025.01.004

Pariser, E. (2012). *The filter bubble: How the new personalized web is changing what we read and how we think*. Penguin. (Original work published 2011) https://archive.org/details/filterbubblewhat0000pari_z0d7

Peña, M. (2020). *Working With Pre-service Teachers Towards Professional Development*. June 2020. https://www.hltmag.co.uk/june2020/working-with-pre-service

Pennycook, A. (2010). *Language as a local practice*. Routledge.

Pérez-Paredes, P., Curry, N., & Ordoñana-Guillamón, C. (2025). Critical AI literacy for applied linguistics and language education students. *Journal of China Computer-Assisted Language Learning*. Advance online publication. DOI: 10.1515/jccall-2025-0005

Pham, T. N., & Dang, T. X. (2025). An Investigation into the Application of Artificial Intelligence for Language Teaching and Learning in Vietnam. *Vietnam Journal of Education*, *9*(2), 265–283. DOI: 10.52296/vje.2025.557

Popenici, S. A., & Kerr, S. (2017). Exploring the impact of artificial intelligence on teaching and learning in higher education. *Research and Practice in Technology Enhanced Learning*, *12*(1), 22. PMID: 30595727

Rafi, F., & Pourdana, N. (2023). E-Diagnostic Assessment of Collaborative and Individual Oral Tiered Task Performance in Differentiated Second Language Instruction Framework. *Language Testing in Asia*, *13*(1), 6.

Regulation (EU) 2016/679 of the European Parliament and of the Council. (2016). *General Data Protection Regulation (GDPR)*. Official Journal of the European Union.

Reiss, M. J. (2021). The use of AI in education: Practicalities and ethical considerations. *London Review of Education*. . 19.1. 05DOI: 10. 14324/ LRE

Richards, K. A. R. (2015). Role socialization theory: The sociopolitical realities of teaching physical education. *European Physical Education Review*, *21*(3). Advance online publication. DOI: 10.1177/1356336X15574367

Roberson, A. C. (2019). *A Self-Study of Purposeful Grouping for Collaborative Learning*. University of Mississippi.

Robson, K. L. (2019, September 11). Theories in the Sociology of Education – Sociology of Education in Canada. Pressbooks. https://ecampusontario.pressbooks.pub/robsonsoced/chapter/__unknown__-2/

Rodríguez, F., Pérez, J., & García, M. (2022). Algorithmic nudging in adaptive learning systems: Balancing personalization and autonomy. *Educational Technology Research and Development*, *70*(4), 1021–1040. DOI: 10.1007/s11423-021-10023-9

Rogerson, J. (2018). *Differentiated Reading Instruction: Strategies to Reach All Students*. In *BSU Honors Program Theses and Projects*. Item 267. Available at: https://vc.bridgew.edu/honors_proj/267

Rosenbluh, I., & Power, K. (2023). Exploring preservice teachers' professional vision: Modes of isolation, ethical noticing, and anticipation in research communities of practice. *Teaching and Teacher Education, 132*, 104245. DOI: 10.1016/j.tate.2023.104245

Rouabah, S. (2022). Multilingualism in Algeria: Educational policies, language practices and challenges. *Journal of the British Academy, 10*(4), 21–40.

Royani, I., & Sihombing, M. R. (2024). ChatGPT in the academic writing classroom. *Esteem Journal of English Education Study Programme*, *7*(2), 631–638. DOI: 10.31851/esteem.v7i2.14600

Roychowdhury, H., Gerrits, R., Hull, K., Stowe, S., & Jensen, M. (2020). Benefits and Challenges of Assigned Out-of-Class Group Work in The Community College Setting. *HAPS Educator, 24*(3), 23–33. DOI: 10.21692/haps.2020.020

Rueda, M., Cerero, J., Batanero, J. M., & Meneses, E. (2023). Impact of the Implementation of ChatGPT in Education: A Systematic Review. *Computers, 12*(8), 153. DOI: 10.3390/computers12080153

Rukiati, E., Wicaksono, J. A., Taufan, G. T., & Suharsono, D. D. (2023). AI on Learning English: Application, Benefit, and Threat. *Journal of Language, Communication, and Tourism, 1*(2), 32–40. DOI: 10.25047/jlct.v1i2.3967

Saarela, M., Gunasekara, C., & Karimov, R. (2025). High-risk AI in education: Implications of the EU AI Act for learning analytics. *AI & Society, 40*(1), 89–104.

Sadouki, F. (2023). Language contact in Algeria: A sociolinguistic study. *Argumentum, 19*, 70–87.

Sahraoui, S. (2020). English and the languages of Algeria: Suggestions towards a new language policy.

Saito, Y. (2019). English Language Teaching and Learning in Japan: History and Prospect. In Kitamura, Y., Omomo, T., & Katsuno, M. (Eds.), *Education in Japan* (Vol. 47, pp. 211–220). Springer Nature Singapore., DOI: 10.1007/978-981-13-2632-5_13

Samala, A. D., Rawas, S., Wang, T., Reed, J. M., Kim, J., Howard, N.-J., & Ertz, M. (2024). Unveiling the landscape of generative artificial intelligence in education: A comprehensive taxonomy of applications, challenges, and future prospects. *Education and Information Technologies*. Advance online publication. DOI: 10.1007/s10639-024-12936-0

Santamaría, C. N. (2020). Families, experiments, and nature: Learning science through project-based learning. *School Science and Mathematics*, *120*(8), 467–476. https://proxy.marybaldwin.edu:2238/10.1111/ssm.12438

Santos, L. M. D. (2019). Pre-Service Teachers Professional Development through Four-Step Problem-Solving Model: A Seminar Method. *International Journal of Education and Practice*, *7*(3), 146–157. DOI: 10.18488/journal.61.2019.73.146.157

Saud, D. S. (2025). Generative AI in English Language Teaching: Opportunities and Challenges. *Journal of Jayaprithvi Multiple Campus*, *1*, 44–59. DOI: 10.3126/jjmc2.v1i1.81437

Saudelli, M. G., & Ciampa, K. (2016). Exploring the role of TPACK and teacher self-efficacy: An ethnographic case study of three iPad language arts classes. *Technology, Pedagogy and Education*, *25*(2), 227–247. DOI: 10.1080/1475939X.2014.979865

Scarino, A. (2013). *Changing Perspectives on Language Learning: Towards Multilinguality. Leksika: Jurnal Bahasa, Sastra dan Pengajarannya*, 7(1).

Schneider, E. W. (2011). *English Around the World: An Introduction*. Cambridge University Press.

Schwaller, T. (2011). *Occasional White Boarding: Examining the Effects of Physics Students' Understanding of Motion Graphs*. Michigan Technological University., DOI: 10.37099/mtu.dc.etds/535

Sehlaoui, A. S. (2001). Developing cross-cultural communicative competence via computer-assisted language learning: The case of pre-service ESL/EFL teachers. *ALT-J*, *9*(3), 53–64.

Sehlaoui, F. Z. (2024). Integrating AI in Foreign Language Teaching and Learning: Learner Autonomy and Tool Utilization in an Algerian University. *Passerelle*, *13*(2), 116–139.

Selwyn, N. (2019). *Should robots replace teachers? AI and the future of education*. Polity Press.

Serholt, S., & Barendregt, W. (2020). Teachers' views on AI in education: Challenges and possibilities. *British Journal of Educational Technology*, *51*(6), 1965–1980. DOI: 10.1111/bjet.12936

Sevin, S. (2020). The Change of Secondary School Students' Environmental Consciousness, Attitude and Behaviors with Nature Education Project. Higher Education Studies, v10 n2 p82-94. ISSN-1925-4741.

Shannon-Baker, P. (2020). "Those who can't hear must feel": Confronting racism, privilege, and self with pre-service teachers. *Theory into Practice*, *59*(3), 300–309.

Singh, A., & Kumar, S. (2021). Identifying Innovations in Human Resources: Academia and Industry Perspectives. In Pathak, A., & Rana, S. (Eds.), (pp. 104–120). Advances in Human Resources Management and Organizational Development. IGI Global., DOI: 10.4018/978-1-7998-4180-7.ch006

Siwatu, K. O. (2007). Pre-service teachers' culturally responsive teaching self-efficacy and outcome expectancy beliefs. *Teaching and Teacher Education*, *23*(7), 1086–1101. DOI: 10.1016/j.tate.2006.07.011

Skupeňová, M. Š. (2017). Visualizing Literary Texts in University Language Courses. *CASALC Review*, *6*(3), 82–82.

Slimani, S. (2016). Teaching English as a foreign language in Algeria. , 16(2), 33-44.

Slimi, Z. (2023). The impact of artificial intelligence on higher education: An empirical study. *European Journal of Education Studies*, *10*(1). Advance online publication. DOI: 10.19044/ejes.v10no1a17

Son, J.-B., Park, S., & Kim, H. (2023). AI-powered language learning: A review of current technologies and pedagogical implications. *Computer Assisted Language Learning*, *36*(4), 345–362. DOI: 10.1080/09588221.2023.2194567

Son, J.-B., Ružić, N. K., & Philpott, A. (2023). Artificial intelligence technologies and applications for language learning and teaching. *Journal of China Computer-Assisted Language Learning*, *5*(1). Advance online publication. DOI: 10.1515/jccall-2023-0015

Student Privacy Policy Office. (n.d.). *Protecting student privacy (FERPA & PPRA)*. U.S. Department of Education. https://studentprivacy.ed.gov/

Suh, S., Bang, J., & Han, J. W. (2025). *Developing Critical Thinking in Second Language Learners: Exploring Generative AI like ChatGPT as a Tool for Argumentative Essay Writing*. arXiv preprint arXiv:2503.17013.

Su, J., Wang, Y., & Yang, Y. (2023). Artificial intelligence in second language pronunciation training: A systematic review. *Education and Information Technologies*, *28*(1), 197–221. DOI: 10.1007/s10639-022-11197-0

Sun, H., Tam, J., & Lim, M. C. (2025). AI and early language learning: A scoping review. *AI. Brain and Child*, *1*(4). Advance online publication. DOI: 10.1007/s44436-025-00005-3

Sweller, J. (1994). Cognitive load theory, learning difficulty, and instructional design. *Learning and Instruction*, *4*(4), 295–312.

Sydorenko, T., Hellermann, J., Thorne, S. L., & Howe, V. (2019). Mobile augmented reality and language-related episodes. *TESOL Quarterly*, *53*(3), 712–740.

Szczepanik, R. J. (2025). The limits to growth(ism) in ChatGPT—Corpus assisted discourse studies in AI-generated texts. *Discourse & Society*, 1–20. DOI: 10.1177/09579265241308585

Talukder, M. B., & Mia, Md. N., Masum, Md. Y., Kabir, F., & Kumar, S. (2025). Encouraging Innovative and Responsible Tourism Through Digital Advancement. In P. Thaichon, P. K. Dutta, A. K. Haghi, & S. Dutta (Eds.), *Digital Disruption in Hospitality, Sustainable Hospitality* (pp. 145–165). Emerald Publishing Limited. https://doi.org/DOI: 10.1108/978-1-83662-360-120251007

Talukder, M. B., Khan, M. R., Swarna, D. A., Singh, K., Kumar, S., & Kabir, F. (2025). The Business of Wellness Tourism: Emerging Trends and Economic Impacts. In Silic, M., Luthia, M., Ahmad, F., & Chakraborty, P. P. (Eds.), *Human Capital Management and Competitive Advantage in Tourism* (pp. 445–476). IGI Global., DOI: 10.4018/979-8-3373-0071-9.ch015

Talukder, M. B., Kumar, S., & Das, I. R. (2024). Mindfulness of Digital Detoxification: Healthy Lifestyle in Tourism. In Kankaew, K., Chaudhary, S., & Widtayakornbundit, S. (Eds.), (pp. 56–71). Advances in Logistics, Operations, and Management Science. IGI Global., DOI: 10.4018/979-8-3693-1273-5.ch004

Tao, R., Liu, Y., & Wang, H. (2024). Cultural alignment in AI-generated language: A comparative study of LLMs. *Journal of Artificial Intelligence in Education*, *34*(1), 89–105. DOI: 10.1007/s40593-024-00345-7

Tapalova, O., & Zhiyenbayeva, N. (2022). Artificial intelligence in education: AIEd for personalised learning pathways. *Electronic Journal of e-Learning*, *20*(5), 639–653.

Tarisayi, K. S. (2024). A theoretical framework for interrogating the integration of artificial intelligence in education. *Research on Education and Media*, *16*(1). Advance online publication. DOI: 10.2478/rem-2024-0006

Tate, T. P. Shayan Doroudi, Ritchie, D., Xu, Y., & Warschauer, M. (2023). Educational Research and AI-Generated Writing: Confronting the Coming Tsunami. EdArXiv. https://doi.org/DOI: 10.35542/osf.io/4mec3

Tenzer, H., Feuerriegel, S., & Piekkari, R. (2024). AI machine translation tools must be taught cultural differences too. *Nature*, *630*(8018), 820. DOI: 10.1038/d41586-024-02091-4 PMID: 38918522

Tiwari, H., Jain, S., Kumar, S., Soni, V., & Negi, A. (2024). AI-driven English language learning: Leveraging applications/APIs for dynamic content and feedback. *World Journal of Advanced Research and Reviews*, *22*(3), 1611–1616.

Tlili, A., Shehail, M., & Asoodar, M.. (2023). What if the devil is in the details? A systematic review of the challenges of generative AI in education. *Computers and Education: Artificial Intelligence*, *6*, 100197. DOI: 10.1016/j.caeai.2023.100197

Tolstykh, O. M., & Oshchepkova, T. (2024). Beyond ChatGPT: Roles that artificial intelligence tools can play in an English language classroom. *Discover Artificial Intelligence*, *4*(1), 60. DOI: 10.1007/s44163-024-00158-9

Trust, T., Whalen, J., & Mouza, C. (2023). Editorial: ChatGPT: Challenges, opportunities, and implications for teacher education. *Contemporary Issues in Technology and Teacher Education, 23*(1). https://citejournal.org/volume-23/issue-1-23/editorial/editorialchatgpt- challenges-opportunities-and-implications-for-teacher-education

Tseng, C.-T. H. (2017). Teaching "Cross-cultural Communication" through Content Based Instruction: Curriculum Design and Learning Outcome from EFL Learners' Perspectives. *English Language Teaching*, *10*(4), 22. DOI: 10.5539/elt.v10n4p22

Tu, J. (2020). Learn to Speak Like A Native: AI-powered Chatbot Simulating Natural Conversation for Language Tutoring. *Journal of Physics: Conference Series*, *1693*(1), 012216. DOI: 10.1088/1742-6596/1693/1/012216

U.S. Department of Education. (2023). *Artificial intelligence and the future of teaching and learning: Insights and recommendations*. Office of Educational Technology. https://tech.ed.gov/ai/

UNESCO. (2021). *AI and education: Guidance for policymakers*. https://unesdoc.unesco.org/ark:/48223/pf0000376709

UNESCO. (2021). AI and education: Guidance for policymakers. United Nations Educational, Scientific and Cultural Organization (UNESCO). https://unesdoc.unesco.org/ark:/48223/pf0000377071

UNESCO. (2021). *Artificial intelligence and the futures of learning*. United Nations Educational, Scientific and Cultural Organization. https://unesdoc.unesco.org/ark:/48223/pf0000377071

UNESCO. (2021). *Recommendation on the ethics of artificial intelligence*. United Nations Educational, Scientific and Cultural Organization. https://unesdoc.unesco.org/ark:/48223/pf0000381137

Uto, M., & Uto, H. (2020). A system for visualizing the effects of spaced repetition learning on students' vocabulary retention. *Research and Practice in Technology Enhanced Learning, 15*(1), 2. DOI: 10.1186/s41039-020-0125-z

Ventures, A. (2024, August 8). *A replication randomized controlled trial (RCT) of ASSISTments* (summary with link to WestEd report). https://www.arnoldventures.org/stories/a-replication-randomized-controlled-trial-rct-of-assistments-an-online-study-tool-to-improve-student-math-outcomes-in-seventh-grade

Viesca, K. M., Teemant, A., Alisaari, J., Ennser-Kananen, J., Flynn, N., Hammer, S., & Routarinne, S. (2022). Quality Content Teaching for Multilingual Students: An International Examination of Excellence in Instructional Practices in Four Countries. *Teaching and Teacher Education, 113*, 103649.

Virtual, M. (2025, August 13). *Have you considered AI in your classroom? A Khanmigo pilot story*. https://michiganvirtual.org/blog/have-you-considered-ai-in-your-classroom-a-khanmigo-pilot-story/

Vozza. (2014). Using Professional Presentations to Improve Cross-Cultural Communication. *The CATESOL Journal*, 26(1), 17–22.

Vygotsky, L. S. (1978). *Mind in society: The development of higher psychological processes*. Harvard University Press.

Wall, T. (2017). L1 Literacy and Its Implications for LESLLA Immigrant Women in Canada.Hamline University. https://digitalcommons.hamline.edu/hse_all/4400

Wang, X. (2023). Bridging the gap between AI and EFL teacher education: Challenges and pathways. *Language Learning & Technology, 27*(2), 123–140. DOI: 10.10125/ltl.13160

Wang, Y., Ong, Y. S., & Kankanhalli, A. (2020). Enhancing reading comprehension with AI-supported intelligent tutoring systems: A classroom study. *British Journal of Educational Technology, 51*(6), 2150–2165. DOI: 10.1111/bjet.12999

Wang, Y., & Tigelaar, D. E. H. (2023). Understanding the complexity of language teachers' adoption of AI: A systematic review of the literature. *Education and Information Technologies, 28*(10), 13349–13380. DOI: 10.1007/s10639-023-11756-3

Warner, R. M. (2010). Differentiation in the Content-Area Classroom for English Language Learners. (Master's Thesis). University of Nebraska–Lincoln. https://digitalcommons.unl.edu/cehsdiss/78

Warshauer, M., & Healey, D. (1998). Computers and language learning: An overview. *Language Teaching, 31*(2), 57–71.

Wei, X. (2025). Cultural Sensitivity in AI language learning: Using NLP to enhance language understanding across cultural contexts. *Proceedings of the TNS Conference*. https://www.ewadirect.com/proceedings/tns/article/view/20110/pdf

Wei, L. (2023). Artificial intelligence in language instruction: Impact on English learning achievement, L2 motivation, and self-regulated learning. *Frontiers in Psychology, 14*, 1261955. DOI: 10.3389/fpsyg.2023.1261955 PMID: 38023040

Weinstein, N., Balmford, A., DeHaan, C. R., Gladwell, V., Bradbury, R. B., & Aman, T. (2015). Seeing the Community for the Trees: The Links Among. *Contact (Thousand Oaks, Ventura County, Calif.)*.

Wei, Y. (2023). The impact of AI-mediated instruction on English learning achievement, L2 motivation, and self-regulated learning among Chinese university students. *Frontiers in Psychology, 14*, 1–15. DOI: 10.3389/fpsyg.2023.1234567

Wenger, E. (1998). *Communities of practice: Learning, meaning, and identity.* Cambridge University Press.

WestEd. (2024). *Implementing and evaluating ASSISTments…* (North Carolina RCT report). https://files.eric.ed.gov/fulltext/ED631720.pdf

Widiati, U., & Hayati, N. (2019). *Teacher Education for English as a Lingua Franca: How well prepared are Indonesian pre-service teachers to develop their future students' intercultural communicative competence? A study of English as a lingua franca*. Routledge., DOI: 10.4324/9780203730522-5

Willard-Holt, C. (2001). The impact of short-term international experience for pre-service teachers. *Teaching and Teacher Education, 17*(4), 505–517. DOI: 10.1016/S0742-051X(01)00009-9

Williamson, B. (2020). Education and the "datafication" of learning: Big data, AI and education governance. *Learning, Media and Technology, 45*(3), 219–232. DOI: 10.1080/17439884.2020.1686014

Williamson, B. (2025). Governing AI in education: Ethics, policy, and the limits of automation. *Learning, Media and Technology, 50*(1), 1–17.

Williamson, B., & Eynon, R. (2020). Historical Threads, Missing Links, and Future Directions in AI in Education. *Learning, Media and Technology, 45*(3), 223–235.

Wu, Y. (2021). *Critical thinking in argumentative essays*. Babel Publishing., DOI: 10.52288/bp.27089851.2021.12.10

Xiao, F., Zhu, S., & Xin, W. (2025). Exploring the landscape of generative AI (ChatGPT) powered writing instruction in English as a foreign language education: A scoping review. *ECNU Review of Education*, *0*(0), 1–19. DOI: 10.1177/20965311241310881

Xiao, Y., Zhang, T., & He, J. (2024). A review of promises and challenges of AI-based chatbots in language education through the lens of learner emotions. *Heliyon*.

Xia, Y., Shin, S.-Y., & Kim, J.-C. (2024). Cross-Cultural Intelligent Language Learning System (CILS): Leveraging AI to facilitate language learning strategies in cross-cultural communication. *Applied Sciences (Basel, Switzerland)*, *14*(13), 5651. DOI: 10.3390/app14135651

Yadav, S. (2025). Leveraging AI to Enhance Teaching and Learning in Education: The Role of Artificial Intelligence in Modernizing Classroom Practices. In Basha, J. S., Alade, T. O., Al Khazimi, M. O. A., Vasudevan, R., & Khan, J. B. (Eds.), *Optimizing Research Techniques and Learning Strategies With Digital Technologies* (pp. 211–238). IGI Global., DOI: 10.4018/979-8-3693-7863-2.ch008

Yang, C. T.-Y., Lai, S.-L., & Chen, H. H.-J. (2022). The impact of intelligent personal assistants on learners' autonomous learning of second language listening and speaking. . *Interactive Learning Environments*. Advance online publication. DOI: 10.1080/10494820.2022.2141266

Yan, W., Li, B., & Lowell, V. L. (2025). Integrating artificial intelligence and extended reality in language education: A systematic literature review (2017–2024). *Education Sciences*, *15*(8), 1066. DOI: 10.3390/educsci15081066

Yılmaz Virlan, A., & Tomak, B. (2024). A Q method study on Turkish EFL learners' perspectives on the use of AI tools for writing: Benefits, concerns, and ethics. *Language Teaching Research*, •••, 1–24. DOI: 10.1177/13621688241308836

Yuniari, N. M. (2024). Students' Perception toward Chat PDF AI Applied in Critical Reading Course. *Indonesian Journal of Foreign Language Studies*, *1*(1), 35–44.

Zawacki-Richter, O., Cefa, B., & Bai, J. Y. (2025). Towards reproducible systematic reviews in Open, Distance, and Digital Education An umbrella mapping review. *Review of Education*, *13*(1), e70031.

Zawacki-Richter, O., Marín, V. I., Bond, M., & Gouverneur, F. (2019). Systematic review of research on artificial intelligence applications in higher education – where are the educators? *International Journal of Educational Technology in Higher Education*, *16*(1), 39.

Zawacki-Richter, O., Marín, V. I., Bond, M., & Gouverneur, F. (2019). Systematic review of research on artificial intelligence applications in higher education — Where are the educators? *International Journal of Educational Technology in Higher Education, 16*, 39. Advance online publication. DOI: 10.1186/s41239-019-0171-0

Zawacki-Richter, O., Marín, V. I., Bond, M., & Gouverneur, F. (2019). Systematic review of research on artificial intelligence applications in higher education–where are the educators? *International Journal of Educational Technology in Higher Education, 16*(1), 1–27.

Zhai, X. (2022). A 'teacher-in-the-loop' approach to using artificial intelligence for automated writing evaluation. *Assessment in Education: Principles, Policy & Practice, 29*(4), 481–501. DOI: 10.1080/0969594X.2022.2091484

Zhai, X., Guo, S., & Zheng, Y. (2024). Artificial intelligence in education research during 2013–2023: A review based on bibliometric analysis. *Education and Information Technologies, 29*, 16387–16409. DOI: 10.1007/s10639-024-12491-8

Zhang, K., & Aslan, A. B. (2021). AI technologies for education: Recent research & future directions. *Computers and Education Artificial Intelligence, 2*, 100025. . caeai. 2021. 100025DOI: 10. 1016/j

Zhang, C., Schießl, J., Plößl, L., Hofmann, F., & Gläser-Zikuda, M. (2023). Acceptance of artificial intelligence among pre-service teachers: A multigroup analysis. *International Journal of Educational Technology in Higher Education, 20*(1). Advance online publication. DOI: 10.1186/s41239-023-00420-7 PMID: 36743849

Zhang, L. (2025). Generative AI in Sino-foreign cooperative education: Opportunities and challenges. *International Journal of Educational Technology in Higher Education, 22*(1), 1–20. DOI: 10.1186/s41239-025-00321-9

Zhang, Q., & Zhang, X. (2021). Bridging the gap: Interdisciplinary AI training for educators. *Educational Technology Research and Development, 69*(4), 2117–2136. DOI: 10.1007/s11423-021-10026-9

Zhao, Y. (2003). *What teachers should know about technology: Perspectives and practices*. Information Age Publishing.

Zhou, Y., Tan, R., & Lee, C. (2024). Breaking the bubble: Teaching AI literacy through filter bubble simulations in middle school. *Computers & Education, 205*, 104589. DOI: 10.1016/j.compedu.2023.104589

Zitouni, K. S. (2022). New trends in EFL online learning and teaching through the lens of artificial intelligence. , 7(1), 1065-1080.

About the Contributors

Mohammad Al-Saggaf is currently an Assistant Professor of English Language Studies and Linguistics, School of Arts and Social Sciences, Xiamen University Malaysia (XMUM), Malaysia and was previously A Senior Lecturer at Management & Science University (MSU) and DRB-HICOM University Malaysia (DHU). Born in Hadramout, Yemen, Dr. Al-Saggaf was educated at Hadramout University of Sc. & Tech in Seiyun, Yemen and graduated with a Bachelor's degree in English Language where he was appointed as lecturer for four years. Dr. Al-Saggaf then attended the National University of Malaysia (UKM) gaining his MA and PhD degrees in English Language Studies, before resuming his academic career, which both embraced teaching undergraduate and postgraduate students and research. Dr. Al-Saggaf's research embraced Applied and Sociolinguistics, TESL, Translation, Cognitive & Corpus Linguistics. He is currently an editorial and advisory member of several international journals in the field. He is a certified trainer and expert in Outcome Based Education (OBE) and has extensive experience in supervising final year projects and theses, teaching Research Methodologies, and mentoring young researchers. He is a member of several professional organizations, including the Malaysian Association of Applied Linguistics (MAAL), the Malaysian English Language Teachers Association (MELTA), and the Asian Federation of Translators and Interpreters (AFTI). Dr. Al-Saggaf is also actively involved in various academic and professional activities, such as organizing conferences, training workshops, and serving on editorial boards. ORCID: 0000-0001-7401-0509

ALI Sorayyaei Azar is an assistant professor at the Department of Language and Literacy Education within the Faculty of Education, University of Malaya (UM), Malaysia. He also got his Ph.D. in applied linguistics from the Faculty of Languages and Linguistics, University of Malaya, Malaysia. In a career spanning 27 years, he has worked as an EFL/ESL senior lecturer, researcher, and curriculum developer in Iran, Turkey, Qatar, and Malaysia. He has published and presented research papers on his topic of interest, namely Academic Discourse Analysis, Genre Analysis, Corpus Linguistics, TESL, Educational Technology, and English Language Teaching Strategies in several prestigious journals including GEMA Online@ Journal of Language Studies (UKM, Malaysia), Asian ESP Journal, Asian EFL Journal, Studies in English Language and Education, World Journal of English Language, and Education and Information Technologies (Springer). He is the head of MAAL- SIG (Research Methods in Applied Linguistics). He is also the Editor of several books, including 'Reconceptions of Policies, Strategies, and Challenges in Education 5.0.', 'Innovations in Educational Robotics: Advancing AI for Sustainable Development', and 'Smart Education and Sustainable Learning Environments in Smart Cities' published by IGI Global-Publisher, in the USA. Besides, Dr. Azar has been appointed as a member of the Editorial Board for several journals, including the Asian Journal of University Education (AJUE) indexed in Scopus- Q2, established by Universiti Teknologi MARA, Shah Alam, Malaysia; the International Journal of Modern Languages and Applied Linguistics (IJMAL), established by Akademi Pengajian Bahasa (APB), Universiti Teknologi MARA, Shah Alam, Malaysia; Education Quarterly Reviews, indexed in ERIC, established by the Asian Institute of Research, Indonesia; and the Journal of Pragmatics and Discourse Research, indexed in Sinta 2, established by Perkumpulan Pengelola Jurnal Bahasa Sastra dan Pengajarannya (PPJBSIP), Indonesia. Scopus Author: 55561989000

Tania Hossain is an Assistant Dean of Waseda University, Faculty of Letters, Arts and Sciences, Tokyo, Japan. She is a native of Dhaka, Bangladesh. She completed her doctorate from International Christian University, Tokyo. Prior coming to Tokyo, she completed her B.A. (hons) and M.A. from University of Dhaka. She teaches sociolinguistics, cultural heritage of South Asia and so on. Her research focuses on policy studies. She is a multilingual person. Along with teaching, she works as an interpreter and translator nationally and globally. She is a born traveler. She traveled more than 100 countries of the world. She is a novelist, a travel writer and a poet. She has published more than 10 books,30 articles and attended over 60 conferences in the world.

Mohammed Abdulkhaleq is an esteemed Assistant Professor in the Department of English Language and Literature at Xiamen University Malaysia. Joining the university in 2020, Dr. Abdulkhaleq has been a dedicated member of the academic community, contributing significantly to the field of English language and literature. Currently serving as the Head of the Programme of English Language and Literature, Dr. Abdulkhaleq plays a pivotal role in shaping the academic landscape within the department. With a passion for fostering a rich learning environment, Dr. Abdulkhaleq brings a wealth of knowledge and expertise to both students and colleagues alike. Dr. Abdulkhaleq 's academic journey has been marked by a commitment to excellence in research and teaching. With a focus on teachers' feedback and students' development, Dr. Abdulkhaleq continues to inspire and guide the next generation of scholars. He is currently a holder of research grant at Xiamen university and working on the field of gamification in education. Beyond the classroom, he actively engages in many extracurricular activities and community services, reflecting a dedication to holistic education and community development. As an Assistant Professor at Xiamen University Malaysia, Dr. Abdulkhaleq exemplifies the values of scholarship, leadership, and a passion for English language and literature. With a steadfast commitment to academic excellence, Dr. Abdulkhaleq continues to be an integral part of the vibrant academic community at Xiamen University Malaysia.

Mohammed H. Alaqad is a distinguished associate professor and researcher specializing in translation studies and applied linguistics, with over a decade of academic experience. He currently serves as a postdoctoral research fellow at the University of Malaya. Dr. Alaqad has been an invited speaker and presenter at over 40 international conferences and events. He has published numerous scientific papers and book chapters globally and has authored several articles and a book chapter on Palestinians in the diaspora. Additionally, he serves on the editorial boards of the Cambridge Scholars of Language & Linguistics in the UK and the International Journal of Applied Linguistics and Translation (IJALT) in the USA. He is the founder and CEO of the Asian Federation of Translators and Interpreters, Malaysia. His research interests include AI applications, applied linguistics, education technology, and translation.

Mohammad Ali Al-Saggaf is an Assistant Professor at the Department of English Language & Literature, Xiamen University Malaysia. He earned his Ph.D. in English Language Studies (Linguistics) from Universiti Kebangsaan Malaysia (UKM). With over 13 years of experience in teaching and research, Dr Al-Saggaf has served as an EFL/ESL senior lecturer, researcher, and curriculum developer in Yemen and Malaysia. Dr Al-Saggaf has published and presented research papers on topics such as Applied & Sociolinguistics, Cognitive and Corpus Linguistics, TESL, and Education in several prestigious journals, including the International Journal of Linguistics and Translation Studies, Pedagogical Research, and TESOL and Technology Studies. He is a certified trainer and expert in Outcome Based Education (OBE) and has extensive experience in supervising final year projects and theses, teaching Research Methodologies, and mentoring young researchers. He is a member of several professional organizations, including the Malaysian Association of Applied Linguistics (MAAL), the Malaysian English Language

Teachers Association (MELTA), and the Asian Federation of Translators and Interpreters (AFTI). Dr Al-Saggaf is also actively involved in various academic and professional activities, such as organizing conferences, training workshops, and serving on editorial boards. ORCID: 0000-0001-7401-0509

Bader Abdulaziz Altamimi is an Assistant Professor of Translation and Translation Studies the Department of English Language and Literature at Prince Sattam Bin Abdulaziz University. He holds a PhD in Translation Studies from the University of Leeds and specializes in translation Studies.

Mesfer Ahmed Mesfer Alwadai is an academician with 20 years' experience who is interested in designing educational courses and professional development programs for workers in educational institutions, and a designer of development and community initiatives characterized by creativity and innovation. Ambitious and eagerly zealous about positive change in designing and building organizations, preparing administrative and executive leaders, and unanimous work in designing projects and programs with the aim of developing work environment and raising performance efficiency and improvement of services, besides working on the governance of procedures and implementation of policies within the organization.

Azadeh Amoozegar received her Ph.D. in Educational Technology from Universiti Putra Malaysia (UPM) in 2018. She is currently a senior lecturer at the Faculty of Education and Liberal Arts, INTI International University, with over six years of teaching experience in higher education. In addition to her academic contributions, she actively serves as a peer reviewer for several high-impact journals, reflecting her commitment to advancing scholarly excellence in the field of education. She has presented her research at numerous national and international conferences and published in reputable peer-reviewed journals. Her research interests centre on online learning, with a particular focus on Artificial Intelligence in Education, Education for Sustainable Development, adaptive learning technologies, and learning analytics. Her methodological expertise lies in quantitative research, including statistical modelling, survey design, and the application of data-driven approaches to educational research and policy. She is also actively involved in supervising Ph.D. students, guiding research in areas aligned with her expertise and contributing to the development of future scholars in the field.

Hussein Taha Assaggaf is an Assistant Professor in applied linguistics at the Department of Foreign Languages, College of Arts & Humanities, Al-Baha University, KSA. He has received his PhD from the National University of Malaysia. He has taught English in Yemen, Malaysia and Saudi Arabia. His research interests include English as a foreign language (EFL) writing, pragmatics, discourse analysis and language and technology.

Houda Boumediene is an Associate Professor at the University of Laghouat, specializing in applied linguistics, corpus analysis, and AI-assisted academic writing. Her research interests include second language acquisition, English for Specific Purposes (ESP), and the pedagogical integration of corpus tools in higher education. She has co-authored international publications exploring the intersection of artificial intelligence, language education, and academic integrity in multilingual settings.

Katrina Broughman (pronounced "Bruff-man") is a native of rural Rockbridge County, Virginia. A creative intellectual raised on arts, theater, dance, and music, Katrina actively uses her eclectic talents to advocate for hope with persistent compassion as a changemaker. Professionally trained as an educator, musician, and sociologist, her interests include youth leadership, community development, social justice, global issues, advocacy, the arts, environmental conservation, and empowering marginalized voices. Katrina taught English in Peace Corps Moldova (2015-2017) and wrote grants to develop successful youth-led programs. Katrina received a B.A. '13 is from Mary Baldwin College (MBU) in English and Sociology (minors in Education plus Peacemaking and Conflict Resolution) with emphasis on the environment. She received her Masters in Education (Environment-Based Learning) from MBU with additional M.A. Sociology coursework at Morehead State University (KY) in 2021. She has been certified in secondary English language arts since 2014 and as Central Blue Ridge VA Master Naturalist since 2018. Katrina aspires to begin a Ph.D program for sociology and nature-based learning in 2025 or 2026.

Prodhan Mahbub Ibna Seraj has been working as an Associate Professor at the Department of English, American International University-Bangladesh (AIUB). He completed his Ph.D. in TESL at the Faculty of Education, Universiti Teknologi Malaysia (UTM), and M.A. in Applied Linguistics & ELT from the University of Dhaka. He has achieved the BEST POSTGRADUATE STUDENT AWARD (Ph.D. program) at the 66th UTM Convocation for his outstanding research work. He is particularly interested in how technology could assist English Language Teaching (ELT). He published 60 research works, like articles, conference papers, and book chapters, in prestigious national and international peer-reviewed journals, including Scopus and Web of Science-indexed indexed.

Sajed S. Ingilan is Associate Professor V and Head of the Bachelor of Arts in English Language program at the University of Southeastern Philippines, where he teaches linguistics, indigenous languages, and translation studies. He is the Chief

Editor of the Southeastern Philippines Journal of Research and Development, a Q2 Scopus-indexed journal. Educated at USeP and University of the Philippines Diliman, he is a certified writer and editor by the National Book Development Board-Philippines and associate member of the National Research Council of the Philippines. To give voice to what has been silenced in the discourse of the majority, he has presented papers in onsite conferences in the United States of America, Malaysia, Indonesia, Thailand, Taiwan, Vietnam, and the Philippines, and has published articles and book chapters indexed in Scopus and Web of Science.

Mohamadreza Jafary earned his Ph.D. in Educational Studies from Universiti Putra Malaysia (UPM) and has been dedicated to the fields of English Language Teaching (ELT) and writing studies since 2002. He is currently a full-time researcher in the Language Acquisition Program (LAP) within the Department of Integrated Studies in Education at McGill University, where he also lectures on a contractual basis at both undergraduate and graduate levels. In addition to his academic research, Dr. Jafary holds certifications as a Cambridge language assessor and serves as an official IELTS examiner in Canada. He is a member of the editorial board of the Canadian Center of Science and Education and has contributed to the McGill Language Policy and Planning (LPP) Conference as both a program building committee member and peer reviewer. His research interests include academic writing, AI-integrated writing modules, machine learning, applied and corpus linguistics, critical pedagogy, language assessment, international exit exam preparation, writing assessment, and written feedback in second language acquisition

Sanjeev Kumar Is a Professor in Lovely Professional University Punjab India. He received Undergraduate in Hotel Management from Osmania University, Postgraduate in Tourism Management from Madurai Kamaraj University. He completed Doctor of Philosophy in Hospitality Management in 2019 from Amity University Jaipur India. His research areas lies in food Service Industry, his research focuses on Alcoholic beverages, Event management and Sustainable Management Practices, Metaverse, AI Machine Learning and Artificial Intelligence. He published more than 80 research papers, articles and chapters in Scopus Indexed, UGC Approved and peer reviewed Journals and books. Dr. Sanjeev Kumar participated and acted as resource person in various National and International conferences, seminars, session chair, research workshops and industry talks and his work has been widely cited. Dr. Sanjeev also edited more than 20 books with various International Publishers such as IGI Global, Cambridge Scholars, Emerald, CABI, Bentham Science, Taylor & Francis. Dr Sanjeev is an active researcher and has published numerous research articles in prestigious National and International journals and books.

Froilan D. Mobo, DPA, Ph.D. is a distinguished Filipino educator, researcher, and academic leader known for his outstanding contributions to education, public administration, and development studies. He currently serves as a Full Professor II at the Philippine Merchant Marine Academy (PMMA), where he has devoted over a decade of service in shaping future maritime professionals. In addition to his academic role, he is the Editor-in-Chief of the International Journal of Multidisciplinary: Applied Business and Education Research (IJMABER), a reputable international refereed journal. Prof. Mobo is a strong advocate of lifelong learning, having earned dual doctorate degrees—Doctor of Public Administration from Urdaneta City University and Doctor of Philosophy in Development Education from Central Luzon State University—as well as triple master's degrees, including a Master of Science in Computer Science, Master of Business Administration, and Master of Arts in Social Studies Education from Bicol University Open University. He also holds a Diploma in Social Studies Education from UP Open University and is a Licensed Professional Teacher with a specialization in Social Studies.

Ouafa Ouarniki is an Associate Professor at Ziane Achour University of Djelfa, Algeria. She specializes in the Didactics of teaching English for Specific purposes (ESP), with strong research interests in English as a Medium of Instruction (EMI) and Integrated Content and Language (ICL). She has benefited from professional Development Training at Teacher College, Columbia University, which further enhanced her expertise in innovative and cross-cultural approaches to language education. Dr. Ouarniki actively organizes and participates in national and international conferences, contributing to knowlege exchange and the advancement of language teaching practices.

Sedigheh Shakib is an Associate Professor and Deputy Head of Research in the Department of English Language Teaching (ELT) at Central Asian University. She holds a PhD in Teaching English as a Second Language from the University of Putra Malaysia and is a certified Cambridge DELTA holder. She is dedicated to training prospective ELT teachers and regularly conducts research workshops for both faculty and students. She also supervises doctoral candidates and mentors researchers. Actively engaged in international academic collaboration, she partners with universities worldwide to secure competitive research grants.Her research interests include applied linguistics, language learning technologies, artificial intelligence ineducation, academic writing, and interdisciplinary research at the nexus of education and technology.

Jabulani Sibanda is an Associate Professor of English Education at Rhodes University in the Department of Secondary and Post-School Education. He holds a

PhD in English Education from Rhodes University, and earlier qualifications from the University of Zimbabwe. With extensive experience in higher education, he has served as Senior Lecturer at Sol Plaatje University and Wits University in South Africa, and as Lecturer at the University of Swaziland in Eswatini and Great Zimbabwe University in Zimbabwe. His scholarly contributions include 35 peer-reviewed publications (33 journal articles, one book chapter, and one conference proceeding), 15 examined theses and dissertations, and 20 conference presentations. His academic interests lie in language and literacy education, curriculum studies, and teacher professional development across diverse contexts.

Vino Vasodavan presently holds the position of lecturer within the School of Education at Taylor's University, where her primary commitment lies in delivering high-quality education. Her unwavering passion for education extends beyond the confines of traditional roles, aspiring to serve as an inspiration to both students and colleagues alike. In her prior role, Dr. Vino served as an Instructional Designer (ID) within the eLearning Division of the Faculty of Medicine at the University of Malaya. Within the realm of academic inquiry, Dr. Vino's research pursuits are anchored in the dynamic field of collaborative learning. Her scholarly endeavors are notably influenced by the conceptual framework of Technological Pedagogical Content Knowledge (TPACK), propelling her to devise innovative learning tasks that advance pedagogical practices. Dr. Vino's scholarly contributions have been recognized through various accolades, including the prestigious gold medal and outstanding innovative award for sustainable development goals (SDGIIA, 2021) bestowed upon Project Bacabaca. Additionally, she secured a silver medal at IUCEL (2023) for her project, "Increase Learners Engagement with Walter the Artificial Intelligence (AI) Learning Buddy," and a gold award at e-CONDEV (2022) for the project titled "21st Century Skills Wheels: Re-Designing Learning Tasks Using Collaborative Tools." Beyond her research accomplishments, Dr. Vino possesses a rich array of professional certifications, including being a Certified Training and Development Manager by HRDF, a Train the Trainer certification, and recognition as a Certified Microsoft Innovative Educator and a Certified Nearpod Educator. These certifications underscore her commitment to continuous professional development and proficiency in leveraging innovative educational technology

Joseph Velarde is the Director of the Education for All Impact Lab at Taylor's University and is also a lecturer from School of Education, Taylor's University. He holds a PhD in Education and Master of Educational Leadership from the University of Malaya, Malaysia, while his undergraduate degree of Communication Arts is from the University of the Philippines. For almost 20 years, Dr Joseph has taught in various educational institutions across all levels (primary, secondary, and tertiary) in the Philippines, Singapore, and Malaysia, primarily focusing on the teaching of English language and literature. He has published several articles in high-indexed publications on school leadership and management. Also, he wrote a book entitled, "Leading in Multicultural Schools," published by Routledge. Dr Joseph's passion for teaching and advocacies for inclusive education led him to commit to projects on cross-cultural communications training of student teachers at Taylor's University and body positivity programs in local schools in Subang Jaya, Malaysia. These initiatives led him to win several awards in local conferences and be a finalist in AKRI2022.

Index

Symbols

A

B

C

D

E

W

www.ingramcontent.com/pod-product-compliance
Lightning Source LLC
LaVergne TN
LVHW081534300926
849161LV00006B/1426